THE
MUELLER
REPORT

Volume II

CONTENTS

Introduction

"The beginning of the end for the Trump presidency."
—MSNBC, April 2017

For over two years, Congressional Democrats and their allies in the mainstream media force-fed a dubious narrative to the American public. Rejecting Donald Trump's election on November 8, 2016, left-wingers waited on pins and needles for the other shoe to drop: the bombshell that would end the Trump Administration and erase the original sin of the president's electoral victory. The largest and most promising prospect for wiping the slate clean was Special Counsel Robert Mueller's investigation into potential collusion between the Trump campaign and the Russian government.

Functioning as the public relations wing of the Democratic Party establishment, many of the nation's "leading" journalists, pundits, and analysts only magnified the exuberance and hopeful expectations surrounding the Mueller investigation. *The Washington Post, The New York Times,* CNN, and MSNBC published more than 8,500 articles on the probe since Mueller was appointed in May 2017. During the same time span, television networks devoted a level of reporting to the collusion narrative "normally associated only with a major war or a presidential election," according to the Media Research Center.

The Democrats and America's talking heads went all in, foreseeing the Special Counsel opening the door to impeachment and the total delegitimization of the electoral process that brought Trump to office. For establishment journalists and politicians, it was simply inconceivable that there would be any other result. Consistently, the mantras rang out across CNN, MSNBC, *The Washington Post,* and many more: "The walls were closing in.[1]" The president and his family had a "noose tightening around them.[2]"

But on March 24, 2019, these same self-proclaimed experts got a bitter taste of reality. Mueller's work was done.

After an exhaustive 22-month investigation, fueled by an unlimited taxpayer-funded budget, the Special Counsel found there was no collusion between the Trump campaign and the Kremlin—the diametric opposite of what was, for the left, the inevitable conclusion. Attorney General William Barr's summary of the findings quoted Mueller's report directly: "The investigation did not establish that members of the Trump Campaign conspired or coordinated with the Russian government in its election interference activities."

Two years of unrelenting conspiracy theories, sprawling organizational charts connecting far-flung dots between Vladimir Putin and Trump's extended family, and delirious conjecture about the planning for Trump Tower Moscow—which was never built—all went up in smoke in an instant.

Rather than providing a welcome epiphany for those political and media figures who had assumed and propagated the worst about their president—that he was, absurdly, a "Russian asset"—the findings only caused them to dig their hole deeper. In an astounding replay of the rage and tantrums that filled the airwaves after November 8, 2016, the sages of CNN, the intellectuals of *The New York Times,* and our nation's enlightened Democratic leaders wept and gnashed their teeth upon finding out that the President of the United States… wait for it… *did not commit treason.*

Their objective was never truth or justice. It was removing Donald Trump from the White House—voters be damned.

After Barr publicized his summary of Mueller's findings, the blame game ensued. Barr—experienced to the hilt and an establishment figure to boot—was accused of covering up the true content of the report. From Nancy Pelosi down, Democrats demanded the "full, unredacted" version of the report be released immediately. Adam Schiff moved the

[1] Ghitis, F. (2018, December 19). *The walls are closing in on Trump.* Retrieved from https://www.cnn.com

[2] O'Donnell, L. (2018, January 10). *Trump breaks Mueller promise as "noose is tightening."* Retrieved from https://www.msnbc.com

goalposts out of the stadium, declaring that even with no indictments, collusion could still have happened.[3] Maxine Waters proclaimed that the end of Mueller's investigation was "not the end of anything![4]" Media figures scrambled to explain that perhaps there were sealed indictments ready to drop and finally end the Trump experiment.

The Democrats' ceaseless questioning of the legitimacy of Trump's presidency contrasted sharply with their attitude before the 2016 election occurred. That was when they assumed that Hillary Clinton had it in the bag. During one of the presidential debates, then-candidate Trump was asked if he would accept the results of the election if he lost to Clinton in a close race. When he demurred to preserve his right to a recount, Clinton blasted his stance as "horrifying.[5]" The left and collective mainstream press echoed her sentiment, with *The New York Times* calling Trump's response "a remarkable statement that seemed to cast doubt on American democracy.[6]"

The *bien pensants* who were aghast at Trump's October 2016 comments and claimed that he threatened the pillars of our very republic now threaten the same with their dismissal of the Mueller investigation. Despite clear and concrete conclusions, the narrative simply cannot be allowed to die.

The end of the Mueller saga should prompt deep introspection among the figures responsible for the political nightmare of the last two years. This responsibility does not fall to those cleared by the report. Not on the Trump family. Not on William Barr. Not on Robert Mueller. Academics who pointed fingers still occupy the ivory towers unmolested, legislators still hold positions of influence, and no journalists who recklessly wielded poison pens lost their jobs for malpractice. Their persistent false narrative polluted the nation's political discourse for two long years.

We know, of course, that sadly this introspection will never come.

---

[3] Forgey, Q. (2019, March 24). *Schiff: There is still "significant evidence of collusion."* Retrieved from https://www.politico.com

[4] Hains, T. (2019, March 24). *Maxine Waters of Mueller Report: "This is not the end of anything."* Retrieved from https://www.realclearpolitics.com

[5] Altman, A. (2016, October 20). *Hillary Clinton calls Donald Trump's debate remark "horrifying."* Retrieved from http://time.com

[6] Healy, P. & Martin, J. (2016, October 19). *Donald Trump won't say if he'll accept result of election.* Retrieved from https://www.nytimes.com

So here we are. The two years of intensive conspiracy theories have benefitted the profiles of congressmen like Jerrold Nadler and Ted Lieu, Twitter grifters, and cable news anchors. Chances are that these same figures who have been so wrong, so often, will simply not accept closure following the release of Mueller's report. They will instead continue to insist there is more to come and order Barr to break the law by releasing the raw, unredacted report. The richness of this demand, coming from the same figures who complained just last year that Republicans jeopardized national security by releasing an unredacted memo on alleged FISA abuses, will be completely lost on the Democratic Party and their water carriers.

We should take home a lesson that allegations of high crimes and misdemeanors are serious and should not be politicized. While most conservatives were not supportive of the Mueller investigation, they let it happen and run its course. This was in many respects a concession, exemplified above all by Attorney General Jeff Sessions' recusal. The least we can expect is that now that Mueller's investigation is finished, the party that demanded the inquiry and made it a case about political retribution over justice should be willing to accept the result of the investigation.

As you read the report that follows, even in its redacted form, be sure to keep your pen and paper handy. Ask yourself who had the most to gain by spreading the false collusion story? How many errors did anonymous sources and screaming CNN chyrons represent? Keep tabs on why and how the excesses of Democratic Party-media symbiosis dominated conversations from the halls of Congress to water coolers across the nation. Don't let the pundits or 2020 presidential candidates fool you. Read the whole report—and make up your own mind.

Kristin Tate
The Hill Newspaper

ORDER NO. 3915-2017

APPOINTMENT OF SPECIAL COUNSEL
TO INVESTIGATE RUSSIAN INTERFERENCE WITH THE
2016 PRESIDENTIAL ELECTION AND RELATED MATTERS

By virtue of the authority vested in me as Acting Attorney General, including 28 U.S.C. §§ 509, 510, and 515, in order to discharge my responsibility to provide supervision and management of the Department of Justice, and to ensure a full and thorough investigation of the Russian government's efforts to interfere in the 2016 presidential election, I hereby order as follows:

(a) Robert S. Mueller III is appointed to serve as Special Counsel for the United States Department of Justice.

(b) The Special Counsel is authorized to conduct the investigation confirmed by then-FBI Director James B. Comey in testimony before the House Permanent Select Committee on Intelligence on March 20, 2017, including:

   (i) any links and/or coordination between the Russian government and individuals associated with the campaign of President Donald Trump; and

   (ii) any matters that arose or may arise directly from the investigation; and

   (iii) any other matters within the scope of 28 C.F.R. § 600.4(a).

(c) If the Special Counsel believes it is necessary and appropriate, the Special Counsel is authorized to prosecute federal crimes arising from the investigation of these matters.

(d) Sections 600.4 through 600.10 of Title 28 of the Code of Federal Regulations are applicable to the Special Counsel.

_5/17/17_
Date

Rod J. Rosenstein
Acting Attorney General

The Attorney General

Washington, D.C.

March 24, 2019

The Honorable Lindsey Graham
Chairman, Committee on the Judiciary
United States Senate
290 Russell Senate Office Building
Washington, D.C. 20510

The Honorable Jerrold Nadler
Chairman, Committee on the Judiciary
United States House of Representatives
2132 Rayburn House Office Building
Washington, D.C. 20515

The Honorable Dianne Feinstein
Ranking Member, Committee on the Judiciary
United States Senate
331 Hart Senate Office Building
Washington, D.C. 20510

The Honorable Doug Collins
Ranking Member, Committee on the Judiciary
United States House of Representatives
1504 Longworth House Office Building
Washington, D.C. 20515

Dear Chairman Graham, Chairman Nadler, Ranking Member Feinstein, and Ranking Member Collins:

As a supplement to the notification provided on Friday, March 22, 2019, I am writing today to advise you of the principal conclusions reached by Special Counsel Robert S. Mueller III and to inform you about the status of my initial review of the report he has prepared.

The Special Counsel's Report

On Friday, the Special Counsel submitted to me a "confidential report explaining the prosecution or declination decisions" he has reached, as required by 28 C.F.R. § 600.8(c). This report is entitled "Report on the Investigation into Russian Interference in the 2016 Presidential Election." Although my review is ongoing, I believe that it is in the public interest to describe the report and to summarize the principal conclusions reached by the Special Counsel and the results of his investigation.

The report explains that the Special Counsel and his staff thoroughly investigated allegations that members of the presidential campaign of Donald J. Trump, and others associated with it, conspired with the Russian government in its efforts to interfere in the 2016 U.S. presidential election, or sought to obstruct the related federal investigations. In the report, the Special Counsel noted that, in completing his investigation, he employed 19 lawyers who were assisted by a team of approximately 40 FBI agents, intelligence analysts, forensic accountants, and other professional staff. The Special Counsel issued more than 2,800 subpoenas, executed nearly 500 search warrants, obtained more than 230 orders for communication records, issued almost 50 orders authorizing use of pen registers, made 13 requests to foreign governments for evidence, and interviewed approximately 500 witnesses.

The Special Counsel obtained a number of indictments and convictions of individuals and entities in connection with his investigation, all of which have been publicly disclosed. During the course of his investigation, the Special Counsel also referred several matters to other offices for further action. The report does not recommend any further indictments, nor did the Special Counsel obtain any sealed indictments that have yet to be made public. Below, I summarize the principal conclusions set out in the Special Counsel's report.

Russian Interference in the 2016 U.S. Presidential Election. The Special Counsel's report is divided into two parts. The first describes the results of the Special Counsel's investigation into Russia's interference in the 2016 U.S. presidential election. The report outlines the Russian effort to influence the election and documents crimes committed by persons associated with the Russian government in connection with those efforts. The report further explains that a primary consideration for the Special Counsel's investigation was whether any Americans – including individuals associated with the Trump campaign – joined the Russian conspiracies to influence the election, which would be a federal crime. The Special Counsel's investigation did not find that the Trump campaign or anyone associated with it conspired or coordinated with Russia in its efforts to influence the 2016 U.S. presidential election. As the report states: "[T]he investigation did not establish that members of the Trump Campaign conspired or coordinated with the Russian government in its election interference activities."[1]

The Special Counsel's investigation determined that there were two main Russian efforts to influence the 2016 election. The first involved attempts by a Russian organization, the Internet Research Agency (IRA), to conduct disinformation and social media operations in the United States designed to sow social discord, eventually with the aim of interfering with the election. As noted above, the Special Counsel did not find that any U.S. person or Trump campaign official or associate conspired or knowingly coordinated with the IRA in its efforts, although the Special Counsel brought criminal charges against a number of Russian nationals and entities in connection with these activities.

The second element involved the Russian government's efforts to conduct computer hacking operations designed to gather and disseminate information to influence the election. The Special Counsel found that Russian government actors successfully hacked into computers and obtained emails from persons affiliated with the Clinton campaign and Democratic Party organizations, and publicly disseminated those materials through various intermediaries, including WikiLeaks. Based on these activities, the Special Counsel brought criminal charges against a number of Russian military officers for conspiring to hack into computers in the United States for purposes of influencing the election. But as noted above, the Special Counsel did not find that the Trump campaign, or anyone associated with it, conspired or coordinated with the Russian government in these efforts, despite multiple offers from Russian-affiliated individuals to assist the Trump campaign.

In assessing potential conspiracy charges, the Special Counsel also considered whether members of the Trump campaign "coordinated" with Russian election interference activities. The Special Counsel defined "coordination" as an "agreement—tacit or express—between the Trump Campaign and the Russian government on election interference."

Obstruction of Justice. The report's second part addresses a number of actions by the President – most of which have been the subject of public reporting – that the Special Counsel investigated as potentially raising obstruction-of-justice concerns. After making a "thorough factual investigation" into these matters, the Special Counsel considered whether to evaluate the conduct under Department standards governing prosecution and declination decisions but ultimately determined not to make a traditional prosecutorial judgment. The Special Counsel therefore did not draw a conclusion – one way or the other – as to whether the examined conduct constituted obstruction. Instead, for each of the relevant actions investigated, the report sets out evidence on both sides of the question and leaves unresolved what the Special Counsel views as "difficult issues" of law and fact concerning whether the President's actions and intent could be viewed as obstruction. The Special Counsel states that "while this report does not conclude that the President committed a crime, it also does not exonerate him."

The Special Counsel's decision to describe the facts of his obstruction investigation without reaching any legal conclusions leaves it to the Attorney General to determine whether the conduct described in the report constitutes a crime. Over the course of the investigation, the Special Counsel's office engaged in discussions with certain Department officials regarding many of the legal and factual matters at issue in the Special Counsel's obstruction investigation. After reviewing the Special Counsel's final report on these issues; consulting with Department officials, including the Office of Legal Counsel; and applying the principles of federal prosecution that guide our charging decisions, Deputy Attorney General Rod Rosenstein and I have concluded that the evidence developed during the Special Counsel's investigation is not sufficient to establish that the President committed an obstruction-of-justice offense. Our determination was made without regard to, and is not based on, the constitutional considerations that surround the indictment and criminal prosecution of a sitting president.[2]

In making this determination, we noted that the Special Counsel recognized that "the evidence does not establish that the President was involved in an underlying crime related to Russian election interference," and that, while not determinative, the absence of such evidence bears upon the President's intent with respect to obstruction. Generally speaking, to obtain and sustain an obstruction conviction, the government would need to prove beyond a reasonable doubt that a person, acting with corrupt intent, engaged in obstructive conduct with a sufficient nexus to a pending or contemplated proceeding. In cataloguing the President's actions, many of which took place in public view, the report identifies no actions that, in our judgment, constitute obstructive conduct, had a nexus to a pending or contemplated proceeding, and were done with corrupt intent, each of which, under the Department's principles of federal prosecution guiding charging decisions, would need to be proven beyond a reasonable doubt to establish an obstruction-of-justice offense.

Status of the Department's Review

The relevant regulations contemplate that the Special Counsel's report will be a "confidential report" to the Attorney General. *See* Office of Special Counsel, 64 Fed. Reg. 37,038,

---

See A Sitting President's Amenability to Indictment and Criminal Prosecution, 24 Op. O.L.C. 222 (2000).

37,040-41 (July 9, 1999). As I have previously stated, however, I am mindful of the public interest in this matter. For that reason, my goal and intent is to release as much of the Special Counsel's report as I can consistent with applicable law, regulations, and Departmental policies.

Based on my discussions with the Special Counsel and my initial review, it is apparent that the report contains material that is or could be subject to Federal Rule of Criminal Procedure 6(e), which imposes restrictions on the use and disclosure of information relating to "matter[s] occurring before [a] grand jury." Fed. R. Crim. P. 6(e)(2)(B). Rule 6(e) generally limits disclosure of certain grand jury information in a criminal investigation and prosecution. *Id.* Disclosure of 6(e) material beyond the strict limits set forth in the rule is a crime in certain circumstances. *See, e.g.*, 18 U.S.C. § 401(3). This restriction protects the integrity of grand jury proceedings and ensures that the unique and invaluable investigative powers of a grand jury are used strictly for their intended criminal justice function.

Given these restrictions, the schedule for processing the report depends in part on how quickly the Department can identify the 6(e) material that by law cannot be made public. I have requested the assistance of the Special Counsel in identifying all 6(e) information contained in the report as quickly as possible. Separately, I also must identify any information that could impact other ongoing matters, including those that the Special Counsel has referred to other offices. As soon as that process is complete, I will be in a position to move forward expeditiously in determining what can be released in light of applicable law, regulations, and Departmental policies.

*   *   *

As I observed in my initial notification, the Special Counsel regulations provide that "the Attorney General may determine that public release of" notifications to your respective Committees "would be in the public interest." 28 C.F.R. § 600.9(c). I have so determined, and I will disclose this letter to the public after delivering it to you.

Sincerely,

William P. Barr
Attorney General

Report On The Investigation Into Russian Interference In The 2016 Presidential Election

Volume II of II

Special Counsel Robert S. Mueller, III

Submitted Pursuant to 28 C.F.R. § 600.8(c)

Washington, D.C.

March 2019

TABLE OF CONTENTS – VOLUME II

U.S. Department of Justice

~~Attorney-Work-Product // May Contain Material Protected Under Fed. R. Crim. P. 6(e)~~

INTRODUCTION TO VOLUME II

This report is submitted to the Attorney General pursuant to 28 C.F.R. § 600.8(c), which states that, "[a]t the conclusion of the Special Counsel's work, he . . . shall provide the Attorney General a confidential report explaining the prosecution or declination decisions [the Special Counsel] reached."

Beginning in 2017, the President of the United States took a variety of actions towards the ongoing FBI investigation into Russia's interference in the 2016 presidential election and related matters that raised questions about whether he had obstructed justice. The Order appointing the Special Counsel gave this Office jurisdiction to investigate matters that arose directly from the FBI's Russia investigation, including whether the President had obstructed justice in connection with Russia-related investigations. The Special Counsel's jurisdiction also covered potentially obstructive acts related to the Special Counsel's investigation itself. This Volume of our report summarizes our obstruction-of-justice investigation of the President.

We first describe the considerations that guided our obstruction-of-justice investigation, and then provide an overview of this Volume:

First, a traditional prosecution or declination decision entails a binary determination to initiate or decline a prosecution, but we determined not to make a traditional prosecutorial judgment. The Office of Legal Counsel (OLC) has issued an opinion finding that "the indictment or criminal prosecution of a sitting President would impermissibly undermine the capacity of the executive branch to perform its constitutionally assigned functions" in violation of "the constitutional separation of powers."[1] Given the role of the Special Counsel as an attorney in the Department of Justice and the framework of the Special Counsel regulations, *see* 28 U.S.C. § 515; 28 C.F.R. § 600.7(a), this Office accepted OLC's legal conclusion for the purpose of exercising prosecutorial jurisdiction. And apart from OLC's constitutional view, we recognized that a federal criminal accusation against a sitting President would place burdens on the President's capacity to govern and potentially preempt constitutional processes for addressing presidential misconduct.[2]

Second, while the OLC opinion concludes that a sitting President may not be prosecuted, it recognizes that a criminal investigation during the President's term is permissible.[3] The OLC opinion also recognizes that a President does not have immunity after he leaves office.[4] And if individuals other than the President committed an obstruction offense, they may be prosecuted at this time. Given those considerations, the facts known to us, and the strong public interest in

---

[1] *A Sitting President's Amenability to Indictment and Criminal Prosecution,* 24 Op. O.L.C. 222, 222, 260 (2000) (OLC Op.).

[2] *See* U.S. CONST. Art. I § 2, cl. 5; § 3, cl. 6; *cf.* OLC Op. at 257-258 (discussing relationship between impeachment and criminal prosecution of a sitting President).

[3] OLC Op. at 257 n.36 ("A grand jury could continue to gather evidence throughout the period of immunity").

[4] OLC Op. at 255 ("Recognizing an immunity from prosecution for a sitting President would not preclude such prosecution once the President's term is over or he is otherwise removed from office by resignation or impeachment").

U.S. Department of Justice

~~Attorney Work Product // May Contain Material Protected Under Fed. R. Crim. P. 6(e)~~

safeguarding the integrity of the criminal justice system, we conducted a thorough factual investigation in order to preserve the evidence when memories were fresh and documentary materials were available.

Third, we considered whether to evaluate the conduct we investigated under the Justice Manual standards governing prosecution and declination decisions, but we determined not to apply an approach that could potentially result in a judgment that the President committed crimes. The threshold step under the Justice Manual standards is to assess whether a person's conduct "constitutes a federal offense." U.S. Dep't of Justice, Justice Manual § 9-27.220 (2018) (Justice Manual). Fairness concerns counseled against potentially reaching that judgment when no charges can be brought. The ordinary means for an individual to respond to an accusation is through a speedy and public trial, with all the procedural protections that surround a criminal case. An individual who believes he was wrongly accused can use that process to seek to clear his name. In contrast, a prosecutor's judgment that crimes were committed, but that no charges will be brought, affords no such adversarial opportunity for public name-clearing before an impartial adjudicator.[5]

The concerns about the fairness of such a determination would be heightened in the case of a sitting President, where a federal prosecutor's accusation of a crime, even in an internal report, could carry consequences that extend beyond the realm of criminal justice. OLC noted similar concerns about sealed indictments. Even if an indictment were sealed during the President's term, OLC reasoned, "it would be very difficult to preserve [an indictment's] secrecy," and if an indictment became public, "[t]he stigma and opprobrium" could imperil the President's ability to govern."[6] Although a prosecutor's internal report would not represent a formal public accusation akin to an indictment, the possibility of the report's public disclosure and the absence of a neutral adjudicatory forum to review its findings counseled against potentially determining "that the person's conduct constitutes a federal offense." Justice Manual § 9-27.220.

Fourth, if we had confidence after a thorough investigation of the facts that the President clearly did not commit obstruction of justice, we would so state. Based on the facts and the applicable legal standards, however, we are unable to reach that judgment. The evidence we obtained about the President's actions and intent presents difficult issues that prevent us from conclusively determining that no criminal conduct occurred. Accordingly, while this report does not conclude that the President committed a crime, it also does not exonerate him.

*   *

This report on our investigation consists of four parts. Section I provides an overview of obstruction-of-justice principles and summarizes certain investigatory and evidentiary considerations. Section II sets forth the factual results of our obstruction investigation and analyzes the evidence. Section III addresses statutory and constitutional defenses. Section IV states our conclusion.

---

[5] For that reason, criticisms have been lodged against the practice of naming unindicted co-conspirators in an indictment. *See United States v. Briggs*, 514 F.2d 794, 802 (5th Cir. 1975) ("The courts have struck down with strong language efforts by grand juries to accuse persons of crime while affording them no forum in which to vindicate themselves."); *see also* Justice Manual § 9-11.130.

[6] OLC Op. at 259 & n.38 (citation omitted).

U.S. Department of Justice

~~Attorney Work Product // May Contain Material Protected Under Fed. R. Crim. P. 6(e)~~

EXECUTIVE SUMMARY TO VOLUME II

Our obstruction-of-justice inquiry focused on a series of actions by the President that related to the Russian-interference investigations, including the President's conduct towards the law enforcement officials overseeing the investigations and the witnesses to relevant events.

FACTUAL RESULTS OF THE OBSTRUCTION INVESTIGATION

The key issues and events we examined include the following:

The Campaign's response to reports about Russian support for Trump. During the 2016 presidential campaign, questions arose about the Russian government's apparent support for candidate Trump. After WikiLeaks released politically damaging Democratic Party emails that were reported to have been hacked by Russia, Trump publicly expressed skepticism that Russia was responsible for the hacks at the same time that he and other Campaign officials privately sought information ████████████████████ about any further planned WikiLeaks releases. Trump also denied having any business in or connections to Russia, even though as late as June 2016 the Trump Organization had been pursuing a licensing deal for a skyscraper to be built in Russia called Trump Tower Moscow. After the election, the President expressed concerns to advisors that reports of Russia's election interference might lead the public to question the legitimacy of his election.

Conduct involving FBI Director Comey and Michael Flynn. In mid-January 2017, incoming National Security Advisor Michael Flynn falsely denied to the Vice President, other administration officials, and FBI agents that he had talked to Russian Ambassador Sergey Kislyak about Russia's response to U.S. sanctions on Russia for its election interference. On January 27, the day after the President was told that Flynn had lied to the Vice President and had made similar statements to the FBI, the President invited FBI Director Comey to a private dinner at the White House and told Comey that he needed loyalty. On February 14, the day after the President requested Flynn's resignation, the President told an outside advisor, "Now that we fired Flynn, the Russia thing is over." The advisor disagreed and said the investigations would continue.

Later that afternoon, the President cleared the Oval Office to have a one-on-one meeting with Comey. Referring to the FBI's investigation of Flynn, the President said, "I hope you can see your way clear to letting this go, to letting Flynn go. He is a good guy. I hope you can let this go." Shortly after requesting Flynn's resignation and speaking privately to Comey, the President sought to have Deputy National Security Advisor K.T. McFarland draft an internal letter stating that the President had not directed Flynn to discuss sanctions with Kislyak. McFarland declined because she did not know whether that was true, and a White House Counsel's Office attorney thought that the request would look like a quid pro quo for an ambassadorship she had been offered.

The President's reaction to the continuing Russia investigation. In February 2017, Attorney General Jeff Sessions began to assess whether he had to recuse himself from campaign-related investigations because of his role in the Trump Campaign. In early March, the President told White House Counsel Donald McGahn to stop Sessions from recusing. And after Sessions announced his recusal on March 2, the President expressed anger at the decision and told advisors that he should have an Attorney General who would protect him. That weekend, the President took Sessions aside at an event and urged him to "unrecuse." Later in March, Comey publicly

U.S. Department of Justice

~~Attorney Work Product // May Contain Material Protected Under Fed. R. Crim. P. 6(e)~~

disclosed at a congressional hearing that the FBI was investigating "the Russian government's efforts to interfere in the 2016 presidential election," including any links or coordination between the Russian government and the Trump Campaign. In the following days, the President reached out to the Director of National Intelligence and the leaders of the Central Intelligence Agency (CIA) and the National Security Agency (NSA) to ask them what they could do to publicly dispel the suggestion that the President had any connection to the Russian election-interference effort. The President also twice called Comey directly, notwithstanding guidance from McGahn to avoid direct contacts with the Department of Justice. Comey had previously assured the President that the FBI was not investigating him personally, and the President asked Comey to "lift the cloud" of the Russia investigation by saying that publicly.

The President's termination of Comey. On May 3, 2017, Comey testified in a congressional hearing, but declined to answer questions about whether the President was personally under investigation. Within days, the President decided to terminate Comey. The President insisted that the termination letter, which was written for public release, state that Comey had informed the President that he was not under investigation. The day of the firing, the White House maintained that Comey's termination resulted from independent recommendations from the Attorney General and Deputy Attorney General that Comey should be discharged for mishandling the Hillary Clinton email investigation. But the President had decided to fire Comey before hearing from the Department of Justice. The day after firing Comey, the President told Russian officials that he had "faced great pressure because of Russia," which had been "taken off" by Comey's firing. The next day, the President acknowledged in a television interview that he was going to fire Comey regardless of the Department of Justice's recommendation and that when he "decided to just do it," he was thinking that "this thing with Trump and Russia is a made-up story." In response to a question about whether he was angry with Comey about the Russia investigation, the President said, "As far as I'm concerned, I want that thing to be absolutely done properly," adding that firing Comey "might even lengthen out the investigation."

The appointment of a Special Counsel and efforts to remove him. On May 17, 2017, the Acting Attorney General for the Russia investigation appointed a Special Counsel to conduct the investigation and related matters. The President reacted to news that a Special Counsel had been appointed by telling advisors that it was "the end of his presidency" and demanding that Sessions resign. Sessions submitted his resignation, but the President ultimately did not accept it. The President told aides that the Special Counsel had conflicts of interest and suggested that the Special Counsel therefore could not serve. The President's advisors told him the asserted conflicts were meritless and had already been considered by the Department of Justice.

On June 14, 2017, the media reported that the Special Counsel's Office was investigating whether the President had obstructed justice. Press reports called this "a major turning point" in the investigation: while Comey had told the President he was not under investigation, following Comey's firing, the President now was under investigation. The President reacted to this news with a series of tweets criticizing the Department of Justice and the Special Counsel's investigation. On June 17, 2017, the President called McGahn at home and directed him to call the Acting Attorney General and say that the Special Counsel had conflicts of interest and must be removed. McGahn did not carry out the direction, however, deciding that he would resign rather than trigger what he regarded as a potential Saturday Night Massacre.

U.S. Department of Justice

~~Attorney Work Product // May Contain Material Protected Under Fed. R. Crim. P. 6(e)~~

Efforts to curtail the Special Counsel's investigation. Two days after directing McGahn to have the Special Counsel removed, the President made another attempt to affect the course of the Russia investigation. On June 19, 2017, the President met one-on-one in the Oval Office with his former campaign manager Corey Lewandowski, a trusted advisor outside the government, and dictated a message for Lewandowski to deliver to Sessions. The message said that Sessions should publicly announce that, notwithstanding his recusal from the Russia investigation, the investigation was "very unfair" to the President, the President had done nothing wrong, and Sessions planned to meet with the Special Counsel and "let [him] move forward with investigating election meddling for future elections." Lewandowski said he understood what the President wanted Sessions to do.

One month later, in another private meeting with Lewandowski on July 19, 2017, the President asked about the status of his message for Sessions to limit the Special Counsel investigation to future election interference. Lewandowski told the President that the message would be delivered soon. Hours after that meeting, the President publicly criticized Sessions in an interview with the New York Times, and then issued a series of tweets making it clear that Sessions's job was in jeopardy. Lewandowski did not want to deliver the President's message personally, so he asked senior White House official Rick Dearborn to deliver it to Sessions. Dearborn was uncomfortable with the task and did not follow through.

Efforts to prevent public disclosure of evidence. In the summer of 2017, the President learned that media outlets were asking questions about the June 9, 2016 meeting at Trump Tower between senior campaign officials, including Donald Trump Jr., and a Russian lawyer who was said to be offering damaging information about Hillary Clinton as "part of Russia and its government's support for Mr. Trump." On several occasions, the President directed aides not to publicly disclose the emails setting up the June 9 meeting, suggesting that the emails would not leak and that the number of lawyers with access to them should be limited. Before the emails became public, the President edited a press statement for Trump Jr. by deleting a line that acknowledged that the meeting was with "an individual who [Trump Jr.] was told might have information helpful to the campaign" and instead said only that the meeting was about adoptions of Russian children. When the press asked questions about the President's involvement in Trump Jr.'s statement, the President's personal lawyer repeatedly denied the President had played any role.

Further efforts to have the Attorney General take control of the investigation. In early summer 2017, the President called Sessions at home and again asked him to reverse his recusal from the Russia investigation. Sessions did not reverse his recusal. In October 2017, the President met privately with Sessions in the Oval Office and asked him to "take [a] look" at investigating Clinton. In December 2017, shortly after Flynn pleaded guilty pursuant to a cooperation agreement, the President met with Sessions in the Oval Office and suggested, according to notes taken by a senior advisor, that if Sessions unrecused and took back supervision of the Russia investigation, he would be a "hero." The President told Sessions, "I'm not going to do anything or direct you to do anything. I just want to be treated fairly." In response, Sessions volunteered that he had never seen anything "improper" on the campaign and told the President there was a "whole new leadership team" in place. He did not unrecuse.

Efforts to have McGahn deny that the President had ordered him to have the Special Counsel removed. In early 2018, the press reported that the President had directed McGahn to

U.S. Department of Justice

~~Attorney Work Product // May Contain Material Protected Under Fed. R. Crim. P. 6(e)~~

have the Special Counsel removed in June 2017 and that McGahn had threatened to resign rather than carry out the order. The President reacted to the news stories by directing White House officials to tell McGahn to dispute the story and create a record stating he had not been ordered to have the Special Counsel removed. McGahn told those officials that the media reports were accurate in stating that the President had directed McGahn to have the Special Counsel removed. The President then met with McGahn in the Oval Office and again pressured him to deny the reports. In the same meeting, the President also asked McGahn why he had told the Special Counsel about the President's effort to remove the Special Counsel and why McGahn took notes of his conversations with the President. McGahn refused to back away from what he remembered happening and perceived the President to be testing his mettle.

Conduct towards Flynn, Manafort, ███████. After Flynn withdrew from a joint defense agreement with the President and began cooperating with the government, the President's personal counsel left a message for Flynn's attorneys reminding them of the President's warm feelings towards Flynn, which he said "still remains," and asking for a "heads up" if Flynn knew "information that implicates the President." When Flynn's counsel reiterated that Flynn could no longer share information pursuant to a joint defense agreement, the President's personal counsel said he would make sure that the President knew that Flynn's actions reflected "hostility" towards the President. During Manafort's prosecution and when the jury in his criminal trial was deliberating, the President praised Manafort in public, said that Manafort was being treated unfairly, and declined to rule out a pardon. After Manafort was convicted, the President called Manafort "a brave man" for refusing to "break" and said that "flipping" "almost ought to be outlawed." ████████████████████████

████████████████████

Conduct involving Michael Cohen. The President's conduct towards Michael Cohen, a former Trump Organization executive, changed from praise for Cohen when he falsely minimized the President's involvement in the Trump Tower Moscow project, to castigation of Cohen when he became a cooperating witness. From September 2015 to June 2016, Cohen had pursued the Trump Tower Moscow project on behalf of the Trump Organization and had briefed candidate Trump on the project numerous times, including discussing whether Trump should travel to Russia to advance the deal. In 2017, Cohen provided false testimony to Congress about the project, including stating that he had only briefed Trump on the project three times and never discussed travel to Russia with him, in an effort to adhere to a "party line" that Cohen said was developed to minimize the President's connections to Russia. While preparing for his congressional testimony, Cohen had extensive discussions with the President's personal counsel, who, according to Cohen, said that Cohen should "stay on message" and not contradict the President. After the FBI searched Cohen's home and office in April 2018, the President publicly asserted that Cohen would not "flip," contacted him directly to tell him to "stay strong," and privately passed messages of support to him. Cohen also discussed pardons with the President's personal counsel and believed that if he stayed on message he would be taken care of. But after Cohen began cooperating with the government in the summer of 2018, the President publicly criticized him, called him a "rat," and suggested that his family members had committed crimes.

U.S. Department of Justice

Attorney Work Product // May Contain Material Protected Under Fed. R. Crim. P. 6(e)

Overarching factual issues. We did not make a traditional prosecution decision about these facts, but the evidence we obtained supports several general statements about the President's conduct.

Several features of the conduct we investigated distinguish it from typical obstruction-of-justice cases. First, the investigation concerned the President, and some of his actions, such as firing the FBI director, involved facially lawful acts within his Article II authority, which raises constitutional issues discussed below. At the same time, the President's position as the head of the Executive Branch provided him with unique and powerful means of influencing official proceedings, subordinate officers, and potential witnesses—all of which is relevant to a potential obstruction-of-justice analysis. Second, unlike cases in which a subject engages in obstruction of justice to cover up a crime, the evidence we obtained did not establish that the President was involved in an underlying crime related to Russian election interference. Although the obstruction statutes do not require proof of such a crime, the absence of that evidence affects the analysis of the President's intent and requires consideration of other possible motives for his conduct. Third, many of the President's acts directed at witnesses, including discouragement of cooperation with the government and suggestions of possible future pardons, took place in public view. That circumstance is unusual, but no principle of law excludes public acts from the reach of the obstruction laws. If the likely effect of public acts is to influence witnesses or alter their testimony, the harm to the justice system's integrity is the same.

Although the series of events we investigated involved discrete acts, the overall pattern of the President's conduct towards the investigations can shed light on the nature of the President's acts and the inferences that can be drawn about his intent. In particular, the actions we investigated can be divided into two phases, reflecting a possible shift in the President's motives. The first phase covered the period from the President's first interactions with Comey through the President's firing of Comey. During that time, the President had been repeatedly told he was not personally under investigation. Soon after the firing of Comey and the appointment of the Special Counsel, however, the President became aware that his own conduct was being investigated in an obstruction-of-justice inquiry. At that point, the President engaged in a second phase of conduct, involving public attacks on the investigation, non-public efforts to control it, and efforts in both public and private to encourage witnesses not to cooperate with the investigation. Judgments about the nature of the President's motives during each phase would be informed by the totality of the evidence.

STATUTORY AND CONSTITUTIONAL DEFENSES

The President's counsel raised statutory and constitutional defenses to a possible obstruction-of-justice analysis of the conduct we investigated. We concluded that none of those legal defenses provided a basis for declining to investigate the facts.

Statutory defenses. Consistent with precedent and the Department of Justice's general approach to interpreting obstruction statutes, we concluded that several statutes could apply here. *See* 18 U.S.C. §§ 1503, 1505, 1512(b)(3), 1512(c)(2). Section 1512(c)(2) is an omnibus obstruction-of-justice provision that covers a range of obstructive acts directed at pending or contemplated official proceedings. No principle of statutory construction justifies narrowing the provision to cover only conduct that impairs the integrity or availability of evidence. Sections 1503 and 1505 also offer broad protection against obstructive acts directed at pending grand jury,

U.S. Department of Justice

~~Attorney Work Product // May Contain Material Protected Under Fed. R. Crim. P. 6(e)~~

judicial, administrative, and congressional proceedings, and they are supplemented by a provision in Section 1512(b) aimed specifically at conduct intended to prevent or hinder the communication to law enforcement of information related to a federal crime.

Constitutional defenses. As for constitutional defenses arising from the President's status as the head of the Executive Branch, we recognized that the Department of Justice and the courts have not definitively resolved these issues. We therefore examined those issues through the framework established by Supreme Court precedent governing separation-of-powers issues. The Department of Justice and the President's personal counsel have recognized that the President is subject to statutes that prohibit obstruction of justice by bribing a witness or suborning perjury because that conduct does not implicate his constitutional authority. With respect to whether the President can be found to have obstructed justice by exercising his powers under Article II of the Constitution, we concluded that Congress has authority to prohibit a President's corrupt use of his authority in order to protect the integrity of the administration of justice.

Under applicable Supreme Court precedent, the Constitution does not categorically and permanently immunize a President for obstructing justice through the use of his Article II powers. The separation-of-powers doctrine authorizes Congress to protect official proceedings, including those of courts and grand juries, from corrupt, obstructive acts regardless of their source. We also concluded that any inroad on presidential authority that would occur from prohibiting corrupt acts does not undermine the President's ability to fulfill his constitutional mission. The term "corruptly" sets a demanding standard. It requires a concrete showing that a person acted with an intent to obtain an improper advantage for himself or someone else, inconsistent with official duty and the rights of others. A preclusion of "corrupt" official action does not diminish the President's ability to exercise Article II powers. For example, the proper supervision of criminal law does not demand freedom for the President to act with a corrupt intention of shielding himself from criminal punishment, avoiding financial liability, or preventing personal embarrassment. To the contrary, a statute that prohibits official action undertaken for such corrupt purposes furthers, rather than hinders, the impartial and evenhanded administration of the law. It also aligns with the President's constitutional duty to faithfully execute the laws. Finally, we concluded that in the rare case in which a criminal investigation of the President's conduct is justified, inquiries to determine whether the President acted for a corrupt motive should not impermissibly chill his performance of his constitutionally assigned duties. The conclusion that Congress may apply the obstruction laws to the President's corrupt exercise of the powers of office accords with our constitutional system of checks and balances and the principle that no person is above the law.

CONCLUSION

Because we determined not to make a traditional prosecutorial judgment, we did not draw ultimate conclusions about the President's conduct. The evidence we obtained about the President's actions and intent presents difficult issues that would need to be resolved if we were making a traditional prosecutorial judgment. At the same time, if we had confidence after a thorough investigation of the facts that the President clearly did not commit obstruction of justice, we would so state. Based on the facts and the applicable legal standards, we are unable to reach that judgment. Accordingly, while this report does not conclude that the President committed a crime, it also does not exonerate him.

I. BACKGROUND LEGAL AND EVIDENTIARY PRINCIPLES

A.   Legal Framework of Obstruction of Justice

The May 17, 2017 Appointment Order and the Special Counsel regulations provide this Office with jurisdiction to investigate "federal crimes committed in the course of, and with intent to interfere with, the Special Counsel's investigation, such as perjury, obstruction of justice, destruction of evidence, and intimidation of witnesses." 28 C.F.R. § 600.4(a). Because of that description of our jurisdiction, we sought evidence for our obstruction-of-justice investigation with the elements of obstruction offenses in mind. Our evidentiary analysis is similarly focused on the elements of such offenses, although we do not draw conclusions on the ultimate questions that govern a prosecutorial decision under the Principles of Federal Prosecution. *See* Justice Manual § 9-27.000 *et seq.* (2018).

Here, we summarize the law interpreting the elements of potentially relevant obstruction statutes in an ordinary case. This discussion does not address the unique constitutional issues that arise in an inquiry into official acts by the President. Those issues are discussed in a later section of this report addressing constitutional defenses that the President's counsel have raised. *See* Volume II, Section III.B, *infra*.

Three basic elements are common to most of the relevant obstruction statutes: (1) an obstructive act; (2) a nexus between the obstructive act and an official proceeding; and (3) a corrupt intent. *See, e.g.*, 18 U.S.C. §§ 1503, 1505, 1512(c)(2). We describe those elements as they have been interpreted by the courts. We then discuss a more specific statute aimed at witness tampering, *see* 18 U.S.C. § 1512(b), and describe the requirements for attempted offenses and endeavors to obstruct justice, *see* 18 U.S.C. §§ 1503, 1512(c)(2).

Obstructive act.   Obstruction-of-justice law "reaches all corrupt conduct capable of producing an effect that prevents justice from being duly administered, regardless of the means employed." *United States v. Silverman*, 745 F.2d 1386, 1393 (11th Cir. 1984) (interpreting 18 U.S.C. § 1503). An "effort to influence" a proceeding can qualify as an endeavor to obstruct justice even if the effort was "subtle or circuitous" and "however cleverly or with whatever cloaking of purpose" it was made. *United States v. Roe*, 529 F.2d 629, 632 (4th Cir. 1975); *see also United States v. Quattrone*, 441 F.3d 153, 173 (2d Cir. 2006). The verbs "'obstruct or impede' are broad" and "can refer to anything that blocks, makes difficult, or hinders." *Marinello v. United States*, 138 S. Ct. 1101, 1106 (2018) (internal brackets and quotation marks omitted).

An improper motive can render an actor's conduct criminal even when the conduct would otherwise be lawful and within the actor's authority. *See United States v. Cueto*, 151 F.3d 620, 631 (7th Cir. 1998) (affirming obstruction conviction of a criminal defense attorney for "litigation-related conduct"); *United States v. Cintolo*, 818 F.2d 980, 992 (1st Cir. 1987) ("any act by any party—whether lawful or unlawful on its face—may abridge § 1503 if performed with a corrupt motive").

Nexus to a pending or contemplated official proceeding.   Obstruction-of-justice law generally requires a nexus, or connection, to an official proceeding. In Section 1503, the nexus must be to pending "judicial or grand jury proceedings." *United States v. Aguilar*, 515 U.S. 593,

U.S. Department of Justice

Attorney Work Product // May Contain Material Protected Under Fed. R. Crim. P. 6(e)

599 (1995). In Section 1505, the nexus can include a connection to a "pending" federal agency proceeding or a congressional inquiry or investigation. Under both statutes, the government must demonstrate "a relationship in time, causation, or logic" between the obstructive act and the proceeding or inquiry to be obstructed. *Id.* at 599; *see also Arthur Andersen LLP v. United States*, 544 U.S. 696, 707-708 (2005). Section 1512(c) prohibits obstructive efforts aimed at official proceedings including judicial or grand jury proceedings. 18 U.S.C. § 1515(a)(1)(A). "For purposes of" Section 1512, "an official proceeding need not be pending or about to be instituted at the time of the offense." 18 U.S.C. § 1512(f)(1). Although a proceeding need not already be in progress to trigger liability under Section 1512(c), a nexus to a contemplated proceeding still must be shown. *United States v. Young*, 916 F.3d 368, 386 (4th Cir. 2019); *United States v. Petruk*, 781 F.3d 438, 445 (8th Cir. 2015); *United States v. Phillips*, 583 F.3d 1261, 1264 (10th Cir. 2009); *United States v. Reich*, 479 F.3d 179, 186 (2d Cir. 2007). The nexus requirement narrows the scope of obstruction statutes to ensure that individuals have "fair warning" of what the law proscribes. *Aguilar*, 515 U.S. at 600 (internal quotation marks omitted).

The nexus showing has subjective and objective components. As an objective matter, a defendant must act "in a manner that is *likely* to obstruct justice," such that the statute "excludes defendants who have an evil purpose but use means that would only unnaturally and improbably be successful." *Aguilar*, 515 U.S. at 601-602 (emphasis added; internal quotation marks omitted). "[T]he endeavor must have the natural and probable effect of interfering with the due administration of justice." *Id.* at 599 (citation and internal quotation marks omitted). As a subjective matter, the actor must have "contemplated a particular, foreseeable proceeding." *Petruk*, 781 F.3d at 445-446. A defendant need not directly impede the proceeding. Rather, a nexus exists if "discretionary actions of a third person would be required to obstruct the judicial proceeding if it was foreseeable to the defendant that the third party would act on the [defendant's] communication in such a way as to obstruct the judicial proceeding." *United States v. Martinez*, 862 F.3d 223, 238 (2d Cir. 2017) (brackets, ellipses, and internal quotation marks omitted).

Corruptly. The word "corruptly" provides the intent element for obstruction of justice and means acting "knowingly and dishonestly" or "with an improper motive." *United States v. Richardson*, 676 F.3d 491, 508 (5th Cir. 2012); *United States v. Gordon*, 710 F.3d 1124, 1151 (10th Cir. 2013) (to act corruptly means to "act[] with an improper purpose and to engage in conduct knowingly and dishonestly with the specific intent to subvert, impede or obstruct" the relevant proceeding) (some quotation marks omitted); *see* 18 U.S.C. § 1515(b) ("As used in section 1505, the term 'corruptly' means acting with an improper purpose, personally or by influencing another."); *see also Arthur Andersen*, 544 U.S. at 705-706 (interpreting "corruptly" to mean "wrongful, immoral, depraved, or evil" and holding that acting "knowingly . . . corruptly" in 18 U.S.C. § 1512(b) requires "consciousness of wrongdoing"). The requisite showing is made when a person acted with an intent to obtain an "improper advantage for [him]self or someone else, inconsistent with official duty and the rights of others." BALLENTINE'S LAW DICTIONARY 276 (3d ed. 1969); *see United States v. Pasha*, 797 F.3d 1122, 1132 (D.C. Cir. 2015); *Aguilar*, 515 U.S. at 616 (Scalia, J., concurring in part and dissenting in part) (characterizing this definition as the "longstanding and well-accepted meaning" of "corruptly").

Witness tampering. A more specific provision in Section 1512 prohibits tampering with a witness. *See* 18 U.S.C. § 1512(b)(1), (3) (making it a crime to "knowingly use[] intimidation . . . or corruptly persuade[] another person," or "engage[] in misleading conduct towards another

U.S. Department of Justice

~~Attorney Work Product // May Contain Material Protected Under Fed. R. Crim. P. 6(e)~~

person," with the intent to "influence, delay, or prevent the testimony of any person in an official proceeding" or to "hinder, delay, or prevent the communication to a law enforcement officer . . . of information relating to the commission or possible commission of a Federal offense"). To establish corrupt persuasion, it is sufficient that the defendant asked a potential witness to lie to investigators in contemplation of a likely federal investigation into his conduct. *United States v. Edlind*, 887 F.3d 166, 174 (4th Cir. 2018); *United States v. Sparks*, 791 F.3d 1188, 1191-1192 (10th Cir. 2015); *United States v. Byrne*, 435 F.3d 16, 23-26 (1st Cir. 2006); *United States v. LaShay*, 417 F.3d 715, 718-719 (7th Cir. 2005); *United States v. Burns*, 298 F.3d 523, 539-540 (6th Cir. 2002); *United States v. Pennington*, 168 F.3d 1060, 1066 (8th Cir. 1999). The "persuasion" need not be coercive, intimidating, or explicit; it is sufficient to "urge," "induce," "ask[]," "argu[e]," "giv[e] reasons," *Sparks*, 791 F.3d at 1192, or "coach[] or remind[] witnesses by planting misleading facts," *Edlind*, 887 F.3d at 174. Corrupt persuasion is shown "where a defendant tells a potential witness a false story as if the story were true, intending that the witness believe the story and testify to it." *United States v. Rodolitz*, 786 F.2d 77, 82 (2d Cir. 1986); *see United States v. Gabriel*, 125 F.3d 89, 102 (2d Cir. 1997). It also covers urging a witness to recall a fact that the witness did not know, even if the fact was actually true. *See LaShay*, 417 F.3d at 719. Corrupt persuasion also can be shown in certain circumstances when a person, with an improper motive, urges a witness not to cooperate with law enforcement. *See United States v. Shotts*, 145 F.3d 1289, 1301 (11th Cr. 1998) (telling Secretary "not to [say] anything [to the FBI] and [she] would not be bothered").

When the charge is acting with the intent to hinder, delay, or prevent the communication of information to law enforcement under Section 1512(b)(3), the "nexus" to a proceeding inquiry articulated in *Aguilar*—that an individual have "knowledge that his actions are likely to affect the judicial proceeding," 515 U.S. at 599—does not apply because the obstructive act is aimed at the communication of information to investigators, not at impeding an official proceeding.

Acting "knowingly . . . corruptly" requires proof that the individual was "conscious of wrongdoing." *Arthur Andersen*, 544 U.S. at 705-706 (declining to explore "[t]he outer limits of this element" but indicating that an instruction was infirm where it permitted conviction even if the defendant "honestly and sincerely believed that [the] conduct was lawful"). It is an affirmative defense that "the conduct consisted solely of lawful conduct and that the defendant's sole intention was to encourage, induce, or cause the other person to testify truthfully." 18 U.S.C. § 1512(e).

Attempts and endeavors. Section 1512(c)(2) covers both substantive obstruction offenses and attempts to obstruct justice. Under general principles of attempt law, a person is guilty of an attempt when he has the intent to commit a substantive offense and takes an overt act that constitutes a substantial step towards that goal. *See United States v. Resendiz-Ponce*, 549 U.S. 102, 106-107 (2007). "[T]he act [must be] substantial, in that it was strongly corroborative of the defendant's criminal purpose." *United States v. Pratt*, 351 F.3d 131, 135 (4th Cir. 2003). While "mere abstract talk" does not suffice, any "concrete and specific" acts that corroborate the defendant's intent can constitute a "substantial step." *United States v. Irving*, 665 F.3d 1184, 1198-1205 (10th Cir. 2011). Thus, "soliciting an innocent agent to engage in conduct constituting an element of the crime" may qualify as a substantial step. Model Penal Code § 5.01(2)(g); *see United States v. Lucas*, 499 F.3d 769, 781 (8th Cir. 2007).

U.S. Department of Justice

Attorney Work Product // May Contain Material Protected Under Fed. R. Crim. P. 6(e)

The omnibus clause of 18 U.S.C. § 1503 prohibits an "endeavor" to obstruct justice, which sweeps more broadly than Section 1512's attempt provision. *See United States v. Sampson*, 898 F.3d 287, 302 (2d Cir. 2018); *United States v. Leisure*, 844 F.2d 1347, 1366-1367 (8th Cir. 1988) (collecting cases). "It is well established that a[n] [obstruction-of-justice] offense is complete when one corruptly endeavors to obstruct or impede the due administration of justice; the prosecution need not prove that the due administration of justice was actually obstructed or impeded." *UnitedStates v. Davis*, 854 F.3d 1276, 1292 (11th Cir. 2017) (internal quotation marks omitted).

B. Investigative and Evidentiary Considerations

After the appointment of the Special Counsel, this Office obtained evidence about the following events relating to potential issues of obstruction of justice involving the President:

(a) The President's January 27, 2017 dinner with former FBI Director James Comey in which the President reportedly asked for Comey's loyalty, one day after the White House had been briefed by the Department of Justice on contacts between former National Security Advisor Michael Flynn and the Russian Ambassador;

(b) The President's February 14, 2017 meeting with Comey in which the President reportedly asked Comey not to pursue an investigation of Flynn;

(c) The President's private requests to Comey to make public the fact that the President was not the subject of an FBI investigation and to lift what the President regarded as a cloud;

(d) The President's outreach to the Director of National Intelligence and the Directors of the National Security Agency and the Central Intelligence Agency about the FBI's Russia investigation;

(e) The President's stated rationales for terminating Comey on May 9, 2017, including statements that could reasonably be understood as acknowledging that the FBI's Russia investigation was a factor in Comey's termination; and

(f) The President's reported involvement in issuing a statement about the June 9, 2016 Trump Tower meeting between Russians and senior Trump Campaign officials that said the meeting was about adoption and omitted that the Russians had offered to provide the Trump Campaign with derogatory information about Hillary Clinton.

Taking into account that information and our analysis of applicable statutory and constitutional principles (discussed below in Volume II, Section III, *infra*), we determined that there was a sufficient factual and legal basis to further investigate potential obstruction-of-justice issues involving the President.

Many of the core issues in an obstruction-of-justice investigation turn on an individual's actions and intent. We therefore requested that the White House provide us with documentary evidence in its possession on the relevant events. We also sought and obtained the White House's concurrence in our conducting interviews of White House personnel who had relevant information. And we interviewed other witnesses who had pertinent knowledge, obtained documents on a

U.S. Department of Justice

~~Attorney Work Product // May Contain Material Protected Under Fed. R. Crim. P. 6(e)~~

voluntary basis when possible, and used legal process where appropriate. These investigative steps allowed us to gather a substantial amount of evidence.

We also sought a voluntary interview with the President. After more than a year of discussion, the President declined to be interviewed. ████████████████████████████

████████████████████████████ During the course of our discussions, the President did agree to answer written questions on certain Russia-related topics, and he provided us with answers. He did not similarly agree to provide written answers to questions on obstruction topics or questions on events during the transition. Ultimately, while we believed that we had the authority and legal justification to issue a grand jury subpoena to obtain the President's testimony, we chose not to do so. We made that decision in view of the substantial delay that such an investigative step would likely produce at a late stage in our investigation. We also assessed that based on the significant body of evidence we had already obtained of the President's actions and his public and private statements describing or explaining those actions, we had sufficient evidence to understand relevant events and to make certain assessments without the President's testimony. The Office's decision-making process on this issue is described in more detail in Appendix C, *infra*, in a note that precedes the President's written responses.

In assessing the evidence we obtained, we relied on common principles that apply in any investigation. The issue of criminal intent is often inferred from circumstantial evidence. *See, e.g., United States v. Croteau*, 819 F.3d 1293, 1305 (11th Cir. 2016) ("[G]uilty knowledge can rarely be established by direct evidence. . . . Therefore, mens rea elements such as knowledge or intent may be proved by circumstantial evidence.") (internal quotation marks omitted); *United States v. Robinson*, 702 F.3d 22, 36 (2d Cir. 2012) ("The government's case rested on circumstantial evidence, but the *mens rea* elements of knowledge and intent can often be proved through circumstantial evidence and the reasonable inferences drawn therefrom.") (internal quotation marks omitted). The principle that intent can be inferred from circumstantial evidence is a necessity in criminal cases, given the right of a subject to assert his privilege against compelled self-incrimination under the Fifth Amendment and therefore decline to testify. Accordingly, determinations on intent are frequently reached without the opportunity to interview an investigatory subject.

Obstruction-of-justice cases are consistent with this rule. *See, e.g., Edlind*, 887 F.3d at 174, 176 (relying on "significant circumstantial evidence that [the defendant] was conscious of her wrongdoing" in an obstruction case; "[b]ecause evidence of intent will almost always be circumstantial, a defendant may be found culpable where the reasonable and foreseeable consequences of her acts are the obstruction of justice") (internal quotation marks, ellipses, and punctuation omitted); *Quattrone*, 441 F.3d at 173-174. Circumstantial evidence that illuminates intent may include a pattern of potentially obstructive acts. Fed. R. Evid. 404(b) ("Evidence of a crime, wrong, or other act . . . may be admissible . . . [to] prov[e] motive, opportunity, intent, preparation, plan, knowledge, identity, absence of mistake, or lack of accident."); *see, e.g., United States v. Frankhauser*, 80 F.3d 641, 648-650 (1st Cir. 1996); *United States v. Arnold*, 773 F.2d 823, 832-834 (7th Cir. 1985); *Cintolo*, 818 F.2d at 1000.

Credibility judgments may also be made based on objective facts and circumstantial evidence. Standard jury instructions highlight a variety of factors that are often relevant in assessing credibility. These include whether a witness had a reason not to tell the truth; whether the witness had a good memory; whether the witness had the opportunity to observe the events about which he testified; whether the witness's testimony was corroborated by other witnesses; and whether anything the witness said or wrote previously contradicts his testimony. *See, e.g., First Circuit Pattern Jury Instructions* § 1.06 (2018); *Fifth Circuit Pattern Jury Instructions (Criminal Cases)* § 1.08 (2012); *Seventh Circuit Pattern Jury Instruction* § 3.01 (2012).

In addition to those general factors, we took into account more specific factors in assessing the credibility of conflicting accounts of the facts. For example, contemporaneous written notes can provide strong corroborating evidence. *See United States v. Nobles*, 422 U.S. 225, 232 (1975) (the fact that a "statement appeared in the contemporaneously recorded report . . . would tend strongly to corroborate the investigator's version of the interview"). Similarly, a witness's recitation of his account before he had any motive to fabricate also supports the witness's credibility. *See Tome v. United States*, 513 U.S. 150, 158 (1995) ("A consistent statement that predates the motive is a square rebuttal of the charge that the testimony was contrived as a consequence of that motive."). Finally, a witness's false description of an encounter can imply consciousness of wrongdoing. *See Al-Adahi v. Obama*, 613 F.3d 1102, 1107 (D.C. Cir. 2010) (noting the "well-settled principle that false exculpatory statements are evidence—often strong evidence—of guilt"). We applied those settled legal principles in evaluating the factual results of our investigation.

U.S. Department of Justice

~~Attorney-Work-Product // May-Contain-Material-Protected-Under-Fed. R. Crim. P. 6(e)~~

II. FACTUAL RESULTS OF THE OBSTRUCTION INVESTIGATION

This section of the report details the evidence we obtained. We first provide an overview of how Russia became an issue in the 2016 presidential campaign, and how candidate Trump responded. We then turn to the key events that we investigated: the President's conduct concerning the FBI investigation of Michael Flynn; the President's reaction to public confirmation of the FBI's Russia investigation; events leading up to and surrounding the termination of FBI Director Comey; efforts to terminate the Special Counsel; efforts to curtail the scope of the Special Counsel's investigation; efforts to prevent disclosure of information about the June 9, 2016 Trump Tower meeting between Russians and senior campaign officials; efforts to have the Attorney General unrecuse; and conduct towards McGahn, Cohen, and other witnesses.

We summarize the evidence we found and then analyze it by reference to the three statutory obstruction-of-justice elements: obstructive act, nexus to a proceeding, and intent. We focus on elements because, by regulation, the Special Counsel has "jurisdiction . . . to investigate . . . federal crimes committed in the course of, and with intent to interfere with, the Special Counsel's investigation, such as perjury, obstruction of justice, destruction of evidence, and intimidation of witnesses." 28 C.F.R. § 600.4(a). Consistent with our jurisdiction to investigate federal obstruction crimes, we gathered evidence that is relevant to the elements of those crimes and analyzed them within an elements framework—while refraining from reaching ultimate conclusions about whether crimes were committed, for the reasons explained above. This section also does not address legal and constitutional defenses raised by counsel for the President; those defenses are analyzed in Volume II, Section III, *infra*.

A. The Campaign's Response to Reports About Russian Support for Trump

During the 2016 campaign, the media raised questions about a possible connection between the Trump Campaign and Russia.[7] The questions intensified after WikiLeaks released politically damaging Democratic Party emails that were reported to have been hacked by Russia. Trump responded to questions about possible connections to Russia by denying any business involvement in Russia—even though the Trump Organization had pursued a business project in Russia as late as June 2016. Trump also expressed skepticism that Russia had hacked the emails at the same time as he and other Campaign advisors privately sought information ▮▮▮▮▮▮▮▮ about any further planned WikiLeaks releases. After the election, when questions persisted about possible links between Russia and the Trump Campaign, the President-Elect continued to deny any connections to Russia and privately expressed concerns that reports of Russian election interference might lead the public to question the legitimacy of his election.[8]

---

[7] This section summarizes and cites various news stories not for the truth of the information contained in the stories, but rather to place candidate Trump's response to those stories in context. Volume I of this report analyzes the underlying facts of several relevant events that were reported on by the media during the campaign.

[8] As discussed in Volume I, while the investigation identified numerous links between individuals with ties to the Russian government and individuals associated with the Trump Campaign, the evidence was not sufficient to charge that any member of the Trump Campaign conspired or coordinated with representatives of the Russian government to interfere in the 2016 election.

U.S. Department of Justice

Attorney Work Product // May Contain Material Protected Under Fed. R. Crim. P. 6(e)

1. Press Reports Allege Links Between the Trump Campaign and Russia

On June 16, 2015, Donald J. Trump declared his intent to seek nomination as the Republican candidate for President.[9] By early 2016, he distinguished himself among Republican candidates by speaking of closer ties with Russia,[10] saying he would get along well with Russian President Vladimir Putin,[11] questioning whether the NATO alliance was obsolete,[12] and praising Putin as a "strong leader."[13] The press reported that Russian political analysts and commentators perceived Trump as favorable to Russia.[14]

Beginning in February 2016 and continuing through the summer, the media reported that several Trump campaign advisors appeared to have ties to Russia. For example, the press reported that campaign advisor Michael Flynn was seated next to Vladimir Putin at an RT gala in Moscow in December 2015 and that Flynn had appeared regularly on RT as an analyst.[15] The press also reported that foreign policy advisor Carter Page had ties to a Russian state-run gas company,[16] and that campaign chairman Paul Manafort had done work for the "Russian-backed former Ukrainian president Viktor Yanukovych."[17] In addition, the press raised questions during the Republican

---

[9] @realDonaldTrump 6/16/15 (11:57 a.m. ET) Tweet.

[10] *See, e.g.*, Meet the Press Interview with Donald J. Trump, NBC (Dec. 20, 2015) (Trump: "I think it would be a positive thing if Russia and the United States actually got along"); *Presidential Candidate Donald Trump News Conference, Hanahan, South Carolina*, C-SPAN (Feb. 15, 2016) ("You want to make a good deal for the country, you want to deal with Russia.").

[11] *See, e.g.*, *Anderson Cooper 360 Degrees*, CNN (July 8, 2015) ("I think I get along with [Putin] fine."); Andrew Rafferty, *Trump Says He Would "Get Along Very Well" With Putin*, NBC (July 30, 2015) (quoting Trump as saying, "I think I would get along very well with Vladimir Putin.").

[12] *See, e.g.*, @realDonaldTrump Tweet 3/24/16 (7:47 a.m. ET); @realDonaldTrump Tweet 3/24/16 (7:59 a.m. ET).

[13] *See, e.g.*, Meet the Press Interview with Donald J. Trump, NBC (Dec. 20, 2015) ("[Putin] is a strong leader. What am I gonna say, he's a weak leader? He's making mincemeat out of our President."); *Donald Trump Campaign Rally in Vandalia, Ohio*, C-SPAN (Mar. 12, 2016) ("I said [Putin] was a strong leader, which he is. I mean, he might be bad, he might be good. But he's a strong leader.").

[14] *See, e.g.*, Andrew Osborn, *From Russia with love: why the Kremlin backs Trump*, Reuters (Mar. 24, 2016); Robert Zubrin, *Trump: The Kremlin's Candidate*, National Review (Apr. 4, 2016).

[15] *See, e.g.*, Mark Hosenball & Steve Holland, *Trump being advised by ex-U.S. Lieutenant General who favors closer Russia ties*, Reuters (Feb. 26, 2016); Tom Hamburger et al., *Inside Trump's financial ties to Russia and his unusual flattery of Vladimir Putin*, Washington Post (June 17, 2016). Certain matters pertaining to Flynn are described in Volume I, Section IV.B.7, *supra*.

[16] *See, e.g.*, Zachary Mider, *Trump's New Russia Advisor Has Deep Ties to Kremlin's Gazprom*, Bloomberg (Mar. 30, 2016); Julia Iofee, *Who is Carter Page?*, Politico (Sep. 23, 2016). Certain matters pertaining to Page are described in Volume I, Section IV.A.3, *supra*.

[17] Tracy Wilkinson, *In a shift, Republican platform doesn't call for arming Ukraine against Russia, spurring outrage*, Los Angeles Times (July 21, 2016); Josh Rogin, *Trump campaign guts GOP's anti-Russia stance on Ukraine*, Washington Post (July 18, 2016).

National Convention about the Trump Campaign's involvement in changing the Republican platform's stance on giving "weapons to Ukraine to fight Russian and rebel forces."[18]

2. The Trump Campaign Reacts to WikiLeaks's Release of Hacked Emails

On June 14, 2016, a cybersecurity firm that had conducted in-house analysis for the Democratic National Committee (DNC) posted an announcement that Russian government hackers had infiltrated the DNC's computer and obtained access to documents.[19]

On July 22, 2016, the day before the Democratic National Convention, WikiLeaks posted thousands of hacked DNC documents revealing sensitive internal deliberations.[20] Soon thereafter, Hillary Clinton's campaign manager publicly contended that Russia had hacked the DNC emails and arranged their release in order to help candidate Trump.[21] On July 26, 2016, the New York Times reported that U.S. "intelligence agencies ha[d] told the White House they now have 'high confidence' that the Russian government was behind the theft of emails and documents from the Democratic National Committee."[22]

Within the Trump Campaign, aides reacted with enthusiasm to reports of the hacks.[23] ▮▮▮▮▮▮▮▮▮▮▮▮▮▮▮▮▮▮▮▮▮▮▮▮▮▮ discussed with Campaign officials that WikiLeaks would release the hacked material.[24] Some witnesses said that Trump himself discussed the possibility of upcoming releases ▮▮▮▮▮▮. Michael Cohen, then-executive vice president of the Trump Organization and special counsel to Trump, recalled hearing ▮▮.[25] Cohen recalled that Trump responded, "oh good, alright,"

---

[18] Josh Rogin, *Trump campaign guts GOP's anti-Russia stance on Ukraine*, Washington Post, Opinions (July 18, 2016). The Republican Platform events are described in Volume I, Section IV.A.6, *supra*.

[19] *Bears in the Midst: Intrusion into the Democratic National Committee*, CrowdStrike (June 15, 2016) (post originally appearing on June 14, 2016, according to records of the timing provided by CrowdStrike); Ellen Nakashima, *Russian government hackers penetrated DNC, stole opposition research on Trump*, Washington Post (June 14, 2016).

[20] Tom Hamburger and Karen Tumulty, *WikiLeaks releases thousands of documents about Clinton and internal deliberations*, Washington Post (July 22, 2016).

[21] Amber Phillips, *Clinton campaign manager: Russians leaked Democrats' emails to help Donald Trump*, Washington Post (July 24, 2016).

[22] David E. Sanger and Eric Schmitt, *Spy Agency Consensus Grows That Russia Hacked D.N.C.*, New York Times (July 26, 2016).

[23] Gates 4/10/18 302, at 5; Newman 8/23/18 302, at 1.

[24] Gates 4/11/18 302, at 2-3 (SM-2180998); Gates 10/25/18 302, at 2; *see also* Volume I, Section III.D.1, *supra*.

[25] Cohen 8/7/18 302, at 8; *see also* Volume I, Section III.D.1, *supra*. According to Cohen, after WikiLeaks's subsequent release of stolen DNC emails on July 22, 2016, Trump said to Cohen words to the effect ▮▮▮▮▮▮▮▮▮▮▮▮▮▮▮▮▮▮▮▮ Cohen 9/18/18 302, at 10. Cohen's role in the candidate's and later

and ███████████████████████████.[26] Manafort said that shortly after WikiLeaks's July 22, 2016 release of hacked documents, he spoke to ███████████████████████████████████; Manafort recalled that Trump responded that Manafort should ███████████████████ keep Trump updated.[27] Deputy campaign manager Rick Gates said that Manafort was getting pressure about ████████████████████ and that Manafort instructed ██████████████████████████ updates on upcoming releases.[28] Around the same time, Gates was with Trump on a trip to an airport ████████████████████████ ███████, and shortly after the call ended, Trump told Gates that more releases of damaging information would be coming.[29] █████████████████████████████ were discussed within the Campaign,[30] and in the summer of 2016, the Campaign was planning a communications strategy based on the possible release of Clinton emails by WikiLeaks.[31]

3. The Trump Campaign Reacts to Allegations That Russia was Seeking to Aid Candidate Trump

In the days that followed WikiLeaks's July 22, 2016 release of hacked DNC emails, the Trump Campaign publicly rejected suggestions that Russia was seeking to aid candidate Trump. On July 26, 2016, Trump tweeted that it was "[c]razy" to suggest that Russia was "dealing with Trump"[32] and that "[f]or the record," he had "ZERO investments in Russia."[33]

In a press conference the next day, July 27, 2016, Trump characterized "this whole thing with Russia" as "a total deflection" and stated that it was "farfetched" and "ridiculous."[34] Trump said that the assertion that Russia had hacked the emails was unproven, but stated that it would give him "no pause" if Russia had Clinton's emails.[35] Trump added, "Russia, if you're listening, I hope you're able to find the 30,000 emails that are missing. I think you will probably be rewarded

---

President's activities, and his own criminal conduct, is described in Volume II, Section II.K, *infra*, and in Volume I, Section IV.A.1, *supra*.

[26] Cohen 8/7/18 302, at 8.

[27] ███████████████████████████████████████. As explained in footnote 197 of Volume I, Section III.D.1.b, *supra*, this Office has included Manafort's account of these events because it aligns with those of other witnesses and is corroborated to that extent.

[28] Gates 10/25/18 302, at 4.

[29] Gates 10/25/18 302, at 4.

[30] Bannon 1/18/19 302, at 3.

[31] Gates 4/11/18 302, at 1-2 (SM-2180998); ███ ███

[32] @realDonaldTrump 7/26/16 (6:47 p.m. ET) Tweet.

[33] @realDonaldTrump 7/26/16 (6:50 p.m. ET) Tweet.

[34] *Donald Trump News Conference, Doral, Florida*, C-SPAN (July 27, 2016).

[35] *Donald Trump News Conference, Doral, Florida*, C-SPAN (July 27, 2016).

U.S. Department of Justice

~~Attorney Work Product // May Contain Material Protected Under Fed. R. Crim. P. 6(e)~~

mightily by our press."[36] Trump also said that "there's nothing that I can think of that I'd rather do than have Russia friendly as opposed to the way they are right now," and in response to a question about whether he would recognize Crimea as Russian territory and consider lifting sanctions, Trump replied, "We'll be looking at that. Yeah, we'll be looking."[37]

During the press conference, Trump repeated "I have nothing to do with Russia" five times.[38] He stated that "the closest [he] came to Russia" was that Russians may have purchased a home or condos from him.[39] He said that after he held the Miss Universe pageant in Moscow in 2013 he had been interested in working with Russian companies that "wanted to put a lot of money into developments in Russia" but "it never worked out."[40] He explained, "[f]rankly, I didn't want to do it for a couple of different reasons. But we had a major developer . . . that wanted to develop property in Moscow and other places. But we decided not to do it."[41] The Trump Organization, however, had been pursuing a building project in Moscow—the Trump Tower Moscow project— from approximately September 2015 through June 2016, and the candidate was regularly updated on developments, including possible trips by Michael Cohen to Moscow to promote the deal and by Trump himself to finalize it.[42]

Cohen recalled speaking with Trump after the press conference about Trump's denial of any business dealings in Russia, which Cohen regarded as untrue.[43] Trump told Cohen that Trump Tower Moscow was not a deal yet and said, "Why mention it if it is not a deal?"[44] According to Cohen, at around this time, in response to Trump's disavowal of connections to Russia, campaign

---

[36] *Donald Trump News Conference, Doral, Florida*, C-SPAN (July 27, 2016). Within five hours of Trump's remark, a Russian intelligence service began targeting email accounts associated with Hillary Clinton for possible hacks. *See* Volume I, Section III, *supra*. In written answers submitted in this investigation, the President stated that he made the "Russia, if you're listening" statement "in jest and sarcastically, as was apparent to any objective observer." Written Responses of Donald J. Trump (Nov. 20, 2018), at 13 (Response to Question II, Part (d)).

[37] *Donald Trump News Conference, Doral, Florida*, C-SPAN (July 27, 2016). In his written answers submitted in this investigation, the President said that his statement that "we'll be looking" at Crimea and sanctions "did not communicate any position." Written Responses of Donald J. Trump (Nov. 20, 2018), at 17 (Response to Question IV, Part (g)).

[38] *Donald Trump News Conference, Doral, Florida*, C-SPAN (July 27, 2016).

[39] *Donald Trump News Conference, Doral, Florida*, C-SPAN (July 27, 2016).

[40] *Donald Trump News Conference, Doral, Florida*, C-SPAN (July 27, 2016).

[41] *Donald Trump News Conference, Doral, Florida*, C-SPAN (July 27, 2016).

[42] The Trump Tower Moscow project and Trump's involvement in it is discussed in detail in Volume I, Section IV.A.1, *supra*, and Volume II, Section II.K, *infra*.

[43] Cohen 9/18/18 302, at 4.

[44] Cohen 9/18/18 302, at 4-5.

advisors had developed a "party line" that Trump had no business with Russia and no connections to Russia.[45]

In addition to denying any connections with Russia, the Trump Campaign reacted to reports of Russian election interference in aid of the Campaign by seeking to distance itself from Russian contacts. For example, in August 2016, foreign policy advisor J.D. Gordon declined an invitation to Russian Ambassador Sergey Kislyak's residence because the timing was "not optimal" in view of media reports about Russian interference.[46] On August 19, 2016, Manafort was asked to resign amid media coverage scrutinizing his ties to a pro-Russian political party in Ukraine and links to Russian business.[47] And when the media published stories about Page's connections to Russia in September 2016, Trump Campaign officials terminated Page's association with the Campaign and told the press that he had played "no role" in the Campaign.[48]

On October 7, 2016, WikiLeaks released the first set of emails stolen by a Russian intelligence agency from Clinton Campaign chairman John Podesta.[49] The same day, the federal government announced that "the Russian Government directed the recent compromises of e-mails from US persons and institutions, including from US political organizations."[50] The government statement directly linked Russian hacking to the releases on WikiLeaks, with the goal of interfering with the presidential election, and concluded "that only Russia's senior-most officials could have authorized these activities" based on their "scope and sensitivity."[51]

On October 11, 2016, Podesta stated publicly that the FBI was investigating Russia's hacking and said that candidate Trump might have known in advance that the hacked emails were going to be released.[52] Vice Presidential Candidate Mike Pence was asked whether the Trump

---

[45] Cohen 11/20/18 302, at 1; Cohen 9/18/18 302, at 3-5. The formation of the "party line" is described in greater detail in Volume II, Section II.K, *infra*.

[46] DJTFP00004953 (8/8/16 Email, Gordon to Pchelyakov) (stating that "[t]hese days are not optimal for us, as we are busily knocking down a stream of false media stories"). The invitation and Gordon's response are discussed in Volume I, Section IV.A.7.*a*, *supra*.

[47] *See, e.g.*, Amber Phillips, *Paul Manafort's complicated ties to Ukraine, explained*, Washington Post (Aug. 19, 2016) ("There were also a wave of fresh headlines dealing with investigations into [Manafort's] ties to a pro-Russian political party in Ukraine."); Tom Winter & Ken Dilanian, *Donald Trump Aide Paul Manafort Scrutinized for Russian Business Ties*, NBC (Aug. 18, 2016). Relevant events involving Manafort are discussed in Volume I, Section IV.A.8, *supra*.

[48] Michael Isikoff, *U.S. intel officials probe ties between Trump adviser and Kremlin*, Yahoo News (Sep. 23, 2016); *see, e.g.*, 9/25/16 Email, Hicks to Conway & Bannon; 9/23/16 Email, J. Miller to Bannon & S. Miller; Page 3/16/17 302, at 2.

[49] @WikiLeaks 10/7/16 (4:32 p.m. ET) Tweet.

[50] Joint Statement from the Department Of Homeland Security and Office of the Director of National Intelligence on Election Security, DHS (Oct. 7, 2016).

[51] Joint Statement from the Department Of Homeland Security and Office of the Director of National Intelligence on Election Security, DHS (Oct. 7, 2016).

[52] John Wagner & Anne Gearan, *Clinton campaign chairman ties email hack to Russians, suggests Trump had early warning*, Washington Post (Oct. 11, 2016).

Campaign was "in cahoots" with WikiLeaks in releasing damaging Clinton-related information and responded, "Nothing could be further from the truth."[53]

4. After the Election, Trump Continues to Deny Any Contacts or Connections with Russia or That Russia Aided his Election

On November 8, 2016, Trump was elected President. Two days later, Russian officials told the press that the Russian government had maintained contacts with Trump's "immediate entourage" during the campaign.[54] In response, Hope Hicks, who had been the Trump Campaign spokesperson, said, "We are not aware of any campaign representatives that were in touch with any foreign entities before yesterday, when Mr. Trump spoke with many world leaders."[55] Hicks gave an additional statement denying any contacts between the Campaign and Russia: "It never happened. There was no communication between the campaign and any foreign entity during the campaign."[56]

On December 10, 2016, the press reported that U.S. intelligence agencies had "concluded that Russia interfered in last month's presidential election to boost Donald Trump's bid for the White House."[57] Reacting to the story the next day, President-Elect Trump stated, "I think it's ridiculous. I think it's just another excuse."[58] He continued that no one really knew who was responsible for the hacking, suggesting that the intelligence community had "no idea if it's Russia or China or somebody. It could be somebody sitting in a bed some place."[59] The President-Elect

---

[53] Louis Nelson, *Pence denies Trump camp in cahoots with WikiLeaks*, Politico (Oct. 14, 2016).

[54] Ivan Nechepurenko, *Russian Officials Were in Contact With Trump Allies, Diplomat Says*, New York Times (Nov. 10, 2016) (quoting Russian Deputy Foreign Minister Sergey Ryabkov saying, "[t]here were contacts" and "I cannot say that all, but a number of them maintained contacts with Russian representatives"); Jim Heintz & Matthew Lee, *Russia eyes better ties with Trump; says contacts underway*, Associated Press (Nov. 11, 2016) (quoting Ryabkov saying, "I don't say that all of them, but a whole array of them supported contacts with Russian representatives").

[55] Ivan Nechepurenko, *Russian Officials Were in Contact With Trump Allies, Diplomat Says*, New York Times (Nov. 11, 2016) (quoting Hicks).

[56] Jim Heintz & Matthew Lee, *Russia eyes better ties with Trump; says contacts underway*, Associated Press (Nov. 10, 2016) (quoting Hicks). Hicks recalled that after she made that statement, she spoke with Campaign advisors Kellyanne Conway, Stephen Miller, Jason Miller, and probably Kushner and Bannon to ensure it was accurate, and there was no hesitation or pushback from any of them. Hicks 12/8/17 302, at 4.

[57] Damien Gayle, *CIA concludes Russia interfered to help Trump win election, say reports*, Guardian (Dec. 10, 2016).

[58] *Chris Wallace Hosts "Fox News Sunday," Interview with President-Elect Donald Trump*, CQ Newsmaker Transcripts (Dec. 11, 2016).

[59] *Chris Wallace Hosts "Fox News Sunday," Interview with President-Elect Donald Trump*, CQ Newsmaker Transcripts (Dec. 11, 2016).

U.S. Department of Justice

~~Attorney Work Product // May Contain Material Protected Under Fed. R. Crim. P. 6(e)~~

also said that Democrats were "putting [] out" the story of Russian interference "because they suffered one of the greatest defeats in the history of politics."[60]

On December 18, 2016, Podesta told the press that the election was "distorted by the Russian intervention" and questioned whether Trump Campaign officials had been "in touch with the Russians."[61] The same day, incoming Chief of Staff Reince Priebus appeared on Fox News Sunday and declined to say whether the President-Elect accepted the intelligence community's determination that Russia intervened in the election.[62] When asked about any contact or coordination between the Campaign and Russia, Priebus said, "Even this question is insane. Of course we didn't interface with the Russians."[63] Priebus added that "this whole thing is a spin job" and said, "the real question is, why the Democrats . . . are doing everything they can to delegitimize the outcome of the election?"[64]

On December 29, 2016, the Obama Administration announced that in response to Russian cyber operations aimed at the U.S. election, it was imposing sanctions and other measures on several Russian individuals and entities.[65] When first asked about the sanctions, President-Elect Trump said, "I think we ought to get on with our lives."[66] He then put out a statement that said "It's time for our country to move on to bigger and better things," but indicated that he would meet with intelligence community leaders the following week for a briefing on Russian interference.[67] The briefing occurred on January 6, 2017.[68] Following the briefing, the intelligence community released the public version of its assessment, which concluded with high confidence that Russia had intervened in the election through a variety of means with the goal of harming Clinton's

---

[60] *Chris Wallace Hosts "Fox News Sunday," Interview with President-Elect Donald Trump*, CQ Newsmaker Transcripts (Dec. 11, 2016).

[61] David Morgan, *Clinton campaign: It's an 'open question' if Trump team colluded with Russia*, Reuters Business Insider (Dec. 18, 2016).

[62] *Chris Wallace Hosts "Fox News Sunday," Interview with Incoming White House Chief of Staff Reince Priebus*, Fox News (Dec. 18, 2016).

[63] *Chris Wallace Hosts "Fox News Sunday," Interview with Incoming White House Chief of Staff Reince Priebus*, Fox News (Dec. 18, 2016).

[64] *Chris Wallace Hosts "Fox News Sunday," Interview with Incoming White House Chief of Staff Reince Priebus*, Fox News (Dec. 18, 2016).

[65] *Statement by the President on Actions in Response to Russian Malicious Cyber Activity and Harassment*, White House (Dec. 29, 2016); *see also* Missy Ryan et al., *Obama administration announces measures to punish Russia for 2016 election interference*, Washington Post (Dec. 29, 2016).

[66] John Wagner, *Trump on alleged election interference by Russia: 'Get on with our lives,'* Washington Post (Dec. 29, 2016).

[67] Missy Ryan et al., *Obama administration announces measures to punish Russia for 2016 election interference*, Washington Post (Dec. 29, 2016).

[68] Comey 11/15/17 302, at 3.

U.S. Department of Justice

Attorney Work Product // May Contain Material Protected Under Fed. R. Crim. P. 6(e)

electability.[69] The assessment further concluded with high confidence that Putin and the Russian government had developed a clear preference for Trump.[70]

Several days later, BuzzFeed published unverified allegations compiled by former British intelligence officer Christopher Steele during the campaign about candidate Trump's Russia connections under the headline "These Reports Allege Trump Has Deep Ties To Russia."[71] In a press conference the next day, the President-Elect called the release "an absolute disgrace" and said, "I have no dealings with Russia. I have no deals that could happen in Russia, because we've stayed away.... So I have no deals, I have no loans and I have no dealings. We could make deals in Russia very easily if we wanted to, I just don't want to because I think that would be a conflict."[72]

Several advisors recalled that the President-Elect viewed stories about his Russian connections, the Russia investigations, and the intelligence community assessment of Russian interference as a threat to the legitimacy of his electoral victory.[73] Hicks, for example, said that the President-Elect viewed the intelligence community assessment as his "Achilles heel" because, even if Russia had no impact on the election, people would think Russia helped him win, taking away from what he had accomplished.[74] Sean Spicer, the first White House communications director, recalled that the President thought the Russia story was developed to undermine the legitimacy of his election.[75] Gates said the President viewed the Russia investigation as an attack on the legitimacy of his win.[76] And Priebus recalled that when the intelligence assessment came out, the President-Elect was concerned people would question the legitimacy of his win.[77]

---

[69] Office of the Director of National Intelligence, *Russia's Influence Campaign Targeting the 2016 US Presidential Election*, at 1 (Jan. 6, 2017).

[70] Office of the Director of National Intelligence, *Russia's Influence Campaign Targeting the 2016 US Presidential Election*, at 1 (Jan. 6, 2017).

[71] Ken Bensinger et al., *These Reports Allege Trump Has Deep Ties To Russia*, BuzzFeed (Jan. 10, 2017).

[72] *Donald Trump's News Conference: Full Transcript and Video*, New York Times (Jan. 11, 2017), *available at* https://www.nytimes.com/2017/01/11/us/politics/trump-press-conference-transcript.html.

[73] Priebus 10/13/17 302, at 7; Hicks 3/13/18 302, at 18; Spicer 10/16/17 302, at 6; Bannon 2/14/18 302, at 2; Gates 4/18/18 302, at 3; *see* Pompeo 6/28/17 302, at 2 (the President believed that the purpose of the Russia investigation was to delegitimize his presidency).

[74] Hicks 3/13/18 302, at 18.

[75] Spicer 10/17/17 302, at 6.

[76] Gates 4/18/18 302, at 3.

[77] Priebus 10/13/17 302, at 7.

23

U.S. Department of Justice

~~Attorney Work Product // May Contain Material Protected Under Fed. R. Crim. P. 6(e)~~

B. The President's Conduct Concerning the Investigation of Michael Flynn

Overview

During the presidential transition, incoming National Security Advisor Michael Flynn had two phone calls with the Russian Ambassador to the United States about the Russian response to U.S. sanctions imposed because of Russia's election interference. After the press reported on Flynn's contacts with the Russian Ambassador, Flynn lied to incoming Administration officials by saying he had not discussed sanctions on the calls. The officials publicly repeated those lies in press interviews. The FBI, which previously was investigating Flynn for other matters, interviewed him about the calls in the first week after the inauguration, and Flynn told similar lies to the FBI. On January 26, 2017, Department of Justice (DOJ) officials notified the White House that Flynn and the Russian Ambassador had discussed sanctions and that Flynn had been interviewed by the FBI. The next night, the President had a private dinner with FBI Director James Comey in which he asked for Comey's loyalty. On February 13, 2017, the President asked Flynn to resign. The following day, the President had a one-on-one conversation with Comey in which he said, "I hope you can see your way clear to letting this go, to letting Flynn go."

Evidence

1. Incoming National Security Advisor Flynn Discusses Sanctions on Russia with Russian Ambassador Sergey Kislyak

Shortly after the election, President-Elect Trump announced he would appoint Michael Flynn as his National Security Advisor.[78] For the next two months, Flynn played an active role on the Presidential Transition Team (PTT) coordinating policy positions and communicating with foreign government officials, including Russian Ambassador to the United States Sergey Kislyak.[79]

On December 29, 2016, as noted in Volume II, Section II.A.4, *supra*, the Obama Administration announced that it was imposing sanctions and other measures on several Russian individuals and entities.[80] That day, multiple members of the PTT exchanged emails about the sanctions and the impact they would have on the incoming Administration, and Flynn informed members of the PTT that he would be speaking to the Russian Ambassador later in the day.[81]

---

[78] Flynn 11/16/17 302, at 7; *President-Elect Donald J. Trump Selects U.S. Senator Jeff Sessions for Attorney General, Lt. Gen. Michael Flynn as Assistant to the President for National Security Affairs and U.S. Rep. Mike Pompeo as Director of the Central Intelligence Agency*, President-Elect Donald J. Trump Press Release (Nov. 18, 2016); *see also, e.g.*, Bryan Bender, *Trump names Mike Flynn national security adviser*, Politico, (Nov. 17, 2016).

[79] Flynn 11/16/17 302, at 8-14; Priebus 10/13/17 302, at 3-5.

[80] *Statement by the President on Actions in Response to Russian Malicious Cyber Activity and Harassment*, The White House, Office of the Press Secretary (Dec. 29, 2016).

[81] 12/29/16 Email, O'Brien to McFarland et al.; 12/29/16 Email, Bossert to Flynn et al.; 12/29/16 Email, McFarland to Flynn et al.; SF000001 (12/29/16 Text Message, Flynn to Flaherty) ("Tit for tat w Russia not good. Russian AMBO reaching out to me today."); Flynn 1/19/18 302, at 2.

Flynn, who was in the Dominican Republic at the time, and K.T. McFarland, who was slated to become the Deputy National Security Advisor and was at the Mar-a-Lago resort in Florida with the President-Elect and other senior staff, talked by phone about what, if anything, Flynn should communicate to Kislyak about the sanctions.[82]   McFarland had spoken with incoming Administration officials about the sanctions and Russia's possible responses and thought she had mentioned in those conversations that Flynn was scheduled to speak with Kislyak.[83] Based on those conversations, McFarland informed Flynn that incoming Administration officials at Mar-a-Lago did not want Russia to escalate the situation.[84] At 4:43 p.m. that afternoon, McFarland sent an email to several officials about the sanctions and informed the group that "Gen [F]lynn is talking to russian ambassador this evening."[85]

Approximately one hour later, McFarland met with the President-Elect and senior officials and briefed them on the sanctions and Russia's possible responses.[86] Incoming Chief of Staff Reince Priebus recalled that McFarland may have mentioned at the meeting that the sanctions situation could be "cooled down" and not escalated.[87] McFarland recalled that at the end of the meeting, someone may have mentioned to the President-Elect that Flynn was speaking to the Russian Ambassador that evening.[88] McFarland did not recall any response by the President-Elect.[89] Priebus recalled that the President-Elect viewed the sanctions as an attempt by the Obama Administration to embarrass him by delegitimizing his election.[90]

Immediately after discussing the sanctions with McFarland on December 29, 2016, Flynn called Kislyak and requested that Russia respond to the sanctions only in a reciprocal manner, without escalating the situation.[91] After the call, Flynn briefed McFarland on its substance.[92] Flynn told McFarland that the Russian response to the sanctions was not going to be escalatory because Russia wanted a good relationship with the Trump Administration.[93] On December 30, 2016, Russian President Vladimir Putin announced that Russia would not take retaliatory measures

---

[82] Statement of Offense at 2-3, *United States v. Michael T. Flynn*, 1:17-cr-232 (D.D.C. Dec. 1, 2017), Doc. 4 (*Flynn* Statement of Offense); Flynn 11/17/17 302, at 3-4; Flynn 11/20/17 302, at 3; McFarland 12/22/17 302, at 6-7.

[83] McFarland 12/22/17 302, at 4-7 (recalling discussions about this issue with Bannon and Priebus).

[84] *Flynn* Statement of Offense, at 3; Flynn 11/17/17 302, at 3-4; McFarland 12/22/17 302, at 6-7.

[85] 12/29/16 Email, McFarland to Flynn et al.

[86] McFarland 12/22/17 302, at 7.

[87] Priebus 1/18/18 302, at 3.

[88] McFarland 12/22/17 302, at 7. Priebus thought it was possible that McFarland had mentioned Flynn's scheduled call with Kislyak at this meeting, although he was not certain. Priebus 1/18/18 302, at 3.

[89] McFarland 12/22/17 302, at 7.

[90] Priebus 1/18/18 302, at 3.

[91] *Flynn* Statement of Offense, at 3; Flynn 11/17/17 302, at 3-4.

[92] *Flynn* Statement of Offense, at 3; McFarland 12/22/17 302, at 7-8; Flynn 11/17/17 302, at 4.

[93] McFarland 12/22/17 302, at 8.

U.S. Department of Justice

~~Attorney Work Product // May Contain Material Protected Under Fed. R. Crim. P. 6(e)~~

in response to the sanctions at that time and would instead "plan . . . further steps to restore Russian-US relations based on the policies of the Trump Administration."[94] Following that announcement, the President-Elect tweeted, "Great move on delay (by V. Putin) - I always knew he was very smart!"[95]

On December 31, 2016, Kislyak called Flynn and told him that Flynn's request had been received at the highest levels and Russia had chosen not to retaliate in response to the request.[96] Later that day, Flynn told McFarland about this follow-up conversation with Kislyak and Russia's decision not to escalate the sanctions situation based on Flynn's request.[97] McFarland recalled that Flynn thought his phone call had made a difference.[98] Flynn spoke with other incoming Administration officials that day, but does not recall whether they discussed the sanctions.[99]

Flynn recalled discussing the sanctions issue with incoming Administration official Stephen Bannon the next day.[100] Flynn said that Bannon appeared to know about Flynn's conversations with Kislyak, and he and Bannon agreed that they had "stopped the train on Russia's response" to the sanctions.[101] On January 3, 2017, Flynn saw the President-Elect in person and thought they discussed the Russian reaction to the sanctions, but Flynn did not have a specific recollection of telling the President-Elect about the substance of his calls with Kislyak.[102]

Members of the intelligence community were surprised by Russia's decision not to retaliate in response to the sanctions.[103] When analyzing Russia's response, they became aware of Flynn's discussion of sanctions with Kislyak.[104] Previously, the FBI had opened an investigation of Flynn based on his relationship with the Russian government.[105] Flynn's contacts with Kislyak became a key component of that investigation.[106]

---

[94] *Statement by the President of Russia*, President of Russia (Dec. 30, 2016) 12/30/16.

[95] @realDonaldTrump 12/30/16 (2:41 p.m. ET) Tweet.

[96] Flynn 1/19/18 302, at 3; *Flynn* Statement of Offense, at 3.

[97] Flynn 1/19/18 302, at 3; Flynn 11/17/17 302, at 6; McFarland 12/22/17 302, at 10; *Flynn* Statement of Offense, at 3.

[98] McFarland 12/22/17 302, at 10; *see* Flynn 1/19/18 302, at 4.

[99] Flynn 11/17/17 302, at 5-6.

[100] Flynn 1/19/18 302, at 4-5. Bannon recalled meeting with Flynn that day, but said he did not remember discussing sanctions with him. Bannon 2/12/18 302, at 9.

[101] Flynn 11/21/17 302, at 1; Flynn 1/19/18 302, at 5.

[102] Flynn 1/19/18 302, at 6; Flynn 11/17/17 302, at 6.

[103] McCord 7/17/17 302, at 2.

[104] McCord 7/17/17 302, at 2.

[105] McCord 7/17/17 302, at 2-3; Comey 11/15/17 302, at 5.

[106] McCord 7/17/17 302, at 2-3.

U.S. Department of Justice

~~Attorney Work Product // May Contain Material Protected Under Fed. R. Crim. P. 6(e)~~

2. President-Elect Trump is Briefed on the Intelligence Community's Assessment of Russian Interference in the Election and Congress Opens Election-Interference Investigations

On January 6, 2017, as noted in Volume II, Section II.A.4, *supra*, intelligence officials briefed President-Elect Trump and the incoming Administration on the intelligence community's assessment that Russia had interfered in the 2016 presidential election.[107] When the briefing concluded, Comey spoke with the President-Elect privately to brief him on unverified, personally sensitive allegations compiled by Steele.[108] According to a memorandum Comey drafted immediately after their private discussion, the President-Elect began the meeting by telling Comey he had conducted himself honorably over the prior year and had a great reputation.[109] The President-Elect stated that he thought highly of Comey, looked forward to working with him, and hoped that he planned to stay on as FBI director.[110] Comey responded that he intended to continue serving in that role.[111] Comey then briefed the President-Elect on the sensitive material in the Steele reporting.[112] Comey recalled that the President-Elect seemed defensive, so Comey decided

---

[107] *Hearing on Russian Election Interference Before the Senate Select Intelligence Committee*, 115th Cong. (June 8, 2017) (Statement for the Record of James B. Comey, former Director of the FBI, at 1-2).

[108] Comey 11/15/17 302, at 3; *Hearing on Russian Election Interference Before the Senate Select Intelligence Committee*, 115th Cong. (June 8, 2017) (Statement for the Record of James B. Comey, former Director of the FBI, at 1-2).

[109] Comey 1/7/17 Memorandum, at 1. Comey began drafting the memorandum summarizing the meeting immediately after it occurred. Comey 11/15/17 302, at 4. He finished the memorandum that evening and finalized it the following morning. Comey 11/15/17 302, at 4.

[110] Comey 1/7/17 Memorandum, at 1; Comey 11/15/17 302, at 3. Comey identified several other occasions in January 2017 when the President reiterated that he hoped Comey would stay on as FBI director. On January 11, President-Elect Trump called Comey to discuss the Steele reports and stated that he thought Comey was doing great and the President-Elect hoped he would remain in his position as FBI director. Comey 11/15/17 302, at 4; *Hearing on Russian Election Interference Before the Senate Select Intelligence Committee*, 115th Cong. (June 8, 2017) (testimony of James B. Comey, former Director of the FBI), CQ Cong. Transcripts, at 90. ("[D]uring that call, he asked me again, 'Hope you're going to stay, you're doing a great job.' And I told him that I intended to."). On January 22, at a White House reception honoring law enforcement, the President greeted Comey and said he looked forward to working with him. *Hearing on Russian Election Interference Before the Senate Select Intelligence Committee*, 115th Cong. (June 8, 2017) (testimony of James B. Comey, former Director of the FBI), CQ Cong. Transcripts, at 22. And as discussed in greater detail in Volume II, Section II.D, *infra*, on January 27, the President invited Comey to dinner at the White House and said he was glad Comey wanted to stay on as FBI Director.

[111] Comey 1/7/17 Memorandum, at 1; Comey 11/15/17 302, at 3.

[112] Comey 1/7/17 Memorandum, at 1-2; Comey 11/15/17 302, at 3. Comey's briefing included the Steele reporting's unverified allegation that the Russians had compromising tapes of the President involving conduct when he was a private citizen during a 2013 trip to Moscow for the Miss Universe Pageant. During the 2016 presidential campaign, a similar claim may have reached candidate Trump. On October 30, 2016, Michael Cohen received a text from Russian businessman Giorgi Rtskhiladze that said, "Stopped flow of tapes from Russia but not sure if there's anything else. Just so you know . . . ." 10/30/16 Text Message, Rtskhiladze to Cohen. Rtskhiladze said "tapes" referred to compromising tapes of Trump rumored to be held by persons associated with the Russian real estate conglomerate Crocus Group, which had helped host

to assure him that the FBI was not investigating him personally.[113] Comey recalled he did not want the President-Elect to think of the conversation as a "J. Edgar Hoover move."[114]

On January 10, 2017, the media reported that Comey had briefed the President-Elect on the Steele reporting,[115] and BuzzFeed News published information compiled by Steele online, stating that the information included "specific, unverified, and potentially unverifiable allegations of contact between Trump aides and Russian operatives."[116] The next day, the President-Elect expressed concern to intelligence community leaders about the fact that the information had leaked and asked whether they could make public statements refuting the allegations in the Steele reports.[117]

In the following weeks, three Congressional committees opened investigations to examine Russia's interference in the election and whether the Trump Campaign had colluded with Russia.[118] On January 13, 2017, the Senate Select Committee on Intelligence (SSCI) announced that it would conduct a bipartisan inquiry into Russian interference in the election, including any "links between Russia and individuals associated with political campaigns."[119] On January 25, 2017, the House Permanent Select Committee on Intelligence (HPSCI) announced that it had been conducting an investigation into Russian election interference and possible coordination with the political campaigns.[120] And on February 2, 2017, the Senate Judiciary Committee announced that it too would investigate Russian efforts to intervene in the election.[121]

---

the 2013 Miss Universe Pageant in Russia. Rtskhiladze 4/4/18 302, at 12. Cohen said he spoke to Trump about the issue after receiving the texts from Rtskhiladze. Cohen 9/12/18 302, at 13. Rtskhiladze said he was told the tapes were fake, but he did not communicate that to Cohen. Rtskhiladze 5/10/18 302, at 7.

[113] Comey 11/15/17 302, at 3-4; *Hearing on Russian Election Interference Before the Senate Select Intelligence Committee*, 115th Cong. (June 8, 2017) (Statement for the Record of James B. Comey, former Director of the FBI, at 2).

[114] Comey 11/15/17 302, at 3.

[115] *See, e.g.,* Evan Perez et al., *Intel chiefs presented Trump with claims of Russian efforts to compromise him,* CNN (Jan. 10, 2017; updated Jan. 12, 2017).

[116] Ken Bensinger et al., *These Reports Allege Trump Has Deep Ties To Russia,* BuzzFeed News (Jan. 10, 2017).

[117] *See* 1/11/17 Email, Clapper to Comey ("He asked if I could put out a statement. He would prefer of course that I say the documents are bogus, which, of course, I can't do."); 1/12/17 Email, Comey to Clapper ("He called me at 5 yesterday and we had a very similar conversation."); Comey 11/15/17 302, at 4-5.

[118] *See 2016 Presidential Election Investigation Fast Facts,* CNN (first published Oct. 12, 2017; updated Mar. 1, 2019) (summarizing starting dates of Russia-related investigations).

[119] *Joint Statement on Committee Inquiry into Russian Intelligence Activities,* SSCI (Jan. 13, 2017).

[120] *Joint Statement on Progress of Bipartisan HPSCI Inquiry into Russian Active Measures,* HPSCI (Jan. 25, 2017).

[121] *Joint Statement from Senators Graham and Whitehouse on Investigation into Russian Influence on Democratic Nations' Elections* (Feb. 2, 2017).

U.S. Department of Justice

~~Attorney Work Product // May Contain Material Protected Under Fed. R. Crim. P. 6(e)~~

3. Flynn Makes False Statements About his Communications with Kislyak to Incoming Administration Officials, the Media, and the FBI

On January 12, 2017, a Washington Post columnist reported that Flynn and Kislyak communicated on the day the Obama Administration announced the Russia sanctions.[122] The column questioned whether Flynn had said something to "undercut the U.S. sanctions" and whether Flynn's communications had violated the letter or spirit of the Logan Act.[123]

President-Elect Trump called Priebus after the story was published and expressed anger about it.[124] Priebus recalled that the President-Elect asked, "What the hell is this all about?"[125] Priebus called Flynn and told him that the President-Elect was angry about the reporting on Flynn's conversations with Kislyak.[126] Flynn recalled that he felt a lot of pressure because Priebus had spoken to the "boss" and said Flynn needed to "kill the story."[127] Flynn directed McFarland to call the Washington Post columnist and inform him that no discussion of sanctions had occurred.[128] McFarland recalled that Flynn said words to the effect of, "I want to kill the story."[129] McFarland made the call as Flynn had requested although she knew she was providing false information, and the Washington Post updated the column to reflect that a "Trump official" had denied that Flynn and Kislyak discussed sanctions.[130]

When Priebus and other incoming Administration officials questioned Flynn internally about the Washington Post column, Flynn maintained that he had not discussed sanctions with Kislyak.[131] Flynn repeated that claim to Vice President-Elect Michael Pence and to incoming press secretary Sean Spicer.[132] In subsequent media interviews in mid-January, Pence, Priebus, and

---

[122] David Ignatius, *Why did Obama dawdle on Russia's hacking?*, Washington Post (Jan. 12, 2017).

[123] David Ignatius, *Why did Obama dawdle on Russia's hacking?*, Washington Post (Jan. 12, 2017). The Logan Act makes it a crime for "[a]ny citizen of the United States, wherever he may be" to "without authority of the United States, directly or indirectly commence[] or carr[y] on any correspondence or intercourse with any foreign government or any officer or agent thereof, in relation to any disputes or controversies with the United States, or to defeat the measures of the United States." 18 U.S.C. § 953.

[124] Priebus 1/18/18 302, at 6.

[125] Priebus 1/18/18 302, at 6.

[126] Priebus 1/18/18 302, at 6.

[127] Flynn 11/21/17 302, at 1; Flynn 11/20/17 302, at 6.

[128] McFarland 12/22/17 302, at 12-13.

[129] McFarland 12/22/17 302, at 12.

[130] McFarland 12/22/17 302, at 12-13; McFarland 8/29/17 302, at 8; *see* David Ignatius, *Why did Obama dawdle on Russia's hacking?*, Washington Post (Jan. 12, 2017).

[131] Flynn 11/17/17 302, at 1, 8; Flynn 1/19/18 302, at 7; Priebus 10/13/17 302, at 7-8; S. Miller 8/31/17 302, at 8-11.

[132] Flynn 11/17/17 302, at 1, 8; Flynn 1/19/18 302, at 7; S. Miller 8/31/17 302, at 10-11.

Spicer denied that Flynn and Kislyak had discussed sanctions, basing those denials on their conversations with Flynn.[133]

The public statements of incoming Administration officials denying that Flynn and Kislyak had discussed sanctions alarmed senior DOJ officials, who were aware that the statements were not true.[134] Those officials were concerned that Flynn had lied to his colleagues—who in turn had unwittingly misled the American public—creating a compromise situation for Flynn because the Department of Justice assessed that the Russian government could prove Flynn lied.[135] The FBI investigative team also believed that Flynn's calls with Kislyak and subsequent denials about discussing sanctions raised potential Logan Act issues and were relevant to the FBI's broader Russia investigation.[136]

On January 20, 2017, President Trump was inaugurated and Flynn was sworn in as National Security Advisor. On January 23, 2017, Spicer delivered his first press briefing and stated that he had spoken with Flynn the night before, who confirmed that the calls with Kislyak were about topics unrelated to sanctions.[137] Spicer's statements added to the Department of Justice's concerns that Russia had leverage over Flynn based on his lies and could use that derogatory information to compromise him.[138]

On January 24, 2017, Flynn agreed to be interviewed by agents from the FBI.[139] During the interview, which took place at the White House, Flynn falsely stated that he did not ask Kislyak to refrain from escalating the situation in response to the sanctions on Russia imposed by the Obama Administration.[140] Flynn also falsely stated that he did not remember a follow-up conversation in which Kislyak stated that Russia had chosen to moderate its response to those sanctions as a result of Flynn's request.[141]

---

[133] *Face the Nation Interview with Vice President-Elect Pence,* CBS (Jan. 15, 2017); Julie Hirschfield Davis et al., *Trump National Security Advisor Called Russian Envoy Day Before Sanctions Were Imposed,* Washington Post (Jan. 13, 2017); *Meet the Press Interview with Reince Priebus,* NBC (Jan. 15, 2017).

[134] Yates 8/15/17 302, at 2-3; McCord 7/17/17 302, at 3-4; McCabe 8/17/17 302, at 5 (DOJ officials were "really freaked out about it").

[135] Yates 8/15/17 302, at 3; McCord 7/17/17 302, at 4.

[136] McCord 7/17/17 302, at 4; McCabe 8/17/17 302, at 5-6.

[137] Sean Spicer, *White House Daily Briefing,* C-SPAN (Jan. 23, 2017).

[138] Yates 8/15/17 302, at 4; Axelrod 7/20/17 302, at 5.

[139] *Flynn* Statement of Offense, at 2.

[140] *Flynn* Statement of Offense, at 2.

[141] *Flynn* Statement of Offense, at 2. On December 1, 2017, Flynn admitted to making these false statements and pleaded guilty to violating 18 U.S.C. § 1001, which makes it a crime to knowingly and willfully "make[] any materially false, fictitious, or fraudulent statement or representation" to federal law enforcement officials. *See* Volume I, Section IV.A.7, *supra*.

U.S. Department of Justice

~~Attorney Work Product // May Contain Material Protected Under Fed. R. Crim. P. 6(e)~~

4. DOJ Officials Notify the White House of Their Concerns About Flynn

On January 26, 2017, Acting Attorney General Sally Yates contacted White House Counsel Donald McGahn and informed him that she needed to discuss a sensitive matter with him in person.[142] Later that day, Yates and Mary McCord, a senior national security official at the Department of Justice, met at the White House with McGahn and White House Counsel's Office attorney James Burnham.[143] Yates said that the public statements made by the Vice President denying that Flynn and Kislyak discussed sanctions were not true and put Flynn in a potentially compromised position because the Russians would know he had lied.[144] Yates disclosed that Flynn had been interviewed by the FBI.[145] She declined to answer a specific question about how Flynn had performed during that interview,[146] but she indicated that Flynn's statements to the FBI were similar to the statements he had made to Pence and Spicer denying that he had discussed sanctions.[147] McGahn came away from the meeting with the impression that the FBI had not pinned Flynn down in lies,[148] but he asked John Eisenberg, who served as legal advisor to the National Security Council, to examine potential legal issues raised by Flynn's FBI interview and his contacts with Kislyak.[149]

That afternoon, McGahn notified the President that Yates had come to the White House to discuss concerns about Flynn.[150] McGahn described what Yates had told him, and the President asked him to repeat it, so he did.[151] McGahn recalled that when he described the FBI interview of Flynn, he said that Flynn did not disclose having discussed sanctions with Kislyak, but that there may not have been a clear violation of 18 U.S.C. § 1001.[152] The President asked about Section 1001, and McGahn explained the law to him, and also explained the Logan Act.[153] The President

---

[142] Yates 8/15/17 302, at 6.

[143] Yates 8/15/17 302, at 6; McCord 7/17/17 302, at 6; SCR015_000198 (2/15/17 Draft Memorandum to file from the Office of the Counsel to the President).

[144] Yates 8/15/17 302, at 6-8; McCord 7/17/17 302, at 6-7; Burnham 11/3/17 302, at 4; SCR015_000198 (2/15/17 Draft Memorandum to file from the Office of the Counsel to the President).

[145] McGahn 11/30/17 302, at 5; Yates 8/15/17 302, at 7; McCord 7/17/17 302, at 7; Burnham 11/3/17 302, at 4.

[146] Yates 8/15/17 302, at 7; McCord 7/17/17 302, at 7.

[147] SCR015_000198 (2/15/17 Draft Memorandum to file from the Office of the Counsel to the President); Burnham 11/3/17 302, at 4.

[148] McGahn 11/30/17 302, at 5.

[149] SCR015_000198 (2/15/17 Draft Memorandum to file from the Office of the Counsel to the President); McGahn 11/30/17 302, at 6, 8.

[150] McGahn 11/30/17 302, at 6; SCR015_000278 (White House Counsel's Office Memorandum re: "Flynn Tick Tock") (on January 26, "McGahn IMMEDIATELY advises POTUS"); SCR015_000198 (2/15/17 Draft Memorandum to file from the Office of the Counsel to the President).

[151] McGahn 11/30/17 302, at 6.

[152] McGahn 11/30/17 302, at 7.

[153] McGahn 11/30/17 302, at 7.

U.S. Department of Justice

~~Attorney Work Product // May Contain Material Protected Under Fed. R. Crim. P. 6(e)~~

instructed McGahn to work with Priebus and Bannon to look into the matter further and directed that they not discuss it with any other officials.[154] Priebus recalled that the President was angry with Flynn in light of what Yates had told the White House and said, "not again, this guy, this stuff."[155]

That evening, the President dined with several senior advisors and asked the group what they thought about FBI Director Comey.[156] According to Director of National Intelligence Dan Coats, who was at the dinner, no one openly advocated terminating Comey but the consensus on him was not positive.[157] Coats told the group that he thought Comey was a good director.[158] Coats encouraged the President to meet Comey face-to-face and spend time with him before making a decision about whether to retain him.[159]

5. McGahn has a Follow-Up Meeting About Flynn with Yates; President Trump has Dinner with FBI Director Comey

The next day, January 27, 2017, McGahn and Eisenberg discussed the results of Eisenberg's initial legal research into Flynn's conduct, and specifically whether Flynn may have violated the Espionage Act, the Logan Act, or 18 U.S.C. § 1001.[160] Based on his preliminary research, Eisenberg informed McGahn that there was a possibility that Flynn had violated 18 U.S.C. § 1001 and the Logan Act.[161] Eisenberg noted that the United States had never successfully prosecuted an individual under the Logan Act and that Flynn could have possible defenses, and

---

[154] McGahn 11/30/17 302, at 7; SCR015_000198-99 (2/15/17 Draft Memorandum to file from the Office of the Counsel to the President).

[155] Priebus 10/13/17 302, at 8. Several witnesses said that the President was unhappy with Flynn for other reasons at this time. Bannon said that Flynn's standing with the President was not good by December 2016. Bannon 2/12/18 302, at 12. The President-Elect had concerns because President Obama had warned him about Flynn shortly after the election. Bannon 2/12/18 302, at 4-5; Hicks 12/8/17 302, at 7 (President Obama's comment sat with President-Elect Trump more than Hicks expected). Priebus said that the President had become unhappy with Flynn even before the story of his calls with Kislyak broke and had become so upset with Flynn that he would not look at him during intelligence briefings. Priebus 1/18/18 302, at 8. Hicks said that the President thought Flynn had bad judgment and was angered by tweets sent by Flynn and his son, and she described Flynn as "being on thin ice" by early February 2017. Hicks 12/8/17 302, at 7, 10.

[156] Coats 6/14/17 302, at 2.

[157] Coats 6/14/17 302, at 2.

[158] Coats 6/14/17 302, at 2.

[159] Coats 6/14/17 302, at 2.

[160] SCR015_000199 (2/15/17 Draft Memorandum to file from the Office of the Counsel to the President); McGahn 11/30/17 302, at 8.

[161] SCR015_000199 (2/15/17 Draft Memorandum to file from the Office of the Counsel to the President); Eisenberg 11/29/17 302, at 9.

told McGahn that he believed it was unlikely that a prosecutor would pursue a Logan Act charge under the circumstances.[162]

That same morning, McGahn asked Yates to return to the White House to discuss Flynn again.[163] In that second meeting, McGahn expressed doubts that the Department of Justice would bring a Logan Act prosecution against Flynn, but stated that the White House did not want to take action that would interfere with an ongoing FBI investigation of Flynn.[164] Yates responded that Department of Justice had notified the White House so that it could take action in response to the information provided.[165] McGahn ended the meeting by asking Yates for access to the underlying information the Department of Justice possessed pertaining to Flynn's discussions with Kislyak.[166]

Also on January 27, the President called FBI Director Comey and invited him to dinner that evening.[167] Priebus recalled that before the dinner, he told the President something like, "don't talk about Russia, whatever you do," and the President promised he would not talk about Russia at the dinner.[168] McGahn had previously advised the President that he should not communicate directly with the Department of Justice to avoid the perception or reality of political interference in law enforcement.[169] When Bannon learned about the President's planned dinner with Comey, he suggested that he or Priebus also attend, but the President stated that he wanted to dine with Comey alone.[170] Comey said that when he arrived for the dinner that evening, he was surprised and concerned to see that no one else had been invited.[171]

---

[162] SCR015_000199 (2/15/17 Draft Memorandum to file from the Office of the Counsel to the President); Eisenberg 11/29/17 302, at 9.

[163] SCR015_000199 (2/15/17 Draft Memorandum to file from the Office of the Counsel to the President); McGahn 11/30/17 302, at 8; Yates 8/15/17 302, at 8.

[164] Yates 8/15/17 302, at 9; McGahn 11/30/17 302, at 8.

[165] Yates 8/15/17 302, at 9; Burnham 11/3/17 302, at 5; see SCR015_00199 (2/15/17 Draft Memorandum to file from the Office of the Counsel to the President) ("Yates was unwilling to confirm or deny that there was an ongoing investigation but did indicate that the Department of Justice would not object to the White House taking action against Flynn.").

[166] Yates 9/15/17 302, at 9; Burnham 11/3/17 302, at 5. In accordance with McGahn's request, the Department of Justice made the underlying information available and Eisenberg viewed the information in early February. Eisenberg 11/29/17 302, at 5; FBI 2/7/17 Electronic Communication, at 1 (documenting 2/2/17 meeting with Eisenberg).

[167] Comey 11/15/17 302, at 6; SCR012b_000001 (President's Daily Diary, 1/27/17); *Hearing on Russian Election Interference Before the Senate Select Intelligence Committee*, 115th Cong. (June 8, 2017) (Statement for the Record of James B. Comey, former Director of the FBI, at 2-3).

[168] Priebus 10/13/17 302, at 17.

[169] *See* McGahn 11/30/17 302, at 9; Dhillon 11/21/17 302, at 2; Bannon 2/12/18 302, at 17.

[170] Bannon 2/12/18 302, at 17.

[171] *Hearing on Russian Election Interference Before the Senate Select Intelligence Committee*, 115th Cong. (June 8, 2017) (Statement for the Record of James B. Comey, former Director of the FBI, at 3); *see* Comey 11/15/17 302, at 6.

U.S. Department of Justice

~~Attorney Work Product // May Contain Material Protected Under Fed. R. Crim. P. 6(e)~~

Comey provided an account of the dinner in a contemporaneous memo, an interview with this Office, and congressional testimony. According to Comey's account of the dinner, the President repeatedly brought up Comey's future, asking whether he wanted to stay on as FBI director.[172] Because the President had previously said he wanted Comey to stay on as FBI director, Comey interpreted the President's comments as an effort to create a patronage relationship by having Comey ask for his job.[173] The President also brought up the Steele reporting that Comey had raised in the January 6, 2017 briefing and stated that he was thinking about ordering the FBI to investigate the allegations to prove they were false.[174] Comey responded that the President should think carefully about issuing such an order because it could create a narrative that the FBI was investigating him personally, which was incorrect.[175] Later in the dinner, the President brought up Flynn and said, "the guy has serious judgment issues."[176] Comey did not comment on Flynn and the President did not acknowledge any FBI interest in or contact with Flynn.[177]

According to Comey's account, at one point during the dinner the President stated, "I need loyalty, I expect loyalty."[178] Comey did not respond and the conversation moved on to other topics, but the President returned to the subject of Comey's job at the end of the dinner and repeated, "I need loyalty."[179] Comey responded, "You will always get honesty from me."[180] The

---

[172] Comey 11/15/17 302, at 7; Comey 1/28/17 Memorandum, at 1, 3; *Hearing on Russian Election Interference Before the Senate Select Intelligence Committee*, 115th Cong. (June 8, 2017) (Statement for the Record of James B. Comey, former Director of the FBI, at 3).

[173] Comey 11/15/17 302, at 7; *Hearing on Russian Election Interference Before the Senate Select Intelligence Committee*, 115th Cong. (June 8, 2017) (Statement for the Record of James B. Comey, former Director of the FBI, at 3).

[174] Comey 1/28/17 Memorandum, at 3; *Hearing on Russian Election Interference Before the Senate Select Intelligence Committee*, 115th Cong. (June 8, 2017) (Statement for the Record of James B. Comey, former Director of the FBI, at 4).

[175] Comey 1/28/17 Memorandum, at 3; *Hearing on Russian Election Interference Before the Senate Select Intelligence Committee*, 115th Cong. (June 8, 2017) (Statement for the Record of James B. Comey, former Director of the FBI, at 4).

[176] Comey 1/28/17 Memorandum, at 4; Comey 11/15/17 302, at 7.

[177] Comey 1/28/17 Memorandum, at 4; Comey 11/15/17 302, at 7.

[178] Comey 1/28/18 Memorandum, at 2; Comey 11/15/17 302, at 7; *Hearing on Russian Election Interference Before the Senate Select Intelligence Committee*, 115th Cong. (June 8, 2017) (Statement for the Record of James B. Comey, former Director of the FBI, at 3).

[179] Comey 1/28/17 Memorandum, at 3; Comey 11/15/17 302, at 7; *Hearing on Russian Election Interference Before the Senate Select Intelligence Committee*, 115th Cong. (June 8, 2017) (Statement for the Record of James B. Comey, former Director of the FBI, at 3-4).

[180] Comey 1/28/17 Memorandum, at 3; Comey 11/15/17 302, at 7; *Hearing on Russian Election Interference Before the Senate Select Intelligence Committee*, 115th Cong. (June 8, 2017) (Statement for the Record of James B. Comey, former Director of the FBI, at 4).

President said, "That's what I want, honest loyalty."[181] Comey said, "You will get that from me."[182]

After Comey's account of the dinner became public, the President and his advisors disputed that he had asked for Comey's loyalty.[183] The President also indicated that he had not invited Comey to dinner, telling a reporter that he thought Comey had "asked for the dinner" because "he wanted to stay on."[184] But substantial evidence corroborates Comey's account of the dinner invitation and the request for loyalty. The President's Daily Diary confirms that the President "extend[ed] a dinner invitation" to Comey on January 27.[185] With respect to the substance of the dinner conversation, Comey documented the President's request for loyalty in a memorandum he began drafting the night of the dinner;[186] senior FBI officials recall that Comey told them about the loyalty request shortly after the dinner occurred;[187] and Comey described the request while

---

[181] Comey 1/28/17 Memorandum, at 3; Comey 11/15/17 302, at 7; *Hearing on Russian Election Interference Before the Senate Select Intelligence Committee*, 115th Cong. (June 8, 2017) (Statement for the Record of James B. Comey, former Director of the FBI, at 4).

[182] Comey 1/28/17 Memorandum, at 3; Comey 11/15/17 302, at 7; *Hearing on Russian Election Interference Before the Senate Select Intelligence Committee*, 115th Cong. (June 8, 2017) (Statement for the Record of James B. Comey, former Director of the FBI, at 4).

[183] *See, e.g.*, Michael S. Schmidt, *In a Private Dinner, Trump Demanded Loyalty. Comey Demurred.*, New York Times (May 11, 2017) (quoting Sarah Sanders as saying, "[The President] would never even suggest the expectation of personal loyalty"); Ali Vitali, *Trump Never Asked for Comey's Loyalty, President's Personal Lawyer Says*, NBC (June 8, 2017) (quoting the President's personal counsel as saying, "The president also never told Mr. Comey, 'I need loyalty, I expect loyalty,' in form or substance."); Remarks by President Trump in Press Conference, White House (June 9, 2017) ("I hardly know the man. I'm not going to say 'I want you to pledge allegiance.' Who would do that? Who would ask a man to pledge allegiance under oath?"). In a private conversation with Spicer, the President stated that he had never asked for Comey's loyalty, but added that if he had asked for loyalty, "Who cares?" Spicer 10/16/17 302, at 4. The President also told McGahn that he never said what Comey said he had. McGahn 12/12/17 302, at 17.

[184] *Interview of Donald J. Trump*, NBC (May 11, 2017).

[185] SCR012b_000001 (President's Daily Diary, 1/27/17) (reflecting that the President called Comey in the morning on January 27 and "[t]he purpose of the call was to extend a dinner invitation"). In addition, two witnesses corroborate Comey's account that the President reached out to schedule the dinner, without Comey having asked for it. Priebus 10/13/17 302, at 17 (the President asked to schedule the January 27 dinner because he did not know much about Comey and intended to ask him whether he wanted to stay on as FBI Director); Rybicki 11/21/18 302, at 3 (recalling that Comey told him about the President's dinner invitation on the day of the dinner).

[186] Comey 11/15/17 302, at 8; *Hearing on Russian Election Interference Before the Senate Select Intelligence Committee*, 115th Cong. (June 8, 2017) (Statement for the Record of James B. Comey, former Director of the FBI, at 4).

[187] McCabe 8/17/17 302, at 9-10; Rybicki 11/21/18 302, at 3. After leaving the White House, Comey called Deputy Director of the FBI Andrew McCabe, summarized what he and the President had discussed, including the President's request for loyalty, and expressed shock over the President's request. McCabe 8/17/17 302, at 9. Comey also convened a meeting with his senior leadership team to discuss what the President had asked of him during the dinner and whether he had handled the request for loyalty properly. McCabe 8/17/17 302, at 10; Rybicki 11/21/18 302, at 3. In addition, Comey distributed his

U.S. Department of Justice

~~Attorney Work Product // May Contain Material Protected Under Fed. R. Crim. P. 6(e)~~

under oath in congressional proceedings and in a subsequent interview with investigators subject to penalties for lying under 18 U.S.C. § 1001. Comey's memory of the details of the dinner, including that the President requested loyalty, has remained consistent throughout.[188]

6. Flynn's Resignation

On February 2, 2017, Eisenberg reviewed the underlying information relating to Flynn's calls with Kislyak.[189] Eisenberg recalled that he prepared a memorandum about criminal statutes that could apply to Flynn's conduct, but he did not believe the White House had enough information to make a definitive recommendation to the President.[190] Eisenberg and McGahn discussed that Eisenberg's review of the underlying information confirmed his preliminary conclusion that Flynn was unlikely to be prosecuted for violating the Logan Act.[191] Because White House officials were uncertain what Flynn had told the FBI, however, they could not assess his exposure to prosecution for violating 18 U.S.C. § 1001.[192]

The week of February 6, Flynn had a one-on-one conversation with the President in the Oval Office about the negative media coverage of his contacts with Kislyak.[193] Flynn recalled that the President was upset and asked him for information on the conversations.[194] Flynn listed the specific dates on which he remembered speaking with Kislyak, but the President corrected one of the dates he listed.[195] The President asked Flynn what he and Kislyak discussed and Flynn responded that he might have talked about sanctions.[196]

---

memorandum documenting the dinner to his senior leadership team, and McCabe confirmed that the memorandum captured what Comey said on the telephone call immediately following the dinner. McCabe 8/17/17 302, at 9-10.

[188] There also is evidence that corroborates other aspects of the memoranda Comey wrote documenting his interactions with the President. For example, Comey recalled, and his memoranda reflect, that he told the President in his January 6, 2017 meeting, and on phone calls on March 30 and April 11, 2017, that the FBI was not investigating the President personally. On May 8, 2017, during White House discussions about firing Comey, the President told Rosenstein and others that Comey had told him three times that he was not under investigation, including once in person and twice on the phone. Gauhar-000058 (Gauhar 5/16/17 Notes).

[189] Eisenberg 11/29/17 302, at 5; FBI 2/7/17 Electronic Communication, at 1 (documenting 2/2/17 meeting with Eisenberg).

[190] Eisenberg 11/29/17 302, at 6.

[191] Eisenberg 11/29/17 302, at 9; SCR015_000200 (2/15/17 Draft Memorandum to file from the Office of the Counsel to the President).

[192] Eisenberg 11/29/17 302, at 9.

[193] Flynn 11/21/17 302, at 2.

[194] Flynn 11/21/17 302, at 2.

[195] Flynn 11/21/17 302, at 2.

[196] Flynn 11/21/17 302, at 2-3.

On February 9, 2017, the Washington Post reported that Flynn discussed sanctions with Kislyak the month before the President took office.[197] After the publication of that story, Vice President Pence learned of the Department of Justice's notification to the White House about the content of Flynn's calls.[198] He and other advisors then sought access to and reviewed the underlying information about Flynn's contacts with Kislyak.[199] FBI Deputy Director Andrew McCabe, who provided the White House officials access to the information and was present when they reviewed it, recalled the officials asking him whether Flynn's conduct violated the Logan Act.[200] McCabe responded that he did not know, but the FBI was investigating the matter because it was a possibility.[201] Based on the evidence of Flynn's contacts with Kislyak, McGahn and Priebus concluded that Flynn could not have forgotten the details of the discussions of sanctions and had instead been lying about what he discussed with Kislyak.[202] Flynn had also told White House officials that the FBI had told him that the FBI was closing out its investigation of him,[203] but Eisenberg did not believe him.[204] After reviewing the materials and speaking with Flynn, McGahn and Priebus concluded that Flynn should be terminated and recommended that course of action to the President.[205]

That weekend, Flynn accompanied the President to Mar-a-Lago.[206] Flynn recalled that on February 12, 2017, on the return flight to D.C. on Air Force One, the President asked him whether he had lied to the Vice President.[207] Flynn responded that he may have forgotten details of his calls, but he did not think he lied.[208] The President responded, "Okay. That's fine. I got it."[209]

---

[197] Greg Miller et al., *National security adviser Flynn discussed sanctions with Russian ambassador, despite denials, officials say*, Washington Post (Feb. 9, 2017).

[198] SCR015_000202 (2/15/17 Draft Memorandum to file from the Office of the Counsel to the President); McGahn 11/30/17 302, at 12.

[199] SCR015_000202 (2/15/17 Draft Memorandum to file from the Office of the Counsel to the President); McCabe 8/17/17 302, at 11-13; Priebus 10/13/17 302, at 10; McGahn 11/30/17 302, at 12.

[200] McCabe 8/17/17 302, at 13.

[201] McCabe 8/17/17 302, at 13.

[202] McGahn 11/30/17 302, at 12; Priebus 1/18/18 302, at 8; Priebus 10/13/17 302, at 10; SCR015_000202 (2/15/17 Draft Memorandum to file from the Office of the Counsel to the President).

[203] McGahn 11/30/17 302, at 11; Eisenberg 11/29/17 302, at 9; Priebus 10/13/17 302, at 11.

[204] Eisenberg 11/29/17 302, at 9.

[205] SCR015_000202 (2/15/17 Draft Memorandum to file from the Office of the Counsel to the President); Priebus 10/13/17 302, at 10; McGahn 11/30/17 302, at 12.

[206] Flynn 11/17/17 302, at 8.

[207] Flynn 1/19/18 302, at 9; Flynn 11/17/17 302, at 8.

[208] Flynn 11/17/17 302, at 8; Flynn 1/19/18 302, at 9.

[209] Flynn 1/19/18 302, at 9.

U.S. Department of Justice

~~Attorney Work Product // May Contain Material Protected Under Fed. R. Crim. P. 6(e)~~

On February 13, 2017, Priebus told Flynn he had to resign.[210] Flynn said he wanted to say goodbye to the President, so Priebus brought him to the Oval Office.[211] Priebus recalled that the President hugged Flynn, shook his hand, and said, "We'll give you a good recommendation. You're a good guy. We'll take care of you."[212]

Talking points on the resignation prepared by the White House Counsel's Office and distributed to the White House communications team stated that McGahn had advised the President that Flynn was unlikely to be prosecuted, and the President had determined that the issue with Flynn was one of trust.[213] Spicer told the press the next day that Flynn was forced to resign "not based on a legal issue, but based on a trust issue, [where] a level of trust between the President and General Flynn had eroded to the point where [the President] felt he had to make a change."[214]

7. The President Discusses Flynn with FBI Director Comey

On February 14, 2017, the day after Flynn's resignation, the President had lunch at the White House with New Jersey Governor Chris Christie.[215] According to Christie, at one point during the lunch the President said, "Now that we fired Flynn, the Russia thing is over."[216] Christie laughed and responded, "No way."[217] He said, "this Russia thing is far from over" and "[w]e'll be here on Valentine's Day 2018 talking about this."[218] The President said, "[w]hat do you mean? Flynn met with the Russians. That was the problem. I fired Flynn. It's over."[219] Christie recalled responding that based on his experience both as a prosecutor and as someone who had been investigated, firing Flynn would not end the investigation.[220] Christie said there was no way to make an investigation shorter, but a lot of ways to make it longer.[221] The President asked Christie what he meant, and Christie told the President not to talk about the investigation even if he was

---

[210] Priebus 1/18/18 302, at 9.

[211] Priebus 1/18/18 302, at 9; Flynn 11/17/17 302, at 10.

[212] Priebus 1/18/18 302, at 9; Flynn 11/17/17 302, at 10.

[213] SCR004_00600 (2/16/17 Email, Burnham to Donaldson).

[214] Sean Spicer, *White House Daily Briefing*, C-SPAN (Feb. 14, 2017). After Flynn pleaded guilty to violating 18 U.S.C. § 1001 in December 2017, the President tweeted, "I had to fire General Flynn because he lied to the Vice President and the FBI." @realDonaldTrump 12/2/17 (12:14 p.m. ET) Tweet. The next day, the President's personal counsel told the press that he had drafted the tweet. Maegan Vazquez et al., *Trump's lawyer says he was behind President's tweet about firing Flynn*, CNN (Dec. 3, 2017).

[215] Christie 2/13/19 302, at 2-3; SCR012b_000022 (President's Daily Diary, 2/14/17).

[216] Christie 2/13/19 302, at 3.

[217] Christie 2/13/19 302, at 3.

[218] Christie 2/13/19 302, at 3. Christie said he thought when the President said "the Russia thing" he was referring to not just the investigations but also press coverage about Russia. Christie thought the more important thing was that there was an investigation. Christie 2/13/19 302, at 4.

[219] Christie 2/13/19 302, at 3.

[220] Christie 2/13/19 302, at 3.

[221] Christie 2/13/19 302, at 3.

U.S. Department of Justice

Attorney Work Product // May Contain Material Protected Under Fed. R. Crim. P. 6(e)

frustrated at times.[222] Christie also told the President that he would never be able to get rid of Flynn, "like gum on the bottom of your shoe."[223]

Towards the end of the lunch, the President brought up Comey and asked if Christie was still friendly with him.[224] Christie said he was.[225] The President told Christie to call Comey and tell him that the President "really like[s] him. Tell him he's part of the team."[226] At the end of the lunch, the President repeated his request that Christie reach out to Comey.[227] Christie had no intention of complying with the President's request that he contact Comey.[228] He thought the President's request was "nonsensical" and Christie did not want to put Comey in the position of having to receive such a phone call.[229] Christie thought it would have been uncomfortable to pass on that message.[230]

At 4 p.m. that afternoon, the President met with Comey, Sessions, and other officials for a homeland security briefing.[231] At the end of the briefing, the President dismissed the other attendees and stated that he wanted to speak to Comey alone.[232] Sessions and senior advisor to the President Jared Kushner remained in the Oval Office as other participants left, but the President

---

[222] Christie 2/13/19 302, at 3-4.

[223] Christie 2/13/19 302, at 3. Christie also recalled that during the lunch, Flynn called Kushner, who was at the lunch, and complained about what Spicer had said about Flynn in his press briefing that day. Kushner told Flynn words to the effect of, "You know the President respects you. The President cares about you. I'll get the President to send out a positive tweet about you later." Kushner looked at the President when he mentioned the tweet, and the President nodded his assent. Christie 2/13/19 302, at 3. Flynn recalled getting upset at Spicer's comments in the press conference and calling Kushner to say he did not appreciate the comments. Flynn 1/19/18 302, at 9.

[224] Christie 2/13/19 302, at 4.

[225] Christie 2/13/19 302, at 4.

[226] Christie 2/13/19 302, at 4-5.

[227] Christie 2/13/19 302, at 5.

[228] Christie 2/13/19 302, at 5.

[229] Christie 2/13/19 302, at 5.

[230] Christie 2/13/19 302, at 5.

[231] SCR012b_000022 (President's Daily Diary, 2/14/17); Comey 11/15/17 302, at 9.

[232] Comey 11/15/17 302, at 10; 2/14/17 Comey Memorandum, at 1; *Hearing on Russian Election Interference Before the Senate Select Intelligence Committee*, 115th Cong. (June 8, 2017) (Statement for the Record of James B. Comey, former Director of the FBI, at 4); Priebus 10/13/17 302, at 18 (confirming that everyone was shooed out "like Comey said" in his June testimony).

U.S. Department of Justice

~~Attorney Work Product // May Contain Material Protected Under Fed. R. Crim. P. 6(e)~~

excused them, repeating that he wanted to speak only with Comey.[233] At some point after others had left the Oval Office, Priebus opened the door, but the President sent him away.[234]

According to Comey's account of the meeting, once they were alone, the President began the conversation by saying, "I want to talk about Mike Flynn."[235] The President stated that Flynn had not done anything wrong in speaking with the Russians, but had to be terminated because he had misled the Vice President.[236] The conversation turned to the topic of leaks of classified information, but the President returned to Flynn, saying "he is a good guy and has been through a lot."[237] The President stated, "I hope you can see your way clear to letting this go, to letting Flynn go. He is a good guy. I hope you can let this go."[238] Comey agreed that Flynn "is a good guy," but did not commit to ending the investigation of Flynn.[239] Comey testified under oath that he took the President's statement "as a direction" because of the President's position and the circumstances of the one-on-one meeting.[240]

---

[233] Comey 11/15/17 302, at 10; Comey 2/14/17 Memorandum, at 1; *Hearing on Russian Election Interference Before the Senate Select Intelligence Committee*, 115th Cong. (June 8, 2017) (Statement for the Record of James B. Comey, former Director of the FBI, at 4). Sessions recalled that the President asked to speak to Comey alone and that Sessions was one of the last to leave the room; he described Comey's testimony about the events leading up to the private meeting with the President as "pretty accurate." Sessions 1/17/18 302, at 6. Kushner had no recollection of whether the President asked Comey to stay behind. Kushner 4/11/18 302, at 24.

[234] Comey 2/14/17 Memorandum, at 2; Priebus 10/13/17 302, at 18.

[235] Comey 11/15/17 302, at 10; Comey 2/14/17 Memorandum, at 1; *Hearing on Russian Election Interference Before the Senate Select Intelligence Committee*, 115th Cong. (June 8, 2017) (Statement for the Record of James B. Comey, former Director of the FBI, at 4).

[236] Comey 2/14/17 Memorandum, at 1; *Hearing on Russian Election Interference Before the Senate Select Intelligence Committee*, 115th Cong. (June 8, 2017) (Statement for the Record of James B. Comey, former Director of the FBI, at 5).

[237] Comey 11/15/17 302, at 10; Comey 2/14/17 Memorandum, at 2; *Hearing on Russian Election Interference Before the Senate Select Intelligence Committee*, 115th Cong. (June 8, 2017) (Statement for the Record of James B. Comey, former Director of the FBI, at 5).

[238] *Hearing on Russian Election Interference Before the Senate Select Intelligence Committee*, 115th Cong. (June 8, 2017) (Statement for the Record of James B. Comey, former Director of the FBI, at 5); Comey 2/14/17 Memorandum, at 2. Comey said he was highly confident that the words in quotations in his Memorandum documenting this meeting were the exact words used by the President. He said he knew from the outset of the meeting that he was about to have a conversation of consequence, and he remembered the words used by the President and wrote them down soon after the meeting. Comey 11/15/17 302, at 10-11.

[239] Comey 11/15/17 302, at 10; Comey 2/14/17 Memorandum, at 2.

[240] *Hearing on Russian Election Interference Before the Senate Select Intelligence Committee*, 115th Cong. (June 8, 2017) (CQ Cong. Transcripts, at 31) (testimony of James B. Comey, former Director of the FBI). Comey further stated, "I mean, this is the president of the United States, with me alone, saying, 'I hope' this. I took it as, this is what he wants me to do." *Id.*; *see also* Comey 11/15/17 302, at 10 (Comey took the statement as an order to shut down the Flynn investigation).

U.S. Department of Justice

Attorney Work Product // May Contain Material Protected Under Fed. R. Crim. P. 6(e)

Shortly after meeting with the President, Comey began drafting a memorandum documenting their conversation.[241] Comey also met with his senior leadership team to discuss the President's request, and they agreed not to inform FBI officials working on the Flynn case of the President's statements so the officials would not be influenced by the request.[242] Comey also asked for a meeting with Sessions and requested that Sessions not leave Comey alone with the President again.[243]

8. The Media Raises Questions About the President's Delay in Terminating Flynn

After Flynn was forced to resign, the press raised questions about why the President waited more than two weeks after the DOJ notification to remove Flynn and whether the President had known about Flynn's contacts with Kislyak before the DOJ notification.[244] The press also continued to raise questions about connections between Russia and the President's campaign.[245] On February 15, 2017, the President told reporters, "General Flynn is a wonderful man. I think he's been treated very, very unfairly by the media."[246] On February 16, 2017, the President held

---

[241] Comey 11/15/17 302, at 11; *Hearing on Russian Election Interference Before the Senate Select Intelligence Committee*, 115th Cong. (June 8, 2017) (Statement for the record of James B. Comey, former Director of the FBI, at 5).

[242] Comey 11/15/17 302, at 11; Rybicki 6/9/17 302, at 4; Rybicki 6/22/17 302, at 1; *Hearing on Russian Election Interference Before the Senate Select Intelligence Committee*, 115th Cong. (June 8, 2017) (Statement for the record of James B. Comey, former Director of the FBI, at 5-6).

[243] Comey 11/15/17 302, at 11; Rybicki 6/9/17 302, at 4-5; Rybicki 6/22/17 302, at 1-2; Sessions 1/17/18 302, at 6 (confirming that later in the week following Comey's one-on-one meeting with the President in the Oval Office, Comey told the Attorney General that he did not want to be alone with the President); Hunt 2/1/18 302, at 6 (within days of the February 14 Oval Office meeting, Comey told Sessions he did not think it was appropriate for the FBI Director to meet alone with the President); Rybicki 11/21/18 302, at 4 (Rybicki helped to schedule the meeting with Sessions because Comey wanted to talk about his concerns about meeting with the President alone); *Hearing on Russian Election Interference Before the Senate Select Intelligence Committee*, 115th Cong. (June 8, 2017) (Statement for the record of James B. Comey, former Director of the FBI, at 6).

[244] *See, e.g.*, Sean Spicer, *White House Daily Briefing*, C-SPAN (Feb. 14, 2017) (questions from the press included, "if [the President] was notified 17 days ago that Flynn had misled the Vice President, other officials here, and that he was a potential threat to blackmail by the Russians, why would he be kept on for almost three weeks?" and "Did the President instruct [Flynn] to talk about sanctions with the [Russian ambassador]?"). Priebus recalled that the President initially equivocated on whether to fire Flynn because it would generate negative press to lose his National Security Advisor so early in his term. Priebus 1/18/18 302, at 8.

[245] *E.g.*, Sean Sullivan et al., *Senators from both parties pledge to deepen probe of Russia and the 2016 election*, Washington Post (Feb. 14, 2017); Aaron Blake, *5 times Donald Trump's team denied contact with Russia*, Washington Post (Feb. 15, 2017); Oren Dorell, *Donald Trump's ties to Russia go back 30 years*, USA Today (Feb. 15, 2017); Pamela Brown et al., *Trump aides were in constant touch with senior Russian officials during campaign*, CNN (Feb. 15, 2017); Austin Wright, *Comey briefs senators amid furor over Trump-Russia ties*, Politico (Feb. 17, 2017); Megan Twohey & Scott Shane, *A Back-Channel Plan for Ukraine and Russia, Courtesy of Trump Associates*, New York Times (Feb. 19, 2017).

[246] Remarks by President Trump and Prime Minister Netanyahu of Israel in Joint Press Conference, White House (Feb. 15, 2017).

U.S. Department of Justice

Attorney Work Product // May Contain Material Protected Under Fed. R. Crim. P. 6(e)

a press conference and said that he removed Flynn because Flynn "didn't tell the Vice President of the United States the facts, and then he didn't remember. And that just wasn't acceptable to me."[247] The President said he did not direct Flynn to discuss sanctions with Kislyak, but "it certainly would have been okay with me if he did. I would have directed him to do it if I thought he wasn't doing it. I didn't direct him, but I would have directed him because that's his job."[248] In listing the reasons for terminating Flynn, the President did not say that Flynn had lied to him.[249] The President also denied having any connection to Russia, stating, "I have nothing to do with Russia. I told you, I have no deals there. I have no anything."[250] The President also said he "had nothing to do with" WikiLeaks's publication of information hacked from the Clinton campaign.[251]

9. The President Attempts to Have K.T. McFarland Create a Witness Statement Denying that he Directed Flynn's Discussions with Kislyak

On February 22, 2017, Priebus and Bannon told McFarland that the President wanted her to resign as Deputy National Security Advisor, but they suggested to her that the Administration could make her the ambassador to Singapore.[252] The next day, the President asked Priebus to have McFarland draft an internal email that would confirm that the President did not direct Flynn to call the Russian Ambassador about sanctions.[253] Priebus said he told the President he would only direct McFarland to write such a letter if she were comfortable with it.[254] Priebus called McFarland into his office to convey the President's request that she memorialize in writing that the President did not direct Flynn to talk to Kislyak.[255] McFarland told Priebus she did not know whether the President had directed Flynn to talk to Kislyak about sanctions, and she declined to say yes or no

---

[247] Remarks by President Trump in Press Conference, White House (Feb. 16, 2017).

[248] Remarks by President Trump in Press Conference, White House (Feb. 16, 2017). The President also said that Flynn's conduct "wasn't wrong – what he did in terms of the information he saw." The President said that Flynn was just "doing the job," and "if anything, he did something right."

[249] Remarks by President Trump in Press Conference, White House (Feb. 16, 2017); Priebus 1/18/18 302, at 9.

[250] Remarks by President Trump in Press Conference, White House (Feb. 16, 2017).

[251] Remarks by President Trump in Press Conference, White House (Feb. 16, 2017).

[252] KTMF_00000047 (McFarland 2/26/17 Memorandum for the Record); McFarland 12/22/17 302, at 16-17.

[253] See Priebus 1/18/18 302, at 11; see also KTMF_00000048 (McFarland 2/26/17 Memorandum for the Record); McFarland 12/22/17 302, at 17.

[254] Priebus 1/18/18 302, at 11.

[255] KTMF_00000048 (McFarland 2/26/17 Memorandum for the Record); McFarland 12/22/17 302, at 17.

to the request.[256] Priebus understood that McFarland was not comfortable with the President's request, and he recommended that she talk to attorneys in the White House Counsel's Office.[257]

McFarland then reached out to Eisenberg.[258] McFarland told him that she had been fired from her job as Deputy National Security Advisor and offered the ambassadorship in Singapore but that the President and Priebus wanted a letter from her denying that the President directed Flynn to discuss sanctions with Kislyak.[259] Eisenberg advised McFarland not to write the requested letter.[260] As documented by McFarland in a contemporaneous "Memorandum for the Record" that she wrote because she was concerned by the President's request: "Eisenberg . . . thought the requested email and letter would be a bad idea – from my side because the email would be awkward. Why would I be emailing Priebus to make a statement for the record? But it would also be a bad idea for the President because it looked as if my ambassadorial appointment was in some way a quid pro quo."[261] Later that evening, Priebus stopped by McFarland's office and told her not to write the email and to forget he even mentioned it.[262]

Around the same time, the President asked Priebus to reach out to Flynn and let him know that the President still cared about him.[263] Priebus called Flynn and said that he was checking in and that Flynn was an American hero.[264] Priebus thought the President did not want Flynn saying bad things about him.[265]

On March 31, 2017, following news that Flynn had offered to testify before the FBI and congressional investigators in exchange for immunity, the President tweeted, "Mike Flynn should ask for immunity in that this is a witch hunt (excuse for big election loss), by media & Dems, of

---

[256] KTMF_00000047 (McFarland 2/26/17 Memorandum for the Record) ("I said I did not know whether he did or didn't, but was in Maralago the week between Christmas and New Year's (while Flynn was on vacation in Carribean) and I was not aware of any Flynn-Trump, or Trump-Russian phone calls"); McFarland 12/22/17 302, at 17.

[257] Priebus 1/18/18 302, at 11.

[258] McFarland 12/22/17 302, at 17.

[259] McFarland 12/22/17 302, at 17.

[260] KTMF_00000048 (McFarland 2/26/17 Memorandum for the Record); McFarland 12/22/17 302, at 17.

[261] KTMF_00000048 (McFarland 2/26/17 Memorandum for the Record); *see* McFarland 12/22/17 302, at 17.

[262] McFarland 12/22/17 302, at 17; KTMF_00000048 (McFarland 2/26/17 Memorandum for the Record).

[263] Priebus 1/18/18 302, at 9.

[264] Priebus 1/18/18 302, at 9; Flynn 1/19/18 302, at 9.

[265] Priebus 1/18/18 302, at 9-10.

U.S. Department of Justice

~~Attorney Work Product // May Contain Material Protected Under Fed. R. Crim. P. 6(e)~~

historic proportion!"[266] In late March or early April, the President asked McFarland to pass a message to Flynn telling him the President felt bad for him and that he should stay strong.[267]

Analysis

In analyzing the President's conduct related to the Flynn investigation, the following evidence is relevant to the elements of obstruction of justice:

a.   Obstructive act. According to Comey's account of his February 14, 2017 meeting in the Oval Office, the President told him, "I hope you can see your way clear to letting this go, to letting Flynn go. . . . I hope you can let this go." In analyzing whether these statements constitute an obstructive act, a threshold question is whether Comey's account of the interaction is accurate, and, if so, whether the President's statements had the tendency to impede the administration of justice by shutting down an inquiry that could result in a grand jury investigation and a criminal charge.

After Comey's account of the President's request to "let[] Flynn go" became public, the President publicly disputed several aspects of the story. The President told the New York Times that he did not "shoo other people out of the room" when he talked to Comey and that he did not remember having a one-on-one conversation with Comey.[268] The President also publicly denied that he had asked Comey to "let[] Flynn go" or otherwise communicated that Comey should drop the investigation of Flynn.[269] In private, the President denied aspects of Comey's account to White House advisors, but acknowledged to Priebus that he brought Flynn up in the meeting with Comey and stated that Flynn was a good guy.[270] Despite those denials, substantial evidence corroborates Comey's account.

---

[266] @realDonaldTrump 3/31/17 (7:04 a.m. ET) Tweet; *see* Shane Harris at al., *Mike Flynn Offers to Testify in Exchange for Immunity*, Wall Street Journal (Mar. 30, 2017).

[267] McFarland 12/22/17 302, at 18.

[268] *Excerpts From The Times's Interview With Trump*, New York Times (July 19, 2017). Hicks recalled that the President told her he had never asked Comey to stay behind in his office. Hicks 12/8/17 302, at 12.

[269] In a statement on May 16, 2017, the White House said: "While the President has repeatedly expressed his view that General Flynn is a decent man who served and protected our country, the President has never asked Mr. Comey or anyone else to end any investigation, including any investigation involving General Flynn.   This is not a truthful or accurate portrayal of the conversation between the President and Mr. Comey." *See* Michael S. Schmidt, *Comey Memorandum Says Trump Asked Him to End Flynn Investigation*, New York Times (May 16, 2017) (quoting White House statement); @realDonaldTrump 12/3/17 (6:15 a.m. ET) Tweet ("I never asked Comey to stop investigating Flynn. Just more Fake News covering another Comey lie!").

[270] Priebus recalled that the President acknowledged telling Comey that Flynn was a good guy and he hoped "everything worked out for him." Priebus 10/13/17 302, at 19. McGahn recalled that the President denied saying to Comey that he hoped Comey would let Flynn go, but added that he was "allowed to hope." The President told McGahn he did not think he had crossed any lines. McGahn 12/14/17 302, at 8.

U.S. Department of Justice

~~Attorney Work Product // May Contain Material Protected Under Fed. R. Crim. P. 6(e)~~

First, Comey wrote a detailed memorandum of his encounter with the President on the same day it occurred. Comey also told senior FBI officials about the meeting with the President that day, and their recollections of what Comey told them at the time are consistent with Comey's account.[271]

Second, Comey provided testimony about the President's request that he "let[] Flynn go" under oath in congressional proceedings and in interviews with federal investigators subject to penalties for lying under 18 U.S.C. § 1001. Comey's recollections of the encounter have remained consistent over time.

Third, the objective, corroborated circumstances of how the one-on-one meeting came to occur support Comey's description of the event. Comey recalled that the President cleared the room to speak with Comey alone after a homeland security briefing in the Oval Office, that Kushner and Sessions lingered and had to be shooed out by the President, and that Priebus briefly opened the door during the meeting, prompting the President to wave him away. While the President has publicly denied those details, other Administration officials who were present have confirmed Comey's account of how he ended up in a one-on-one meeting with the President.[272] And the President acknowledged to Priebus and McGahn that he in fact spoke to Comey about Flynn in their one-on-one meeting.

Fourth, the President's decision to clear the room and, in particular, to exclude the Attorney General from the meeting signals that the President wanted to be alone with Comey, which is consistent with the delivery of a message of the type that Comey recalls, rather than a more innocuous conversation that could have occurred in the presence of the Attorney General.

Finally, Comey's reaction to the President's statements is consistent with the President having asked him to "let[] Flynn go." Comey met with the FBI leadership team, which agreed to keep the President's statements closely held and not to inform the team working on the Flynn investigation so that they would not be influenced by the President's request. Comey also promptly met with the Attorney General to ask him not to be left alone with the President again, an account verified by Sessions, FBI Chief of Staff James Rybicki, and Jody Hunt, who was then the Attorney General's chief of staff.

A second question is whether the President's statements, which were not phrased as a direct order to Comey, could impede or interfere with the FBI's investigation of Flynn. While the President said he "hope[d]" Comey could "let[] Flynn go," rather than affirmatively directing him to do so, the circumstances of the conversation show that the President was asking Comey to close the FBI's investigation into Flynn. First, the President arranged the meeting with Comey so that they would be alone and purposely excluded the Attorney General, which suggests that the President meant to make a request to Comey that he did not want anyone else to hear. Second, because the President is the head of the Executive Branch, when he says that he "hopes" a subordinate will do something, it is reasonable to expect that the subordinate will do what the President wants. Indeed, the President repeated a version of "let this go" three times, and Comey

---

[271] Rybicki 11/21/18 302, at 4; McCabe 8/17/17 302, at 13-14.

[272] *See* Priebus 10/13/17 302, at 18; Sessions 1/17/18 302, at 6.

testified that he understood the President's statements as a directive, which is corroborated by the way Comey reacted at the time.

b. Nexus to a proceeding. To establish a nexus to a proceeding, it would be necessary to show that the President could reasonably foresee and actually contemplated that the investigation of Flynn was likely to lead to a grand jury investigation or prosecution.

At the time of the President's one-on-one meeting with Comey, no grand jury subpoenas had been issued as part of the FBI's investigation into Flynn. But Flynn's lies to the FBI violated federal criminal law, ██████████████████████████ and resulted in Flynn's prosecution for violating 18 U.S.C. § 1001. By the time the President spoke to Comey about Flynn, DOJ officials had informed McGahn, who informed the President, that Flynn's statements to senior White House officials about his contacts with Kislyak were not true and that Flynn had told the same version of events to the FBI. McGahn also informed the President that Flynn's conduct could violate 18 U.S.C. § 1001. After the Vice President and senior White House officials reviewed the underlying information about Flynn's calls on February 10, 2017, they believed that Flynn could not have forgotten his conversations with Kislyak and concluded that he had been lying. In addition, the President's instruction to the FBI Director to "let[] Flynn go" suggests his awareness that Flynn could face criminal exposure for his conduct and was at risk of prosecution.

c. Intent. As part of our investigation, we examined whether the President had a personal stake in the outcome of an investigation into Flynn—for example, whether the President was aware of Flynn's communications with Kislyak close in time to when they occurred, such that the President knew that Flynn had lied to senior White House officials and that those lies had been passed on to the public. Some evidence suggests that the President knew about the existence and content of Flynn's calls when they occurred, but the evidence is inconclusive and could not be relied upon to establish the President's knowledge. In advance of Flynn's initial call with Kislyak, the President attended a meeting where the sanctions were discussed and an advisor may have mentioned that Flynn was scheduled to talk to Kislyak. Flynn told McFarland about the substance of his calls with Kislyak and said they may have made a difference in Russia's response, and Flynn recalled talking to Bannon in early January 2017 about how they had successfully "stopped the train on Russia's response" to the sanctions. It would have been reasonable for Flynn to have wanted the President to know of his communications with Kislyak because Kislyak told Flynn his request had been received at the highest levels in Russia and that Russia had chosen not to retaliate in response to the request, and the President was pleased by the Russian response, calling it a "[g]reat move." And the President never said publicly or internally that Flynn had lied to him about the calls with Kislyak.

But McFarland did not recall providing the President-Elect with Flynn's read-out of his calls with Kislyak, and Flynn does not have a specific recollection of telling the President-Elect directly about the calls. Bannon also said he did not recall hearing about the calls from Flynn. And in February 2017, the President asked Flynn what was discussed on the calls and whether he had lied to the Vice President, suggesting that he did not already know. Our investigation accordingly did not produce evidence that established that the President knew about Flynn's discussions of sanctions before the Department of Justice notified the White House of those discussions in late January 2017. The evidence also does not establish that Flynn otherwise

possessed information damaging to the President that would give the President a personal incentive to end the FBI's inquiry into Flynn's conduct.

Evidence does establish that the President connected the Flynn investigation to the FBI's broader Russia investigation and that he believed, as he told Christie, that terminating Flynn would end "the whole Russia thing." Flynn's firing occurred at a time when the media and Congress were raising questions about Russia's interference in the election and whether members of the President's campaign had colluded with Russia. Multiple witnesses recalled that the President viewed the Russia investigations as a challenge to the legitimacy of his election. The President paid careful attention to negative coverage of Flynn and reacted with annoyance and anger when the story broke disclosing that Flynn had discussed sanctions with Kislyak. Just hours before meeting one-on-one with Comey, the President told Christie that firing Flynn would put an end to the Russia inquiries. And after Christie pushed back, telling the President that firing Flynn would not end the Russia investigation, the President asked Christie to reach out to Comey and convey that the President liked him and he was part of "the team." That afternoon, the President cleared the room and asked Comey to "let[] Flynn go."

We also sought evidence relevant to assessing whether the President's direction to Comey was motivated by sympathy towards Flynn. In public statements the President repeatedly described Flynn as a good person who had been harmed by the Russia investigation, and the President directed advisors to reach out to Flynn to tell him the President "care[d]" about him and felt bad for him. At the same time, multiple senior advisors, including Bannon, Priebus, and Hicks, said that the President had become unhappy with Flynn well before Flynn was forced to resign and that the President was frequently irritated with Flynn. Priebus said he believed the President's initial reluctance to fire Flynn stemmed not from personal regard, but from concern about the negative press that would be generated by firing the National Security Advisor so early in the Administration. And Priebus indicated that the President's post-firing expressions of support for Flynn were motivated by the President's desire to keep Flynn from saying negative things about him.

The way in which the President communicated the request to Comey also is relevant to understanding the President's intent. When the President first learned about the FBI investigation into Flynn, he told McGahn, Bannon, and Priebus not to discuss the matter with anyone else in the White House. The next day, the President invited Comey for a one-on-one dinner against the advice of an aide who recommended that other White House officials also attend. At the dinner, the President asked Comey for "loyalty" and, at a different point in the conversation, mentioned that Flynn had judgment issues. When the President met with Comey the day after Flynn's termination—shortly after being told by Christie that firing Flynn would not end the Russia investigation—the President cleared the room, even excluding the Attorney General, so that he could again speak to Comey alone. The President's decision to meet one-on-one with Comey contravened the advice of the White House Counsel that the President should not communicate directly with the Department of Justice to avoid any appearance of interfering in law enforcement activities. And the President later denied that he cleared the room and asked Comey to "let[] Flynn go"—a denial that would have been unnecessary if he believed his request was a proper exercise of prosecutorial discretion.

U.S. Department of Justice

~~Attorney Work Product // May Contain Material Protected Under Fed. R. Crim. P. 6(e)~~

Finally, the President's effort to have McFarland write an internal email denying that the President had directed Flynn to discuss sanctions with Kislyak highlights the President's concern about being associated with Flynn's conduct. The evidence does not establish that the President was trying to have McFarland lie. The President's request, however, was sufficiently irregular that McFarland—who did not know the full extent of Flynn's communications with the President and thus could not make the representation the President wanted—felt the need to draft an internal memorandum documenting the President's request, and Eisenberg was concerned that the request would look like a quid pro quo in exchange for an ambassadorship.

C. The President's Reaction to Public Confirmation of the FBI's Russia Investigation

Overview

In early March 2017, the President learned that Sessions was considering recusing from the Russia investigation and tried to prevent the recusal. After Sessions announced his recusal on March 2, the President expressed anger at Sessions for the decision and then privately asked Sessions to "unrecuse." On March 20, 2017, Comey publicly disclosed the existence of the FBI's Russia investigation. In the days that followed, the President contacted Comey and other intelligence agency leaders and asked them to push back publicly on the suggestion that the President had any connection to the Russian election-interference effort in order to "lift the cloud" of the ongoing investigation.

Evidence

1. Attorney General Sessions Recuses From the Russia Investigation

In late February 2017, the Department of Justice began an internal analysis of whether Sessions should recuse from the Russia investigation based on his role in the 2016 Trump Campaign.[273] On March 1, 2017, the press reported that, in his January confirmation hearing to become Attorney General, Senator Sessions had not disclosed two meetings he had with Russian Ambassador Kislyak before the presidential election, leading to congressional calls for Sessions to recuse or for a special counsel to investigate Russia's interference in the presidential election.[274]

Also on March 1, the President called Comey and said he wanted to check in and see how Comey was doing.[275] According to an email Comey sent to his chief of staff after the call, the President "talked about Sessions a bit," said that he had heard Comey was "doing great," and said that he hoped Comey would come by to say hello when he was at the White House.[276] Comey

---

[273] Sessions 1/17/18 302, at 1; Hunt 2/1/18 302, at 3.

[274] *E.g.*, Adam Entous et al., *Sessions met with Russian envoy twice last year, encounters he later did not disclose*, Washington Post (Mar. 1, 2017).

[275] 3/1/17 Email, Comey to Rybicki; SCR012b_000030 (President's Daily Diary, 3/1/17, reflecting call with Comey at 11:55 am.)

[276] 3/1/17 Email, Comey to Rybicki; *see Hearing on Russian Election Interference Before the Senate Select Intelligence Committee*, 115th Cong. (June 8, 2017) (CQ Cong. Transcripts, at 86) (testimony

U.S. Department of Justice

~~Attorney Work Product // May Contain Material Protected Under Fed. R. Crim. P. 6(e)~~

interpreted the call as an effort by the President to "pull [him] in," but he did not perceive the call as an attempt by the President to find out what Comey was doing with the Flynn investigation.[277]

The next morning, the President called McGahn and urged him to contact Sessions to tell him not to recuse himself from the Russia investigation.[278] McGahn understood the President to be concerned that a recusal would make Sessions look guilty for omitting details in his confirmation hearing; leave the President unprotected from an investigation that could hobble the presidency and derail his policy objectives; and detract from favorable press coverage of a Presidential Address to Congress the President had delivered earlier in the week.[279] McGahn reached out to Sessions and reported that the President was not happy about the possibility of recusal.[280] Sessions replied that he intended to follow the rules on recusal.[281] McGahn reported back to the President about the call with Sessions, and the President reiterated that he did not want Sessions to recuse.[282] Throughout the day, McGahn continued trying on behalf of the President to avert Sessions's recusal by speaking to Sessions's personal counsel, Sessions's chief of staff, and Senate Majority Leader Mitch McConnell, and by contacting Sessions himself two more times.[283] Sessions recalled that other White House advisors also called him that day to argue against his recusal.[284]

That afternoon, Sessions announced his decision to recuse "from any existing or future investigations of any matters related in any way to the campaigns for President of the United States."[285] Sessions believed the decision to recuse was not a close call, given the applicable

---

of James B. Comey, former Director of the FBI) ("[H]e called me one day. . . . [H]e just called to check in and tell me I was doing an awesome job, and wanted to see how I was doing.").

[277] Comey 11/15/17 302, at 17-18.

[278] McGahn 11/30/17 302, at 16.

[279] McGahn 11/30/17 302, at 16-17; see SC_AD_00123 (Donaldson 3/2/17 Notes) ("Just in the middle of another Russia Fiasco.").

[280] Sessions 1/17/18 302, at 3.

[281] McGahn 11/30/17 302, at 17.

[282] McGahn 11/30/17 302, at 17.

[283] McGahn 11/30/17 302, at 18-19; Sessions 1/17/18 302, at 3; Hunt 2/1/18 302, at 4; Donaldson 11/6/17 302, at 8-10; see Hunt-000017; SC_AD_00121 (Donaldson 3/2/17 Notes).

[284] Sessions 1/17/18 302, at 3.

[285] Attorney General Sessions Statement on Recusal, Department of Justice Press Release (Mar. 2, 2017) ("During the course of the last several weeks, I have met with the relevant senior career Department officials to discuss whether I should recuse myself from any matters arising from the campaigns for President of the United States. Having concluded those meetings today, I have decided to recuse myself from any existing or future investigations of any matters related in any way to the campaigns for President of the United States."). At the time of Sessions's recusal, Dana Boente, then the Acting Deputy Attorney General and U.S. Attorney for the Eastern District of Virginia, became the Acting Attorney General for campaign-related matters pursuant to an executive order specifying the order of succession at the Department of Justice. Id. ("Consistent with the succession order for the Department of Justice, . . . Dana Boente shall act as and perform the functions of the Attorney General with respect to any matters from

language in the Code of Federal Regulations (CFR), which Sessions considered to be clear and decisive.[286] Sessions thought that any argument that the CFR did not apply to him was "very thin."[287] Sessions got the impression, based on calls he received from White House officials, that the President was very upset with him and did not think he had done his duty as Attorney General.[288]

Shortly after Sessions announced his recusal, the White House Counsel's Office directed that Sessions should not be contacted about the matter.[289] Internal White House Counsel's Office notes from March 2, 2017, state "No contact w/Sessions" and "No comms / Serious concerns about obstruction."[290]

On March 3, the day after Sessions's recusal, McGahn was called into the Oval Office.[291] Other advisors were there, including Priebus and Bannon.[292] The President opened the conversation by saying, "I don't have a lawyer."[293] The President expressed anger at McGahn about the recusal and brought up Roy Cohn, stating that he wished Cohn was his attorney.[294] McGahn interpreted this comment as directed at him, suggesting that Cohn would fight for the

---

which I have recused myself to the extent they exist."); *see* Exec. Order No. 13775, 82 Fed. Reg. 10697 (Feb. 14, 2017).

[286] Sessions 1/17/18 302, at 1-2. 28 C.F.R. § 45.2 provides that "no employee shall participate in a criminal investigation or prosecution if he has a personal or political relationship with . . . [a]ny person or organization substantially involved in the conduct that is the subject of the investigation or prosecution," and defines "political relationship" as "a close identification with an elected official, a candidate (whether or not successful) for elective, public office, a political party, or a campaign organization, arising from service as a principal adviser thereto or a principal official thereof."

[287] Sessions 1/17/18 302, at 2.

[288] Sessions 1/17/18 302, at 3.

[289] Donaldson 11/6/17 302, at 11; SC_AD_00123 (Donaldson 3/2/17 Notes). It is not clear whether the President was aware of the White House Counsel's Office direction not to contact Sessions about his recusal.

[290] SC_AD_00123 (Donaldson 3/2/17 Notes). McGahn said he believed the note "No comms / Serious concerns about obstruction" may have referred to concerns McGahn had about the press team saying "crazy things" and trying to spin Sessions's recusal in a way that would raise concerns about obstruction. McGahn 11/30/17 302, at 19. Donaldson recalled that "No comms" referred to the order that no one should contact Sessions. Donaldson 11/6/17 302, at 11.

[291] McGahn 12/12/17 302, at 2.

[292] McGahn 12/12/17 302, at 2.

[293] McGahn 12/12/17 302, at 2.

[294] McGahn 12/12/17 302, at 2. Cohn had previously served as a lawyer for the President during his career as a private businessman. Priebus recalled that when the President talked about Cohn, he said Cohn would win cases for him that had no chance, and that Cohn had done incredible things for him. Priebus 4/3/18 302, at 5. Bannon recalled the President describing Cohn as a winner and a fixer, someone who got things done. Bannon 2/14/18 302, at 6.

U.S. Department of Justice

~~Attorney Work Product // May Contain Material Protected Under Fed. R. Crim. P. 6(e)~~

President whereas McGahn would not.[295] The President wanted McGahn to talk to Sessions about the recusal, but McGahn told the President that DOJ ethics officials had weighed in on Sessions's decision to recuse.[296] The President then brought up former Attorneys General Robert Kennedy and Eric Holder and said that they had protected their presidents.[297] The President also pushed back on the DOJ contacts policy, and said words to the effect of, "You're telling me that Bobby and Jack didn't talk about investigations? Or Obama didn't tell Eric Holder who to investigate?"[298] Bannon recalled that the President was as mad as Bannon had ever seen him and that he screamed at McGahn about how weak Sessions was.[299] Bannon recalled telling the President that Sessions's recusal was not a surprise and that before the inauguration they had discussed that Sessions would have to recuse from campaign-related investigations because of his work on the Trump Campaign.[300]

That weekend, Sessions and McGahn flew to Mar-a-Lago to meet with the President.[301] Sessions recalled that the President pulled him aside to speak to him alone and suggested that Sessions should "unrecuse" from the Russia investigation.[302] The President contrasted Sessions with Attorneys General Holder and Kennedy, who had developed a strategy to help their presidents where Sessions had not.[303] Sessions said he had the impression that the President feared that the investigation could spin out of control and disrupt his ability to govern, which Sessions could have helped avert if he were still overseeing it.[304]

On March 5, 2017, the White House Counsel's Office was informed that the FBI was asking for transition-period records relating to Flynn—indicating that the FBI was still actively investigating him.[305] On March 6, the President told advisors he wanted to call the Acting Attorney

---

[295] McGahn 12/12/17 302, at 2.

[296] McGahn 12/12/17 302, at 2.

[297] McGahn 12/12/17 302, at 3. Bannon said the President saw Robert Kennedy and Eric Holder as Attorneys General who protected the presidents they served. The President thought Holder always stood up for President Obama and even took a contempt charge for him, and Robert Kennedy always had his brother's back. Bannon 2/14/18 302, at 5. Priebus recalled that the President said he had been told his entire life he needed to have a great lawyer, a "bulldog," and added that Holder had been willing to take a contempt-of-Congress charge for President Obama. Priebus 4/3/18 302, at 5.

[298] McGahn 12/12/17 302, at 3.

[299] Bannon 2/14/18 302, at 5.

[300] Bannon 2/14/18 302, at 5.

[301] Sessions 1/17/18 302, at 3; Hunt 2/1/18 302, at 5; McGahn 12/12/17 302, at 3.

[302] Sessions 1/17/18 302, at 3-4.

[303] Sessions 1/17/18 302, at 3-4

[304] Sessions 1/17/18 302, at 3-4. Hicks recalled that after Sessions recused, the President was angry and scolded Sessions in her presence, but she could not remember exactly when that conversation occurred. Hicks 12/8/17 302, at 13.

[305] SC_AD_000137 (Donaldson 3/5/17 Notes); *see* Donaldson 11/6/17 302, at 13.

U.S. Department of Justice

~~Attorney Work-Product // May Contain Material Protected Under Fed. R. Crim. P. 6(e)~~

General to find out whether the White House or the President was being investigated, although it is not clear whether the President knew at that time of the FBI's recent request concerning Flynn.[306]

2. FBI Director Comey Publicly Confirms the Existence of the Russia Investigation in Testimony Before HPSCI

On March 9, 2017, Comey briefed the "Gang of Eight" congressional leaders about the FBI's investigation of Russian interference, including an identification of the principal U.S. subjects of the investigation.[307] Although it is unclear whether the President knew of that briefing at the time, notes taken by Annie Donaldson, then McGahn's chief of staff, on March 12, 2017, state, "POTUS in panic/chaos . . . Need binders to put in front of POTUS. (1) All things related to Russia."[308] The week after Comey's briefing, the White House Counsel's Office was in contact with SSCI Chairman Senator Richard Burr about the Russia investigations and appears to have received information about the status of the FBI investigation.[309]

On March 20, 2017, Comey was scheduled to testify before HPSCI.[310] In advance of Comey's testimony, congressional officials made clear that they wanted Comey to provide information about the ongoing FBI investigation.[311] Dana Boente, who at that time was the Acting Attorney General for the Russia investigation, authorized Comey to confirm the existence of the Russia investigation and agreed that Comey should decline to comment on whether any particular individuals, including the President, were being investigated.[312]

---

[306] Donaldson 11/6/17 302, at 14; *see* SC_AD_000168 (Donaldson 3/6/17 Notes) ("POTUS wants to call Dana [then the Acting Attorney General for campaign-related investigations] / Is investigation / No / We know something on Flynn / GSA got contacted by FBI / There's something hot").

[307] Comey 11/15/17 302, at 13-14; SNS-Classified-0000140-44 (3/8/17 Email, Gauhar to Page et al.).

[308] SC_AD_00188 (Donaldson 3/12/18 Notes). Donaldson said she was not part of the conversation that led to these notes, and must have been told about it from others. Donaldson 11/6/17 302, at 13.

[309] Donaldson 11/6/17 302, at 14-15. On March 16, 2017, the White House Counsel's Office was briefed by Senator Burr on the existence of "4-5 targets." Donaldson 11/6/17 302, at 15. The "targets" were identified in notes taken by Donaldson as "Flynn (FBI was in—wrapping up)→DOJ looking for phone records"; "Comey→Manafort (Ukr + Russia, not campaign)"; ███████ "Carter Page ($ game)"; and "Greek Guy" (potentially referring to George Papadopoulos, later charged with violating 18 U.S.C. § 1001 for lying to the FBI). SC_AD_00198 (Donaldson 3/16/17 Notes). Donaldson and McGahn both said they believed these were targets of SSCI. Donaldson 11/6/17 302, at 15; McGahn 12/12/17 302, at 4. But SSCI does not formally investigate individuals as "targets"; the notes on their face reference the FBI, the Department of Justice, and Comey; and the notes track the background materials prepared by the FBI for Comey's briefing to the Gang of 8 on March 9. *See* SNS-Classified-0000140-44 (3/8/17 Email, Gauhar to Page et al.); *see also* Donaldson 11/6/17 302, at 15 (Donaldson could not rule out that Burr had told McGahn those individuals were the FBI's targets).

[310] *Hearing on Russian Election Tampering Before the House Permanent Select Intelligence Committee*, 115th Cong. (Mar. 20, 2017).

[311] Comey 11/15/17 302, at 16; McCabe 8/17/17, at 15; McGahn 12/14/17 302, at 1.

[312] Boente 1/31/18 302, at 5; Comey 11/15/17 302, at 16-17.

In his opening remarks at the HPSCI hearing, which were drafted in consultation with the Department of Justice, Comey stated that he had "been authorized by the Department of Justice to confirm that the FBI, as part of [its] counterintelligence mission, is investigating the Russian government's efforts to interfere in the 2016 presidential election and that includes investigating the nature of any links between individuals associated with the Trump campaign and the Russian government and whether there was any coordination between the campaign and Russia's efforts. As with any counterintelligence investigation, this will also include an assessment of whether any crimes were committed."[313] Comey added that he would not comment further on what the FBI was "doing and whose conduct [it] [was] examining" because the investigation was ongoing and classified—but he observed that he had "taken the extraordinary step in consultation with the Department of Justice of briefing this Congress's leaders . . . in a classified setting in detail about the investigation."[314] Comey was specifically asked whether President Trump was "under investigation during the campaign" or "under investigation now."[315] Comey declined to answer, stating, "Please don't over interpret what I've said as—as the chair and ranking know, we have briefed him in great detail on the subjects of the investigation and what we're doing, but I'm not gonna answer about anybody in this forum."[316] Comey was also asked whether the FBI was investigating the information contained in the Steele reporting, and he declined to answer.[317]

According to McGahn and Donaldson, the President had expressed frustration with Comey before his March 20 testimony, and the testimony made matters worse.[318] The President had previously criticized Comey for too frequently making headlines and for not attending intelligence briefings at the White House, and the President suspected Comey of leaking certain information to the media.[319] McGahn said the President thought Comey was acting like "his own branch of government."[320]

---

[313] *Hearing on Russian Election Tampering Before the House Permanent Select Intelligence Committee*, 115th Cong. (Mar. 20, 2017) (CQ Cong. Transcripts, at 11) (testimony by FBI Director James B. Comey); Comey 11/15/17 302, at 17; Boente 1/31/18 302, at 5 (confirming that the Department of Justice authorized Comey's remarks).

[314] *Hearing on Russian Election Tampering Before the House Permanent Select Intelligence Committee*, 115th Cong. (Mar. 20, 2017) (CQ Cong. Transcripts, at 11) (testimony by FBI Director James B. Comey).

[315] *Hearing on Russian Election Tampering Before the House Permanent Select Intelligence Committee*, 115th Cong. (Mar. 20, 2017) (CQ Cong. Transcripts, at 130) (question by Rep. Swalwell).

[316] *Hearing on Russian Election Tampering Before the House Permanent Select Intelligence Committee*, 115th Cong. (Mar. 20, 2017) (CQ Cong. Transcripts, at 130) (testimony by FBI Director James B. Comey).

[317] *Hearing on Russian Election Tampering Before the House Permanent Select Intelligence Committee*, 115th Cong. (Mar. 20, 2017) (CQ Cong. Transcripts, at 143) (testimony by FBI Director James B. Comey).

[318] Donaldson 11/6/17 302, at 21; McGahn 12/12/17 302, at 7.

[319] Donaldson 11/6/17 302, at 21; McGahn 12/12/17 302, at 6-9.

[320] McGahn 12/12/17 302, at 7.

U.S. Department of Justice

~~Attorney Work Product // May Contain Material Protected Under Fed. R. Crim. P. 6(e)~~

Press reports following Comey's March 20 testimony suggested that the FBI was investigating the President, contrary to what Comey had told the President at the end of the January 6, 2017 intelligence assessment briefing.[321] McGahn, Donaldson, and senior advisor Stephen Miller recalled that the President was upset with Comey's testimony and the press coverage that followed because of the suggestion that the President was under investigation.[322] Notes from the White House Counsel's Office dated March 21, 2017, indicate that the President was "beside himself" over Comey's testimony.[323] The President called McGahn repeatedly that day to ask him to intervene with the Department of Justice, and, according to the notes, the President was "getting hotter and hotter, get rid?"[324] Officials in the White House Counsel's Office became so concerned that the President would fire Comey that they began drafting a memorandum that examined whether the President needed cause to terminate the FBI director.[325]

At the President's urging, McGahn contacted Boente several times on March 21, 2017, to seek Boente's assistance in having Comey or the Department of Justice correct the misperception that the President was under investigation.[326] Boente did not specifically recall the conversations, although he did remember one conversation with McGahn around this time where McGahn asked if there was a way to speed up or end the Russia investigation as quickly as possible.[327] Boente said McGahn told him the President was under a cloud and it made it hard for him to govern.[328] Boente recalled telling McGahn that there was no good way to shorten the investigation and attempting to do so could erode confidence in the investigation's conclusions.[329] Boente said McGahn agreed and dropped the issue.[330] The President also sought to speak with Boente directly, but McGahn told the President that Boente did not want to talk to the President about the request

---

[321] *E.g.*, Matt Apuzzo et al., *F.B.I. Is Investigating Trump's Russia Ties, Comey Confirms*, New York Times (Mar. 20, 2017); Andy Greenberg. *The FBI Has Been Investigating Trump's Russia Ties Since July*, Wired (Mar. 20, 2017); Julie Borger & Spencer Ackerman, *Trump-Russia collusion is being investigated by FBI, Comey confirms*, Guardian (Mar. 20, 2017); *see* Comey 1/6/17 Memorandum, at 2.

[322] Donaldson 11/6/17 302, at 16-17; S. Miller 10/31/17 302, at 4; McGahn 12/12/17 302, at 5-7.

[323] SC_AD_00213 (Donaldson 3/21/17 Notes). The notes from that day also indicate that the President referred to the "Comey bombshell" which "made [him] look like a fool." SC_AD_00206 (Donaldson 3/21/17 Notes).

[324] SC_AD_00210 (Donaldson 3/21/17 Notes).

[325] SCR016_000002-05 (White House Counsel's Office Memorandum). White House Counsel's Office attorney Uttam Dhillon did not recall a triggering event causing the White House Counsel's Office to begin this research. Dhillon 11/21/17 302, at 5. Metadata from the document, which was provided by the White House, establishes that it was created on March 21, 2017.

[326] Donaldson 11/6/17 302, at 16-21; McGahn 12/12/17 302, at 5-7.

[327] Boente 1/31/18 302, at 5.

[328] Boente 1/31/18 302, at 5.

[329] Boente 1/31/18 302, at 5.

[330] Boente 1/31/18 302, at 5.

U.S. Department of Justice

~~Attorney Work Product // May Contain Material Protected Under Fed. R. Crim. P. 6(e)~~

to intervene with Comey.[331] McGahn recalled Boente telling him in calls that day that he did not think it was sustainable for Comey to stay on as FBI director for the next four years, which McGahn said he conveyed to the President.[332] Boente did not recall discussing with McGahn or anyone else the idea that Comey should not continue as FBI director.[333]

3. The President Asks Intelligence Community Leaders to Make Public Statements that he had No Connection to Russia

In the weeks following Comey's March 20, 2017 testimony, the President repeatedly asked intelligence community officials to push back publicly on any suggestion that the President had a connection to the Russian election-interference effort.

On March 22, 2017, the President asked Director of National Intelligence Daniel Coats and CIA Director Michael Pompeo to stay behind in the Oval Office after a Presidential Daily Briefing.[334] According to Coats, the President asked them whether they could say publicly that no link existed between him and Russia.[335] Coats responded that the Office of the Director of National Intelligence (ODNI) has nothing to do with investigations and it was not his role to make a public statement on the Russia investigation.[336] Pompeo had no recollection of being asked to stay behind after the March 22 briefing, but he recalled that the President regularly urged officials to get the word out that he had not done anything wrong related to Russia.[337]

Coats told this Office that the President never asked him to speak to Comey about the FBI investigation.[338] Some ODNI staffers, however, had a different recollection of how Coats described the meeting immediately after it occurred. According to senior ODNI official Michael Dempsey, Coats said after the meeting that the President had brought up the Russia investigation and asked him to contact Comey to see if there was a way to get past the investigation, get it over with, end it, or words to that effect.[339] Dempsey said that Coats described the President's comments as falling "somewhere between musing about hating the investigation" and wanting Coats to "do something to stop it."[340] Dempsey said Coats made it clear that he would not get involved with an ongoing FBI investigation.[341] Edward Gistaro, another ODNI official, recalled

---

[331] SC_AD_00210 (Donaldson 3/21/17 Notes); McGahn 12/12/17 302, at 7; Donaldson 11/6/17 302, at 19.

[332] McGahn 12/12/17 302, at 7; Burnham 11/03/17 302, at 11.

[333] Boente 1/31/18 302, at 3.

[334] Coats 6/14/17 302, at 3; Culver 6/14/17 302, at 2.

[335] Coats 6/14/17 302, at 3.

[336] Coats 6/14/17 302, at 3.

[337] Pompeo 6/28/17 302, at 1-3.

[338] Coats 6/14/17 302, at 3.

[339] Dempsey 6/14/17 302, at 2.

[340] Dempsey 6/14/17 302, at 2-3.

[341] Dempsey 6/14/17 302, at 3.

U.S. Department of Justice

~~Attorney Work Product // May Contain Material Protected Under Fed. R. Crim. P. 6(e)~~

that right after Coats's meeting with the President, on the walk from the Oval Office back to the Eisenhower Executive Office Building, Coats said that the President had kept him behind to ask him what he could do to "help with the investigation."[342] Another ODNI staffer who had been waiting for Coats outside the Oval Office talked to Gistaro a few minutes later and recalled Gistaro reporting that Coats was upset because the President had asked him to contact Comey to convince him there was nothing to the Russia investigation.[343]

On Saturday, March 25, 2017, three days after the meeting in the Oval Office, the President called Coats and again complained about the Russia investigations, saying words to the effect of, "I can't do anything with Russia, there's things I'd like to do with Russia, with trade, with ISIS, they're all over me with this."[344] Coats told the President that the investigations were going to go on and the best thing to do was to let them run their course.[345] Coats later testified in a congressional hearing that he had "never felt pressure to intervene or interfere in any way and shape—with shaping intelligence in a political way, or in relationship . . . to an ongoing investigation."[346]

On March 26, 2017, the day after the President called Coats, the President called NSA Director Admiral Michael Rogers.[347] The President expressed frustration with the Russia investigation, saying that it made relations with the Russians difficult.[348] The President told Rogers "the thing with the Russians [wa]s messing up" his ability to get things done with Russia.[349] The President also said that the news stories linking him with Russia were not true and asked Rogers if he could do anything to refute the stories.[350] Deputy Director of the NSA Richard Ledgett, who was present for the call, said it was the most unusual thing he had experienced in 40 years of government service.[351] After the call concluded, Ledgett prepared a memorandum that he and Rogers both signed documenting the content of the conversation and the President's request, and they placed the memorandum in a safe.[352] But Rogers did not perceive the President's request to be an order, and the President did not ask Rogers to push back on the Russia

---

[342] Gistaro 6/14/17 302, at 2.

[343] Culver 6/14/17 302, at 2-3.

[344] Coats 6/14/17 302, at 4.

[345] Coats 6/14/17 302, at 4; Dempsey 6/14/17 302, at 3 (Coats relayed that the President had asked several times what Coats could do to help "get [the investigation] done," and Coats had repeatedly told the President that fastest way to "get it done" was to let it run its course).

[346] *Hearing on Foreign Intelligence Surveillance Act Before the Senate Select Intelligence Committee*, 115th Cong. (June 7, 2017) (CQ Cong. Transcripts, at 25) (testimony by Daniel Coats, Director of National Intelligence).

[347] Rogers 6/12/17 302, at 3-4.

[348] Rogers 6/12/17 302, at 4.

[349] Ledgett 6/13/17 302, at 1-2; *see* Rogers 6/12/17 302, at 4.

[350] Rogers 6/12/17 302, at 4-5; Ledgett 6/13/17 302, at 2.

[351] Ledgett 6/13/17 302, at 2.

[352] Ledgett 6/13/17 302, at 2-3; Rogers 6/12/17 302, at 4.

U.S. Department of Justice

~~Attorney Work Product // May Contain Material Protected Under Fed. R. Crim. P. 6(e)~~

investigation itself.[353] Rogers later testified in a congressional hearing that as NSA Director he had "never been directed to do anything [he] believe[d] to be illegal, immoral, unethical or inappropriate" and did "not recall ever feeling pressured to do so."[354]

In addition to the specific comments made to Coats, Pompeo, and Rogers, the President spoke on other occasions in the presence of intelligence community officials about the Russia investigation and stated that it interfered with his ability to conduct foreign relations.[355] On at least two occasions, the President began Presidential Daily Briefings by stating that there was no collusion with Russia and he hoped a press statement to that effect could be issued.[356] Pompeo recalled that the President vented about the investigation on multiple occasions, complaining that there was no evidence against him and that nobody would publicly defend him.[357] Rogers recalled a private conversation with the President in which he "vent[ed]" about the investigation, said he had done nothing wrong, and said something like the "Russia thing has got to go away."[358] Coats recalled the President bringing up the Russia investigation several times, and Coats said he finally told the President that Coats's job was to provide intelligence and not get involved in investigations.[359]

4. The President Asks Comey to "Lift the Cloud" Created by the Russia Investigation

On the morning of March 30, 2017, the President reached out to Comey directly about the Russia investigation.[360] According to Comey's contemporaneous record of the conversation, the President said "he was trying to run the country and the cloud of this Russia business was making

---

[353] Rogers 6/12/17 302, at 5; Ledgett 6/13/17 302, at 2.

[354] *Hearing on Foreign Intelligence Surveillance Act Before the Senate Select Intelligence Committee*, 115th Cong. (June 7, 2017) (CQ Cong. Transcripts, at 20) (testimony by Admiral Michael Rogers, Director of the National Security Agency).

[355] Gistaro 6/14/17 302, at 1, 3; Pompeo 6/28/17 302, at 2-3.

[356] Gistaro 6/14/17 302, at 1.

[357] Pompeo 6/28/17 302, at 2.

[358] Rogers 6/12/17 302, at 6.

[359] Coats 6/14/17 302, at 3-4.

[360] SCR012b_000044 (President's Daily Diary, 3/30/17, reflecting call to Comey from 8:14 - 8:24 a.m.); Comey 3/30/17 Memorandum, at 1 ("The President called me on my CMS phone at 8:13 am today . . . . The call lasted 11 minutes (about 10 minutes when he was connected)."; *Hearing on Russian Election Interference Before the Senate Select Intelligence Committee*, 115th Cong. (June 8, 2017) (Statement for the Record of James B. Comey, former Director of the FBI, at 6).

that difficult."[361] The President asked Comey what could be done to "lift the cloud."[362] Comey explained "that we were running it down as quickly as possible and that there would be great benefit, if we didn't find anything, to our Good Housekeeping seal of approval, but we had to do our work."[363] Comey also told the President that congressional leaders were aware that the FBI was not investigating the President personally.[364] The President said several times, "We need to get that fact out."[365] The President commented that if there was "some satellite" (which Comey took to mean an associate of the President's or the campaign) that did something, "it would be good to find that out" but that he himself had not done anything wrong and he hoped Comey "would find a way to get out that we weren't investigating him."[366] After the call ended, Comey called Boente and told him about the conversation, asked for guidance on how to respond, and said he was uncomfortable with direct contact from the President about the investigation.[367]

On the morning of April 11, 2017, the President called Comey again.[368] According to Comey's contemporaneous record of the conversation, the President said he was "following up to see if [Comey] did what [the President] had asked last time—getting out that he personally is not under investigation."[369] Comey responded that he had passed the request to Boente but not heard back, and he informed the President that the traditional channel for such a request would be to

---

[361] Comey 3/30/17 Memorandum, at 1. Comey subsequently testified before Congress about this conversation and described it to our Office; his recollections were consistent with his memorandum. *Hearing on Russian Election Interference Before the Senate Select Intelligence Committee*, 115th Cong. (June 8, 2017) (Statement for the Record of James B. Comey, former Director of the FBI, at 6); Comey 11/15/17 302, at 18.

[362] Comey 3/30/17 Memorandum, at 1; Comey 11/15/17 302, at 18.

[363] Comey 3/30/17 Memorandum, at 1; Comey 11/15/17 302, at 18.

[364] Comey 3/30/17 Memorandum, at 1; *Hearing on Russian Election Interference Before the Senate Select Intelligence Committee*, 115th Cong. (June 8, 2017) (Statement for the Record of James B. Comey, former Director of the FBI, at 6).

[365] Comey 3/30/17 Memorandum, at 1; *Hearing on Russian Election Interference Before the Senate Select Intelligence Committee*, 115th Cong. (June 8, 2017) (Statement for the Record of James B. Comey, former Director of the FBI, at 6).

[366] Comey 3/30/17 Memorandum, at 1; *Hearing on Russian Election Interference Before the Senate Select Intelligence Committee*, 115th Cong. (June 8, 2017) (Statement for the Record of James B. Comey, former Director of the FBI, at 6-7).

[367] Comey 3/30/17 Memorandum, at 2; Boente 1/31/18 302, at 6-7; *Hearing on Russian Election Interference Before the Senate Select Intelligence Committee*, 115th Cong. (June 8, 2017) (Statement for the Record of James B. Comey, former Director of the FBI, at 7).

[368] SCR012b_000053 (President's Daily Diary, 4/11/17, reflecting call to Comey from 8:27 – 8:31 a.m.); Comey 4/11/17 Memorandum, at 1 ("I returned the president's call this morning at 8:26 am EDT. We spoke for about four minutes.").

[369] Comey 4/11/17 Memorandum, at 1. Comey subsequently testified before Congress about this conversation and his recollections were consistent with his memo. *Hearing on Russian Election Interference Before the Senate Select Intelligence Committee*, 115th Cong. (June 8, 2017) (Statement for the Record of James B. Comey, former Director of the FBI, at 7).

U.S. Department of Justice

~~Attorney Work Product // May Contain Material Protected Under Fed. R. Crim. P. 6(e)~~

have the White House Counsel contact DOJ leadership.[370] The President said he would take that step.[371] The President then added, "Because I have been very loyal to you, very loyal, we had that thing, you know."[372] In a televised interview that was taped early that afternoon, the President was asked if it was too late for him to ask Comey to step down; the President responded, "No, it's not too late, but you know, I have confidence in him. We'll see what happens. You know, it's going to be interesting."[373] After the interview, Hicks told the President she thought the President's comment about Comey should be removed from the broadcast of the interview, but the President wanted to keep it in, which Hicks thought was unusual.[374]

Later that day, the President told senior advisors, including McGahn and Priebus, that he had reached out to Comey twice in recent weeks.[375] The President acknowledged that McGahn would not approve of the outreach to Comey because McGahn had previously cautioned the President that he should not talk to Comey directly to prevent any perception that the White House was interfering with investigations.[376] The President told McGahn that Comey had indicated the FBI could make a public statement that the President was not under investigation if the Department of Justice approved that action.[377] After speaking with the President, McGahn followed up with Boente to relay the President's understanding that the FBI could make a public announcement if the Department of Justice cleared it.[378] McGahn recalled that Boente said Comey had told him there was nothing obstructive about the calls from the President, but they made Comey uncomfortable.[379] According to McGahn, Boente responded that he did not want to issue a statement about the President not being under investigation because of the potential political ramifications and did not want to order Comey to do it because that action could prompt the

---

[370] Comey 4/11/17 Memorandum, at 1.

[371] Comey 4/11/17 Memorandum, at 1.

[372] Comey 4/11/17 Memorandum, at 1. In a footnote to this statement in his memorandum, Comey wrote, "His use of these words did not fit with the flow of the call, which at that point had moved away from any request of me, but I have recorded it here as it happened."

[373] Maria Bartiromo, *Interview with President Trump*, Fox Business Network (Apr. 12, 2017); SCR012b_000054 (President's Daily Diary, 4/11/17, reflecting Bartiromo interview from 12:30 - 12:55 p.m.).

[374] Hicks 12/8/17 302, at 13.

[375] Priebus 10/13/17 302, at 23; McGahn 12/12/17 302, at 9.

[376] Priebus 10/13/17 302, at 23; McGahn 12/12/17 302, at 9; *see* McGahn 11/30/17 302, at 9; Dhillon 11/21/17 302, at 2 (stating that White House Counsel attorneys had advised the President not to contact the FBI Director directly because it could create a perception he was interfering with investigations). Later in April, the President told other attorneys in the White House Counsel's Office that he had called Comey even though he knew they had advised against direct contact. Dhillon 11/21/17 302, at 2 (recalling that the President said, "I know you told me not to, but I called Comey anyway.").

[377] McGahn 12/12/17 302, at 9.

[378] McGahn 12/12/17 302, at 9.

[379] McGahn 12/12/17 302, at 9; *see* Boente 1/31/18 302, at 6 (recalling that Comey told him after the March 30, 2017 call that it was not obstructive).

appointment of a Special Counsel.[380] Boente did not recall that aspect of his conversation with McGahn, but did recall telling McGahn that the direct outreaches from the President to Comey were a problem.[381] Boente recalled that McGahn agreed and said he would do what he could to address that issue.[382]

Analysis

In analyzing the President's reaction to Sessions's recusal and the requests he made to Coats, Pompeo, Rogers, and Comey, the following evidence is relevant to the elements of obstruction of justice:

a.   Obstructive act.   The evidence shows that, after Comey's March 20, 2017 testimony, the President repeatedly reached out to intelligence agency leaders to discuss the FBI's investigation. But witnesses had different recollections of the precise content of those outreaches. Some ODNI officials recalled that Coats told them immediately after the March 22 Oval Office meeting that the President asked Coats to intervene with Comey and "stop" the investigation. But the first-hand witnesses to the encounter remember the conversation differently. Pompeo had no memory of the specific meeting, but generally recalled the President urging officials to get the word out that the President had not done anything wrong related to Russia. Coats recalled that the President asked that Coats state publicly that no link existed between the President and Russia, but did not ask him to speak with Comey or to help end the investigation. The other outreaches by the President during this period were similar in nature. The President asked Rogers if he could do anything to refute the stories linking the President to Russia, and the President asked Comey to make a public statement that would "lift the cloud" of the ongoing investigation by making clear that the President was not personally under investigation. These requests, while significant enough that Rogers thought it important to document the encounter in a written memorandum, were not interpreted by the officials who received them as directives to improperly interfere with the investigation.

b.   Nexus to a proceeding. At the time of the President's outreaches to leaders of the intelligence agencies in late March and early April 2017, the FBI's Russia investigation did not yet involve grand jury proceedings. The outreaches, however, came after and were in response to Comey's March 20, 2017 announcement that the FBI, as a part of its counterintelligence mission, was conducting an investigation into Russian interference in the 2016 presidential election. Comey testified that the investigation included any links or coordination with Trump campaign officials and would "include an assessment of whether any crimes were committed."

c.   Intent. As described above, the evidence does not establish that the President asked or directed intelligence agency leaders to stop or interfere with the FBI's Russia investigation—and the President affirmatively told Comey that if "some satellite" was involved in Russian election interference "it would be good to find that out." But the President's intent in trying to prevent Sessions's recusal, and in reaching out to Coats, Pompeo, Rogers, and Comey following

---

[380] McGahn 12/12/17 302, at 9-10.

[381] Boente 1/31/18 302, at 7; McGahn 12/12/17 302, at 9.

[382] Boente 1/31/18 302, at 7.

U.S. Department of Justice

Attorney Work Product // May Contain Material Protected Under Fed. R. Crim. P. 6(e)

Comey's public announcement of the FBI's Russia investigation, is nevertheless relevant to understanding what motivated the President's other actions towards the investigation.

The evidence shows that the President was focused on the Russia investigation's implications for his presidency—and, specifically, on dispelling any suggestion that he was under investigation or had links to Russia. In early March, the President attempted to prevent Sessions's recusal, even after being told that Sessions was following DOJ conflict-of-interest rules. After Sessions recused, the White House Counsel's Office tried to cut off further contact with Sessions about the matter, although it is not clear whether that direction was conveyed to the President. The President continued to raise the issue of Sessions's recusal and, when he had the opportunity, he pulled Sessions aside and urged him to unrecuse. The President also told advisors that he wanted an Attorney General who would protect him, the way he perceived Robert Kennedy and Eric Holder to have protected their presidents. The President made statements about being able to direct the course of criminal investigations, saying words to the effect of, "You're telling me that Bobby and Jack didn't talk about investigations? Or Obama didn't tell Eric Holder who to investigate?"

After Comey publicly confirmed the existence of the FBI's Russia investigation on March 20, 2017, the President was "beside himself" and expressed anger that Comey did not issue a statement correcting any misperception that the President himself was under investigation. The President sought to speak with Acting Attorney General Boente directly and told McGahn to contact Boente to request that Comey make a clarifying statement. The President then asked other intelligence community leaders to make public statements to refute the suggestion that the President had links to Russia, but the leaders told him they could not publicly comment on the investigation. On March 30 and April 11, against the advice of White House advisors who had informed him that any direct contact with the FBI could be perceived as improper interference in an ongoing investigation, the President made personal outreaches to Comey asking him to "lift the cloud" of the Russia investigation by making public the fact that the President was not personally under investigation.

Evidence indicates that the President was angered by both the existence of the Russia investigation and the public reporting that he was under investigation, which he knew was not true based on Comey's representations. The President complained to advisors that if people thought Russia helped him with the election, it would detract from what he had accomplished.

Other evidence indicates that the President was concerned about the impact of the Russia investigation on his ability to govern. The President complained that the perception that he was under investigation was hurting his ability to conduct foreign relations, particularly with Russia. The President told Coats he "can't do anything with Russia," he told Rogers that "the thing with the Russians" was interfering with his ability to conduct foreign affairs, and he told Comey that "he was trying to run the country and the cloud of this Russia business was making that difficult."

U.S. Department of Justice

~~Attorney Work Product // May Contain Material Protected Under Fed. R. Crim. P. 6(e)~~

D. Events Leading Up To and Surrounding the Termination of FBI Director Comey

Overview

Comey was scheduled to testify before Congress on May 3, 2017. Leading up to that testimony, the President continued to tell advisors that he wanted Comey to make public that the President was not under investigation. At the hearing, Comey declined to answer questions about the scope or subjects of the Russia investigation and did not state publicly that the President was not under investigation. Two days later, on May 5, 2017, the President told close aides he was going to fire Comey, and on May 9, he did so, using his official termination letter to make public that Comey had on three occasions informed the President that he was not under investigation. The President decided to fire Comey before receiving advice or a recommendation from the Department of Justice, but he approved an initial public account of the termination that attributed it to a recommendation from the Department of Justice based on Comey's handling of the Clinton email investigation. After Deputy Attorney General Rod Rosenstein resisted attributing the firing to his recommendation, the President acknowledged that he intended to fire Comey regardless of the DOJ recommendation and was thinking of the Russia investigation when he made the decision. The President also told the Russian Foreign Minister, "I just fired the head of the F.B.I. He was crazy, a real nut job. I faced great pressure because of Russia. That's taken off. . . . . I'm not under investigation."

Evidence

1. Comey Testifies Before the Senate Judiciary Committee and Declines to Answer Questions About Whether the President is Under Investigation

On May 3, 2017, Comey was scheduled to testify at an FBI oversight hearing before the Senate Judiciary Committee.[383] McGahn recalled that in the week leading up to the hearing, the President said that it would be the last straw if Comey did not take the opportunity to set the record straight by publicly announcing that the President was not under investigation.[384] The President had previously told McGahn that the perception that the President was under investigation was hurting his ability to carry out his presidential duties and deal with foreign leaders.[385] At the hearing, Comey declined to answer questions about the status of the Russia investigation, stating "[t]he Department of Justice ha[d] authorized [him] to confirm that [the Russia investigation] exists," but that he was "not going to say another word about it" until the investigation was completed.[386] Comey also declined to answer questions about whether investigators had "ruled

---

[383] *Hearing on Oversight of the FBI before the Senate Judiciary Committee*, 115th Cong. (May 3, 2017).

[384] McGahn 12/12/17 302, at 10-11.

[385] McGahn 12/12/17 302, at 7, 10-11 (McGahn believed that two foreign leaders had expressed sympathy to the President for being under investigation); SC_AD_00265 (Donaldson 4/11/17 Notes) ("P Called Comey – Day we told him not to? 'You are not under investigation' NK/China/Sapping Credibility").

[386] *Hearing on FBI Oversight Before the Senate Judiciary Committee*, 115th Cong. (CQ Cong. Transcripts, at 70) (May 3, 2017) (testimony by FBI Director James Comey). Comey repeated this point

U.S. Department of Justice

Attorney Work Product // May Contain Material Protected Under Fed. R. Crim. P. 6(e)

out anyone in the Trump campaign as potentially a target of th[e] criminal investigation," including whether the FBI had "ruled out the president of the United States."[387]

Comey was also asked at the hearing about his decision to announce 11 days before the presidential election that the FBI was reopening the Clinton email investigation.[388] Comey stated that it made him "mildly nauseous to think that we might have had some impact on the election," but added that "even in hindsight" he "would make the same decision."[389] He later repeated that he had no regrets about how he had handled the email investigation and believed he had "done the right thing at each turn."[390]

In the afternoon following Comey's testimony, the President met with McGahn, Sessions, and Sessions's Chief of Staff Jody Hunt.[391] At that meeting, the President asked McGahn how Comey had done in his testimony and McGahn relayed that Comey had declined to answer questions about whether the President was under investigation.[392] The President became very upset and directed his anger at Sessions.[393] According to notes written by Hunt, the President said, "This is terrible Jeff. It's all because you recused. AG is supposed to be most important appointment. Kennedy appointed his brother. Obama appointed Holder. I appointed you and you recused yourself. You left me on an island. I can't do anything."[394] The President said that the recusal was unfair and that it was interfering with his ability to govern and undermining his authority with foreign leaders.[395] Sessions responded that he had had no choice but to recuse, and it was a mandatory rather than discretionary decision.[396] Hunt recalled that Sessions also stated at

_____

several times during his testimony. *See id.* at 26 (explaining that he was "not going to say another peep about [the investigation] until we're done"); *id.* at 90 (stating that he would not provide any updates about the status of investigation "before the matter is concluded").

[387] *Hearing on FBI Oversight Before the Senate Judiciary Committee*, 115th Cong. (May 3, 2017) (CQ Cong. Transcripts, at 87-88) (questions by Sen. Blumenthal and testimony by FBI Director James B. Comey).

[388] *Hearing on FBI Oversight Before the Senate Judiciary Committee*, 115th Cong. (May 3, 2017) (CQ Cong. Transcripts, at 15) (question by Sen. Feinstein).

[389] *Hearing on FBI Oversight Before the Senate Judiciary Committee*, 115th Cong. (May 3, 2017) (CQ Cong. Transcripts, at 17) (testimony by FBI Director James B. Comey).

[390] *Hearing on FBI Oversight Before the Senate Judiciary Committee*, 115th Cong. (May 3, 2017) (CQ Cong. Transcripts, at 92) (testimony by FBI Director James B. Comey).

[391] Sessions 1/17/18 302, at 8; Hunt 2/1/18 302, at 8.

[392] Sessions 1/17/18 302, at 8; Hunt-000021 (Hunt 5/3/17 Notes); McGahn 3/8/18 302, at 6.

[393] Sessions 1/17/18 302, at 8-9.

[394] Hunt-000021 (Hunt 5/3/17 Notes). Hunt said that he wrote down notes describing this meeting and others with the President after the events occurred. Hunt 2/1/17 302, at 2.

[395] Hunt-000021-22 (Hunt 5/3/17 Notes) ("I have foreign leaders saying they are sorry I am being investigated."); Sessions 1/17/18 302, at 8 (Sessions recalled that a Chinese leader had said to the President that he was sorry the President was under investigation, which the President interpreted as undermining his authority); Hunt 2/1/18 302, at 8.

[396] Sessions 1/17/18 302, at 8; Hunt-000022 (Hunt 5/3/17 Notes).

U.S. Department of Justice

~~Attorney Work Product // May Contain Material Protected Under Fed. R. Crim. P. 6(e)~~

some point during the conversation that a new start at the FBI would be appropriate and the President should consider replacing Comey as FBI director.[397] According to Sessions, when the meeting concluded, it was clear that the President was unhappy with Comey, but Sessions did not think the President had made the decision to terminate Comey.[398]

Bannon recalled that the President brought Comey up with him at least eight times on May 3 and May 4, 2017.[399] According to Bannon, the President said the same thing each time: "He told me three times I'm not under investigation. He's a showboater. He's a grandstander. I don't know any Russians. There was no collusion."[400] Bannon told the President that he could not fire Comey because "that ship had sailed."[401] Bannon also told the President that firing Comey was not going to stop the investigation, cautioning him that he could fire the FBI director but could not fire the FBI.[402]

2. The President Makes the Decision to Terminate Comey

The weekend following Comey's May 3, 2017 testimony, the President traveled to his resort in Bedminster, New Jersey.[403] At a dinner on Friday, May 5, attended by the President and various advisors and family members, including Jared Kushner and senior advisor Stephen Miller, the President stated that he wanted to remove Comey and had ideas for a letter that would be used to make the announcement.[404] The President dictated arguments and specific language for the letter, and Miller took notes.[405] As reflected in the notes, the President told Miller that the letter should start, "While I greatly appreciate you informing me that I am not under investigation concerning what I have often stated is a fabricated story on a Trump-Russia relationship — pertaining to the 2016 presidential election, please be informed that I, and I believe the American public – including Ds and Rs – have lost faith in you as Director of the FBI."[406] Following the dinner, Miller prepared a termination letter based on those notes and research he conducted to support the President's arguments.[407] Over the weekend, the President provided several rounds of

---

[397] Hunt-000022 (Hunt 5/3/17 Notes).

[398] Sessions 1/17/18 302, at 9.

[399] Bannon 2/12/18 302, at 20.

[400] Bannon 2/12/18 302, at 20.

[401] Bannon 2/12/18 302, at 20.

[402] Bannon 2/12/18 302, at 20-21; see Priebus 10/13/17 302, at 28.

[403] S. Miller 10/31/17 302, at 4-5; SCR025_000019 (President's Daily Diary, 5/4/17).

[404] S. Miller 10/31/17 302, at 5.

[405] S. Miller 10/31/17 302, at 5-6.

[406] S. Miller 5/5/17 Notes, at 1; see S. Miller 10/31/17 302, at 8.

[407] S. Miller 10/31/17 302, at 6.

U.S. Department of Justice

Attorney Work Product // May Contain Material Protected Under Fed. R. Crim. P. 6(e)

edits on the draft letter.[408] Miller said the President was adamant that he not tell anyone at the White House what they were preparing because the President was worried about leaks.[409]

In his discussions with Miller, the President made clear that he wanted the letter to open with a reference to him not being under investigation.[410] Miller said he believed that fact was important to the President to show that Comey was not being terminated based on any such investigation.[411] According to Miller, the President wanted to establish as a factual matter that Comey had been under a "review period" and did not have assurance from the President that he would be permitted to keep his job.[412]

The final version of the termination letter prepared by Miller and the President began in a way that closely tracked what the President had dictated to Miller at the May 5 dinner: "Dear Director Comey, While I greatly appreciate your informing me, on three separate occasions, that I am not under investigation concerning the fabricated and politically-motivated allegations of a Trump-Russia relationship with respect to the 2016 Presidential Election, please be informed that I, along with members of both political parties and, most importantly, the American Public, have lost faith in you as the Director of the FBI and you are hereby terminated."[413] The four-page letter went on to critique Comey's judgment and conduct, including his May 3 testimony before the Senate Judiciary Committee, his handling of the Clinton email investigation, and his failure to hold leakers accountable.[414] The letter stated that Comey had "asked [the President] at dinner shortly after inauguration to let [Comey] stay on in the Director's role, and [the President] said that [he] would consider it," but the President had "concluded that [he] ha[d] no alternative but to find new leadership for the Bureau – a leader that restores confidence and trust."[415]

In the morning of Monday, May 8, 2017, the President met in the Oval Office with senior advisors, including McGahn, Priebus, and Miller, and informed them he had decided to terminate Comey.[416] The President read aloud the first paragraphs of the termination letter he wrote with

---

[408] S. Miller 10/31/17 302, at 6-8.

[409] S. Miller 10/31/17 302, at 7. Miller said he did not want Priebus to be blindsided, so on Sunday night he called Priebus to tell him that the President had been thinking about the "Comey situation" and there would be an important discussion on Monday. S. Miller 10/31/17 302, at 7.

[410] S. Miller 10/31/17 302, at 8.

[411] S. Miller 10/31/17 302, at 8.

[412] S. Miller 10/31/17 302, at 10.

[413] SCR013c_000003-06 (Draft Termination Letter to FBI Director Comey).

[414] SCR013c_000003-06 (Draft Termination Letter to FBI Director Comey). Kushner said that the termination letter reflected the reasons the President wanted to fire Comey and was the truest representation of what the President had said during the May 5 dinner. Kushner 4/11/18 302, at 25.

[415] SCR013c_000003 (Draft Termination Letter to FBI Director Comey).

[416] McGahn 12/12/17 302, at 11; Priebus 10/13/17 302, at 24; S. Miller 10/31/17 302, at 11; Dhillon 11/21/17 302, at 6; Eisenberg 11/29/17 302, at 13.

Miller and conveyed that the decision had been made and was not up for discussion.[417] The President told the group that Miller had researched the issue and determined the President had the authority to terminate Comey without cause.[418] In an effort to slow down the decision-making process, McGahn told the President that DOJ leadership was currently discussing Comey's status and suggested that White House Counsel's Office attorneys should talk with Sessions and Rod Rosenstein, who had recently been confirmed as the Deputy Attorney General.[419] McGahn said that previously scheduled meetings with Sessions and Rosenstein that day would be an opportunity to find out what they thought about firing Comey.[420]

At noon, Sessions, Rosenstein, and Hunt met with McGahn and White House Counsel's Office attorney Uttam Dhillon at the White House.[421] McGahn said that the President had decided to fire Comey and asked for Sessions's and Rosenstein's views.[422] Sessions and Rosenstein criticized Comey and did not raise concerns about replacing him.[423] McGahn and Dhillon said the fact that neither Sessions nor Rosenstein objected to replacing Comey gave them peace of mind that the President's decision to fire Comey was not an attempt to obstruct justice.[424] An Oval Office meeting was scheduled later that day so that Sessions and Rosenstein could discuss the issue with the President.[425]

At around 5 p.m., the President and several White House officials met with Sessions and Rosenstein to discuss Comey.[426] The President told the group that he had watched Comey's May

---

[417] S. Miller 10/31/17 302, at 11 (observing that the President started the meeting by saying, "I'm going to read you a letter. Don't talk me out of this. I've made my decision."); Dhillon 11/21/17 302, at 6 (the President announced in an irreversible way that he was firing Comey); Eisenberg 11/29/17 302, at 13 (the President did not leave whether or not to fire Comey up for discussion); Priebus 10/13/17 302, at 25; McGahn 12/12/17 302, at 11-12.

[418] Dhillon 302 11/21/17, at 6; Eisenberg 11/29/17 302, at 13; McGahn 12/12/17 302, at 11.

[419] McGahn 12/12/17 302, at 12, 13; S. Miller 10/31/17 302, at 11; Dhillon 11/21/17 302, at 7. Because of the Attorney General's recusal, Rosenstein became the Acting Attorney General for the Russia investigation upon his confirmation as Deputy Attorney General. See 28 U.S.C. § 508(a) ("In case of a vacancy in the office of Attorney General, or of his absence or disability, the Deputy Attorney General may exercise all the duties of that office").

[420] McGahn 12/12/17 302, at 12.

[421] Dhillon 11/21/17 302, at 7; McGahn 12/12/17 302, at 13; Gauhar-000056 (Gauhar 5/16/17 Notes); see Gauhar-000056-72 (2/11/19 Memorandum to File attaching Gauhar handwritten notes) ("Ms. Gauhar determined that she likely recorded all these notes during one or more meetings on Tuesday, May 16, 2017.").

[422] McGahn 12/12/17 302, at 13; see Gauhar-000056 (Gauhar 5/16/17 Notes).

[423] Dhillon 11/21/17 302, at 7-9; Sessions 1/17/18 302, at 9; McGahn 12/12/17 302, at 13.

[424] McGahn 12/12/17 302, at 13; Dhillon 11/21/17 302, at 9.

[425] Hunt-000026 (Hunt 5/8/17 Notes); see Gauhar-000057 (Gauhar 5/16/17 Notes).

[426] Rosenstein 5/23/17 302, at 2; McGahn 12/12/17 302, at 14; see Gauhar-000057 (Gauhar 5/16/17 Notes).

3 testimony over the weekend and thought that something was "not right" with Comey.[427] The President said that Comey should be removed and asked Sessions and Rosenstein for their views.[428] Hunt, who was in the room, recalled that Sessions responded that he had previously recommended that Comey be replaced.[429] McGahn and Dhillon said Rosenstein described his concerns about Comey's handling of the Clinton email investigation.[430]

The President then distributed copies of the termination letter he had drafted with Miller, and the discussion turned to the mechanics of how to fire Comey and whether the President's letter should be used.[431] McGahn and Dhillon urged the President to permit Comey to resign, but the President was adamant that he be fired.[432] The group discussed the possibility that Rosenstein and Sessions could provide a recommendation in writing that Comey should be removed.[433] The President agreed and told Rosenstein to draft a memorandum, but said he wanted to receive it first thing the next morning.[434] Hunt's notes reflect that the President told Rosenstein to include in his recommendation the fact that Comey had refused to confirm that the President was not personally under investigation.[435] According to notes taken by a senior DOJ official of Rosenstein's description of his meeting with the President, the President said, "Put the Russia stuff in the memo."[436] Rosenstein responded that the Russia investigation was not the basis of his recommendation, so he did not think Russia should be mentioned.[437] The President told Rosenstein he would appreciate it if Rosenstein put it in his letter anyway.[438] When Rosenstein

---

[427] Hunt-000026-27 (Hunt 5/8/17 Notes).

[428] Sessions 1/17/18 302, at 10; *see* Gauhar-000058 (Gauhar 5/16/17 Notes) ("POTUS to AG: What is your rec?").

[429] Hunt-000027 (Hunt 5/8/17 Notes).

[430] McGahn 12/12/17 302, at 14; Dhillon 11/21/17 302, at 7.

[431] Hunt-000028 (Hunt 5/8/17 Notes).

[432] McGahn 12/12/17 302, at 13.

[433] Hunt-000028-29 (Hunt 5/8/17 Notes).

[434] McCabe 9/26/17 302, at 13; Rosenstein 5/23/17 302, at 2; *see* Gauhar-000059 (Gauhar 5/16/17 Notes) ("POTUS tells DAG to write a memo").

[435] Hunt-000028-29 (Hunt 5/8/17 Notes) ("POTUS asked if Rod's recommendation would include the fact that although Comey talks about the investigation he refuses to say that the President is not under investigation. . . . So it would be good if your recommendation would make mention of the fact that Comey refuses to say public[ly] what he said privately 3 times.").

[436] Gauhar-000059 (Gauhar 5/16/17 Notes).

[437] Sessions 1/17/18 302 at 10; McCabe 9/26/17 302, at 13; *see* Gauhar-000059 (Gauhar 5/16/17 Notes).

[438] Gauhar-000059 (Gauhar 5/16/17 Notes); McCabe 5/16/17 Memorandum 1; McCabe 9/26/17 302, at 13.

left the meeting, he knew that Comey would be terminated, and he told DOJ colleagues that his own reasons for replacing Comey were "not [the President's] reasons."[439]

On May 9, Hunt delivered to the White House a letter from Sessions recommending Comey's removal and a memorandum from Rosenstein, addressed to the Attorney General, titled "Restoring Public Confidence in the FBI."[440] McGahn recalled that the President liked the DOJ letters and agreed that they should provide the foundation for a new cover letter from the President accepting the recommendation to terminate Comey.[441] Notes taken by Donaldson on May 9 reflected the view of the White House Counsel's Office that the President's original termination letter should "[n]ot [see the] light of day" and that it would be better to offer "[n]o other rationales" for the firing than what was in Rosenstein's and Sessions's memoranda.[442] The President asked Miller to draft a new termination letter and directed Miller to say in the letter that Comey had informed the President three times that he was not under investigation.[443] McGahn, Priebus, and Dhillon objected to including that language, but the President insisted that it be included.[444] McGahn, Priebus, and others perceived that language to be the most important part of the letter to

---

[439] Rosenstein 5/23/17 302, at 2; Gauhar-000059 (Gauhar 5/16/17 Notes) ("DAG reasons not their reasons [POTUS]"); Gauhar-000060 (Gauhar 5/16/17 Notes) ("1st draft had a recommendation. Took it out b/c knew decision had already been made.").

[440] Rosenstein 5/23/17 302, at 4; McGahn 12/12/17 302, at 15; 5/9/17 Letter, Sessions to President Trump ("Based on my evaluation, and for the reasons expressed by the Deputy Attorney General in the attached memorandum, I have concluded that a fresh start is needed at the leadership of the FBI."); 5/9/17 Memorandum, Rosenstein to Sessions (concluding with, "The way the Director handled the conclusion of the email investigation was wrong. As a result, the FBI is unlikely to regain public and congressional trust until it has a Director who understands the gravity of the mistakes and pledges never to repeat them. Having refused to admit his errors, the Director cannot be expected to implement the necessary corrective actions.").

[441] S. Miller 10/31/17 302, at 12; McGahn 12/12/17 302, at 15; Hunt-000031 (Hunt 5/9/17 Notes).

[442] SC_AD_00342 (Donaldson 5/9/17 Notes). Donaldson also wrote "[i]s this the beginning of the end?" because she was worried that the decision to terminate Comey and the manner in which it was carried out would be the end of the presidency. Donaldson 11/6/17 302, at 25.

[443] S. Miller 10/31/17 302, at 12; McGahn 12/12/17 302, at 15; Hunt-000032 (Hunt 5/9/17 Notes).

[444] McGahn 12/12/17 302, at 15; S. Miller 10/31/17 302, at 12; Dhillon 11/21/17 302, at 8, 10; Priebus 10/13/17 302, at 27; Hunt 2/1/18 302, at 14-15; Hunt-000032 (Hunt 5/9/17 Notes).

the President.[445] Dhillon made a final pitch to the President that Comey should be permitted to resign, but the President refused.[446]

Around the time the President's letter was finalized, Priebus summoned Spicer and the press team to the Oval Office, where they were told that Comey had been terminated for the reasons stated in the letters by Rosenstein and Sessions.[447] To announce Comey's termination, the White House released a statement, which Priebus thought had been dictated by the President.[448] In full, the statement read: "Today, President Donald J. Trump informed FBI Director James Comey that he has been terminated and removed from office. President Trump acted based on the clear recommendations of both Deputy Attorney General Rod Rosenstein and Attorney General Jeff Sessions."[449]

That evening, FBI Deputy Director Andrew McCabe was summoned to meet with the President at the White House.[450] The President told McCabe that he had fired Comey because of the decisions Comey had made in the Clinton email investigation and for many other reasons.[451] The President asked McCabe if he was aware that Comey had told the President three times that he was not under investigation.[452] The President also asked McCabe whether many people in the FBI disliked Comey and whether McCabe was part of the "resistance" that had disagreed with Comey's decisions in the Clinton investigation.[453] McCabe told the President that he knew Comey had told the President he was not under investigation, that most people in the FBI felt positively about Comey, and that McCabe worked "very closely" with Comey and was part of all the decisions that had been made in the Clinton investigation.[454]

---

[445] Dhillon 11/21/17 302, at 10; Eisenberg 11/29/17 302, at 15 (providing the view that the President's desire to include the language about not being under investigation was the "driving animus of the whole thing"); Burnham 11/3/17 302, at 16 (Burnham knew the only line the President cared about was the line that said Comey advised the President on three separate occasions that the President was not under investigation). According to Hunt's notes, the reference to Comey's statement would indicate that "notwithstanding" Comey's having informed the President that he was not under investigation, the President was terminating Comey. Hunt-000032 (Hunt 5/9/17 Notes). McGahn said he believed the President wanted the language included so that people would not think that the President had terminated Comey because the President was under investigation. McGahn 12/12/17 302, at 15.

[446] McGahn 12/12/17 302, at 15; Donaldson 11/6/17 302, at 25; see SC_AD_00342 (Donaldson 5/9/17 Notes) ("Resign vs. Removal. -- POTUS/removal.").

[447] Spicer 10/16/17 302, at 9; McGahn 12/12/17 302, at 16.

[448] Priebus 10/13/17 302, at 28.

[449] *Statement of the Press Secretary*, The White House, Office of the Press Secretary (May 9, 2017).

[450] McCabe 9/26/17 302, at 4; SCR025_000044 (President's Daily Diary, 5/9/17); McCabe 5/10/17 Memorandum, at 1.

[451] McCabe 9/26/17 302, at 5; McCabe 5/10/17 Memorandum, at 1.

[452] McCabe 9/26/17 302, at 5; McCabe 5/10/17 Memorandum, at 1-2.

[453] McCabe 9/26/17 302, at 5; McCabe 5/10/17 Memorandum, at 1-2.

[454] McCabe 9/26/17 302, at 5; McCabe 5/10/17 Memorandum, at 1-2.

U.S. Department of Justice

~~Attorney Work Product // May Contain Material Protected Under Fed. R. Crim. P. 6(e)~~

Later that evening, the President told his communications team he was unhappy with the press coverage of Comey's termination and ordered them to go out and defend him.[455] The President also called Chris Christie and, according to Christie, said he was getting "killed" in the press over Comey's termination.[456] The President asked what he should do.[457] Christie asked, "Did you fire [Comey] because of what Rod wrote in the memo?", and the President responded, "Yes."[458] Christie said that the President should "get Rod out there" and have him defend the decision.[459] The President told Christie that this was a "good idea" and said he was going to call Rosenstein right away.[460]

That night, the White House Press Office called the Department of Justice and said the White House wanted to put out a statement saying that it was Rosenstein's idea to fire Comey.[461] Rosenstein told other DOJ officials that he would not participate in putting out a "false story."[462] The President then called Rosenstein directly and said he was watching Fox News, that the coverage had been great, and that he wanted Rosenstein to do a press conference.[463] Rosenstein responded that this was not a good idea because if the press asked him, he would tell the truth that Comey's firing was not his idea.[464] Sessions also informed the White House Counsel's Office that evening that Rosenstein was upset that his memorandum was being portrayed as the reason for Comey's termination.[465]

In an unplanned press conference late in the evening of May 9, 2017, Spicer told reporters, "It was all [Rosenstein]. No one from the White House. It was a DOJ decision."[466] That evening and the next morning, White House officials and spokespeople continued to maintain that the

---

[455] Spicer 10/16/17 302, at 11; Hicks 12/8/17, at 18; Sanders 7/3/18 302, at 2.

[456] Christie 2/13/19 302, at 6.

[457] Christie 2/13/19 302, at 6.

[458] Christie 2/13/19 302, at 6.

[459] Christie 2/13/19 302, at 6.

[460] Christie 2/13/19 302, at 6.

[461] Gauhar-000071 (Gauhar 5/16/17 Notes); Page Memorandum, at 3 (recording events of 5/16/17); McCabe 9/26/17 302, at 14.

[462] Rosenstein 5/23/17 302, at 4-5; Gauhar-000059 (Gauhar 5/16/17 Notes).

[463] Rosenstein 5/23/17 302, at 4-5; Gauhar-000071 (Gauhar 5/16/17 Notes).

[464] Gauhar-000071 (Gauhar 5/16/17 Notes). DOJ notes from the week of Comey's firing indicate that Priebus was "screaming" at the DOJ public affairs office trying to get Rosenstein to do a press conference, and the DOJ public affairs office told Priebus that Rosenstein had told the President he was not doing it. Gauhar-000071-72 (Gauhar 5/16/17 Notes).

[465] McGahn 12/12/17 302, at 16-17; Donaldson 11/6/17 302, at 26-27; Dhillon 11/21/17 302, at 11.

[466] Jenna Johnson, *After Trump fired Comey, White House staff scrambled to explain why,* Washington Post (May 10, 2017) (quoting Spicer).

U.S. Department of Justice

~~Attorney Work Product // May Contain Material Protected Under Fed. R. Crim. P. 6(e)~~

President's decision to terminate Comey was driven by the recommendations the President received from Rosenstein and Sessions.[467]

In the morning on May 10, 2017, President Trump met with Russian Foreign Minister Sergey Lavrov and Russian Ambassador Sergey Kislyak in the Oval Office.[468] The media subsequently reported that during the May 10 meeting the President brought up his decision the prior day to terminate Comey, telling Lavrov and Kislyak: "I just fired the head of the F.B.I. He was crazy, a real nut job. I faced great pressure because of Russia. That's taken off. . . . I'm not under investigation."[469] The President never denied making those statements, and the White House did not dispute the account, instead issuing a statement that said: "By grandstanding and politicizing the investigation into Russia's actions, James Comey created unnecessary pressure on our ability to engage and negotiate with Russia. The investigation would have always continued, and obviously, the termination of Comey would not have ended it. Once again, the real story is that our national security has been undermined by the leaking of private and highly classified information."[470] Hicks said that when she told the President about the reports on his meeting with Lavrov, he did not look concerned and said of Comey, "he *is* crazy."[471] When McGahn asked the President about his comments to Lavrov, the President said it was good that Comey was fired because that took the pressure off by making it clear that he was not under investigation so he could get more work done.[472]

That same morning, on May 10, 2017, the President called McCabe.[473] According to a memorandum McCabe wrote following the call, the President asked McCabe to come over to the White House to discuss whether the President should visit FBI headquarters and make a speech to

---

[467] *See, e.g.,* Sarah Sanders, *White House Daily Briefing,* C-SPAN (May 10, 2017); SCR013_001088 (5/10/17 Email, Hemming to Cheung et al.) (internal White House email describing comments on the Comey termination by Vice President Pence).

[468] SCR08_000353 (5/9/17 White House Document, "Working Visit with Foreign Minister Sergey Lavrov of Russia"); SCR08_001274 (5/10/17 Email, Ciaramella to Kelly et al.). The meeting had been planned on May 2, 2017, during a telephone call between the President and Russian President Vladimir Putin, and the meeting date was confirmed on May 5, 2017, the same day the President dictated ideas for the Comey termination letter to Stephen Miller. SCR08_001274 (5/10/17 Email, Ciaramella to Kelly et al.).

[469] Matt Apuzzo et al., *Trump Told Russians That Firing "Nut Job" Comey Eased Pressure From Investigation,* New York Times (May 19, 2017).

[470] SCR08_002117 (5/19/17 Email, Walters to Farhi (CBS News)); *see* Spicer 10/16/17 302, at 13 (noting he would have been told to "clean it up" if the reporting on the meeting with the Russian Foreign Minister was inaccurate, but he was never told to correct the reporting); Hicks 12/8/17 302, at 19 (recalling that the President never denied making the statements attributed to him in the Lavrov meeting and that the President had said similar things about Comey in an off-the-record meeting with reporters on May 18, 2017, calling Comey a "nut job" and "crazy").

[471] Hicks 12/8/17 302, at 19.

[472] McGahn 12/12/17 302, at 18.

[473] SCR025_000046 (President's Daily Diary, 5/10/17); McCabe 5/10/17 Memorandum, at 1.

U.S. Department of Justice

~~Attorney Work Product // May Contain Material Protected Under Fed. R. Crim. P. 6(e)~~

employees.[474] The President said he had received "hundreds" of messages from FBI employees indicating their support for terminating Comey.[475] The President also told McCabe that Comey should not have been permitted to travel back to Washington, D.C. on the FBI's airplane after he had been terminated and that he did not want Comey "in the building again," even to collect his belongings.[476] When McCabe met with the President that afternoon, the President, without prompting, told McCabe that people in the FBI loved the President, estimated that at least 80% of the FBI had voted for him, and asked McCabe who he had voted for in the 2016 presidential election.[477]

In the afternoon of May 10, 2017, deputy press secretary Sarah Sanders spoke to the President about his decision to fire Comey and then spoke to reporters in a televised press conference.[478] Sanders told reporters that the President, the Department of Justice, and bipartisan members of Congress had lost confidence in Comey, "[a]nd most importantly, the rank and file of the FBI had lost confidence in their director. Accordingly, the President accepted the recommendation of his Deputy Attorney General to remove James Comey from his position."[479] In response to questions from reporters, Sanders said that Rosenstein decided "on his own" to review Comey's performance and that Rosenstein decided "on his own" to come to the President on Monday, May 8 to express his concerns about Comey. When a reporter indicated that the "vast majority" of FBI agents supported Comey, Sanders said, "Look, we've heard from countless members of the FBI that say very different things."[480] Following the press conference, Sanders spoke to the President, who told her she did a good job and did not point out any inaccuracies in her comments.[481] Sanders told this Office that her reference to hearing from "countless members of the FBI" was a "slip of the tongue."[482] She also recalled that her statement in a separate press interview that rank-and-file FBI agents had lost confidence in Comey was a comment she made "in the heat of the moment" that was not founded on anything.[483]

Also on May 10, 2017, Sessions and Rosenstein each spoke to McGahn and expressed concern that the White House was creating a narrative that Rosenstein had initiated the decision to

---

[474] McCabe 5/10/17 Memorandum, at 1.

[475] McCabe 5/10/17 Memorandum, at 1.

[476] McCabe 5/10/17 Memorandum, at 1; Rybicki 6/13/17 302, at 2. Comey had been visiting the FBI's Los Angeles office when he found out he had been terminated. Comey 11/15/17 302, at 22.

[477] McCabe 5/10/17 Memorandum, at 1-2. McCabe's memorandum documenting his meeting with the President is consistent with notes taken by the White House Counsel's Office. See SC_AD_00347 (Donaldson 5/10/17 Notes).

[478] Sanders 7/3/18 302, at 4; Sarah Sanders, White House Daily Briefing, C-SPAN (May 10, 2017).

[479] Sarah Sanders, White House Daily Briefing, C-SPAN (May 10, 2017); Sanders 7/3/18 302, at 4.

[480] Sarah Sanders, White House Daily Briefing, C-SPAN (May 10, 2017).

[481] Sanders 7/3/18 302, at 4.

[482] Sanders 7/3/18 302, at 4.

[483] Sanders 7/3/18 302, at 3.

fire Comey.[484] The White House Counsel's Office agreed that it was factually wrong to say that the Department of Justice had initiated Comey's termination,[485] and McGahn asked attorneys in the White House Counsel's Office to work with the press office to correct the narrative.[486]

The next day, on May 11, 2017, the President participated in an interview with Lester Holt. The President told White House Counsel's Office attorneys in advance of the interview that the communications team could not get the story right, so he was going on Lester Holt to say what really happened.[487] During the interview, the President stated that he had made the decision to fire Comey before the President met with Rosenstein and Sessions. The President told Holt, "I was going to fire regardless of recommendation . .   [Rosenstein] made a recommendation. But regardless of recommendation, I was going to fire Comey knowing there was no good time to do it."[488] The President continued, "And in fact, when I decided to just do it, I said to myself—I said, you know, this Russia thing with Trump and Russia is a made-up story. It's an excuse by the Democrats for having lost an election that they should've won."[489]

In response to a question about whether he was angry with Comey about the Russia investigation, the President said, "As far as I'm concerned, I want that thing to be absolutely done properly."[490] The President added that he realized his termination of Comey "probably maybe will confuse people" with the result that it "might even lengthen out the investigation," but he "ha[d] to do the right thing for the American people" and Comey was "the wrong man for that position."[491] The President described Comey as "a showboat" and "a grandstander," said that "[t]he FBI has been in turmoil," and said he wanted "to have a really competent, capable director."[492] The President affirmed that he expected the new FBI director to continue the Russia investigation.[493]

On the evening of May 11, 2017, following the Lester Holt interview, the President tweeted, "Russia must be laughing up their sleeves watching as the U.S. tears itself apart over a Democrat EXCUSE for losing the election."[494] The same day, the media reported that the President had demanded that Comey pledge his loyalty to the President in a private dinner shortly

---

[484] McGahn 12/12/17 302, at 16-17; Donaldson 11/6/17 302, at 26; *see* Dhillon 11/21/17 302, at 11.

[485] Donaldson 11/6/17 302, at 27.

[486] McGahn 12/12/17 302, at 17.

[487] Dhillon 11/21/17 302, at 11.

[488] *Interview with President Donald Trump*, NBC (May 11, 2017) Transcript, at 2.

[489] *Interview with President Donald Trump*, NBC (May 11, 2017) Transcript, at 2.

[490] *Interview with President Donald Trump*, NBC (May 11, 2017) Transcript, at 3.

[491] *Interview with President Donald Trump*, NBC (May 11, 2017) Transcript, at 3.

[492] *Interview with President Donald Trump*, NBC (May 11, 2017) Transcript, at 1, 5.

[493] *Interview with President Donald Trump*, NBC (May 11, 2017) Transcript, at 7.

[494] @realDonaldTrump 5/11/17 (4:34 p.m. ET) Tweet.

U.S. Department of Justice

~~Attorney Work Product // May Contain Material Protected Under Fed. R. Crim. P. 6(e)~~

after being sworn in.[495] Late in the morning of May 12, 2017, the President tweeted, "Again, the story that there was collusion between the Russians & Trump campaign was fabricated by Dems as an excuse for losing the election."[496] The President also tweeted, "James Comey better hope that there are no 'tapes' of our conversations before he starts leaking to the press!" and "When James Clapper himself, and virtually everyone else with knowledge of the witch hunt, says there is no collusion, when does it end?"[497]

Analysis

In analyzing the President's decision to fire Comey, the following evidence is relevant to the elements of obstruction of justice:

a.   Obstructive act. The act of firing Comey removed the individual overseeing the FBI's Russia investigation. The President knew that Comey was personally involved in the investigation based on Comey's briefing of the Gang of Eight, Comey's March 20, 2017 public testimony about the investigation, and the President's one-on-one conversations with Comey.

Firing Comey would qualify as an obstructive act if it had the natural and probable effect of interfering with or impeding the investigation   for example, if the termination would have the effect of delaying or disrupting the investigation or providing the President with the opportunity to appoint a director who would take a different approach to the investigation that the President perceived as more protective of his personal interests. Relevant circumstances bearing on that issue include whether the President's actions had the potential to discourage a successor director or other law enforcement officials in their conduct of the Russia investigation. The President fired Comey abruptly without offering him an opportunity to resign, banned him from the FBI building, and criticized him publicly, calling him a "showboat" and claiming that the FBI was "in turmoil" under his leadership. And the President followed the termination with public statements that were highly critical of the investigation; for example, three days after firing Comey, the President referred to the investigation as a "witch hunt" and asked, "when does it end?" Those actions had the potential to affect a successor director's conduct of the investigation.

The anticipated effect of removing the FBI director, however, would not necessarily be to prevent or impede the FBI from continuing its investigation. As a general matter, FBI investigations run under the operational direction of FBI personnel levels below the FBI director. Bannon made a similar point when he told the President that he could fire the FBI director, but could not fire the FBI. The White House issued a press statement the day after Comey was fired that said, "The investigation would have always continued, and obviously, the termination of Comey would not have ended it." In addition, in his May 11 interview with Lester Holt, the President stated that he understood when he made the decision to fire Comey that the action might prolong the investigation. And the President chose McCabe to serve as interim director, even

---

[495] Michael S. Schmidt, *In a Private Dinner, Trump Demanded Loyalty. Comey Demurred.*, New York Times (May 11, 2017).

[496] @realDonaldTrump 5/12/17 (7:51 a.m. ET) Tweet.

[497] @realDonaldTrump 5/12/17 (8:26 a.m. ET) Tweet; @realDonaldTrump 5/12/17 (8:54 a.m. ET) Tweet.

though McCabe told the President he had worked "very closely" with Comey and was part of all the decisions made in the Clinton investigation.

      b.   Nexus to a proceeding. The nexus element would be satisfied by evidence showing that a grand jury proceeding or criminal prosecution arising from an FBI investigation was objectively foreseeable and actually contemplated by the President when he terminated Comey.

Several facts would be relevant to such a showing. At the time the President fired Comey, a grand jury had not begun to hear evidence related to the Russia investigation and no grand jury subpoenas had been issued. On March 20, 2017, however, Comey had announced that the FBI was investigating Russia's interference in the election, including "an assessment of whether any crimes were committed." It was widely known that the FBI, as part of the Russia investigation, was investigating the hacking of the DNC's computers—a clear criminal offense.

In addition, at the time the President fired Comey, evidence indicates the President knew that Flynn was still under criminal investigation and could potentially be prosecuted, despite the President's February 14, 2017 request that Comey "let[] Flynn go." On March 5, 2017, the White House Counsel's Office was informed that the FBI was asking for transition-period records relating to Flynn—indicating that the FBI was still actively investigating him. The same day, the President told advisors he wanted to call Dana Boente, then the Acting Attorney General for the Russia investigation, to find out whether the White House or the President was being investigated. On March 31, 2017, the President signaled his awareness that Flynn remained in legal jeopardy by tweeting that "Mike Flynn should ask for immunity" before he agreed to provide testimony to the FBI or Congress. And in late March or early April, the President asked McFarland to pass a message to Flynn telling him that the President felt bad for him and that he should stay strong, further demonstrating the President's awareness of Flynn's criminal exposure.

      c.   Intent. Substantial evidence indicates that the catalyst for the President's decision to fire Comey was Comey's unwillingness to publicly state that the President was not personally under investigation, despite the President's repeated requests that Comey make such an announcement. In the week leading up to Comey's May 3, 2017 Senate Judiciary Committee testimony, the President told McGahn that it would be the last straw if Comey did not set the record straight and publicly announce that the President was not under investigation. But during his May 3 testimony, Comey refused to answer questions about whether the President was being investigated. Comey's refusal angered the President, who criticized Sessions for leaving him isolated and exposed, saying "You left me on an island." Two days later, the President told advisors he had decided to fire Comey and dictated a letter to Stephen Miller that began with a reference to the fact that the President was not being investigated: "While I greatly appreciate you informing me that I am not under investigation concerning what I have often stated is a fabricated story on a Trump-Russia relationship . . . ." The President later asked Rosenstein to include "Russia" in his memorandum and to say that Comey had told the President that he was not under investigation. And the President's final termination letter included a sentence, at the President's insistence and against McGahn's advice, stating that Comey had told the President on three separate occasions that he was not under investigation.

The President's other stated rationales for why he fired Comey are not similarly supported by the evidence. The termination letter the President and Stephen Miller prepared in Bedminster

U.S. Department of Justice

~~Attorney Work Product // May Contain Material Protected Under Fed. R. Crim. P. 6(e)~~

cited Comey's handling of the Clinton email investigation, and the President told McCabe he fired Comey for that reason. But the facts surrounding Comey's handling of the Clinton email investigation were well known to the President at the time he assumed office, and the President had made it clear to both Comey and the President's senior staff in early 2017 that he wanted Comey to stay on as director. And Rosenstein articulated his criticism of Comey's handling of the Clinton investigation after the President had already decided to fire Comey. The President's draft termination letter also stated that morale in the FBI was at an all-time low and Sanders told the press after Comey's termination that the White House had heard from "countless" FBI agents who had lost confidence in Comey. But the evidence does not support those claims. The President told Comey at their January 27 dinner that "the people of the FBI really like [him]," no evidence suggests that the President heard otherwise before deciding to terminate Comey, and Sanders acknowledged to investigators that her comments were not founded on anything.

We also considered why it was important to the President that Comey announce publicly that he was not under investigation. Some evidence indicates that the President believed that the erroneous perception he was under investigation harmed his ability to manage domestic and foreign affairs, particularly in dealings with Russia. The President told Comey that the "cloud" of "this Russia business" was making it difficult to run the country. The President told Sessions and McGahn that foreign leaders had expressed sympathy to him for being under investigation and that the perception he was under investigation was hurting his ability to address foreign relations issues. The President complained to Rogers that "the thing with the Russians [was] messing up" his ability to get things done with Russia, and told Coats, "I can't do anything with Russia, there's things I'd like to do with Russia, with trade, with ISIS, they're all over me with this." The President also may have viewed Comey as insubordinate for his failure to make clear in the May 3 testimony that the President was not under investigation.

Other evidence, however, indicates that the President wanted to protect himself from an investigation into his campaign. The day after learning about the FBI's interview of Flynn, the President had a one-on-one dinner with Comey, against the advice of senior aides, and told Comey he needed Comey's "loyalty." When the President later asked Comey for a second time to make public that he was not under investigation, he brought up loyalty again, saying "Because I have been very loyal to you, very loyal, we had that thing, you know." After the President learned of Sessions's recusal from the Russia investigation, the President was furious and said he wanted an Attorney General who would protect him the way he perceived Robert Kennedy and Eric Holder to have protected their presidents. The President also said he wanted to be able to tell his Attorney General "who to investigate."

In addition, the President had a motive to put the FBI's Russia investigation behind him. The evidence does not establish that the termination of Comey was designed to cover up a conspiracy between the Trump Campaign and Russia: As described in Volume I, the evidence uncovered in the investigation did not establish that the President or those close to him were involved in the charged Russian computer-hacking or active-measure conspiracies, or that the President otherwise had an unlawful relationship with any Russian official. But the evidence does indicate that a thorough FBI investigation would uncover facts about the campaign and the President personally that the President could have understood to be crimes or that would give rise to personal and political concerns. Although the President publicly stated during and after the election that he had no connection to Russia, the Trump Organization, through Michael Cohen,

U.S. Department of Justice

Attorney Work Product // May Contain Material Protected Under Fed. R. Crim. P. 6(e)

was pursuing the proposed Trump Tower Moscow project through June 2016 and candidate Trump was repeatedly briefed on the progress of those efforts.[498] In addition, some witnesses said that Trump was aware that ███████████████████████████████████ ██████ at a time when public reports stated that Russian intelligence officials were behind the hacks, and that Trump privately sought information about future WikiLeaks releases.[499] More broadly, multiple witnesses described the President's preoccupation with press coverage of the Russia investigation and his persistent concern that it raised questions about the legitimacy of his election.[500]

Finally, the President and White House aides initially advanced a pretextual reason to the press and the public for Comey's termination. In the immediate aftermath of the firing, the President dictated a press statement suggesting that he had acted based on the DOJ recommendations, and White House press officials repeated that story. But the President had decided to fire Comey before the White House solicited those recommendations. Although the President ultimately acknowledged that he was going to fire Comey regardless of the Department of Justice's recommendations, he did so only after DOJ officials made clear to him that they would resist the White House's suggestion that they had prompted the process that led to Comey's termination. The initial reliance on a pretextual justification could support an inference that the President had concerns about providing the real reason for the firing, although the evidence does not resolve whether those concerns were personal, political, or both.

E.   The President's Efforts to Remove the Special Counsel

Overview

The Acting Attorney General appointed a Special Counsel on May 17, 2017, prompting the President to state that it was the end of his presidency and that Attorney General Sessions had failed to protect him and should resign. Sessions submitted his resignation, which the President ultimately did not accept. The President told senior advisors that the Special Counsel had conflicts of interest, but they responded that those claims were "ridiculous" and posed no obstacle to the Special Counsel's service. Department of Justice ethics officials similarly cleared the Special Counsel's service. On June 14, 2017, the press reported that the President was being personally investigated for obstruction of justice and the President responded with a series of tweets

---

[498] *See* Volume II, Section II.K.1, *infra.*

[499] *See* Volume I, Section III.D.1, *supra.*

[500] In addition to whether the President had a motive related to Russia-related matters that an FBI investigation could uncover, we considered whether the President's intent in firing Comey was connected to other conduct that could come to light as a result of the FBI's Russian-interference investigation. In particular, Michael Cohen was a potential subject of investigation because of his pursuit of the Trump Tower Moscow project and involvement in other activities. And facts uncovered in the Russia investigation, which our Office referred to the U.S. Attorney's Office for the Southern District of New York, ultimately led to the conviction of Cohen in the Southern District of New York for campaign-finance offenses related to payments he said he made at the direction of the President. *See* Volume II, Section II.K.5, *infra.* The investigation, however, did not establish that when the President fired Comey, he was considering the possibility that the FBI's investigation would uncover these payments or that the President's intent in firing Comey was otherwise connected to a concern about these matters coming to light.

U.S. Department of Justice

Attorney Work Product // May Contain Material Protected Under Fed. R. Crim. P. 6(e)

criticizing the Special Counsel's investigation. That weekend, the President called McGahn and directed him to have the Special Counsel removed because of asserted conflicts of interest. McGahn did not carry out the instruction for fear of being seen as triggering another Saturday Night Massacre and instead prepared to resign. McGahn ultimately did not quit and the President did not follow up with McGahn on his request to have the Special Counsel removed.

Evidence

1. The Appointment of the Special Counsel and the President's Reaction

On May 17, 2017, Acting Attorney General Rosenstein appointed Robert S. Mueller, III as Special Counsel and authorized him to conduct the Russia investigation and matters that arose from the investigation.[501] The President learned of the Special Counsel's appointment from Sessions, who was with the President, Hunt, and McGahn conducting interviews for a new FBI Director.[502] Sessions stepped out of the Oval Office to take a call from Rosenstein, who told him about the Special Counsel appointment, and Sessions then returned to inform the President of the news.[503] According to notes written by Hunt, when Sessions told the President that a Special Counsel had been appointed, the President slumped back in his chair and said, "Oh my God. This is terrible. This is the end of my Presidency. I'm fucked."[504] The President became angry and lambasted the Attorney General for his decision to recuse from the investigation, stating, "How could you let this happen, Jeff?"[505] The President said the position of Attorney General was his most important appointment and that Sessions had "let [him] down," contrasting him to Eric Holder and Robert Kennedy.[506] Sessions recalled that the President said to him, "you were supposed to protect me," or words to that effect.[507] The President returned to the consequences of the appointment and said, "Everyone tells me if you get one of these independent counsels it ruins your presidency. It takes years and years and I won't be able to do anything. This is the worst thing that ever happened to me."[508]

---

[501] Office of the Deputy Attorney General, Order No. 3915-2017, *Appointment of Special Counsel to Investigate Russian Interference with the 2016 Presidential Election and Related Matters* (May 17, 2017).

[502] Sessions 1/17/18 302, at 13; Hunt 2/1/18 302, at 18; McGahn 12/14/17 302, at 4; Hunt-000039 (Hunt 5/17/17 Notes).

[503] Sessions 1/17/18 302, at 13; Hunt 2/1/18 302, at 18; McGahn 12/14/17 302, at 4; Hunt-000039 (Hunt 5/17/17 Notes).

[504] Hunt-000039 (Hunt 5/17/17 Notes).

[505] Hunt-000039 (Hunt 5/17/17 Notes); Sessions 1/17/18 302, at 13-14.

[506] Hunt-000040; *see* Sessions 1/17/18 302, at 14.

[507] Sessions 1/17/18 302, at 14.

[508] Hunt-000040 (Hunt 5/17/17 Notes); *see* Sessions 1/17/18 302, at 14. Early the next morning, the President tweeted, "This is the single greatest witch hunt of a politician in American history!" @realDonaldTrump 5/18/17 (7:52 a.m. ET) Tweet.

The President then told Sessions he should resign as Attorney General.[509] Sessions agreed to submit his resignation and left the Oval Office.[510] Hicks saw the President shortly after Sessions departed and described the President as being extremely upset by the Special Counsel's appointment.[511] Hicks said that she had only seen the President like that one other time, when the Access Hollywood tape came out during the campaign.[512]

The next day, May 18, 2017, FBI agents delivered to McGahn a preservation notice that discussed an investigation related to Comey's termination and directed the White House to preserve all relevant documents.[513] When he received the letter, McGahn issued a document hold to White House staff and instructed them not to send out any burn bags over the weekend while he sorted things out.[514]

Also on May 18, Sessions finalized a resignation letter that stated, "Pursuant to our conversation of yesterday, and at your request, I hereby offer my resignation."[515] Sessions, accompanied by Hunt, brought the letter to the White House and handed it to the President.[516] The President put the resignation letter in his pocket and asked Sessions several times whether he wanted to continue serving as Attorney General.[517] Sessions ultimately told the President he wanted to stay, but it was up to the President.[518] The President said he wanted Sessions to stay.[519] At the conclusion of the meeting, the President shook Sessions's hand but did not return the resignation letter.[520]

When Priebus and Bannon learned that the President was holding onto Sessions's resignation letter, they became concerned that it could be used to influence the Department of Justice.[521] Priebus told Sessions it was not good for the President to have the letter because it

---

[509] Hunt-000041 (Hunt 5/17/17 Notes); Sessions 1/17/18 302, at 14.

[510] Hunt-000041 (Hunt 5/17/17 Notes); Sessions 1/17/18 302, at 14.

[511] Hicks 12/8/17 302, at 21.

[512] Hicks 12/8/17 302, at 21. The Access Hollywood tape was released on October 7, 2016, as discussed in Volume I, Section III.D.1, *supra*.

[513] McGahn 12/14/17 302, at 9; SCR015_000175-82 (Undated Draft Memoranda to White House Staff).

[514] McGahn 12/14/17 302, at 9; SCR015_000175-82 (Undated Draft Memoranda to White House Staff). The White House Counsel's Office had previously issued a document hold on February 27, 2017. SCR015_000171 (2/17/17 Memorandum from McGahn to Executive Office of the President Staff).

[515] Hunt-000047 (Hunt 5/18/17 Notes); 5/18/17 Letter, Sessions to President Trump (resigning as Attorney General).

[516] Hunt-000047-49 (Hunt 5/18/17 Notes); Sessions 1/17/18 302, at 14.

[517] Hunt-000047-49 (Hunt 5/18/17 Notes); Sessions 1/17/18 302, at 14.

[518] Hunt-000048-49 (Hunt 5/18/17 Notes); Sessions 1/17/18 302, at 14.

[519] Sessions 1/17/18 302, at 14.

[520] Hunt-000049 (Hunt 5/18/17 Notes).

[521] Hunt-000050-51 (Hunt 5/18/17 Notes).

U.S. Department of Justice

~~Attorney-Work-Product // May-Contain-Material-Protected-Under-Fed. R. Crim. P. 6(e)~~

would function as a kind of "shock collar" that the President could use any time he wanted; Priebus said the President had "DOJ by the throat."[522] Priebus and Bannon told Sessions they would attempt to get the letter back from the President with a notation that he was not accepting Sessions's resignation.[523]

On May 19, 2017, the President left for a trip to the Middle East.[524] Hicks recalled that on the President's flight from Saudi Arabia to Tel Aviv, the President pulled Sessions's resignation letter from his pocket, showed it to a group of senior advisors, and asked them what he should do about it.[525] During the trip, Priebus asked about the resignation letter so he could return it to Sessions, but the President told him that the letter was back at the White House, somewhere in the residence.[526] It was not until May 30, three days after the President returned from the trip, that the President returned the letter to Sessions with a notation saying, "Not accepted."[527]

2. The President Asserts that the Special Counsel has Conflicts of Interest

In the days following the Special Counsel's appointment, the President repeatedly told advisors, including Priebus, Bannon, and McGahn, that Special Counsel Mueller had conflicts of interest.[528] The President cited as conflicts that Mueller had interviewed for the FBI Director position shortly before being appointed as Special Counsel, that he had worked for a law firm that represented people affiliated with the President, and that Mueller had disputed certain fees relating to his membership in a Trump golf course in Northern Virginia.[529] The President's advisors pushed

---

[522] Hunt-000050 (Hunt 5/18/17 Notes); Priebus 10/13/17 302, at 21; Hunt 2/1/18 302, at 21.

[523] Hunt-000051 (Hunt 5/18/17 Notes).

[524] SCR026_000110 (President's Daily Diary, 5/19/17).

[525] Hicks 12/8/17 302, at 22.

[526] Priebus 10/13/17 302, at 21. Hunt's notes state that when Priebus returned from the trip, Priebus told Hunt that the President was supposed to have given him the letter, but when he asked for it, the President "slapped the desk" and said he had forgotten it back at the hotel. Hunt-000052 (Hunt Notes, undated).

[527] Hunt-000052-53 (Hunt 5/30/17 Notes); 5/18/17 Letter, Sessions to President Trump (resignation letter). Robert Porter, who was the White House Staff Secretary at the time, said that in the days after the President returned from the Middle East trip, the President took Sessions's letter out of a drawer in the Oval Office and showed it to Porter. Porter 4/13/18 302, at 8. ▮▮▮

[528] Priebus 1/18/18 302, at 12; Bannon 2/14/18 302, at 10; McGahn 3/8/18 302, at 1; McGahn 12/14/17 302, at 10; Bannon 10/26/18 302, at 12.

[529] Priebus 1/18/18 302, at 12; Bannon 2/14/18 302, at 10. In October 2011, Mueller resigned his family's membership from Trump National Golf Club in Sterling, Virginia, in a letter that noted that "we live in the District and find that we are unable to make full use of the Club" and that inquired "whether we would be entitled to a refund of a portion of our initial membership fee," which was paid in 1994. 10/12/11 Letter, Muellers to Trump National Golf Club. About two weeks later, the controller of the club responded that the Muellers' resignation would be effective October 31, 2011, and that they would be "placed on a waitlist to be refunded on a first resigned / first refunded basis" in accordance with the club's legal

back on his assertion of conflicts, telling the President they did not count as true conflicts.[530] Bannon recalled telling the President that the purported conflicts were "ridiculous" and that none of them was real or could come close to justifying precluding Mueller from serving as Special Counsel.[531] As for Mueller's interview for FBI Director, Bannon recalled that the White House had invited Mueller to speak to the President to offer a perspective on the institution of the FBI.[532] Bannon said that, although the White House thought about beseeching Mueller to become Director again, he did not come in looking for the job.[533] Bannon also told the President that the law firm position did not amount to a conflict in the legal community.[534] And Bannon told the President that the golf course dispute did not rise to the level of a conflict and claiming one was "ridiculous and petty."[535] The President did not respond when Bannon pushed back on the stated conflicts of interest.[536]

On May 23, 2017, the Department of Justice announced that ethics officials had determined that the Special Counsel's prior law firm position did not bar his service, generating media reports that Mueller had been cleared to serve.[537] McGahn recalled that around the same time, the President complained about the asserted conflicts and prodded McGahn to reach out to Rosenstein about the issue.[538] McGahn said he responded that he could not make such a call and that the President should instead consult his personal lawyer because it was not a White House issue.[539] Contemporaneous notes of a May 23, 2017 conversation between McGahn and the President reflect that McGahn told the President that he would not call Rosenstein and that he would suggest that the President not make such a call either.[540] McGahn advised that the President could discuss the issue with his personal attorney but it would "look like still trying to meddle in [the] investigation" and "knocking out Mueller" would be "[a]nother fact used to claim obst[ruction] of

---

documents. 10/27/11 Letter, Muellers to Trump National Golf Club. The Muellers have not had further contact with the club.

[530] Priebus 4/3/18 302, at 3; Bannon 10/26/18 302, at 13 (confirming that he, Priebus, and McGahn pushed back on the asserted conflicts).

[531] Bannon 10/26/18 302, at 12-13.

[532] Bannon 10/26/18 302, at 12.

[533] Bannon 10/26/18 302, at 12.

[534] Bannon 10/26/18 302, at 12.

[535] Bannon 10/26/18 302, at 13.

[536] Bannon 10/26/18 302, at 12.

[537] Matt Zapotosky & Matea Gold, *Justice Department ethics experts clear Mueller to lead Russia probe*, Washington Post (May 23, 2017).

[538] McGahn 3/8/18 302, at 1; McGahn 12/14/17 302, at 10; Priebus 1/18/18 302, at 12.

[539] McGahn 3/8/18 302, at 1. McGahn and Donaldson said that after the appointment of the Special Counsel, they considered themselves potential fact witnesses and accordingly told the President that inquiries related to the investigation should be brought to his personal counsel. McGahn 12/14/17 302, at 7; Donaldson 4/2/18 302, at 5.

[540] SC_AD_00361 (Donaldson 5/31/17 Notes).

U.S. Department of Justice

Attorney Work Product // May Contain Material Protected Under Fed. R. Crim. P. 6(e)

just[ice]."[541] McGahn told the President that his "biggest exposure" was not his act of firing Comey but his "other contacts" and "calls," and his "ask re: Flynn."[542] By the time McGahn provided this advice to the President, there had been widespread reporting on the President's request for Comey's loyalty, which the President publicly denied; his request that Comey "let[] Flynn go," which the President also denied; and the President's statement to the Russian Foreign Minister that the termination of Comey had relieved "great pressure" related to Russia, which the President did not deny.[543]

On June 8, 2017, Comey testified before Congress about his interactions with the President before his termination, including the request for loyalty, the request that Comey "let[] Flynn go," and the request that Comey "lift the cloud" over the presidency caused by the ongoing investigation.[544] Comey's testimony led to a series of news reports about whether the President had obstructed justice.[545] On June 9, 2017, the Special Counsel's Office informed the White House Counsel's Office that investigators intended to interview intelligence community officials who had allegedly been asked by the President to push back against the Russia investigation.[546]

On Monday, June 12, 2017, Christopher Ruddy, the chief executive of Newsmax Media and a longtime friend of the President's, met at the White House with Priebus and Bannon.[547] Ruddy recalled that they told him the President was strongly considering firing the Special Counsel

---

[541] SC_AD_00361 (Donaldson 5/31/17 Notes).

[542] SC_AD_00361 (Donaldson 5/31/17 Notes).

[543] *See, e.g.,* Michael S. Schmidt, *In a Private Dinner, Trump Demanded Loyalty. Comey Demurred.,* New York Times (May 11, 2017); Michael S. Schmidt, *Comey Memorandum Says Trump Asked Him to End Flynn Investigation,* New York Times (May 16, 2017); Matt Apuzzo et al., *Trump Told Russians That Firing 'Nut Job' Comey Eased Pressure From Investigation,* New York Times (May 19, 2017).

[544] *Hearing on Russian Election Interference Before the Senate Select Intelligence Committee,* 115th Cong. (June 8, 2017) (Statement for the Record of James B. Comey, former Director of the FBI, at 5-6). Comey testified that he deliberately caused his memorandum documenting the February 14, 2017 meeting to be leaked to the New York Times in response to a tweet from the President, sent on May 12, 2017, that stated "James Comey better hope that there are no 'tapes' of our conversations before he starts leaking to the press!," and because he thought sharing the memorandum with a reporter "might prompt the appointment of a special counsel." *Hearing on Russian Election Interference Before the Senate Select Intelligence Committee,* 115th Cong. (June 8, 2017) (CQ Cong. Transcripts, at 55) (testimony by James B. Comey, former Director of the FBI).

[545] *See, e.g.,* Matt Zapotosky, *Comey lays out the case that Trump obstructed justice,* Washington Post (June 8, 2017) ("Legal analysts said Comey's testimony clarified and bolstered the case that the president obstructed justice.").

[546] 6/9/17 Email, Special Counsel's Office to the White House Counsel's Office. This Office made the notification to give the White House an opportunity to invoke executive privilege in advance of the interviews. On June 12, 2017, the Special Counsel's Office interviewed Admiral Rogers in the presence of agency counsel. Rogers 6/12/17 302, at 1. On June 13, the Special Counsel's Office interviewed Ledgett. Ledgett 6/13/17 302, at 1. On June 14, the Office interviewed Coats and other personnel from his office. Coats 6/14/17 302, at 1; Gistaro 6/14/17 302, at 1; Culver 6/14/17 302, at 1.

[547] Ruddy 6/6/18 302, at 5.

U.S. Department of Justice

Attorney Work Product // May Contain Material Protected Under Fed. R. Crim. P. 6(e)

and that he would do so precipitously, without vetting the decision through Administration officials.[548] Ruddy asked Priebus if Ruddy could talk publicly about the discussion they had about the Special Counsel, and Priebus said he could.[549] Priebus told Ruddy he hoped another blow up like the one that followed the termination of Comey did not happen.[550] Later that day, Ruddy stated in a televised interview that the President was "considering perhaps terminating the Special Counsel" based on purported conflicts of interest.[551] Ruddy later told another news outlet that "Trump is definitely considering" terminating the Special Counsel and "it's not something that's being dismissed."[552] Ruddy's comments led to extensive coverage in the media that the President was considering firing the Special Counsel.[553]

White House officials were unhappy with that press coverage and Ruddy heard from friends that the President was upset with him.[554] On June 13, 2017, Sanders asked the President for guidance on how to respond to press inquiries about the possible firing of the Special Counsel.[555] The President dictated an answer, which Sanders delivered, saying that "[w]hile the president has every right to" fire the Special Counsel, "he has no intention to do so."[556]

Also on June 13, 2017, the President's personal counsel contacted the Special Counsel's Office and raised concerns about possible conflicts.[557] The President's counsel cited Mueller's previous partnership in his law firm, his interview for the FBI Director position, and an asserted personal relationship he had with Comey.[558] That same day, Rosenstein had testified publicly before Congress and said he saw no evidence of good cause to terminate the Special Counsel, including for conflicts of interest.[559] Two days later, on June 15, 2017, the Special Counsel's

---

[548] Ruddy 6/6/18 302, at 5-6.

[549] Ruddy 6/6/18 302, at 6.

[550] Ruddy 6/6/18 302, at 6.

[551] *Trump Confidant Christopher Ruddy says Mueller has "real conflicts" as special counsel*, PBS (June 12, 2017); Michael D. Shear & Maggie Haberman, *Friend Says Trump Is Considering Firing Mueller as Special Counsel*, New York Times (June 12, 2017).

[552] Katherine Faulders & Veronica Stracqualursi, *Trump friend Chris Ruddy says Spicer's 'bizarre' statement doesn't deny claim Trump seeking Mueller firing*, ABC (June 13, 2017).

[553] *See, e.g.*, Michael D. Shear & Maggie Haberman, *Friend Says Trump Is Considering Firing Mueller as Special Counsel*, New York Times (June 12, 2017).

[554] Ruddy 6/6/18 302, at 6-7.

[555] Sanders 7/3/18 302, at 6-7.

[556] Glenn Thrush et al., *Trump Stews, Staff Steps In, and Mueller Is Safe for Now*, New York Times (June 13, 2017); *see* Sanders 7/3/18 302, at 6 (Sanders spoke with the President directly before speaking to the press on Air Force One and the answer she gave is the answer the President told her to give).

[557] Special Counsel's Office Attorney 6/13/17 Notes.

[558] Special Counsel's Office Attorney 6/13/17 Notes.

[559] *Hearing on Fiscal 2018 Justice Department Budget before the Senate Appropriations Subcommittee on Commerce, Justice, and Science*, 115th Cong. (June 13, 2017) (CQ Cong. Transcripts, at 14) (testimony by Rod Rosenstein, Deputy Attorney General).

Office informed the Acting Attorney General's office about the areas of concern raised by the President's counsel and told the President's counsel that their concerns had been communicated to Rosenstein so that the Department of Justice could take any appropriate action.[560]

3. The Press Reports that the President is Being Investigated for Obstruction of Justice and the President Directs the White House Counsel to Have the Special Counsel Removed

On the evening of June 14, 2017, the Washington Post published an article stating that the Special Counsel was investigating whether the President had attempted to obstruct justice.[561] This was the first public report that the President himself was under investigation by the Special Counsel's Office, and cable news networks quickly picked up on the report.[562] The Post story stated that the Special Counsel was interviewing intelligence community leaders, including Coats and Rogers, about what the President had asked them to do in response to Comey's March 20, 2017 testimony; that the inquiry into obstruction marked "a major turning point" in the investigation; and that while "Trump had received private assurances from then-FBI Director James B. Comey starting in January that he was not personally under investigation," "[o]fficials say that changed shortly after Comey's firing."[563] That evening, at approximately 10:31 p.m., the President called McGahn on McGahn's personal cell phone and they spoke for about 15 minutes.[564] McGahn did not have a clear memory of the call but thought they might have discussed the stories reporting that the President was under investigation.[565]

Beginning early the next day, June 15, 2017, the President issued a series of tweets acknowledging the existence of the obstruction investigation and criticizing it. He wrote: "They made up a phony collusion with the Russians story, found zero proof, so now they go for obstruction of justice on the phony story. Nice";[566] "You are witnessing the single greatest WITCH HUNT in American political history—led by some very bad and conflicted people!";[567] and "Crooked H destroyed phones w/ hammer, 'bleached' emails, & had husband meet w/AG days

---

[560] Special Counsel's Office Attorney 6/15/17 Notes.

[561] Devlin Barrett et al., *Special counsel is investigating Trump for possible obstruction of justice, officials say*, Washington Post (June 14, 2017).

[562] CNN, for example, began running a chyron at 6:55 p.m. that stated: "WASH POST: MUELLER INVESTIGATING TRUMP FOR OBSTRUCTION OF JUSTICE." CNN, (June 14, 2017, published online at 7:15 p.m. ET).

[563] Devlin Barrett et al., *Special counsel is investigating Trump for possible obstruction of justice, officials say*, Washington Post (June 14, 2017).

[564] SCR026_000183 (President's Daily Diary, 6/14/17) (reflecting call from the President to McGahn on 6/14/17 with start time 10:31 p.m. and end time 10:46 p.m.); Call Records of Don McGahn.

[565] McGahn 2/28/19 302, at 1-2. McGahn thought he and the President also probably talked about the investiture ceremony for Supreme Court Justice Neil Gorsuch, which was scheduled for the following day. McGahn 2/28/18 302, at 2.

[566] @realDonaldTrump 6/15/17 (6:55 a.m. ET) Tweet.

[567] @realDonaldTrump 6/15/17 (7:57 a.m. ET) Tweet.

U.S. Department of Justice

~~Attorney Work Product // May Contain Material Protected Under Fed. R. Crim. P. 6(e)~~

before she was cleared—& they talk about obstruction?"[568]   The next day, June 16, 2017, the President wrote additional tweets criticizing the investigation: "After 7 months of investigations & committee hearings about my 'collusion with the Russians,' nobody has been able to show any proof. Sad!";[569] and "I am being investigated for firing the FBI Director by the man who told me to fire the FBI Director! Witch Hunt."[570]

On Saturday, June 17, 2017, the President called McGahn and directed him to have the Special Counsel removed.[571] McGahn was at home and the President was at Camp David.[572] In interviews with this Office, McGahn recalled that the President called him at home twice and on both occasions directed him to call Rosenstein and say that Mueller had conflicts that precluded him from serving as Special Counsel.[573]

On the first call, McGahn recalled that the President said something like, "You gotta do this. You gotta call Rod."[574] McGahn said he told the President that he would see what he could do.[575] McGahn was perturbed by the call and did not intend to act on the request.[576] He and other advisors believed the asserted conflicts were "silly" and "not real," and they had previously communicated that view to the President.[577] McGahn also had made clear to the President that the White House Counsel's Office should not be involved in any effort to press the issue of conflicts.[578] McGahn was concerned about having any role in asking the Acting Attorney General to fire the Special Counsel because he had grown up in the Reagan era and wanted to be more like Judge

---

[568] @realDonaldTrump 6/15/17 (3:56 p.m. ET) Tweet.

[569] @realDonaldTrump 6/16/17 (7:53 a.m. ET) Tweet.

[570] @realDonaldTrump 6/16/17 (9:07 a.m. ET) Tweet.

[571] McGahn 3/8/18 302, at 1-2; McGahn 12/14/17 302, at 10.

[572] McGahn 3/8/18 302, at 1, 3; SCR026_000196 (President's Daily Diary, 6/17/17) (records showing President departed the White House at 11:07 a.m. on June 17, 2017, and arrived at Camp David at 11:37 a.m.).

[573] McGahn 3/8/18 302, at 1-2; McGahn 12/14/17 302, at 10. Phone records show that the President called McGahn in the afternoon on June 17, 2017, and they spoke for approximately 23 minutes. SCR026_000196 (President's Daily Diary, 6/17/17) (reflecting call from the President to McGahn on 6/17/17 with start time 2:23 p.m. and end time 2:46 p.m.); (Call Records of Don McGahn). Phone records do not show another call between McGahn and the President that day. Although McGahn recalled receiving multiple calls from the President on the same day, in light of the phone records he thought it was possible that the first call instead occurred on June 14, 2017, shortly after the press reported that the President was under investigation for obstruction of justice. McGahn 2/28/19 302, at 1-3. While McGahn was not certain of the specific dates of the calls, McGahn was confident that he had at least two phone conversations with the President in which the President directed him to call the Acting Attorney General to have the Special Counsel removed. McGahn 2/28/19 302, at 1-3.

[574] McGahn 3/8/18 302, at 1.

[575] McGahn 3/8/18 302, at 1.

[576] McGahn 3/8/18 302, at 1.

[577] McGahn 3/8/18 302, at 1-2.

[578] McGahn 3/8/18 302, at 1-2.

U.S. Department of Justice

Attorney Work Product // May Contain Material Protected Under Fed. R. Crim. P. 6(e)

Robert Bork and not "Saturday Night Massacre Bork."[579] McGahn considered the President's request to be an inflection point and he wanted to hit the brakes.[580]

When the President called McGahn a second time to follow up on the order to call the Department of Justice, McGahn recalled that the President was more direct, saying something like, "Call Rod, tell Rod that Mueller has conflicts and can't be the Special Counsel."[581] McGahn recalled the President telling him "Mueller has to go" and "Call me back when you do it."[582] McGahn understood the President to be saying that the Special Counsel had to be removed by Rosenstein.[583] To end the conversation with the President, McGahn left the President with the impression that McGahn would call Rosenstein.[584] McGahn recalled that he had already said no to the President's request and he was worn down, so he just wanted to get off the phone.[585]

McGahn recalled feeling trapped because he did not plan to follow the President's directive but did not know what he would say the next time the President called.[586] McGahn decided he had to resign.[587] He called his personal lawyer and then called his chief of staff, Annie Donaldson, to inform her of his decision.[588] He then drove to the office to pack his belongings and submit his resignation letter.[589] Donaldson recalled that McGahn told her the President had called and demanded he contact the Department of Justice and that the President wanted him to do something that McGahn did not want to do.[590] McGahn told Donaldson that the President had called at least twice and in one of the calls asked "have you done it?"[591] McGahn did not tell Donaldson the specifics of the President's request because he was consciously trying not to involve her in the

---

[579] McGahn 3/8/18 302, at 2.

[580] McGahn 3/8/18 302, at 2.

[581] McGahn 3/8/18 302, at 5.

[582] McGahn 3/8/18 302, at 2, 5; McGahn 2/28/19 302, at 3.

[583] McGahn 3/8/18 302, at 1-2, 5.

[584] McGahn 3/8/18 302, at 2.

[585] McGahn 2/28/19 302, at 3; McGahn 3/8/18 302, at 2.

[586] McGahn 3/8/18 302, at 2.

[587] McGahn 3/8/18 302, at 2.

[588] McGahn 3/8/18 302, at 2-3; McGahn 2/28/19 302, at 3; Donaldson 4/2/18 302, at 4; Call Records of Don McGahn.

[589] McGahn 3/8/18 302, at 2; Donaldson 4/2/18 302, at 4.

[590] Donaldson 4/2/18 302, at 4.

[591] Donaldson 4/2/18 302, at 4.

investigation, but Donaldson inferred that the President's directive was related to the Russia investigation.[592] Donaldson prepared to resign along with McGahn.[593]

That evening, McGahn called both Priebus and Bannon and told them that he intended to resign.[594] McGahn recalled that, after speaking with his attorney and given the nature of the President's request, he decided not to share details of the President's request with other White House staff.[595] Priebus recalled that McGahn said that the President had asked him to "do crazy shit," but he thought McGahn did not tell him the specifics of the President's request because McGahn was trying to protect Priebus from what he did not need to know.[596] Priebus and Bannon both urged McGahn not to quit, and McGahn ultimately returned to work that Monday and remained in his position.[597] He had not told the President directly that he planned to resign, and when they next saw each other the President did not ask McGahn whether he had followed through with calling Rosenstein.[598]

Around the same time, Chris Christie recalled a telephone call with the President in which the President asked what Christie thought about the President firing the Special Counsel.[599] Christie advised against doing so because there was no substantive basis for the President to fire the Special Counsel, and because the President would lose support from Republicans in Congress if he did so.[600]

Analysis

In analyzing the President's direction to McGahn to have the Special Counsel removed, the following evidence is relevant to the elements of obstruction of justice:

a.   Obstructive act. As with the President's firing of Comey, the attempt to remove the Special Counsel would qualify as an obstructive act if it would naturally obstruct the

---

[592] McGahn 2/28/19 302, at 3-4; Donaldson 4/2/18 302, at 4-5. Donaldson said she believed McGahn consciously did not share details with her because he did not want to drag her into the investigation. Donaldson 4/2/18 302, at 5; *see* McGahn 2/28/19 302, at 3.

[593] Donaldson 4/2/18 302, at 5.

[594] McGahn 12/14/17 302, at 10; Call Records of Don McGahn; McGahn 2/28/19 302, at 3-4; Priebus 4/3/18 302, at 6-7.

[595] McGahn 2/28/19 302, at 4. Priebus and Bannon confirmed that McGahn did not tell them the specific details of the President's request. Priebus 4/3/18 302, at 7; Bannon 2/14/18 302, at 10.

[596] Priebus 4/3/18 302, at 7.

[597] McGahn 3/8/18 302, at 3; McGahn 2/28/19 302, at 3-4.

[598] McGahn 3/8/18 302, at 3.

[599] Christie 2/13/19 302, at 7. Christie did not recall the precise date of this call, but believed it was after Christopher Wray was announced as the nominee to be the new FBI director, which was on June 7, 2017. Christie 2/13/19 302, at 7. Telephone records show that the President called Christie twice after that time period, on July 4, 2017, and July 14, 2017. Call Records of Chris Christie.

[600] Christie 2/13/19 302, at 7.

investigation and any grand jury proceedings that might flow from the inquiry. Even if the removal of the lead prosecutor would not prevent the investigation from continuing under a new appointee, a factfinder would need to consider whether the act had the potential to delay further action in the investigation, chill the actions of any replacement Special Counsel, or otherwise impede the investigation.

A threshold question is whether the President in fact directed McGahn to have the Special Counsel removed. After news organizations reported that in June 2017 the President had ordered McGahn to have the Special Counsel removed, the President publicly disputed these accounts, and privately told McGahn that he had simply wanted McGahn to bring conflicts of interest to the Department of Justice's attention. *See* Volume II, Section II.I, *infra*. Some of the President's specific language that McGahn recalled from the calls is consistent with that explanation. Substantial evidence, however, supports the conclusion that the President went further and in fact directed McGahn to call Rosenstein to have the Special Counsel removed.

First, McGahn's clear recollection was that the President directed him to tell Rosenstein not only that conflicts existed but also that "Mueller has to go." McGahn is a credible witness with no motive to lie or exaggerate given the position he held in the White House.[601] McGahn spoke with the President twice and understood the directive the same way both times, making it unlikely that he misheard or misinterpreted the President's request. In response to that request, McGahn decided to quit because he did not want to participate in events that he described as akin to the Saturday Night Massacre. He called his lawyer, drove to the White House, packed up his office, prepared to submit a resignation letter with his chief of staff, told Priebus that the President had asked him to "do crazy shit," and informed Priebus and Bannon that he was leaving. Those acts would be a highly unusual reaction to a request to convey information to the Department of Justice.

Second, in the days before the calls to McGahn, the President, through his counsel, had already brought the asserted conflicts to the attention of the Department of Justice. Accordingly, the President had no reason to have McGahn call Rosenstein that weekend to raise conflicts issues that already had been raised.

Third, the President's sense of urgency and repeated requests to McGahn to take immediate action on a weekend—"You gotta do this. You gotta call Rod."—support McGahn's recollection that the President wanted the Department of Justice to take action to remove the Special Counsel. Had the President instead sought only to have the Department of Justice re-examine asserted conflicts to evaluate whether they posed an ethical bar, it would have been unnecessary to set the process in motion on a Saturday and to make repeated calls to McGahn.

Finally, the President had discussed "knocking out Mueller" and raised conflicts of interest in a May 23, 2017 call with McGahn, reflecting that the President connected the conflicts to a plan to remove the Special Counsel. And in the days leading up to June 17, 2017, the President made clear to Priebus and Bannon, who then told Ruddy, that the President was considering terminating

---

[601] When this Office first interviewed McGahn about this topic, he was reluctant to share detailed information about what had occurred and only did so after continued questioning. *See* McGahn 12/14/17 302 (agent notes).

U.S. Department of Justice

~~Attorney Work Product // May Contain Material Protected Under Fed. R. Crim. P. 6(e)~~

the Special Counsel. Also during this time period, the President reached out to Christie to get his thoughts on firing the Special Counsel. This evidence shows that the President was not just seeking an examination of whether conflicts existed but instead was looking to use asserted conflicts as a way to terminate the Special Counsel.

b.   <u>Nexus to an official proceeding.</u> To satisfy the proceeding requirement, it would be necessary to establish a nexus between the President's act of seeking to terminate the Special Counsel and a pending or foreseeable grand jury proceeding.

Substantial evidence indicates that by June 17, 2017, the President knew his conduct was under investigation by a federal prosecutor who could present any evidence of federal crimes to a grand jury. On May 23, 2017, McGahn explicitly warned the President that his "biggest exposure" was not his act of firing Comey but his "other contacts" and "calls," and his "ask re: Flynn." By early June, it was widely reported in the media that federal prosecutors had issued grand jury subpoenas in the Flynn inquiry and that the Special Counsel had taken over the Flynn investigation.[602] On June 9, 2017, the Special Counsel's Office informed the White House that investigators would be interviewing intelligence agency officials who allegedly had been asked by the President to push back against the Russia investigation. On June 14, 2017, news outlets began reporting that the President was himself being investigated for obstruction of justice. Based on widespread reporting, the President knew that such an investigation could include his request for Comey's loyalty; his request that Comey "let[] Flynn go"; his outreach to Coats and Rogers; and his termination of Comey and statement to the Russian Foreign Minister that the termination had relieved "great pressure" related to Russia. And on June 16, 2017, the day before he directed McGahn to have the Special Counsel removed, the President publicly acknowledged that his conduct was under investigation by a federal prosecutor, tweeting, "I am being investigated for firing the FBI Director by the man who told me to fire the FBI Director!"

c.   <u>Intent.</u> Substantial evidence indicates that the President's attempts to remove the Special Counsel were linked to the Special Counsel's oversight of investigations that involved the President's conduct—and, most immediately, to reports that the President was being investigated for potential obstruction of justice.

Before the President terminated Comey, the President considered it critically important that he was not under investigation and that the public not erroneously think he was being investigated. As described in Volume II, Section II.D, *supra*, advisors perceived the President, while he was drafting the Comey termination letter, to be concerned more than anything else about getting out that he was not personally under investigation. When the President learned of the appointment of the Special Counsel on May 17, 2017, he expressed further concern about the investigation, saying "[t]his is the end of my Presidency." The President also faulted Sessions for recusing, saying "you were supposed to protect me."

On June 14, 2017, when the Washington Post reported that the Special Counsel was investigating the President for obstruction of justice, the President was facing what he had wanted

---

[602] *See, e.g.,* Evan Perez et al., *CNN exclusive: Grand jury subpoenas issued in FBI's Russia investigation,* CNN (May 9, 2017); Matt Ford, *Why Mueller Is Taking Over the Michael Flynn Grand Jury,* The Atlantic (June 2, 2017).

to avoid: a criminal investigation into his own conduct that was the subject of widespread media attention. The evidence indicates that news of the obstruction investigation prompted the President to call McGahn and seek to have the Special Counsel removed. By mid-June, the Department of Justice had already cleared the Special Counsel's service and the President's advisors had told him that the claimed conflicts of interest were "silly" and did not provide a basis to remove the Special Counsel. On June 13, 2017, the Acting Attorney General testified before Congress that no good cause for removing the Special Counsel existed, and the President dictated a press statement to Sanders saying he had no intention of firing the Special Counsel. But the next day, the media reported that the President was under investigation for obstruction of justice and the Special Counsel was interviewing witnesses about events related to possible obstruction—spurring the President to write critical tweets about the Special Counsel's investigation. The President called McGahn at home that night and then called him on Saturday from Camp David. The evidence accordingly indicates that news that an obstruction investigation had been opened is what led the President to call McGahn to have the Special Counsel terminated.

There also is evidence that the President knew that he should not have made those calls to McGahn. The President made the calls to McGahn after McGahn had specifically told the President that the White House Counsel's Office—and McGahn himself—could not be involved in pressing conflicts claims and that the President should consult with his personal counsel if he wished to raise conflicts. Instead of relying on his personal counsel to submit the conflicts claims, the President sought to use his official powers to remove the Special Counsel. And after the media reported on the President's actions, he denied that he ever ordered McGahn to have the Special Counsel terminated and made repeated efforts to have McGahn deny the story, as discussed in Volume II, Section II.I, *infra*. Those denials are contrary to the evidence and suggest the President's awareness that the direction to McGahn could be seen as improper.

F.   The President's Efforts to Curtail the Special Counsel Investigation

Overview

Two days after the President directed McGahn to have the Special Counsel removed, the President made another attempt to affect the course of the Russia investigation. On June 19, 2017, the President met one-on-one with Corey Lewandowski in the Oval Office and dictated a message to be delivered to Attorney General Sessions that would have had the effect of limiting the Russia investigation to future election interference only. One month later, the President met again with Lewandowski and followed up on the request to have Sessions limit the scope of the Russia investigation. Lewandowski told the President the message would be delivered soon. Hours later, the President publicly criticized Sessions in an unplanned press interview, raising questions about Sessions's job security.

1.   The President Asks Corey Lewandowski to Deliver a Message to Sessions to Curtail the Special Counsel Investigation

On June 19, 2017, two days after the President directed McGahn to have the Special Counsel removed, the President met one-on-one in the Oval Office with his former campaign

U.S. Department of Justice

~~Attorney-Work-Product // May Contain Material Protected Under Fed. R. Crim. P. 6(e)~~

manager Corey Lewandowski.[603] Senior White House advisors described Lewandowski as a "devotee" of the President and said the relationship between the President and Lewandowski was "close."[604]

During the June 19 meeting, Lewandowski recalled that, after some small talk, the President brought up Sessions and criticized his recusal from the Russia investigation.[605] The President told Lewandowski that Sessions was weak and that if the President had known about the likelihood of recusal in advance, he would not have appointed Sessions.[606] The President then asked Lewandowski to deliver a message to Sessions and said "write this down."[607] This was the first time the President had asked Lewandowski to take dictation, and Lewandowski wrote as fast as possible to make sure he captured the content correctly.[608]

The President directed that Sessions should give a speech publicly announcing:

> I know that I recused myself from certain things having to do with specific areas. But our POTUS . . . is being treated very unfairly. He shouldn't have a Special Prosecutor/Counsel b/c he hasn't done anything wrong. I was on the campaign w/ him for nine months, there were no Russians involved with him. I know it for a fact b/c I was there. He didn't do anything wrong except he ran the greatest campaign in American history.[609]

The dictated message went on to state that Sessions would meet with the Special Counsel to limit his jurisdiction to future election interference:

> Now a group of people want to subvert the Constitution of the United States. I am going to meet with the Special Prosecutor to explain this is very unfair and let the Special Prosecutor move forward with investigating election meddling for future elections so that nothing can happen in future elections.[610]

---

[603] Lewandowski 4/6/18 302, at 2; SCR026_000201 (President's Daily Diary, 6/19/17). ▮

[604] Kelly 8/2/18 302, at 7; Dearborn 6/20/18 302, at 1 (describing Lewandowski as a "comfort to the President" whose loyalty was appreciated). Kelly said that when he was Chief of Staff and the President had meetings with friends like Lewandowski, Kelly tried not to be there and to push the meetings to the residence to create distance from the West Wing. Kelly 8/2/18 302, at 7.

[605] Lewandowski 4/6/18 302, at 2.

[606] Lewandowski 4/6/18 302, at 2.

[607] Lewandowski 4/6/18 302, at 2.

[608] Lewandowski 4/6/18 302, at 3.

[609] Lewandowski 4/6/18 302, at 2-3; Lewandowski 6/19/17 Notes, at 1-2.

[610] Lewandowski 4/6/18 302, at 3; Lewandowski 6/19/17 Notes, at 3.

U.S. Department of Justice

Attorney Work Product // May Contain Material Protected Under Fed. R. Crim. P. 6(e)

The President said that if Sessions delivered that statement he would be the "most popular guy in the country."[611] Lewandowski told the President he understood what the President wanted Sessions to do.[612]

Lewandowski wanted to pass the message to Sessions in person rather than over the phone.[613] He did not want to meet at the Department of Justice because he did not want a public log of his visit and did not want Sessions to have an advantage over him by meeting on what Lewandowski described as Sessions's turf.[614] Lewandowski called Sessions and arranged a meeting for the following evening at Lewandowski's office, but Sessions had to cancel due to a last minute conflict.[615] Shortly thereafter, Lewandowski left Washington, D.C., without having had an opportunity to meet with Sessions to convey the President's message.[616] Lewandowski stored the notes in a safe at his home, which he stated was his standard procedure with sensitive items.[617]

2. The President Follows Up with Lewandowski

Following his June meeting with the President, Lewandowski contacted Rick Dearborn, then a senior White House official, and asked if Dearborn could pass a message to Sessions.[618] Dearborn agreed without knowing what the message was, and Lewandowski later confirmed that Dearborn would meet with Sessions for dinner in late July and could deliver the message then.[619] Lewandowski recalled thinking that the President had asked him to pass the message because the President knew Lewandowski could be trusted, but Lewandowski believed Dearborn would be a better messenger because he had a longstanding relationship with Sessions and because Dearborn was in the government while Lewandowski was not.[620]

On July 19, 2017, the President again met with Lewandowski alone in the Oval Office.[621] In the preceding days, as described in Volume II, Section II.G, *infra*, emails and other information about the June 9, 2016 meeting between several Russians and Donald Trump Jr., Jared Kushner, and Paul Manafort had been publicly disclosed. In the July 19 meeting with Lewandowski, the

---

[611] Lewandowski 4/6/18 302, at 3; Lewandowski 6/19/17 Notes, at 4.

[612] Lewandowski 4/6/18 302, at 3.

[613] Lewandowski 4/6/18 302, at 3-4.

[614] Lewandowski 4/6/18 302, at 4.

[615] Lewandowski 4/6/18 302, at 4.

[616] Lewandowski 4/6/18 302, at 4.

[617] Lewandowski 4/6/18 302, at 4.

[618] Lewandowski 4/6/18 302, at 4; *see* Dearborn 6/20/18 302, at 3.

[619] Lewandowski 4/6/18 302, at 4-5.

[620] Lewandowski 4/6/18 302, at 4, 6.

[621] Lewandowski 4/6/18 302, at 5; SCR029b_000002-03 (6/5/18 Additional Response to Special Counsel Request for Certain Visitor Log Information).

U.S. Department of Justice

~~Attorney Work Product // May Contain Material Protected Under Fed. R. Crim. P. 6(e)~~

President raised his previous request and asked if Lewandowski had talked to Sessions.[622] Lewandowski told the President that the message would be delivered soon.[623] Lewandowski recalled that the President told him that if Sessions did not meet with him, Lewandowski should tell Sessions he was fired.[624]

Immediately following the meeting with the President, Lewandowski saw Dearborn in the anteroom outside the Oval Office and gave him a typewritten version of the message the President had dictated to be delivered to Sessions.[625] Lewandowski told Dearborn that the notes were the message they had discussed, but Dearborn did not recall whether Lewandowski said the message was from the President.[626] The message "definitely raised an eyebrow" for Dearborn, and he recalled not wanting to ask where it came from or think further about doing anything with it.[627] Dearborn also said that being asked to serve as a messenger to Sessions made him uncomfortable.[628] He recalled later telling Lewandowski that he had handled the situation, but he did not actually follow through with delivering the message to Sessions, and he did not keep a copy of the typewritten notes Lewandowski had given him.[629]

3. The President Publicly Criticizes Sessions in a New York Times Interview

Within hours of the President's meeting with Lewandowski on July 19, 2017, the President gave an unplanned interview to the New York Times in which he criticized Sessions's decision to recuse from the Russia investigation.[630] The President said that "Sessions should have never recused himself, and if he was going to recuse himself, he should have told me before he took the job, and I would have picked somebody else."[631] Sessions's recusal, the President said, was "very unfair to the president. How do you take a job and then recuse yourself? If he would have recused himself before the job, I would have said, 'Thanks, Jeff, but I can't, you know, I'm not going to

---

[622] Lewandowski 4/6/18 302, at 5.

[623] Lewandowski 4/6/18 302, at 5.

[624] Lewandowski 4/6/18 302, at 6. Priebus vaguely recalled Lewandowski telling him that in approximately May or June 2017 the President had asked Lewandowski to get Sessions's resignation. Priebus recalled that Lewandowski described his reaction as something like, "What can I do? I'm not an employee of the administration. I'm a nobody." Priebus 4/3/18 302, at 6.

[625] Lewandowski 4/6/18 302, at 5. Lewandowski said he asked Hope Hicks to type the notes when he went in to the Oval Office, and he then retrieved the notes from her partway through his meeting with the President. Lewandowski 4/6/18 302, at 5.

[626] Lewandowski 4/6/18 302, at 5; Dearborn 6/20/18 302, at 3.

[627] Dearborn 6/20/18 302, at 3.

[628] Dearborn 6/20/18 302, at 3.

[629] Dearborn 6/20/18 302, at 3-4.

[630] Peter Baker et al., *Excerpts From The Times's Interview With Trump*, New York Times (July 19, 2017).

[631] Peter Baker et al., *Excerpts From The Times's Interview With Trump*, New York Times (July 19, 2017).

U.S. Department of Justice

Attorney Work Product // May Contain Material Protected Under Fed. R. Crim. P. 6(e)

take you.' It's extremely unfair, and that's a mild word, to the president."[632] Hicks, who was present for the interview, recalled trying to "throw [herself] between the reporters and [the President]" to stop parts of the interview, but the President "loved the interview."[633]

Later that day, Lewandowski met with Hicks and they discussed the President's New York Times interview.[634] Lewandowski recalled telling Hicks about the President's request that he meet with Sessions and joking with her about the idea of firing Sessions as a private citizen if Sessions would not meet with him.[635] As Hicks remembered the conversation, Lewandowski told her the President had recently asked him to meet with Sessions and deliver a message that he needed to do the "right thing" and resign.[636] While Hicks and Lewandowski were together, the President called Hicks and told her he was happy with how coverage of his New York Times interview criticizing Sessions was playing out.[637]

4. The President Orders Priebus to Demand Sessions's Resignation

Three days later, on July 21, 2017, the Washington Post reported that U.S. intelligence intercepts showed that Sessions had discussed campaign-related matters with the Russian ambassador, contrary to what Sessions had said publicly.[638] That evening, Priebus called Hunt to talk about whether Sessions might be fired or might resign.[639] Priebus had previously talked to Hunt when the media had reported on tensions between Sessions and the President, and, after speaking to Sessions, Hunt had told Priebus that the President would have to fire Sessions if he wanted to remove Sessions because Sessions was not going to quit.[640] According to Hunt, who took contemporaneous notes of the July 21 call, Hunt told Priebus that, as they had previously discussed, Sessions had no intention of resigning.[641] Hunt asked Priebus what the President would

---

[632] Peter Baker et al., *Excerpts From The Times's Interview With Trump*, New York Times (July 19, 2017).

[633] Hicks 12/8/17 302, at 23.

[634] Hicks 3/13/18 302, at 10; Lewandowski 4/6/18 302, at 6.

[635] Lewandowski 4/6/18 302, at 6.

[636] Hicks 3/13/18 302, at 10. Hicks thought that the President might be able to make a recess appointment of a new Attorney General because the Senate was about to go on recess. Hicks 3/13/18 302, at 10. Lewandowski recalled that in the afternoon of July 19, 2017, following his meeting with the President, he conducted research on recess appointments but did not share his research with the President. Lewandowski 4/6/18 302, at 7.

[637] Lewandowski 4/6/18 302, at 6.

[638] Adam Entous et al., *Sessions discussed Trump campaign-related matters with Russian ambassador, U.S. intelligence intercepts show*, Washington Post (July 21, 2017). The underlying events concerning the Sessions-Kislyak contacts are discussed in Volume I, Section IV.A.4.c, *supra*.

[639] Hunt 2/1/18 302, at 23.

[640] Hunt 2/1/18 302, at 23.

[641] Hunt 2/1/18 302, at 23-24; Hunt 7/21/17 Notes, at 1.

U.S. Department of Justice

~~Attorney Work Product // May Contain Material Protected Under Fed. R. Crim. P. 6(e)~~

accomplish by firing Sessions, pointing out there was an investigation before and there would be an investigation after.[642]

Early the following morning, July 22, 2017, the President tweeted, "A new INTELLIGENCE LEAK from the Amazon Washington Post, this time against A.G. Jeff Sessions. These illegal leaks, like Comey's, must stop!"[643] Approximately one hour later, the President tweeted, "So many people are asking why isn't the A.G. or Special Council looking at the many Hillary Clinton or Comey crimes. 33,000 e-mails deleted?"[644] Later that morning, while aboard Marine One on the way to Norfolk, Virginia, the President told Priebus that he had to get Sessions to resign immediately.[645] The President said that the country had lost confidence in Sessions and the negative publicity was not tolerable.[646] According to contemporaneous notes taken by Priebus, the President told Priebus to say that he "need[ed] a letter of resignation on [his] desk immediately" and that Sessions had "no choice" but "must immediately resign."[647] Priebus replied that if they fired Sessions, they would never get a new Attorney General confirmed and that the Department of Justice and Congress would turn their backs on the President, but the President suggested he could make a recess appointment to replace Sessions.[648]

Priebus believed that the President's request was a problem, so he called McGahn and asked for advice, explaining that he did not want to pull the trigger on something that was "all wrong."[649] Although the President tied his desire for Sessions to resign to Sessions's negative press and poor performance in congressional testimony, Priebus believed that the President's desire to replace Sessions was driven by the President's hatred of Sessions's recusal from the Russia investigation.[650] McGahn told Priebus not to follow the President's order and said they should consult their personal counsel, with whom they had attorney-client privilege.[651] McGahn

---

[642] Hunt 2/1/18 302, at 23-24; Hunt 7/21/17 Notes, at 1-2.

[643] @realDonaldTrump 7/22/17 (6:33 a.m. ET) Tweet.

[644] @realDonaldTrump 7/22/17 (7:44 a.m. ET) Tweet. Three minutes later, the President tweeted, "What about all of the Clinton ties to Russia, including Podesta Company, Uranium deal, Russian Reset, big dollar speeches etc." @realDonaldTrump 7/22/17 (7:47 a.m. ET) Tweet.

[645] Priebus 1/18/18 302, at 13-14.

[646] Priebus 1/18/18 302, at 14; Priebus 4/3/18 302, at 4-5; see RP_000073 (Priebus 7/22/17 Notes).

[647] RP_000073 (Priebus 7/22/17 Notes).

[648] Priebus 4/3/18 302, at 5.

[649] Priebus 1/18/18 302, at 14; Priebus 4/3/18 302, at 4-5.

[650] Priebus 4/3/18 302, at 5.

[651] RP_C00074 (Priebus 7/22/17 Notes); McGahn 12/14/17 302, at 11; Priebus 1/18/18 302, at 14. Priebus followed McGahn's advice and called his personal attorney to discuss the President's request because he thought it was the type of thing about which one would need to consult an attorney. Priebus 1/18/18 302, at 14.

U.S. Department of Justice

Attorney Work Product // May Contain Material Protected Under Fed. R. Crim. P. 6(e)

and Priebus discussed the possibility that they would both have to resign rather than carry out the President's order to fire Sessions.[652]

That afternoon, the President followed up with Priebus about demanding Sessions's resignation, using words to the effect of, "Did you get it? Are you working on it?"[653] Priebus said that he believed that his job depended on whether he followed the order to remove Sessions, although the President did not directly say so.[654] Even though Priebus did not intend to carry out the President's directive, he told the President he would get Sessions to resign.[655] Later in the day, Priebus called the President and explained that it would be a calamity if Sessions resigned because Priebus expected that Rosenstein and Associate Attorney General Rachel Brand would also resign and the President would be unable to get anyone else confirmed.[656] The President agreed to hold off on demanding Sessions's resignation until after the Sunday shows the next day, to prevent the shows from focusing on the firing.[657]

By the end of that weekend, Priebus recalled that the President relented and agreed not to ask Sessions to resign.[658] Over the next several days, the President tweeted about Sessions. On the morning of Monday, July 24, 2017, the President criticized Sessions for neglecting to investigate Clinton and called him "beleaguered."[659] On July 25, the President tweeted, "Attorney General Jeff Sessions has taken a VERY weak position on Hillary Clinton crimes (where are E-mails & DNC server) & Intel leakers!"[660] The following day, July 26, the President tweeted, "Why didn't A.G. Sessions replace Acting FBI Director Andrew McCabe, a Comey friend who was in charge of Clinton investigation."[661] According to Hunt, in light of the President's frequent public attacks, Sessions prepared another resignation letter and for the rest of the year carried it with him in his pocket every time he went to the White House.[662]

---

[652] McGahn 12/14/17 302, at 11; RP_000074 (Priebus 7/22/17 Notes) ("discuss resigning together").

[653] Priebus 1/18/18 302, at 14; Priebus 4/3/18 302, at 4.

[654] Priebus 4/3/18 302, at 4.

[655] Priebus 1/18/18 302, at 15.

[656] Priebus 1/18/18 302, at 15.

[657] Priebus 1/18/18 302, at 15.

[658] Priebus 1/18/18 302, at 15.

[659] @realDonaldTrump 7/24/17 (8:49 a.m. ET) Tweet ("So why aren't the Committees and investigators, and of course our beleaguered A.G., looking into Crooked Hillarys crimes & Russia relations?").

[660] @realDonaldTrump 7/25/17 (6:12 a.m. ET) Tweet. The President sent another tweet shortly before this one asking "where is the investigation A.G." @realDonaldTrump 7/25/17 (6:03 a.m. ET) Tweet.

[661] @realDonaldTrump 7/26/17 (9:48 a.m. ET) Tweet.

[662] Hunt 2/1/18 302, at 24-25.

Analysis

In analyzing the President's efforts to have Lewandowski deliver a message directing Sessions to publicly announce that the Special Counsel investigation would be confined to future election interference, the following evidence is relevant to the elements of obstruction of justice:

a.   Obstructive act. The President's effort to send Sessions a message through Lewandowski would qualify as an obstructive act if it would naturally obstruct the investigation and any grand jury proceedings that might flow from the inquiry.

The President sought to have Sessions announce that the President "shouldn't have a Special Prosecutor/Counsel" and that Sessions was going to "meet with the Special Prosecutor to explain this is very unfair and let the Special Prosecutor move forward with investigating election meddling for future elections so that nothing can happen in future elections." The President wanted Sessions to disregard his recusal from the investigation, which had followed from a formal DOJ ethics review, and have Sessions declare that he knew "for a fact" that "there were no Russians involved with the campaign" because he "was there." The President further directed that Sessions should explain that the President should not be subject to an investigation "because he hasn't done anything wrong." Taken together, the President's directives indicate that Sessions was being instructed to tell the Special Counsel to end the existing investigation into the President and his campaign, with the Special Counsel being permitted to "move forward with investigating election meddling for future elections."

b.   Nexus to an official proceeding. As described above, by the time of the President's initial one-on-one meeting with Lewandowski on June 19, 2017, the existence of a grand jury investigation supervised by the Special Counsel was public knowledge. By the time of the President's follow-up meeting with Lewandowski, █████████████████████████████ ██████████████████ *See* Volume II, Section II.G, *infra.* To satisfy the nexus requirement, it would be necessary to show that limiting the Special Counsel's investigation would have the natural and probable effect of impeding that grand jury proceeding.

c.   Intent. Substantial evidence indicates that the President's effort to have Sessions limit the scope of the Special Counsel's investigation to future election interference was intended to prevent further investigative scrutiny of the President's and his campaign's conduct.

As previously described, *see* Volume II, Section II.B, *supra,* the President knew that the Russia investigation was focused in part on his campaign, and he perceived allegations of Russian interference to cast doubt on the legitimacy of his election. The President further knew that the investigation had broadened to include his own conduct and whether he had obstructed justice. Those investigations would not proceed if the Special Counsel's jurisdiction were limited to future election interference only.

The timing and circumstances of the President's actions support the conclusion that he sought that result. The President's initial direction that Sessions should limit the Special Counsel's investigation came just two days after the President had ordered McGahn to have the Special Counsel removed, which itself followed public reports that the President was personally under investigation for obstruction of justice. The sequence of those events raises an inference that after seeking to terminate the Special Counsel, the President sought to exclude his and his campaign's conduct from the investigation's scope. The President raised the matter with Lewandowski again on July 19, 2017, just days after emails and information about the June 9, 2016 meeting between Russians and senior campaign officials had been publicly disclosed, generating substantial media coverage and investigative interest.

The manner in which the President acted provides additional evidence of his intent. Rather than rely on official channels, the President met with Lewandowski alone in the Oval Office. The President selected a loyal "devotee" outside the White House to deliver the message, supporting an inference that he was working outside White House channels, including McGahn, who had previously resisted contacting the Department of Justice about the Special Counsel. The President also did not contact the Acting Attorney General, who had just testified publicly that there was no cause to remove the Special Counsel. Instead, the President tried to use Sessions to restrict and redirect the Special Counsel's investigation when Sessions was recused and could not properly take any action on it.

The July 19, 2017 events provide further evidence of the President's intent. The President followed up with Lewandowski in a separate one-on-one meeting one month after he first dictated the message for Sessions, demonstrating he still sought to pursue the request. And just hours after Lewandowski assured the President that the message would soon be delivered to Sessions, the President gave an unplanned interview to the New York Times in which he publicly attacked Sessions and raised questions about his job security. Four days later, on July 22, 2017, the President directed Priebus to obtain Sessions's resignation. That evidence could raise an inference that the President wanted Sessions to realize that his job might be on the line as he evaluated whether to comply with the President's direction that Sessions publicly announce that, notwithstanding his recusal, he was going to confine the Special Counsel's investigation to future election interference.

G. The President's Efforts to Prevent Disclosure of Emails About the June 9, 2016 Meeting Between Russians and Senior Campaign Officials

Overview

By June 2017, the President became aware of emails setting up the June 9, 2016 meeting between senior campaign officials and Russians who offered derogatory information on Hillary Clinton as "part of Russia and its government's support for Mr. Trump." On multiple occasions in late June and early July 2017, the President directed aides not to publicly disclose the emails, and he then dictated a statement about the meeting to be issued by Donald Trump Jr. describing the meeting as about adoption.

Evidence

1. The President Learns About the Existence of Emails Concerning the June 9, 2016 Trump Tower Meeting

In mid-June 2017—the same week that the President first asked Lewandowski to pass a message to Sessions—senior Administration officials became aware of emails exchanged during

U.S. Department of Justice

~~Attorney Work Product // May Contain Material Protected Under Fed. R. Crim. P. 6(e)~~

the campaign arranging a meeting between Donald Trump Jr., Paul Manafort, Jared Kushner, and a Russian attorney.[663] As described in Volume I, Section IV.A.5, *supra*, the emails stated that the "Crown [P]rosecutor of Russia" had offered "to provide the Trump campaign with some official documents and information that would incriminate Hillary and her dealings with Russia" as part of "Russia and its government's support for Mr. Trump."[664] Trump Jr. responded, "[I]f it's what you say I love it,"[665] and he, Kushner, and Manafort met with the Russian attorney and several other Russian individuals at Trump Tower on June 9, 2016.[666] At the meeting, the Russian attorney claimed that funds derived from illegal activities in Russia were provided to Hillary Clinton and other Democrats, and the Russian attorney then spoke about the Magnitsky Act, a 2012 U.S. statute that imposed financial and travel sanctions on Russian officials and that had resulted in a retaliatory ban in Russia on U.S. adoptions of Russian children.[667]

According to written answers submitted by the President in response to questions from this Office, the President had no recollection of learning of the meeting or the emails setting it up at the time the meeting occurred or at any other time before the election.[668]

The Trump Campaign had previously received a document request from SSCI that called for the production of various information, including, "[a] list and a description of all meetings" between any "individual affiliated with the Trump campaign" and "any individual formally or informally affiliated with the Russian government or Russian business interests which took place between June 16, 2015, and 12 pm on January 20, 2017," and associated records.[669] Trump Organization attorneys became aware of the June 9 meeting no later than the first week of June 2017, when they began interviewing the meeting participants, and the Trump Organization attorneys provided the emails setting up the meeting to the President's personal counsel.[670] Mark Corallo, who had been hired as a spokesman for the President's personal legal team, recalled that he learned about the June 9 meeting around June 21 or 22, 2017.[671] Priebus recalled learning about the June 9 meeting from Fox News host Sean Hannity in late June 2017.[672] Priebus notified one

---

[663] Hicks 3/13/18 302, at 1; Raffel 2/8/18 302, at 2.

[664] RG000061 (6/3/16 Email, Goldstone to Trump Jr.); @DonaldJTrumpJR 7/11/17 (11:01 a.m. ET) Tweet.

[665] RG000061 (6/3/16 Email, Trump Jr. to Goldstone); @DonaldJTrumpJR 7/11/17 (11:01 a.m. ET) Tweet.

[666] Samochornov 7/12/17 302, at 4.

[667] *See* Volume I, Section IV.A.5, *supra* (describing meeting in detail).

[668] Written Responses of Donald J. Trump (Nov. 20, 2018), at 8 (Response to Question I, Parts (a) through (c)). The President declined to answer questions about his knowledge of the June 9 meeting or other events after the election.

[669] DJTFP_SCO_PDF_00000001-02 (5/17/17 Letter, SSCI to Donald J. Trump for President, Inc.).

[670] Goldstone 2/8/18 302, at 12; 6/2/17 and 6/5/17 Emails, Goldstone & Garten; Raffel 2/8/18 302, at 3; Hicks 3/13/18 302, at 2.

[671] Corallo 2/15/18 302, at 3.

[672] Priebus 4/3/18 302, at 7.

U.S. Department of Justice

~~Attorney Work Product // May Contain Material Protected Under Fed. R. Crim. P. 6(e)~~

of the President's personal attorneys, who told Priebus he was already working on it.[673] By late June, several advisors recalled receiving media inquiries that could relate to the June 9 meeting.[674]

2. The President Directs Communications Staff Not to Publicly Disclose Information About the June 9 Meeting

Communications advisors Hope Hicks and Josh Raffel recalled discussing with Jared Kushner and Ivanka Trump that the emails were damaging and would inevitably be leaked.[675] Hicks and Raffel advised that the best strategy was to proactively release the emails to the press.[676] On or about June 22, 2017, Hicks attended a meeting in the White House residence with the President, Kushner, and Ivanka Trump.[677] According to Hicks, Kushner said that he wanted to fill the President in on something that had been discovered in the documents he was to provide to the congressional committees involving a meeting with him, Manafort, and Trump Jr.[678] Kushner brought a folder of documents to the meeting and tried to show them to the President, but the President stopped Kushner and said he did not want to know about it, shutting the conversation down.[679]

On June 28, 2017, Hicks viewed the emails at Kushner's attorney's office.[680] She recalled being shocked by the emails because they looked "really bad."[681] The next day, Hicks spoke privately with the President to mention her concern about the emails, which she understood were soon going to be shared with Congress.[682] The President seemed upset because too many people knew about the emails and he told Hicks that just one lawyer should deal with the matter.[683] The President indicated that he did not think the emails would leak, but said they would leak if everyone had access to them.[684]

---

[673] Priebus 4/3/18 302, at 7.

[674] Corallo 2/15/18 302, at 3; Hicks 12/7/17 302, at 8; Raffel 2/8/18 302, at 3.

[675] Raffel 2/8/18 302, at 2-3; Hicks 3/13/18 302, at 2.

[676] Raffel 2/8/18 302, at 2-3, 5; Hicks 3/13/18 302, at 2; Hicks 12/7/17 302, at 8.

[677] Hicks 12/7/17 302, at 6-7; Hicks 3/13/18 302, at 1.

[678] Hicks 12/7/17 302, at 7; Hicks 3/13/18 302, at 1.

[679] Hicks 12/7/17 302, at 7; Hicks 3/13/18 302, at 1. Counsel for Ivanka Trump provided an attorney proffer that is consistent with Hicks's account and with the other events involving Ivanka Trump set forth in this section of the report. Kushner said that he did not recall talking to the President at this time about the June 9 meeting or the underlying emails. Kushner 4/11/18 302, at 30.

[680] Hicks 3/13/18 302, at 1-2.

[681] Hicks 3/13/18 302, at 2.

[682] Hicks 12/7/17 302, at 8.

[683] Hicks 3/13/18 302, at 2-3; Hicks 12/7/17 302, at 8.

[684] Hicks 12/7/17 302, at 8.

U.S. Department of Justice

~~Attorney Work Product // May Contain Material Protected Under Fed. R. Crim. P. 6(e)~~

Later that day, Hicks, Kushner, and Ivanka Trump went together to talk to the President.[685] Hicks recalled that Kushner told the President the June 9 meeting was not a big deal and was about Russian adoption, but that emails existed setting up the meeting.[686] Hicks said she wanted to get in front of the story and have Trump Jr. release the emails as part of an interview with "softball questions."[687] The President said he did not want to know about it and they should not go to the press.[688] Hicks warned the President that the emails were "really bad" and the story would be "massive" when it broke, but the President was insistent that he did not want to talk about it and said he did not want details.[689] Hicks recalled that the President asked Kushner when his document production was due.[690] Kushner responded that it would be a couple of weeks and the President said, "then leave it alone."[691] Hicks also recalled that the President said Kushner's attorney should give the emails to whomever he needed to give them to, but the President did not think they would be leaked to the press.[692] Raffel later heard from Hicks that the President had directed the group not to be proactive in disclosing the emails because the President believed they would not leak.[693]

3. The President Directs Trump Jr.'s Response to Press Inquiries About the June 9 Meeting

The following week, the President departed on an overseas trip for the G20 summit in Hamburg, Germany, accompanied by Hicks, Raffel, Kushner, and Ivanka Trump, among others.[694] On July 7, 2017, while the President was overseas, Hicks and Raffel learned that the New York Times was working on a story about the June 9 meeting.[695] The next day, Hicks told the President about the story and he directed her not to comment.[696] Hicks thought the President's reaction was odd because he usually considered not responding to the press to be the ultimate sin.[697] Later that day, Hicks and the President again spoke about the story.[698] Hicks recalled that the President asked

---

[685] Hicks 12/7/17 302, at 8; Hicks 3/13/18 302, at 2.

[686] Hicks 3/13/18 302, at 2; Hicks 12/7/17 302, at 9.

[687] Hicks 3/13/18 302, at 2-3.

[688] Hicks 3/13/18 302, at 2-3; Hicks 12/7/17 302, at 9.

[689] Hicks 3/13/18 302, at 3; Hicks 12/7/17 302, at 9.

[690] Hicks 3/13/18 302, at 3.

[691] Hicks 3/13/18 302, at 3.

[692] Hicks 12/7/17 302, at 9.

[693] Raffel 2/8/18 302, at 5.

[694] Raffel 2/8/18 302, at 6.

[695] Raffel 2/8/18 302, at 6-7; Hicks 3/13/18 302, at 3.

[696] Hicks 12/7/17 302, at 10; Hicks 3/13/18 302, at 3.

[697] Hicks 12/7/17 302, at 10.

[698] Hicks 3/13/18 302, at 3.

U.S. Department of Justice

~~Attorney Work Product // May Contain Material Protected Under Fed. R. Crim. P. 6(e)~~

her what the meeting had been about, and she said that she had been told the meeting was about Russian adoption.[699] The President responded, "then just say that."[700]

On the flight home from the G20 on July 8, 2017, Hicks obtained a draft statement about the meeting to be released by Trump Jr. and brought it to the President.[701] The draft statement began with a reference to the information that was offered by the Russians in setting up the meeting: "I was asked to have a meeting by an acquaintance I knew from the 2013 Miss Universe pageant with an individual who I was told might have information helpful to the campaign."[702] Hicks again wanted to disclose the entire story, but the President directed that the statement not be issued because it said too much.[703] The President told Hicks to say only that Trump Jr. took a brief meeting and it was about Russian adoption.[704] After speaking with the President, Hicks texted Trump Jr. a revised statement on the June 9 meeting that read:

> It was a short meeting. I asked Jared and Paul to stop by. We discussed a program about the adoption of Russian children that was active and popular with American families years ago and was since ended by the Russian government, but it was not a campaign issue at that time and there was no follow up.[705]

Hicks's text concluded, "Are you ok with this? Attributed to you."[706] Trump Jr. responded by text message that he wanted to add the word "primarily" before "discussed" so that the statement would read, "We primarily discussed a program about the adoption of Russian children."[707] Trump Jr. texted that he wanted the change because "[t]hey started with some Hillary thing which was bs and some other nonsense which we shot down fast."[708] Hicks texted back, "I think that's right too but boss man worried it invites a lot of questions[.] [U]ltimately [d]efer to you and [your attorney] on that word Bc I know it's important and I think the mention of a campaign issue adds something to it in case we have to go further."[709] Trump Jr. responded, "If I don't have it in there it appears as though I'm lying later when they inevitably leak something."[710] Trump Jr.'s statement—adding

---

[699] Hicks 3/13/18 302, at 3; Hicks 12/7/17 302, at 10.

[700] Hicks 3/13/18 302, at 3; *see* Hicks 12/7/17 302, at 10.

[701] Hicks 3/13/18 302, at 4.

[702] Hicks 7/8/17 Notes.

[703] Hicks 3/13/18 302, at 4-5; Hicks 12/7/17 302, at 11.

[704] Hicks 12/7/17 302, at 11.

[705] SCR011a_000004 (7/8/17 Text Message, Hicks to Trump Jr.).

[706] SCR011a_000004 (7/8/17 Text Message, Hicks to Trump Jr.).

[707] SCR011a_000005 (7/8/17 Text Message, Trump Jr. to Hicks).

[708] SCR011a_000005 (7/8/17 Text Message, Trump Jr. to Hicks).

[709] SCR011a_000005 (7/8/17 Text Message, Hicks to Trump Jr.).

[710] SCR011a_000006 (7/8/17 Text Message, Trump Jr. to Hicks).

U.S. Department of Justice

Attorney Work Product // May Contain Material Protected Under Fed. R. Crim. P. 6(e)

the word "primarily" and making other minor additions was then provided to the New York Times.[711] The full statement provided to the *Times* stated:

> It was a short introductory meeting. I asked Jared and Paul to stop by. We primarily discussed a program about the adoption of Russian children that was active and popular with American families years ago and was since ended by the Russian government, but it was not a campaign issue at the time and there was no follow up. I was asked to attend the meeting by an acquaintance, but was not told the name of the person I would be meeting with beforehand.[712]

The statement did not mention the offer of derogatory information about Clinton or any discussion of the Magnitsky Act or U.S. sanctions, which were the principal subjects of the meeting, as described in Volume I, Section IV.A.5, *supra*.

A short while later, while still on Air Force One, Hicks learned that Priebus knew about the emails, which further convinced her that additional information about the June 9 meeting would leak and the White House should be proactive and get in front of the story.[713] Hicks recalled again going to the President to urge him that they should be fully transparent about the June 9 meeting, but he again said no, telling Hicks, "You've given a statement. We're done."[714]

Later on the flight home, Hicks went to the President's cabin, where the President was on the phone with one of his personal attorneys.[715] At one point the President handed the phone to Hicks, and the attorney told Hicks that he had been working with Circa News on a separate story, and that she should not talk to the New York Times.[716]

4. The Media Reports on the June 9, 2016 Meeting

Before the President's flight home from the G20 landed, the New York Times published its story about the June 9, 2016 meeting.[717] In addition to the statement from Trump Jr., the Times story also quoted a statement from Corallo on behalf of the President's legal team suggesting that the meeting might have been a setup by individuals working with the firm that produced the Steele reporting.[718] Corallo also worked with Circa News on a story published an hour later that

[711] Hicks 3/13/18 302, at 6; *see* Jo Becker et al., *Trump Team Met With Lawyer Linked to Kremlin During Campaign,* New York Times (July 8, 2017).

[712] *See* Jo Becker et al., *Trump Team Met With Lawyer Linked to Kremlin During Campaign,* New York Times (July 8, 2017).

[713] Hicks 3/13/18 302, at 6; Raffel 2/8/18 302, at 9-10.

[714] Hicks 12/7/17 302, at 12; Raffel 2/8/18 302, at 10.

[715] Hicks 3/13/18 302, at 7.

[716] Hicks 3/13/18 302, at 7.

[717] *See* Jo Becker et al., *Trump Team Met With Lawyer Linked to Kremlin During Campaign,* New York Times (July 8, 2017); Raffel 2/8/18 302, at 10.

[718] *See* Jo Becker et al., *Trump Team Met With Lawyer Linked to Kremlin During Campaign,* New York Times (July 8, 2017).

U.S. Department of Justice

Attorney Work Product // May Contain Material Protected Under Fed. R. Crim. P. 6(e)

questioned whether Democratic operatives had arranged the June 9 meeting to create the appearance of improper connections between Russia and Trump family members.[719] Hicks was upset about Corallo's public statement and called him that evening to say the President had not approved the statement.[720]

The next day, July 9, 2017, Hicks and the President called Corallo together and the President criticized Corallo for the statement he had released.[721] Corallo told the President the statement had been authorized and further observed that Trump Jr.'s statement was inaccurate and that a document existed that would contradict it.[722] Corallo said that he purposely used the term "document" to refer to the emails setting up the June 9 meeting because he did not know what the President knew about the emails.[723] Corallo recalled that when he referred to the "document" on the call with the President, Hicks responded that only a few people had access to it and said "it will never get out."[724] Corallo took contemporaneous notes of the call that say: "Also mention existence of doc. Hope says 'only a few people have it. It will never get out.'"[725] Hicks later told investigators that she had no memory of making that comment and had always believed the emails would eventually be leaked, but she might have been channeling the President on the phone call because it was clear to her throughout her conversations with the President that he did not think the emails would leak.[726]

On July 11, 2017, Trump Jr. posted redacted images of the emails setting up the June 9 meeting on Twitter; the New York Times reported that he did so "[a]fter being told that The Times was about to publish the content of the emails."[727] Later that day, the media reported that the President had been personally involved in preparing Trump Jr.'s initial statement to the New York Times that had claimed the meeting "primarily" concerned "a program about the adoption of Russian children."[728] Over the next several days, the President's personal counsel repeatedly and

---

[719] See *Donald Trump Jr. gathered members of campaign for meeting with Russian lawyer before election*, Circa News (July 8, 2017).

[720] Hicks 3/13/18 302, at 8; Corallo 2/15/18 302, at 6-7.

[721] Corallo 2/15/18 302, at 7.

[722] Corallo 2/15/18 302, at 7.

[723] Corallo 2/15/18 302, at 7-9.

[724] Corallo 2/15/18 302, at 8.

[725] Corallo 2/15/18 302, at 8; Corallo 7/9/17 Notes ("Sunday 9th -- Hope calls w/ POTUS on line"). Corallo said he is "100% confident" that Hicks said "It will never get out" on the call. Corallo 2/15/18 302, at 9.

[726] Hicks 3/13/18 302, at 9.

[727] @DonaldJTrumpJR 7/11/17 (11:01 a.m. ET) Tweet; Jo Becker et al., *Russian Dirt on Clinton? 'I Love It,' Donald Trump Jr. Said*, New York Times (July 11, 2017).

[728] See, e.g., Peter Baker & Maggie Haberman, *Rancor at White House as Russia Story Refuses to Let the Page Turn*, New York Times (July 11, 2017) (reporting that the President "signed off" on Trump Jr.'s statement).

U.S. Department of Justice

~~Attorney Work Product // May Contain Material Protected Under Fed. R. Crim. P. 6(e)~~

inaccurately denied that the President played any role in drafting Trump Jr.'s statement.[729] After consulting with the President on the issue, White House Press Secretary Sarah Sanders told the media that the President "certainly didn't dictate" the statement, but that "he weighed in, offered suggestions like any father would do."[730] Several months later, the President's personal counsel stated in a private communication to the Special Counsel's Office that "the President dictated a short but accurate response to the New York Times article on behalf of his son, Donald Trump, Jr."[731] The President later told the press that it was "irrelevant" whether he dictated the statement and said, "It's a statement to the New York Times. . . . That's not a statement to a high tribunal of judges."[732]

On July 12, 2017, the Special Counsel's Office ▮▮▮▮▮▮▮▮▮▮▮▮▮▮▮▮ Trump Jr. ▮▮▮▮▮▮▮▮▮▮▮▮▮▮ related to the June 9 meeting and those who attended the June 9 meeting.[733]

On July 19, 2017, the President had his follow-up meeting with Lewandowski and then met with reporters for the New York Times. In addition to criticizing Sessions in his Times interview, the President addressed the June 9, 2016 meeting and said he "didn't know anything about the meeting" at the time.[734] The President added, "As I've said—most other people, you know, when they call up and say, 'By the way, we have information on your opponent,' I think most politicians — I was just with a lot of people, they said . . . , 'Who wouldn't have taken a meeting like that?'"[735]

Analysis

In analyzing the President's actions regarding the disclosure of information about the June 9 meeting, the following evidence is relevant to the elements of obstruction of justice:

a.   Obstructive act. On at least three occasions between June 29, 2017, and July 9, 2017, the President directed Hicks and others not to publicly disclose information about the June

---

[729] *See, e.g.*, David Wright, *Trump lawyer: President was aware of "nothing"*, CNN (July 12, 2017) (quoting the President's personal attorney as saying, "I wasn't involved in the statement drafting at all nor was the President."); *see also* Good Morning America, ABC (July 12, 2017) ("The President didn't sign off on anything. . . . The President wasn't involved in that."); Meet the Press, NBC (July 16, 2017) ("I do want to be clear—the President was not involved in the drafting of the statement.").

[730] Sarah Sanders, *White House Daily Briefing*, C-SPAN (Aug. 1, 2017); Sanders 7/3/18 302, at 9 (the President told Sanders he "weighed in, as any father would" and knew she intended to tell the press what he said).

[731] 1/29/18 Letter, President's Personal Counsel to Special Counsel's Office, at 18.

[732] Remarks by President Trump in Press Gaggle (June 15, 2018).

[733]

[734] Peter Baker et al., *Excerpts From The Times's Interview With Trump*, New York Times (July 19, 2017).

[735] Peter Baker et al., *Excerpts From The Times's Interview With Trump*, New York Times (July 19, 2017).

9, 2016 meeting between senior campaign officials and a Russian attorney. On June 29, Hicks warned the President that the emails setting up the June 9 meeting were "really bad" and the story would be "massive" when it broke, but the President told her and Kushner to "leave it alone." Early on July 8, after Hicks told the President the New York Times was working on a story about the June 9 meeting, the President directed her not to comment, even though Hicks said that the President usually considered not responding to the press to be the ultimate sin. Later that day, the President rejected Trump Jr.'s draft statement that would have acknowledged that the meeting was with "an individual who I was told might have information helpful to the campaign." The President then dictated a statement to Hicks that said the meeting was about Russian adoption (which the President had twice been told was discussed at the meeting). The statement dictated by the President did not mention the offer of derogatory information about Clinton.

Each of these efforts by the President involved his communications team and was directed at the press. They would amount to obstructive acts only if the President, by taking these actions, sought to withhold information from or mislead congressional investigators or the Special Counsel. On May 17, 2017, the President's campaign received a document request from SSCI that clearly covered the June 9 meeting and underlying emails, and those documents also plainly would have been relevant to the Special Counsel's investigation.

But the evidence does not establish that the President took steps to prevent the emails or other information about the June 9 meeting from being provided to Congress or the Special Counsel. The series of discussions in which the President sought to limit access to the emails and prevent their public release occurred in the context of developing a press strategy. The only evidence we have of the President discussing the production of documents to Congress or the Special Counsel is the conversation on June 29, 2017, when Hicks recalled the President acknowledging that Kushner's attorney should provide emails related to the June 9 meeting to whomever he needed to give them to. We do not have evidence of what the President discussed with his own lawyers at that time.

     b.   Nexus to an official proceeding. As described above, by the time of the President's attempts to prevent the public release of the emails regarding the June 9 meeting, the existence of a grand jury investigation supervised by the Special Counsel was public knowledge, and the President had been told that the emails were responsive to congressional inquiries. To satisfy the nexus requirement, however, it would be necessary to show that preventing the release of the emails to the public would have the natural and probable effect of impeding the grand jury proceeding or congressional inquiries. As noted above, the evidence does not establish that the President sought to prevent disclosure of the emails in those official proceedings.

     c.   Intent. The evidence establishes the President's substantial involvement in the communications strategy related to information about his campaign's connections to Russia and his desire to minimize public disclosures about those connections. The President became aware of the emails no later than June 29, 2017, when he discussed them with Hicks and Kushner, and he could have been aware of them as early as June 2, 2017, when lawyers for the Trump Organization began interviewing witnesses who participated in the June 9 meeting. The President thereafter repeatedly rejected the advice of Hicks and other staffers to publicly release information about the June 9 meeting. The President expressed concern that multiple people had access to the emails and instructed Hicks that only one lawyer should deal with the matter. And the President

U.S. Department of Justice

Attorney Work Product // May Contain Material Protected Under Fed. R. Crim. P. 6(e)

dictated a statement to be released by Trump Jr. in response to the first press accounts of the June 9 meeting that said the meeting was about adoption.

But as described above, the evidence does not establish that the President intended to prevent the Special Counsel's Office or Congress from obtaining the emails setting up the June 9 meeting or other information about that meeting. The statement recorded by Corallo—that the emails "will never get out"—can be explained as reflecting a belief that the emails would not be made public if the President's press strategy were followed, even if the emails were provided to Congress and the Special Counsel.

H.   The President's Further Efforts to Have the Attorney General Take Over the Investigation

Overview

From summer 2017 through 2018, the President attempted to have Attorney General Sessions reverse his recusal, take control of the Special Counsel's investigation, and order an investigation of Hillary Clinton.

Evidence

1.   The President Again Seeks to Have Sessions Reverse his Recusal

After returning Sessions's resignation letter at the end of May 2017, but before the President's July 19, 2017 New York Times interview in which he publicly criticized Sessions for recusing from the Russia investigation, the President took additional steps to have Sessions reverse his recusal. In particular, at some point after the May 17, 2017 appointment of the Special Counsel, Sessions recalled, the President called him at home and asked if Sessions would "unrecuse" himself.[736] According to Sessions, the President asked him to reverse his recusal so that Sessions could direct the Department of Justice to investigate and prosecute Hillary Clinton, and the "gist" of the conversation was that the President wanted Sessions to unrecuse from "all of it," including the Special Counsel's Russia investigation.[737] Sessions listened but did not respond, and he did not reverse his recusal or order an investigation of Clinton.[738]

In early July 2017, the President asked Staff Secretary Rob Porter what he thought of Associate Attorney General Rachel Brand.[739] Porter recalled that the President asked him if Brand was good, tough, and "on the team."[740] The President also asked if Porter thought Brand was interested in being responsible for the Special Counsel's investigation and whether she would want

---

[736] Sessions 1/17/18 302, at 15. That was the second time that the President asked Sessions to reverse his recusal from campaign-related investigations. *See* Volume II, Section II.C.1, *supra* (describing President's March 2017 request at Mar-a-Lago for Sessions to unrecuse).

[737] Sessions 1/17/18 302, at 15.

[738] Sessions 1/17/18 302, at 15.

[739] Porter 4/13/18 302, at 11; Porter 5/8/18 302, at 6.

[740] Porter 4/13/18 302, at 11; Porter 5/8/18 302, at 6.

U.S. Department of Justice

Attorney Work Product // May Contain Material Protected Under Fed. R. Crim. P. 6(e)

to be Attorney General one day.[741] Because Porter knew Brand, the President asked him to sound her out about taking responsibility for the investigation and being Attorney General.[742] Contemporaneous notes taken by Porter show that the President told Porter to "Keep in touch with your friend," in reference to Brand.[743] Later, the President asked Porter a few times in passing whether he had spoken to Brand, but Porter did not reach out to her because he was uncomfortable with the task.[744] In asking him to reach out to Brand, Porter understood the President to want to find someone to end the Russia investigation or fire the Special Counsel, although the President never said so explicitly.[745] Porter did not contact Brand because he was sensitive to the implications of that action and did not want to be involved in a chain of events associated with an effort to end the investigation or fire the Special Counsel.[746]

McGahn recalled that during the summer of 2017, he and the President discussed the fact that if Sessions were no longer in his position the Special Counsel would report directly to a non-recused Attorney General.[747] McGahn told the President that things might not change much under a new Attorney General.[748] McGahn also recalled that in or around July 2017, the President frequently brought up his displeasure with Sessions.[749] Hicks recalled that the President viewed Sessions's recusal from the Russia investigation as an act of disloyalty.[750] In addition to criticizing Sessions's recusal, the President raised other concerns about Sessions and his job performance with McGahn and Hicks.[751]

---

[741] Porter 4/13/18 302, at 11; Porter 5/8/18 302, at 6. Because of Sessions's recusal, if Rosenstein were no longer in his position, Brand would, by default, become the DOJ official in charge of supervising the Special Counsel's investigation, and if both Sessions and Rosenstein were removed, Brand would be next in line to become Acting Attorney General for all DOJ matters. *See* 28 U.S.C. § 508.

[742] Porter 4/13/18 302, at 11; Porter 5/8/18 302, at 6.

[743] SC_RRP000020 (Porter 7/10/17 Notes).

[744] Porter 4/13/18 302, at 11-12.

[745] Porter 4/13/18 302, at 11-12.

[746] Porter 4/13/18 302, at 11-12. Brand confirmed that no one ever raised with her the prospect of taking over the Russia investigation or becoming Attorney General. Brand 1/29/19 302, at 2.

[747] McGahn 12/14/17 302, at 11.

[748] McGahn 12/14/17 302, at 11.

[749] McGahn 12/14/17 302, at 9.

[750] Hicks 3/13/18 302, at 10.

[751] McGahn 12/14/17 302, at 9; Hicks 3/13/18 302, at 10.

U.S. Department of Justice

~~Attorney Work Product // May Contain Material Protected Under Fed. R. Crim. P. 6(e)~~

2. Additional Efforts to Have Sessions Unrecuse or Direct Investigations Covered by his Recusal

Later in 2017, the President continued to urge Sessions to reverse his recusal from campaign-related investigations and considered replacing Sessions with an Attorney General who would not be recused.

On October 16, 2017, the President met privately with Sessions and said that the Department of Justice was not investigating individuals and events that the President thought the Department should be investigating.[752] According to contemporaneous notes taken by Porter, who was at the meeting, the President mentioned Clinton's emails and said, "Don't have to tell us, just take [a] look."[753] Sessions did not offer any assurances or promises to the President that the Department of Justice would comply with that request.[754] Two days later, on October 18, 2017, the President tweeted, "Wow, FBI confirms report that James Comey drafted letter exonerating Crooked Hillary Clinton long before investigation was complete. Many people not interviewed, including Clinton herself. Comey stated under oath that he didn't do this-obviously a fix? Where is Justice Dept?"[755] On October 29, 2017, the President tweeted that there was "ANGER & UNITY" over a "lack of investigation" of Clinton and "the Comey fix," and concluded: "DO SOMETHING!"[756]

On December 6, 2017, five days after Flynn pleaded guilty to lying about his contacts with the Russian government, the President asked to speak with Sessions in the Oval Office at the end of a cabinet meeting.[757] During that Oval Office meeting, which Porter attended, the President again suggested that Sessions could "unrecuse," which Porter linked to taking back supervision of the Russia investigation and directing an investigation of Hillary Clinton.[758] According to contemporaneous notes taken by Porter, the President said, "I don't know if you could un-recuse yourself. You'd be a hero. Not telling you to do anything. Dershowitz says POTUS can get involved. Can order AG to investigate. I don't want to get involved. I'm not going to get involved. I'm not going to do anything or direct you to do anything. I just want to be treated fairly."[759] According to Porter's notes, Sessions responded, "We are taking steps; whole new leadership

---

[752] Porter 5/8/18 302, at 10.

[753] SC_RRP000024 (Porter 10/16/17 Notes); *see* Porter 5/8/18 302, at 10.

[754] Porter 5/8/18 302, at 10.

[755] @realDonaldTrump 10/18/17 (6:21 a.m. ET) Tweet; @realDonaldTrump 10/18/17 (6:27 a.m. ET) Tweet.

[756] @realDonaldTrump 10/29/17 (9:53 a.m. ET) Tweet; @realDonaldTrump 10/29/17 (10:02 a.m. ET) Tweet; @realDonaldTrump 10/29/17 (10:17 a.m. ET) Tweet.

[757] Porter 4/13/18 302, at 5-6; *see* SC_RRP000031 (Porter 12/6/17 Notes) ("12:45pm With the President, Gen. Kelly, and Sessions (who I pulled in after the Cabinet meeting)"); SC_RRP000033 (Porter 12/6/17 Notes) ("Post-cabinet meeting – POTUS asked me to get AG Sessions. Asked me to stay. Also COS Kelly.").

[758] Porter 5/8/18 302, at 12; Porter 4/13/18 302, at 5-6.

[759] SC_RRP000033 (Porter 12/6/17 Notes); *see* Porter 4/13/18 302, at 6; Porter 5/8/18 302, at 12.

U.S. Department of Justice

Attorney Work Product // May Contain Material Protected Under Fed. R. Crim. P. 6(e)

team. Professionals; will operate according to the law."[760] Sessions also said, "I never saw anything that was improper," which Porter thought was noteworthy because it did not fit with the previous discussion about Clinton.[761] Porter understood Sessions to be reassuring the President that he was on the President's team.[762]

At the end of December, the President told the New York Times it was "too bad" that Sessions had recused himself from the Russia investigation.[763] When asked whether Holder had been a more loyal Attorney General to President Obama than Sessions was to him, the President said, "I don't want to get into loyalty, but I will tell you that, I will say this: Holder protected President Obama. Totally protected him. When you look at the things that they did, and Holder protected the president. And I have great respect for that, I'll be honest."[764] Later in January, the President brought up the idea of replacing Sessions and told Porter that he wanted to "clean house" at the Department of Justice.[765] In a meeting in the White House residence that Porter attended on January 27, 2018, Porter recalled that the President talked about the great attorneys he had in the past with successful win records, such as Roy Cohn and Jay Goldberg, and said that one of his biggest failings as President was that he had not surrounded himself with good attorneys, citing Sessions as an example.[766] The President raised Sessions's recusal and brought up and criticized the Special Counsel's investigation.[767]

Over the next several months, the President continued to criticize Sessions in tweets and media interviews and on several occasions appeared to publicly encourage him to take action in the Russia investigation despite his recusal.[768] On June 5, 2018, for example, the President

---

[760] SC_RRP000033 (Porter 12/6/17 Notes); *see* Porter 4/13/18 302, at 6.

[761] SC_RRP000033 (Porter 12/6/17 Notes); Porter 4/13/18 302, at 6.

[762] Porter 4/13/18 302, at 6-7.

[763] Michael S. Schmidt & Michael D. Shear, *Trump Says Russia Inquiry Makes U.S. "Look Very Bad"*, New York Times (Dec. 28, 2017).

[764] Michael S. Schmidt & Michael D. Shear, *Trump Says Russia Inquiry Makes U.S. "Look Very Bad"*, New York Times (Dec. 28, 2017).

[765] Porter 4/13/18 302, at 14.

[766] Porter 5/8/18 302, at 15. Contemporaneous notes Porter took of the conversation state, "Roy Cohn (14-0) / Jay Goldberg (12-0)." SC_RRP000047 (Porter 1/27/18 Notes).

[767] Porter 5/8/18 302, at 15-16.

[768] *See, e.g.*, @realDonaldTrump 2/28/18 (9:34 a.m. ET) Tweet ("Why is A.G. Jeff Sessions asking the Inspector General to investigate potentially massive FISA abuse. Will take forever, has no prosecutorial power and already late with reports on Comey etc. Isn't the I.G. an Obama guy? Why not use Justice Department lawyers? DISGRACEFUL!"); @realDonaldTrump 4/7/18 (4:52 p.m. ET) Tweet ("Lawmakers of the House Judiciary Committee are angrily accusing the Department of Justice of missing the Thursday Deadline for turning over UNREDACTED Documents relating to FISA abuse, FBI, Comey, Lynch, McCabe, Clinton Emails and much more. Slow walking – what is going on? BAD!"); @realDonaldTrump 4/22/18 (8:22 a.m. ET) Tweet ("'GOP Lawmakers asking Sessions to Investigate Comey and Hillary Clinton.' @FoxNews Good luck with that request!"); @realDonaldTrump 12/16/18 (3:37 p.m. ET) Tweet

U.S. Department of Justice

~~Attorney Work Product // May Contain Material Protected Under Fed. R. Crim. P. 6(e)~~

tweeted, "The Russian Witch Hunt Hoax continues, all because Jeff Sessions didn't tell me he was going to recuse himself. . . . I would have quickly picked someone else. So much time and money wasted, so many lives ruined . . . and Sessions knew better than most that there was No Collusion!"[769] On August 1, 2018, the President tweeted that "Attorney General Jeff Sessions should stop this Rigged Witch Hunt right now."[770] On August 23, 2018, the President publicly criticized Sessions in a press interview and suggested that prosecutions at the Department of Justice were politically motivated because Paul Manafort had been prosecuted but Democrats had not.[771] The President said, "I put in an Attorney General that never took control of the Justice Department, Jeff Sessions."[772] That day, Sessions issued a press statement that said, "I took control of the Department of Justice the day I was sworn in . . . . While I am Attorney General, the actions of the Department of Justice will not be improperly influenced by political considerations."[773] The next day, the President tweeted a response: "'Department of Justice will not be improperly influenced by political considerations.' Jeff, this is GREAT, what everyone wants, so look into all of the corruption on the 'other side' including deleted Emails, Comey lies & leaks, Mueller conflicts, McCabe, Strzok, Page, Ohr, FISA abuse, Christopher Steele & his phony and corrupt Dossier, the Clinton Foundation, illegal surveillance of Trump campaign, Russian collusion by Dems – and so much more. Open up the papers & documents without redaction? Come on Jeff, you can do it, the country is waiting!"[774]

On November 7, 2018, the day after the midterm elections, the President replaced Sessions with Sessions's chief of staff as Acting Attorney General.[775]

Analysis

In analyzing the President's efforts to have Sessions unrecuse himself and regain control of the Russia investigation, the following considerations and evidence are relevant to the elements of obstruction of justice:

a. <u>Obstructive act.</u> To determine if the President's efforts to have the Attorney General unrecuse could qualify as an obstructive act, it would be necessary to assess evidence on whether those actions would naturally impede the Russia investigation. That inquiry would take into account the supervisory role that the Attorney General, if unrecused, would play in the Russia investigation. It also would have to take into account that the Attorney General's recusal covered

---

("Jeff Sessions should be ashamed of himself for allowing this total HOAX to get started in the first place!").

[769] @realDonaldTrump 6/5/18 (7:31 a.m. ET) Tweet.

[770] @realDonaldTrump 8/1/18 (9:24 a.m. ET) Tweet.

[771] Fox & Friends Interview of President Trump, Fox News (Aug. 23, 2018).

[772] Fox & Friends Interview of President Trump, Fox News (Aug. 23, 2018).

[773] Sessions 8/23/18 Press Statement.

[774] @realDonaldTrump 8/24/18 (6:17 a.m. ET) Tweet; @ realDonaldTrump 8/24/18 (6:28 a.m. ET) Tweet.

[775] @realDonaldTrump 11/7/18 (2:44 p.m. ET) Tweet.

other campaign-related matters. The inquiry would not turn on what Attorney General Sessions would actually do if unrecused, but on whether the efforts to reverse his recusal would naturally have had the effect of impeding the Russia investigation.

On multiple occasions in 2017, the President spoke with Sessions about reversing his recusal so that he could take over the Russia investigation and begin an investigation and prosecution of Hillary Clinton. For example, in early summer 2017, Sessions recalled the President asking him to unrecuse, but Sessions did not take it as a directive. When the President raised the issue again in December 2017, the President said, as recorded by Porter, "Not telling you to do anything. . . . I'm not going to get involved. I'm not going to do anything or direct you to do anything. I just want to be treated fairly." The duration of the President's efforts—which spanned from March 2017 to August 2018 and the fact that the President repeatedly criticized Sessions in public and in private for failing to tell the President that he would have to recuse is relevant to assessing whether the President's efforts to have Sessions unrecuse could qualify as obstructive acts.

b. Nexus to an official proceeding. As described above, by mid-June 2017, the existence of a grand jury investigation supervised by the Special Counsel was public knowledge. In addition, in July 2017, a different grand jury supervised by the Special Counsel was empaneled in the District of Columbia, and the press reported on the existence of this grand jury in early August 2017.[776] Whether the conduct towards the Attorney General would have a foreseeable impact on those proceedings turns on much of the same evidence discussed above with respect to the obstructive-act element.

c. Intent. There is evidence that at least one purpose of the President's conduct toward Sessions was to have Sessions assume control over the Russia investigation and supervise it in a way that would restrict its scope. By the summer of 2017, the President was aware that the Special Counsel was investigating him personally for obstruction of justice. And in the wake of the disclosures of emails about the June 9 meeting between Russians and senior members of the campaign, see Volume II, Section II.G, supra, it was evident that the investigation into the campaign now included the President's son, son-in-law, and former campaign manager. The President had previously and unsuccessfully sought to have Sessions publicly announce that the Special Counsel investigation would be confined to future election interference. Yet Sessions remained recused. In December 2017, shortly after Flynn pleaded guilty, the President spoke to Sessions in the Oval Office with only Porter present and told Sessions that he would be a hero if he unrecused. Porter linked that request to the President's desire that Sessions take back supervision of the Russia investigation and direct an investigation of Hillary Clinton. The President said in that meeting that he "just want[ed] to be treated fairly," which could reflect his perception that it was unfair that he was being investigated while Hillary Clinton was not. But a principal effect of that act would be to restore supervision of the Russia investigation to the Attorney General—a position that the President frequently suggested should be occupied by someone like Eric Holder and Bobby Kennedy, who the President described as protecting their

---

[776] E.g., Del Quentin Wilbur & Byron Tau, *Special Counsel Robert Mueller Impanels Washington Grand Jury in Russia Probe*, Wall Street Journal (Aug. 3, 2017); Carol D. Leonnig et al., *Special Counsel Mueller using grand jury in federal court in Washington as part of Russia investigation*, Washington Post (Aug. 3, 2017).

U.S. Department of Justice

Attorney Work Product // May Contain Material Protected Under Fed. R. Crim. P. 6(e)

presidents. A reasonable inference from those statements and the President's actions is that the President believed that an unrecused Attorney General would play a protective role and could shield the President from the ongoing Russia investigation.

I.   The President Orders McGahn to Deny that the President Tried to Fire the Special Counsel

Overview

In late January 2018, the media reported that in June 2017 the President had ordered McGahn to have the Special Counsel fired based on purported conflicts of interest but McGahn had refused, saying he would quit instead. After the story broke, the President, through his personal counsel and two aides, sought to have McGahn deny that he had been directed to remove the Special Counsel. Each time he was approached, McGahn responded that he would not refute the press accounts because they were accurate in reporting on the President's effort to have the Special Counsel removed. The President later personally met with McGahn in the Oval Office with only the Chief of Staff present and tried to get McGahn to say that the President never ordered him to fire the Special Counsel. McGahn refused and insisted his memory of the President's direction to remove the Special Counsel was accurate. In that same meeting, the President challenged McGahn for taking notes of his discussions with the President and asked why he had told Special Counsel investigators that he had been directed to have the Special Counsel removed.

Evidence

1.   The Press Reports that the President Tried to Fire the Special Counsel

On January 25, 2018, the New York Times reported that in June 2017, the President had ordered McGahn to have the Department of Justice fire the Special Counsel.[777] According to the article, "[a]mid the first wave of news media reports that Mr. Mueller was examining a possible obstruction case, the president began to argue that Mr. Mueller had three conflicts of interest that disqualified him from overseeing the investigation."[778] The article further reported that "[a]fter receiving the president's order to fire Mr. Mueller, the White House counsel . . . refused to ask the Justice Department to dismiss the special counsel, saying he would quit instead."[779] The article stated that the president "ultimately backed down after the White House counsel threatened to resign rather than carry out the directive."[780] After the article was published, the President

---

[777] Michael S. Schmidt & Maggie Haberman, *Trump Ordered Mueller Fired, but Backed Off When White House Counsel Threatened to Quit*, New York Times (Jan. 25. 2018).

[778] Michael S. Schmidt & Maggie Haberman, *Trump Ordered Mueller Fired, but Backed Off When White House Counsel Threatened to Quit*, New York Times (Jan. 25. 2018).

[779] Michael S. Schmidt & Maggie Haberman, *Trump Ordered Mueller Fired, but Backed Off When White House Counsel Threatened to Quit*, New York Times (Jan. 25. 2018).

[780] Michael S. Schmidt & Maggie Haberman, *Trump Ordered Mueller Fired, but Backed Off When White House Counsel Threatened to Quit*, New York Times (Jan. 25. 2018).

U.S. Department of Justice

~~Attorney Work Product // May Contain Material Protected Under Fed. R. Crim. P. 6(e)~~

dismissed the story when asked about it by reporters, saying, "Fake news, folks. Fake news. A typical New York Times fake story."[781]

The next day, the Washington Post reported on the same event but added that McGahn had not told the President directly that he intended to resign rather than carry out the directive to have the Special Counsel terminated.[782] In that respect, the Post story clarified the Times story, which could be read to suggest that McGahn had told the President of his intention to quit, causing the President to back down from the order to have the Special Counsel fired.[783]

2. The President Seeks to Have McGahn Dispute the Press Reports

On January 26, 2018, the President's personal counsel called McGahn's attorney and said that the President wanted McGahn to put out a statement denying that he had been asked to fire the Special Counsel and that he had threatened to quit in protest.[784] McGahn's attorney spoke with McGahn about that request and then called the President's personal counsel to relay that McGahn would not make a statement.[785] McGahn's attorney informed the President's personal counsel that the Times story was accurate in reporting that the President wanted the Special Counsel removed.[786] Accordingly, McGahn's attorney said, although the article was inaccurate in some other respects, McGahn could not comply with the President's request to dispute the story.[787] Hicks recalled relaying to the President that one of his attorneys had spoken to McGahn's attorney about the issue.[788]

---

[781] Sophie Tatum & Kara Scannell, *Trump denies he called for Mueller's firing*, CNN (Jan. 26, 2018); Michael S. Schmidt & Maggie Haberman, *Trump Ordered Mueller Fired, but Backed Off When White House Counsel Threatened to Quit*, New York Times (Jan. 25, 2018).

[782] The *Post* article stated, "Despite internal objections, Trump decided to assert that Mueller had unacceptable conflicts of interest and moved to remove him from his position. . . In response, McGahn said he would not remain at the White House if Trump went through with the move. McGahn did not deliver his resignation threat directly to Trump but was serious about his threat to leave." Rosalind S. Helderman & Josh Dawsey, *Trump moved to fire Mueller in June, bringing White House counsel to the brink of leaving*, Washington Post (Jan. 26, 2018).

[783] Rosalind S. Helderman & Josh Dawsey, *Trump moved to fire Mueller in June, bringing White House counsel to the brink of leaving*, Washington Post (Jan. 26, 2018); *see* McGahn 3/8/17 302, at 3-4.

[784] McGahn 3/8/18 302, at 3 (agent note).

[785] McGahn 3/8/18 302, at 3 (agent note).

[786] McGahn 3/8/18 302, at 3-4 (agent note).

[787] McGahn 3/8/18 302, at 4 (agent note).

[788] Hicks 3/13/18 302, at 11. Hicks also recalled that the President spoke on the phone that day with Chief of Staff John Kelly and that the President said Kelly told him that McGahn had totally refuted the story and was going to put out a statement. Hicks 3/13/18 302, at 11. But Kelly said that he did not speak to McGahn when the article came out and did not tell anyone he had done so. Kelly 8/2/18 302, at 1-2.

Also on January 26, 2017, Hicks recalled that the President asked Sanders to contact McGahn about the story.[789] McGahn told Sanders there was no need to respond and indicated that some of the article was accurate.[790] Consistent with that position, McGahn did not correct the *Times* story.

On February 4, 2018, Priebus appeared on Meet the Press and said he had not heard the President say that he wanted the Special Counsel fired.[791] After Priebus's appearance, the President called Priebus and said he did a great job on Meet the Press.[792] The President also told Priebus that the President had "never said any of those things about" the Special Counsel.[793]

The next day, on February 5, 2018, the President complained about the *Times* article to Porter.[794] The President told Porter that the article was "bullshit" and he had not sought to terminate the Special Counsel.[795] The President said that McGahn leaked to the media to make himself look good.[796] The President then directed Porter to tell McGahn to create a record to make clear that the President never directed McGahn to fire the Special Counsel.[797] Porter thought the matter should be handled by the White House communications office, but the President said he wanted McGahn to write a letter to the file "for our records" and wanted something beyond a press statement to demonstrate that the reporting was inaccurate.[798] The President referred to McGahn as a "lying bastard" and said that he wanted a record from him.[799] Porter recalled the President

---

[789] Hicks 3/13/18 302, at 11. Sanders did not recall whether the President asked her to speak to McGahn or if she did it on her own. Sanders 7/23/18 302, at 2.

[790] Sanders 7/23/18 302, at 1-2.

[791] Meet the Press Interview with Reince Priebus, NBC (Feb. 4, 2018).

[792] Priebus 4/3/18 302, at 10.

[793] Priebus 4/3/18 302, at 10.

[794] Porter 4/13/18 302, at 16-17. Porter did not recall the timing of this discussion with the President. Porter 4/13/18 302, at 17. Evidence indicates it was February 5, 2018. On the back of a pocket card dated February 5, 2018, Porter took notes that are consistent with his description of the discussion: "COS: (1) Letter from DM – Never threatened to quit – DJT never told him to fire M." SC_RRP000053 (Porter Undated Notes). Porter said it was possible he took the notes on a day other than February 5. Porter 4/13/18 302, at 17. But Porter also said that "COS" referred to matters he wanted to discuss with Chief of Staff Kelly, Porter 4/13/18 302, at 17, and Kelly took notes dated February 5, 2018, that state "POTUS – Don McGahn letter – Mueller + resigning." WH000017684 (Kelly 2/5/18 Notes). Kelly said he did not recall what the notes meant, but thought the President may have "mused" about having McGahn write a letter. Kelly 8/2/18 302, at 3. McGahn recalled that Porter spoke with him about the President's request about two weeks after the New York Times story was published, which is consistent with the discussion taking place on or about February 5. McGahn 3/8/18 302, at 4.

[795] Porter 4/13/18 302, at 17.

[796] Porter 4/13/18 302, at 17.

[797] Porter 4/13/18 302, at 17.

[798] Porter 4/13/18 302, at 17; Porter 5/8/18 302, at 18.

[799] Porter 4/13/18 302, at 17; Porter 5/8/18 302, at 18.

U.S. Department of Justice

~~Attorney Work Product // May Contain Material Protected Under Fed. R. Crim. P. 6(e)~~

saying something to the effect of, "If he doesn't write a letter, then maybe I'll have to get rid of him."[800]

Later that day, Porter spoke to McGahn to deliver the President's message.[801] Porter told McGahn that he had to write a letter to dispute that he was ever ordered to terminate the Special Counsel.[802] McGahn shrugged off the request, explaining that the media reports were true.[803] McGahn told Porter that the President had been insistent on firing the Special Counsel and that McGahn had planned to resign rather than carry out the order, although he had not personally told the President he intended to quit.[804] Porter told McGahn that the President suggested that McGahn would be fired if he did not write the letter.[805] McGahn dismissed the threat, saying that the optics would be terrible if the President followed through with firing him on that basis.[806] McGahn said he would not write the letter the President had requested.[807] Porter said that to his knowledge the issue of McGahn's letter never came up with the President again, but Porter did recall telling Kelly about his conversation with McGahn.[808]

The next day, on February 6, 2018, Kelly scheduled time for McGahn to meet with him and the President in the Oval Office to discuss the Times article.[809] The morning of the meeting, the President's personal counsel called McGahn's attorney and said that the President was going to be speaking with McGahn and McGahn could not resign no matter what happened in the meeting.[810]

The President began the Oval Office meeting by telling McGahn that the New York Times story did not "look good" and McGahn needed to correct it.[811] McGahn recalled the President said, "I never said to fire Mueller. I never said 'fire.' This story doesn't look good. You need to correct this. You're the White House counsel."[812]

---

[800] Porter 4/13/18 302, at 17.

[801] Porter 4/13/18 302, at 17; McGahn 3/8/18 302, at 4.

[802] Porter 4/13/18 302, at 17; McGahn 3/8/18 302, at 4.

[803] Porter 4/13/18 302, at 17; McGahn 3/8/18 302, at 4.

[804] Porter 4/13/18 302, at 17; McGahn 3/8/18 302, at 4.

[805] Porter 4/13/18 302, at 17; McGahn 3/8/18 302, at 4.

[806] Porter 4/13/18 302, at 17-18; McGahn 3/8/18 302, at 4.

[807] McGahn 3/8/18 302, at 4.

[808] Porter 4/13/18 302, at 18.

[809] McGahn 3/8/18 302, at 4; WH000017685 (Kelly 2/6/18 Notes). McGahn recalled that, before the Oval Office meeting, he told Kelly that he was not inclined to fix the article. McGahn 3/8/18 302, at 4.

[810] McGahn 3/8/18 302, at 5 (agent note); 2/26/19 Email, Counsel for Don McGahn to Special Counsel's Office (confirming February 6, 2018 date of call from the President's personal counsel).

[811] McGahn 3/8/18 302, at 4; Kelly 8/2/18 302, at 2.

[812] McGahn 3/8/18 302, at 4; Kelly 8/2/18 302, at 2.

U.S. Department of Justice

Attorney Work Product // May Contain Material Protected Under Fed. R. Crim. P. 6(e)

In response, McGahn acknowledged that he had not told the President directly that he planned to resign, but said that the story was otherwise accurate.[813] The President asked McGahn, "Did I say the word 'fire'?"[814] McGahn responded, "What you said is, 'Call Rod [Rosenstein], tell Rod that Mueller has conflicts and can't be the Special Counsel.'"[815] The President responded, "I never said that."[816] The President said he merely wanted McGahn to raise the conflicts issue with Rosenstein and leave it to him to decide what to do.[817] McGahn told the President he did not understand the conversation that way and instead had heard, "Call Rod. There are conflicts. Mueller has to go."[818] The President asked McGahn whether he would "do a correction," and McGahn said no.[819] McGahn thought the President was testing his mettle to see how committed McGahn was to what happened.[820] Kelly described the meeting as "a little tense."[821]

The President also asked McGahn in the meeting why he had told Special Counsel's Office investigators that the President had told him to have the Special Counsel removed.[822] McGahn responded that he had to and that his conversations with the President were not protected by attorney-client privilege.[823] The President then asked, "What about these notes? Why do you take notes? Lawyers don't take notes. I never had a lawyer who took notes."[824] McGahn responded that he keeps notes because he is a "real lawyer" and explained that notes create a record and are not a bad thing.[825] The President said, "I've had a lot of great lawyers, like Roy Cohn. He did not take notes."[826]

After the Oval Office meeting concluded, Kelly recalled McGahn telling him that McGahn and the President "did have that conversation" about removing the Special Counsel.[827] McGahn recalled that Kelly said that he had pointed out to the President after the Oval Office that McGahn

---

[813] McGahn 3/8/18 302, at 4.

[814] McGahn 3/8/18 302, at 4; Kelly 8/2/18 302, at 2.

[815] McGahn 3/8/18 302, at 5.

[816] McGahn 3/8/18 302, at 5.

[817] McGahn 3/8/18 302, at 5.

[818] McGahn 3/8/18 302, at 5.

[819] McGahn 3/8/18 302, at 5; Kelly 8/2/18 302, at 2.

[820] McGahn 3/8/18 302, at 5.

[821] Kelly 8/2/18 302, at 2.

[822] McGahn 3/8/18 302, at 5.

[823] McGahn 3/8/18 302, at 5.

[824] McGahn 3/8/18 302, at 5. McGahn said the President was referring to Donaldson's notes, which the President thought of as McGahn's notes. McGahn 3/8/18 302, at 5.

[825] McGahn 3/8/18 302, at 5.

[826] McGahn 3/8/18 302, at 5.

[827] Kelly 8/2/18 302, at 2.

U.S. Department of Justice

Attorney Work Product // May Contain Material Protected Under Fed. R. Crim. P. 6(e)

had not backed down and would not budge.[828] Following the Oval Office meeting, the President's personal counsel called McGahn's counsel and relayed that the President was "fine" with McGahn.[829]

Analysis

In analyzing the President's efforts to have McGahn deny that he had been ordered to have the Special Counsel removed, the following evidence is relevant to the elements of obstruction of justice:

a.   Obstructive act. The President's repeated efforts to get McGahn to create a record denying that the President had directed him to remove the Special Counsel would qualify as an obstructive act if it had the natural tendency to constrain McGahn from testifying truthfully or to undermine his credibility as a potential witness if he testified consistently with his memory, rather than with what the record said.

There is some evidence that at the time the New York Times and Washington Post stories were published in late January 2018, the President believed the stories were wrong and that he had never told McGahn to have Rosenstein remove the Special Counsel. The President correctly understood that McGahn had not told the President directly that he planned to resign. In addition, the President told Priebus and Porter that he had not sought to terminate the Special Counsel, and in the Oval Office meeting with McGahn, the President said, "I never said to fire Mueller. I never said 'fire.'" That evidence could indicate that the President was not attempting to persuade McGahn to change his story but was instead offering his own—but different—recollection of the substance of his June 2017 conversations with McGahn and McGahn's reaction to them.

Other evidence cuts against that understanding of the President's conduct. As previously described, *see* Volume II, Section II.E, *supra*, substantial evidence supports McGahn's account that the President had directed him to have the Special Counsel removed, including the timing and context of the President's directive; the manner in which McGahn reacted; and the fact that the President had been told the conflicts were insubstantial, were being considered by the Department of Justice, and should be raised with the President's personal counsel rather than brought to McGahn. In addition, the President's subsequent denials that he had told McGahn to have the Special Counsel removed were carefully worded. When first asked about the New York Times story, the President said, "Fake news, folks. Fake news. A typical New York Times fake story." And when the President spoke with McGahn in the Oval Office, he focused on whether he had used the word "fire," saying, "I never said to fire Mueller. I never said 'fire'" and "Did I say the word 'fire'?" The President's assertion in the Oval Office meeting that he had never directed McGahn to have the Special Counsel removed thus runs counter to the evidence.

In addition, even if the President sincerely disagreed with McGahn's memory of the June 17, 2017 events, the evidence indicates that the President knew by the time of the Oval Office

---

[828] McGahn 3/8/18 302, at 5. Kelly did not recall discussing the Oval Office meeting with the President after the fact. Kelly 8/2/18 302, at 2. Handwritten notes taken by Kelly state, "Don[:] Mueller discussion in June. - Bannon Priebus - came out okay." WH000017685 (Kelly 2/6/18 Notes).

[829] McGahn 3/8/18 302, at 5 (agent note).

meeting that McGahn's account differed and that McGahn was firm in his views. Shortly after the story broke, the President's counsel told McGahn's counsel that the President wanted McGahn to make a statement denying he had been asked to fire the Special Counsel, but McGahn responded through his counsel that that aspect of the story was accurate and he therefore could not comply with the President's request. The President then directed Sanders to tell McGahn to correct the story, but McGahn told her he would not do so because the story was accurate in reporting on the President's order. Consistent with that position, McGahn never issued a correction. More than a week later, the President brought up the issue again with Porter, made comments indicating the President thought McGahn had leaked the story, and directed Porter to have McGahn create a record denying that the President had tried to fire the Special Counsel. At that point, the President said he might "have to get rid of" McGahn if McGahn did not comply. McGahn again refused and told Porter, as he had told Sanders and as his counsel had told the President's counsel, that the President had in fact ordered him to have Rosenstein remove the Special Counsel. That evidence indicates that by the time of the Oval Office meeting the President was aware that McGahn did not think the story was false and did not want to issue a statement or create a written record denying facts that McGahn believed to be true. The President nevertheless persisted and asked McGahn to repudiate facts that McGahn had repeatedly said were accurate.

b.   Nexus to an official proceeding. By January 2018, the Special Counsel's use of a grand jury had been further confirmed by the return of several indictments. The President also was aware that the Special Counsel was investigating obstruction-related events because, among other reasons, on January 8, 2018, the Special Counsel's Office provided his counsel with a detailed list of topics for a possible interview with the President.[830] The President knew that McGahn had personal knowledge of many of the events the Special Counsel was investigating and that McGahn had already been interviewed by Special Counsel investigators. And in the Oval Office meeting, the President indicated he knew that McGahn had told the Special Counsel's Office about the President's effort to remove the Special Counsel. The President challenged McGahn for disclosing that information and for taking notes that he viewed as creating unnecessary legal exposure. That evidence indicates the President's awareness that the June 17, 2017 events were relevant to the Special Counsel's investigation and any grand jury investigation that might grow out of it.

To establish a nexus, it would be necessary to show that the President's actions would have the natural tendency to affect such a proceeding or that they would hinder, delay, or prevent the communication of information to investigators. Because McGahn had spoken to Special Counsel investigators before January 2018, the President could not have been seeking to influence his prior statements in those interviews. But because McGahn had repeatedly spoken to investigators and the obstruction inquiry was not complete, it was foreseeable that he would be interviewed again on obstruction-related topics. If the President were focused solely on a press strategy in seeking to have McGahn refute the New York Times article, a nexus to a proceeding or to further investigative interviews would not be shown. But the President's efforts to have McGahn write a letter "for our records" approximately ten days after the stories had come out—well past the typical

---

[830] 1/29/18 Letter, President's Personal Counsel to Special Counsel's Office, at 1-2 ("In our conversation of January 8, your office identified the following topics as areas you desired to address with the President in order to complete your investigation on the subjects of alleged collusion and obstruction of justice"; listing 16 topics).

time to issue a correction for a news story—indicates the President was not focused solely on a press strategy, but instead likely contemplated the ongoing investigation and any proceedings arising from it.

      c.   Intent. Substantial evidence indicates that in repeatedly urging McGahn to dispute that he was ordered to have the Special Counsel terminated, the President acted for the purpose of influencing McGahn's account in order to deflect or prevent further scrutiny of the President's conduct towards the investigation.

      Several facts support that conclusion. The President made repeated attempts to get McGahn to change his story. As described above, by the time of the last attempt, the evidence suggests that the President had been told on multiple occasions that McGahn believed the President had ordered him to have the Special Counsel terminated. McGahn interpreted his encounter with the President in the Oval Office as an attempt to test his mettle and see how committed he was to his memory of what had occurred. The President had already laid the groundwork for pressing McGahn to alter his account by telling Porter that it might be necessary to fire McGahn if he did not deny the story, and Porter relayed that statement to McGahn. Additional evidence of the President's intent may be gleaned from the fact that his counsel was sufficiently alarmed by the prospect of the President's meeting with McGahn that he called McGahn's counsel and said that McGahn could not resign no matter what happened in the Oval Office that day. The President's counsel was well aware of McGahn's resolve not to issue what he believed to be a false account of events despite the President's request. Finally, as noted above, the President brought up the Special Counsel investigation in his Oval Office meeting with McGahn and criticized him for telling this Office about the June 17, 2017 events. The President's statements reflect his understanding—and his displeasure—that those events would be part of an obstruction-of-justice inquiry.

J.   The President's Conduct Towards Flynn, Manafort, ▮▮▮▮▮

Overview

      In addition to the interactions with McGahn described above, the President has taken other actions directed at possible witnesses in the Special Counsel's investigation, including Flynn, Manafort, ▮▮▮ and as described in the next section, Cohen. When Flynn withdrew from a joint defense agreement with the President, the President's personal counsel stated that Flynn's actions would be viewed as reflecting "hostility" towards the President. During Manafort's prosecution and while the jury was deliberating, the President repeatedly stated that Manafort was being treated unfairly and made it known that Manafort could receive a pardon. ▮▮▮▮▮▮▮▮▮▮▮▮▮▮

Evidence

1. Conduct Directed at Michael Flynn

      As previously noted, *see* Volume II, Section II.B, *supra*, the President asked for Flynn's resignation on February 13, 2017. Following Flynn's resignation, the President made positive public comments about Flynn, describing him as a "wonderful man," "a fine person," and a "very

U.S. Department of Justice

~~Attorney Work Product // May Contain Material Protected Under Fed. R. Crim. P. 6(e)~~

good person."[831] The President also privately asked advisors to pass messages to Flynn conveying that the President still cared about him and encouraging him to stay strong.[832]

In late November 2017, Flynn began to cooperate with this Office. On November 22, 2017, Flynn withdrew from a joint defense agreement he had with the President.[833] Flynn's counsel told the President's personal counsel and counsel for the White House that Flynn could no longer have confidential communications with the White House or the President.[834] Later that night, the President's personal counsel left a voicemail for Flynn's counsel that said:

> I understand your situation, but let me see if I can't state it in starker terms. . . . [I]t wouldn't surprise me if you've gone on to make a deal with . . . the government. . . . [I]f . . . there's information that implicates the President, then we've got a national security issue, . . . so, you know, . . . we need some kind of heads up. Um, just for the sake of protecting all our interests if we can. . . . [R]emember what we've always said about the President and his feelings toward Flynn and, that still remains . . . .[835]

On November 23, 2017, Flynn's attorneys returned the call from the President's personal counsel to acknowledge receipt of the voicemail.[836] Flynn's attorneys reiterated that they were no longer in a position to share information under any sort of privilege.[837] According to Flynn's attorneys, the President's personal counsel was indignant and vocal in his disagreement.[838] The President's personal counsel said that he interpreted what they said to him as a reflection of Flynn's

---

[831] *See, e.g., Remarks by President Trump in Press Conference*, White House (Feb. 16, 2018) (stating that "Flynn is a fine person" and "I don't think [Flynn] did anything wrong. If anything, he did something right . . . You know, he was just doing his job"); *Interview of Donald J. Trump*, NBC (May 11, 2017) (stating that Flynn is a "very good person").

[832] *See* Priebus 1/18/17 302, at 9-10 (the President asked Priebus to contact Flynn the week he was terminated to convey that the President still cared about him and felt bad about what happened to him; Priebus thought the President did not want Flynn to have a problem with him); McFarland 12/22/17 302, at 18 (about a month or two after Flynn was terminated, the President asked McFarland to get in touch with Flynn and tell him that he was a good guy, he should stay strong, and the President felt bad for him); Flynn 1/19/18 302, at 9 (recalling the call from Priebus and an additional call from Hicks who said she wanted to relay on behalf of the President that the President hoped Flynn was okay); Christie 2/13/19 302, at 3 (describing a phone conversation between Kushner and Flynn the day after Flynn was fired where Kushner said, "You know the President respects you. The President cares about you. I'll get the President to send out a positive tweet about you later," and the President nodded his assent to Kushner's comment promising a tweet).

[833] Counsel for Flynn 3/1/18 302, at 1.

[834] Counsel for Flynn 3/1/18 302, at 1.

[835] 11/22/17 Voicemail Transcript, President's Personal Counsel to Counsel for Michael Flynn.

[836] Counsel for Flynn 3/1/18 302, at 1.

[837] Counsel for Flynn 3/1/18 302, at 1.

[838] Counsel for Flynn 3/1/18 302, at 1.

U.S. Department of Justice

~~Attorney Work Product // May Contain Material Protected Under Fed. R. Crim. P. 6(e)~~

hostility towards the President and that he planned to inform his client of that interpretation.[839] Flynn's attorneys understood that statement to be an attempt to make them reconsider their position because the President's personal counsel believed that Flynn would be disturbed to know that such a message would be conveyed to the President.[840]

On December 1, 2017, Flynn pleaded guilty to making false statements pursuant to a cooperation agreement.[841] The next day, the President told the press that he was not concerned about what Flynn might tell the Special Counsel.[842] In response to a question about whether the President still stood behind Flynn, the President responded, "We'll see what happens."[843] Over the next several days, the President made public statements expressing sympathy for Flynn and indicating he had not been treated fairly.[844] On December 15, 2017, the President responded to a press inquiry about whether he was considering a pardon for Flynn by saying, "I don't want to talk about pardons for Michael Flynn yet. We'll see what happens. Let's see. I can say this: When you look at what's gone on with the FBI and with the Justice Department, people are very, very angry."[845]

2. Conduct Directed at Paul Manafort

On October 27, 2017, a grand jury in the District of Columbia indicted Manafort and former deputy campaign manager Richard Gates on multiple felony counts, and on February 22, 2018, a grand jury in the Eastern District of Virginia indicted Manafort and Gates on additional felony

---

[839] Counsel for Flynn 3/1/18 302, at 2. Because of attorney-client privilege issues, we did not seek to interview the President's personal counsel about the extent to which he discussed his statements to Flynn's attorneys with the President.

[840] Counsel for Flynn 3/1/18 302, at 2.

[841] Information, *United States v. Michael T. Flynn*, 1:17-cr-232 (D.D.C. Dec. 1, 2017), Doc. 1; Plea Agreement, *United States v. Michael T. Flynn*, 1:17-cr-232 (D.D.C. Dec. 1, 2017), Doc. 3.

[842] *President Trump Remarks on Tax Reform and Michael Flynn's Guilty Plea*, C-SPAN (Dec. 2, 2017).

[843] *President Trump Remarks on Tax Reform and Michael Flynn's Guilty Plea*, C-SPAN (Dec. 2, 2017).

[844] *See* @realDonaldTrump 12/2/17 (9:06 p.m. ET) Tweet ("So General Flynn lies to the FBI and his life is destroyed, while Crooked Hillary Clinton, on that now famous FBI holiday 'interrogation' with no swearing in and no recording, lies many times . . . and nothing happens to her? Rigged system, or just a double standard?"); President Trump Departure Remarks, C-SPAN (Dec. 4, 2017) ("Well, I feel badly for General Flynn. I feel very badly. He's led a very strong life. And I feel very badly.").

[845] *President Trump White House Departure*, C-SPAN (Dec. 15, 2017).

U.S. Department of Justice

~~Attorney Work Product // May Contain Material Protected Under Fed. R. Crim. P. 6(e)~~

counts.[846] The charges in both cases alleged criminal conduct by Manafort that began as early as 2005 and continued through 2018.[847]

In January 2018, Manafort told Gates that he had talked to the President's personal counsel and they were "going to take care of us."[848] Manafort told Gates it was stupid to plead, saying that he had been in touch with the President's personal counsel and repeating that they should "sit tight" and "we'll be taken care of."[849] Gates asked Manafort outright if anyone mentioned pardons and Manafort said no one used that word.[850]

As the proceedings against Manafort progressed in court, the President told Porter that he never liked Manafort and that Manafort did not know what he was doing on the campaign.[851] The President discussed with aides whether and in what way Manafort might be cooperating with the Special Counsel's investigation, and whether Manafort knew any information that would be harmful to the President.[852]

In public, the President made statements criticizing the prosecution and suggesting that Manafort was being treated unfairly. On June 15, 2018, before a scheduled court hearing that day on whether Manafort's bail should be revoked based on new charges that Manafort had tampered with witnesses while out on bail, the President told the press, "I feel badly about a lot of them

---

[846] Indictment, *United States v. Paul J. Manafort, Jr. and Richard W. Gates III*, 1:17-cr-201 (D.D.C. Oct, 27, 2017), Doc. 13 ("*Manafort and Gates* D.D.C. Indictment"); Indictment, *United States v. Paul J. Manafort, Jr. and Richard W. Gates III*, 1:18-cr-83 (E.D. Va. Feb. 22, 2018), Doc. 9 ("*Manafort and Gates* E.D. Va. Indictment")

[847] *Manafort and Gates* D.D.C. Indictment; *Manafort and Gates* E.D. Va. Indictment.

[848] Gates 4/18/18 302, at 4. In February 2018, Gates pleaded guilty, pursuant to a cooperation plea agreement, to a superseding criminal information charging him with conspiring to defraud and commit multiple offenses (*i.e.*, tax fraud, failure to report foreign bank accounts, and acting as an unregistered agent of a foreign principal) against the United States, as well as making false statements to our Office. Superseding Criminal Information, *United States v. Richard W. Gates III*, 1:17-cr-201 (D.D.C. Feb. 23, 2018), Doc. 195; Plea Agreement, *United States v. Richard W. Gates III*, 1:17-cr-201 (D.D.C. Feb. 23, 2018), Doc. 205. Gates has provided information and in-court testimony that the Office has deemed to be reliable.

[849] Gates 4/18/18 302, at 4.

[850] Gates 4/18/18 302, at 4. Manafort told this Office that he never told Gates that he had talked to the President's personal counsel or suggested that they would be taken care of. Manafort also said he hoped for a pardon but never discussed one with the President, although he noticed the President's public comments about pardons. Manafort 10/1/18 302, at 11. As explained in Volume I, Section IV.A.8, *supra*, Manafort entered into a plea agreement with our Office. The U.S. District Court for the District of Columbia determined that he breached the agreement by being untruthful in proffer sessions and before the grand jury. Order, *United States v. Manafort*, 1:17-cr-201 (D.D.C. Feb. 13, 2019), Doc. 503.

[851] Porter 5/8/18 302, at 11. Priebus recalled that the President never really liked Manafort. *See* Priebus 4/3/18 302, at 11. Hicks said that candidate Trump trusted Manafort's judgment while he worked on the Campaign, but she also once heard Trump tell Gates to keep an eye on Manafort. Hicks 3/13/18 302, at 16.

[852] Porter 5/8/18 302, at 11; McGahn 12/14/17 302, at 14.

U.S. Department of Justice

Attorney Work Product // May Contain Material Protected Under Fed. R. Crim. P. 6(e)

because I think a lot of it is very unfair. I mean, I look at some of them where they go back 12 years. Like Manafort has nothing to do with our campaign. But I feel so—I tell you, I feel a little badly about it. They went back 12 years to get things that he did 12 years ago? . . . I feel badly for some people, because they've gone back 12 years to find things about somebody, and I don't think it's right."[853] In response to a question about whether he was considering a pardon for Manafort or other individuals involved in the Special Counsel's investigation, the President said, "I don't want to talk about that. No, I don't want to talk about that. . . . But look, I do want to see people treated fairly. That's what it's all about."[854] Hours later, Manafort's bail was revoked and the President tweeted, "Wow, what a tough sentence for Paul Manafort, who has represented Ronald Reagan, Bob Dole and many other top political people and campaigns. Didn't know Manafort was the head of the Mob. What about Comey and Crooked Hillary and all the others? Very unfair!"[855]

Immediately following the revocation of Manafort's bail, the President's personal lawyer, Rudolph Giuliani, gave a series of interviews in which he raised the possibility of a pardon for Manafort. Giuliani told the New York Daily News that "[w]hen the whole thing is over, things might get cleaned up with some presidential pardons."[856] Giuliani also said in an interview that, although the President should not pardon anyone while the Special Counsel's investigation was ongoing, "when the investigation is concluded, he's kind of on his own, right?"[857] In a CNN interview two days later, Giuliani said, "I guess I should clarify this once and for all. . . . The president has issued no pardons in this investigation. The president is not going to issue pardons in this investigation. . . . When it's over, hey, he's the president of the United States. He retains his pardon power. Nobody is taking that away from him."[858] Giuliani rejected the suggestion that his and the President's comments could signal to defendants that they should not cooperate in a criminal prosecution because a pardon might follow, saying the comments were "certainly not intended that way."[859] Giuliani said the comments only acknowledged that an individual involved in the investigation would not be "excluded from [a pardon], if in fact the president and his advisors . . . come to the conclusion that you have been treated unfairly."[860] Giuliani observed that pardons were not unusual in political investigations but said, "That doesn't mean they're going to happen

---

[853] Remarks by President Trump in Press Gaggle, White House (June 15, 2018).

[854] Remarks by President Trump in Press Gaggle, White House (June 15, 2018).

[855] @realDonaldTrump 6/15/18 (1:41 p.m. ET) Tweet.

[856] Chris Sommerfeldt, *Rudy Giuliani says Mueller probe 'might get cleaned up' with 'presidential pardons' in light of Paul Manafort going to jail*, New York Daily News (June 15, 2018).

[857] Sharon LaFraniere, *Judge Orders Paul Manafort Jailed Before Trial, Citing New Obstruction Charges*, New York Times (June 15, 2018) (quoting Giuliani).

[858] *State of the Union with Jake Tapper Transcript*, CNN (June 17, 2018); *see* Karoun Demirjian, *Giuliani suggests Trump may pardon Manafort after Mueller's probe*, Washington Post (June 17, 2018).

[859] *State of the Union with Jake Tapper Transcript*, CNN (June 17, 2018).

[860] *State of the Union with Jake Tapper Transcript*, CNN (June 17, 2018).

U.S. Department of Justice

~~Attorney Work Product // May Contain Material Protected Under Fed. R. Crim. P. 6(e)~~

here. Doesn't mean that anybody should rely on it. . . . Big signal is, nobody has been pardoned yet."[861]

On July 31, 2018, Manafort's criminal trial began in the Eastern District of Virginia, generating substantial news coverage.[862] The next day, the President tweeted, "This is a terrible situation and Attorney General Jeff Sessions should stop this Rigged Witch Hunt right now, before it continues to stain our country any further. Bob Mueller is totally conflicted, and his 17 Angry Democrats that are doing his dirty work are a disgrace to USA!"[863] Minutes later, the President tweeted, "Paul Manafort worked for Ronald Reagan, Bob Dole and many other highly prominent and respected political leaders. He worked for me for a very short time. Why didn't government tell me that he was under investigation. These old charges have nothing to do with Collusion—a Hoax!"[864] Later in the day, the President tweeted, "Looking back on history, who was treated worse, Alfonse Capone, legendary mob boss, killer and 'Public Enemy Number One,' or Paul Manafort, political operative & Reagan/Dole darling, now serving solitary confinement—although convicted of nothing? Where is the Russian Collusion?"[865] The President's tweets about the Manafort trial were widely covered by the press.[866] When asked about the President's tweets, Sanders told the press, "Certainly, the President's been clear. He thinks Paul Manafort's been treated unfairly."[867]

On August 16, 2018, the Manafort case was submitted to the jury and deliberations began. At that time, Giuliani had recently suggested to reporters that the Special Counsel investigation needed to be "done in the next two or three weeks,"[868] and media stories reported that a Manafort acquittal would add to criticism that the Special Counsel investigation was not worth the time and expense, whereas a conviction could show that ending the investigation would be premature.[869]

[861] *State of the Union with Jake Tapper Transcript*, CNN (June 17, 2018).

[862] *See, e.g.*, Katelyn Polantz, *Takeaways from day one of the Paul Manafort trial*, CNN (July 31, 2018); Frank Bruni, *Paul Manafort's Trial Is Donald Trump's, Too*, New York Times Opinion (July 31, 2018); Rachel Weiner et al., *Paul Manafort trial Day 2: Witnesses describe extravagant clothing purchases, home remodels, lavish cars paid with wire transfers*, Washington Post (Aug. 1, 2018).

[863] @realDonaldTrump 8/1/18 (9:24 a.m. ET) Tweet. Later that day, when Sanders was asked about the President's tweet, she told reporters, "It's not an order. It's the President's opinion." Sarah Sanders, *White House Daily Briefing*, C-SPAN (Aug. 1, 2018).

[864] @realDonaldTrump 8/1/18 (9:34 a.m. ET) Tweet.

[865] @realDonaldTrump 8/1/18 (11:35 a.m. ET) Tweet.

[866] *See, e.g.*, Carol D. Leonnig et al., *Trump calls Manafort prosecution "a hoax," says Sessions should stop Mueller investigation "right now"*, Washington Post (Aug. 1, 2018); Louis Nelson, *Trump claims Manafort case has "nothing to do with collusion"*, Politico (Aug. 1. 2018).

[867] Sarah Sanders, *White House Daily Briefing*, C-SPAN (Aug. 1, 2018).

[868] Chris Strohm & Shannon Pettypiece, *Mueller Probe Doesn't Need to Shut Down Before Midterms, Officials Say*, Bloomberg (Aug. 15, 2018).

[869] *See, e.g.*, Katelyn Polantz et al., *Manafort jury ends first day of deliberations without a verdict*, CNN (Aug. 16, 2018); David Voreacos, *What Mueller's Manafort Case Means for the Trump Battle to*

U.S. Department of Justice

~~Attorney Work Product // May Contain Material Protected Under Fed. R. Crim. P. 6(e)~~

On August 17, 2018, as jury deliberations continued, the President commented on the trial from the South Lawn of the White House. In an impromptu exchange with reporters that lasted approximately five minutes, the President twice called the Special Counsel's investigation a "rigged witch hunt."[870] When asked whether he would pardon Manafort if he was convicted, the President said, "I don't talk about that now. I don't talk about that."[871] The President then added, without being asked a further question, "I think the whole Manafort trial is very sad when you look at what's going on there. I think it's a very sad day for our country. He worked for me for a very short period of time. But you know what, he happens to be a very good person. And I think it's very sad what they've done to Paul Manafort."[872] The President did not take further questions.[873] In response to the President's statements, Manafort's attorney said, "Mr. Manafort really appreciates the support of President Trump."[874]

On August 21, 2018, the jury found Manafort guilty on eight felony counts. Also on August 21, Michael Cohen pleaded guilty to eight offenses, including a campaign-finance violation that he said had occurred "in coordination with, and at the direction of, a candidate for federal office."[875] The President reacted to Manafort's convictions that day by telling reporters, "Paul Manafort's a good man" and "it's a very sad thing that happened."[876] The President described the Special Counsel's investigation as "a witch hunt that ends in disgrace."[877] The next day, the President tweeted, "I feel very badly for Paul Manafort and his wonderful family. 'Justice' took a 12 year old tax case, among other things, applied tremendous pressure on him and, unlike Michael Cohen, he refused to 'break'—make up stories in order to get a 'deal.' Such respect for a brave man!"[878]

In a Fox News interview on August 22, 2018, the President said: "[Cohen] makes a better deal when he uses me, like everybody else. And one of the reasons I respect Paul Manafort so much is he went through that trial—you know they make up stories. People make up stories. This

---

Come, Bloomberg (Aug. 2, 2018); Gabby Morrongiello, *What a guilty verdict for Manafort would mean for Trump and Mueller*, Washington Examiner (Aug. 18, 2018).

[870] President Trump Remarks on John Brennan and Mueller Probe, C-SPAN (Aug. 17, 2018).

[871] President Trump Remarks on John Brennan and Mueller Probe, C-SPAN (Aug. 17, 2018).

[872] President Trump Remarks on John Brennan and Mueller Probe, C-SPAN (Aug. 17, 2018).

[873] President Trump Remarks on John Brennan and Mueller Probe, C-SPAN (Aug. 17, 2018).

[874] *Trump calls Manafort "very good person,"* All In with Chris Hayes (Aug. 17, 2018) (transcript); *Manafort lawyer: We appreciate Trump's support,* CNN (Aug. 17, 2018) (https://www.cnn.com/videos/politics/2018/08/17/paul-manafort-attorney-trump-jury-deliberations-schneider-lead-vpx.cnn).

[875] Transcript at 23, *United States v. Michael Cohen*, 1:18-cr-602 (S.D.N.Y. Aug. 21, 2018), Doc. 7 (*Cohen 8/21/18 Transcript*).

[876] *President Trump Remarks on Manafort Trial*, C-SPAN (Aug. 21, 2018).

[877] *President Trump Remarks on Manafort Trial*, C-SPAN (Aug. 21, 2018).

[878] @realDonaldTrump 8/22/18 (9:21 a.m. ET) Tweet.

U.S. Department of Justice

~~Attorney Work Product // May Contain Material Protected Under Fed. R. Crim. P. 6(e)~~

whole thing about flipping, they call it, I know all about flipping."[879] The President said that flipping was "not fair" and "almost ought to be outlawed."[880] In response to a question about whether he was considering a pardon for Manafort, the President said, "I have great respect for what he's done, in terms of what he's gone through. . . . He worked for many, many people many, many years, and I would say what he did, some of the charges they threw against him, every consultant, every lobbyist in Washington probably does."[881] Giuliani told journalists that the President "really thinks Manafort has been horribly treated" and that he and the President had discussed the political fallout if the President pardoned Manafort.[882] The next day, Giuliani told the Washington Post that the President had asked his lawyers for advice on the possibility of a pardon for Manafort and other aides, and had been counseled against considering a pardon until the investigation concluded.[883]

On September 14, 2018, Manafort pleaded guilty to charges in the District of Columbia and signed a plea agreement that required him to cooperate with investigators.[884] Giuliani was reported to have publicly said that Manafort remained in a joint defense agreement with the President following Manafort's guilty plea and agreement to cooperate, and that Manafort's attorneys regularly briefed the President's lawyers on the topics discussed and the information Manafort had provided in interviews with the Special Counsel's Office.[885] On November 26, 2018, the Special Counsel's Office disclosed in a public court filing that Manafort had breached his plea agreement by lying about multiple subjects.[886] The next day, Giuliani said that the President had been "upset for weeks" about what he considered to be "the un-American, horrible treatment of

---

[879] *Fox & Friends Exclusive Interview with President Trump*, Fox News (Aug. 23, 2018) (recorded the previous day).

[880] *Fox & Friends Exclusive Interview with President Trump*, Fox News (Aug. 23, 2018) (recorded the previous day).

[881] *Fox & Friends Exclusive Interview with President Trump*, Fox News (Aug. 23, 2018) (recorded the previous day).

[882] Maggie Haberman & Katie Rogers, *"How Did We End Up Here?" Trump Wonders as the White House Soldiers On*, New York Times (Aug. 22, 2018).

[883] Carol D. Leonnig & Josh Dawsey, *Trump recently sought his lawyers' advice on possibility of pardoning Manafort, Giuliani says*, Washington Post (Aug. 23, 2018).

[884] Plea Agreement, *United States v. Paul J. Manafort, Jr.*, 1:17-cr-201 (D.D.C. Sept. 14, 2018), Doc. 422.

[885] Karen Freifeld & Nathan Layne, *Trump lawyer: Manafort said nothing damaging in Mueller interviews*, Reuters (Oct. 22, 2018); Michael S. Schmidt et al., *Manafort's Lawyer Said to Brief Trump Attorneys on What He Told Mueller*, New York Times (Nov. 27, 2018); Dana Bash, *Manafort team briefed Giuliani on Mueller meetings*, CNN, Posted 11/28/18, *available at* https://www.cnn.com/videos/politics/2018/11/28/manafort-lawyers-keeping-trump-lawyers-giuliani-updated-mueller-probe-bash-sot-nr-vpx.cnn; *see* Sean Hannity, *Interview with Rudy Giuliani*, Fox News (Sept. 14, 2018) (Giuliani: "[T]here was a quote put out by a source close to Manafort that the plea agreement has, and cooperation agreement has, nothing to do with the Trump campaign. . . . Now, I know that because I've been privy to a lot of facts I can't repeat.").

[886] Joint Status Report, *United States v. Paul J. Manafort, Jr.*, (D.D.C Nov. 26, 2018), Doc. 455.

U.S. Department of Justice

~~Attorney Work Product // May Contain Material Protected Under Fed. R. Crim. P. 6(e)~~

Manafort."[887] In an interview on November 28, 2018, the President suggested that it was "very brave" that Manafort did not "flip":

> If you told the truth, you go to jail. You know this flipping stuff is terrible. You flip and you lie and you get—the prosecutors will tell you 99 percent of the time they can get people to flip. It's rare that they can't. But I had three people: Manafort, Corsi—I don't know Corsi, but he refuses to say what they demanded.[888] Manafort, Corsi ███████████. It's actually very brave.[889]

In response to a question about a potential pardon for Manafort, the President said, "It was never discussed, but I wouldn't take it off the table. Why would I take it off the table?"[890]

3. ████████████████████

---

[887] Stephen Collinson, *Trump appears consumed by Mueller investigation as details emerge*, CNN (Nov. 29, 2018).

[888] "Corsi" is a reference to Jerome Corsi, █████████████████ who was involved in efforts to coordinate with WikiLeaks and Assange, and who stated publicly at that time that he had refused a plea offer from the Special Counsel's Office because he was "not going to sign a lie." Sara Murray & Eli Watkins, ██████████ *says he won't agree to plea deal*, CNN (Nov. 26, 2018).

[889] Marisa Schultz & Nikki Schwab, *Oval Office Interview with President Trump: Trump says pardon for Paul Manafort still a possibility*, New York Post (Nov. 28, 2018). That same day, the President tweeted: "While the disgusting Fake News is doing everything within their power not to report it that way, at least 3 major players are intimating that the Angry Mueller Gang of Dems is viciously telling witnesses to lie about facts & they will get relief. This is our Joseph McCarthy Era!" @realDonaldTrump 11/28/18 (8:39 a.m. ET) Tweet.

[890] Marisa Schultz & Nikki Schwab, *New York Post Oval Office Interview with President Trump: Trump says pardon for Paul Manafort still a possibility*, New York Post (Nov. 28, 2018).

U.S. Department of Justice

~~Attorney-Work-Product // May-Contain-Material-Protected-Under-Fed. R. Crim. P. 6(e)~~

Analysis

In analyzing the President's conduct towards Flynn, Manafort, █████████, the following evidence is relevant to the elements of obstruction of justice:

a. <u>Obstructive act</u>. The President's actions towards witnesses in the Special Counsel's investigation would qualify as obstructive if they had the natural tendency to prevent particular witnesses from testifying truthfully, or otherwise would have the probable effect of influencing, delaying, or preventing their testimony to law enforcement.

With regard to Flynn, the President sent private and public messages to Flynn encouraging him to stay strong and conveying that the President still cared about him before he began to cooperate with the government. When Flynn's attorneys withdrew him from a joint defense agreement with the President, signaling that Flynn was potentially cooperating with the government, the President's personal counsel initially reminded Flynn's counsel of the President's warm feelings towards Flynn and said "that still remains." But when Flynn's counsel reiterated that Flynn could no longer share information under a joint defense agreement, the President's personal counsel stated that the decision would be interpreted as reflecting Flynn's hostility towards the President. That sequence of events could have had the potential to affect Flynn's decision to cooperate, as well as the extent of that cooperation. Because of privilege issues, however, we could not determine whether the President was personally involved in or knew about the specific message his counsel delivered to Flynn's counsel.

With respect to Manafort, there is evidence that the President's actions had the potential to influence Manafort's decision whether to cooperate with the government. The President and his personal counsel made repeated statements suggesting that a pardon was a possibility for Manafort, while also making it clear that the President did not want Manafort to "flip" and cooperate with the government. On June 15, 2018, the day the judge presiding over Manafort's D.C. case was considering whether to revoke his bail, the President said that he "felt badly" for Manafort and stated, "I think a lot of it is very unfair." And when asked about a pardon for Manafort, the President said, "I do want to see people treated fairly. That's what it's all about." Later that day, after Manafort's bail was revoked, the President called it a "tough sentence" that was "Very unfair!" Two days later, the President's personal counsel stated that individuals involved in the Special Counsel's investigation could receive a pardon "if in fact the [P]resident and his advisors . . . come to the conclusion that you have been treated unfairly"—using language that paralleled how the President had already described the treatment of Manafort. Those statements, combined with the President's commendation of Manafort for being a "brave man" who "refused to 'break'," suggested that a pardon was a more likely possibility if Manafort continued not to cooperate with the government. And while Manafort eventually pleaded guilty pursuant to a cooperation agreement, he was found to have violated the agreement by lying to investigators.

The President's public statements during the Manafort trial, including during jury deliberations, also had the potential to influence the trial jury. On the second day of trial, for example, the President called the prosecution a "terrible situation" and a "hoax" that "continues to stain our country" and referred to Manafort as a "Reagan/Dole darling" who was "serving solitary confinement" even though he was "convicted of nothing." Those statements were widely picked up by the press. While jurors were instructed not to watch or read news stories about the case and are presumed to follow those instructions, the President's statements during the trial generated substantial media coverage that could have reached jurors if they happened to see the statements or learned about them from others. And the President's statements during jury deliberations that Manafort "happens to be a very good person" and that "it's very sad what they've done to Paul Manafort" had the potential to influence jurors who learned of the statements, which the President made just as jurors were considering whether to convict or acquit Manafort.

b.   Nexus to an official proceeding. The President's actions towards Flynn, Manafort, ██████ appear to have been connected to pending or anticipated official proceedings involving each individual. The President's conduct towards Flynn ████ principally occurred when both were under criminal investigation by the Special Counsel's Office and press reports speculated about whether they would cooperate with the Special Counsel's investigation. And the President's conduct towards Manafort was directly connected to the official proceedings involving him. The President made statements about Manafort and the charges against him during Manafort's criminal trial. And the President's comments about the prospect of Manafort "flipping" occurred when it was clear the Special Counsel continued to oversee grand jury proceedings.

c.   Intent. Evidence concerning the President's intent related to Flynn as a potential witness is inconclusive. As previously noted, because of privilege issues we do not have evidence establishing whether the President knew about or was involved in his counsel's communications with Flynn's counsel stating that Flynn's decision to withdraw from the joint defense agreement and cooperate with the government would be viewed as reflecting "hostility" towards the President. And regardless of what the President's personal counsel communicated, the President continued to express sympathy for Flynn after he pleaded guilty pursuant to a cooperation agreement, stating that Flynn had "led a very strong life" and the President "fe[lt] very badly" about what had happened to him.

Evidence concerning the President's conduct towards Manafort indicates that the President intended to encourage Manafort to not cooperate with the government. Before Manafort was convicted, the President repeatedly stated that Manafort had been treated unfairly. One day after Manafort was convicted on eight felony charges and potentially faced a lengthy prison term, the President said that Manafort was "a brave man" for refusing to "break" and that "flipping" "almost ought to be outlawed." At the same time, although the President had privately told aides he did not like Manafort, he publicly called Manafort "a good man" and said he had a "wonderful family." And when the President was asked whether he was considering a pardon for Manafort, the President did not respond directly and instead said he had "great respect for what [Manafort]'s done, in terms of what he's gone through." The President added that "some of the charges they threw against him, every consultant, every lobbyist in Washington probably does." In light of the President's counsel's previous statements that the investigations "might get cleaned up with some presidential pardons" and that a pardon would be possible if the President "come[s] to the conclusion that you have been treated unfairly," the evidence supports the inference that the

U.S. Department of Justice

~~Attorney-Work-Product // May Contain Material Protected Under Fed. R. Crim. P. 6(e)~~

President intended Manafort to believe that he could receive a pardon, which would make cooperation with the government as a means of obtaining a lesser sentence unnecessary.

We also examined the evidence of the President's intent in making public statements about Manafort at the beginning of his trial and when the jury was deliberating. Some evidence supports a conclusion that the President intended, at least in part, to influence the jury. The trial generated widespread publicity, and as the jury began to deliberate, commentators suggested that an acquittal would add to pressure to end the Special Counsel's investigation. By publicly stating on the second day of deliberations that Manafort "happens to be a very good person" and that "it's very sad what they've done to Paul Manafort" right after calling the Special Counsel's investigation a "rigged witch hunt," the President's statements could, if they reached jurors, have the natural tendency to engender sympathy for Manafort among jurors, and a factfinder could infer that the President intended that result. But there are alternative explanations for the President's comments, including that he genuinely felt sorry for Manafort or that his goal was not to influence the jury but to influence public opinion. The President's comments also could have been intended to continue sending a message to Manafort that a pardon was possible. As described above, the President made his comments about Manafort being "a very good person" immediately after declining to answer a question about whether he would pardon Manafort.

U.S. Department of Justice

~~Attorney Work Product // May Contain Material Protected Under Fed. R. Crim. P. 6(e)~~

K.   The President's Conduct Involving Michael Cohen

Overview

The President's conduct involving Michael Cohen spans the full period of our investigation. During the campaign, Cohen pursued the Trump Tower Moscow project on behalf of the Trump Organization. Cohen briefed candidate Trump on the project numerous times, including discussing whether Trump should travel to Russia to advance the deal. After the media began questioning Trump's connections to Russia, Cohen promoted a "party line" that publicly distanced Trump from Russia and asserted he had no business there. Cohen continued to adhere to that party line in 2017, when Congress asked him to provide documents and testimony in its Russia investigation. In an attempt to minimize the President's connections to Russia, Cohen submitted a letter to Congress falsely stating that he only briefed Trump on the Trump Tower Moscow project three times, that he did not consider asking Trump to travel to Russia, that Cohen had not received a response to an outreach he made to the Russian government, and that the project ended in January 2016, before the first Republican caucus or primary. While working on the congressional statement, Cohen had extensive discussions with the President's personal counsel, who, according to Cohen, said that Cohen should not contradict the President and should keep the statement short and "tight." After the FBI searched Cohen's home and office in April 2018, the President publicly asserted that Cohen would not "flip" and privately passed messages of support to him. Cohen also discussed pardons with the President's personal counsel and believed that if he stayed on message, he would get a pardon or the President would do "something else" to make the investigation end. But after Cohen began cooperating with the government in July 2018, the President publicly criticized him, called him a "rat," and suggested his family members had committed crimes.

Evidence

1. Candidate Trump's Awareness of and Involvement in the Trump Tower Moscow Project

The President's interactions with Cohen as a witness took place against the background of the President's involvement in the Trump Tower Moscow project.

As described in detail in Volume I, Section IV.A.1, *supra,* from September 2015 until at least June 2016, the Trump Organization pursued a Trump Tower Moscow project in Russia, with negotiations conducted by Cohen, then-executive vice president of the Trump Organization and special counsel to Donald J. Trump.[909] The Trump Organization had previously and

---

[909] In August 2018 and November 2018, Cohen pleaded guilty to multiple crimes of deception, including making false statements to Congress about the Trump Tower Moscow project, as described later in this section. When Cohen first met with investigators from this Office, he repeated the same lies he told Congress about the Trump Tower Moscow project. Cohen 8/7/18 302, at 12-17. But after Cohen pleaded guilty to offenses in the Southern District of New York on August 21, 2018, he met with investigators again and corrected the record. The Office found Cohen's testimony in these subsequent proffer sessions to be consistent with and corroborated by other information obtained in the course of the Office's investigation. The Office's sentencing submission in Cohen's criminal case stated: "Starting with his second meeting with the [Special Counsel's Office] in September 2018, the defendant has accepted responsibility not only for

U.S. Department of Justice

Attorney Work Product // May Contain Material Protected Under Fed. R. Crim. P. 6(e)

unsuccessfully pursued a building project in Moscow.[910] According to Cohen, in approximately September 2015 he obtained internal approval from Trump to negotiate on behalf of the Trump Organization to have a Russian corporation build a tower in Moscow that licensed the Trump name and brand.[911] Cohen thereafter had numerous brief conversations with Trump about the project.[912] Cohen recalled that Trump wanted to be updated on any developments with Trump Tower Moscow and on several occasions brought the project up with Cohen to ask what was happening on it.[913] Cohen also discussed the project on multiple occasions with Donald Trump Jr. and Ivanka Trump.[914]

In the fall of 2015, Trump signed a Letter of Intent for the project that specified highly lucrative terms for the Trump Organization.[915] In December 2015, Felix Sater, who was handling negotiations between Cohen and the Russian corporation, asked Cohen for a copy of his and Trump's passports to facilitate travel to Russia to meet with government officials and possible financing partners.[916] Cohen recalled discussing the trip with Trump and requesting a copy of Trump's passport from Trump's personal secretary, Rhona Graff.[917]

By January 2016, Cohen had become frustrated that Sater had not set up a meeting with Russian government officials, so Cohen reached out directly by email to the office of Dmitry

---

his false statements concerning the [Trump Tower] Moscow Project, but also his broader efforts through public statements and testimony before Congress to minimize his role in, and what he knew about, contacts between the [Trump Organization] and Russian interests during the course of the campaign. The information provided by Cohen about the [Trump Tower] Moscow Project in these proffer sessions is consistent with and corroborated by other information obtained in the course of the [Special Counsel's Office's] investigation. . . . The defendant, without prompting by the [Special Counsel's Office], also corrected other false and misleading statements that he had made concerning his outreach to and contacts with Russian officials during the course of the campaign." Gov't Sentencing Submission at 4, *United States v. Michael Cohen*, 1:18-cr-850 (S.D.N.Y. Dec. 7, 2018), Doc. 14. At Cohen's sentencing, our Office further explained that Cohen had "provided valuable information . . . while taking care and being careful to note what he knows and what he doesn't know." Transcript at 19, *United States v. Michael Cohen*, 1:18-cr-850 (S.D.N.Y. Dec. 12, 2018), Doc. 17 (*Cohen 12/12/18 Transcript*).

[910] *See* Volume I, Section IV.A.1, *supra* (noting that starting in at least 2013, several employees of the Trump Organization, including then-president of the organization Donald J. Trump, pursued a Trump Tower Moscow deal with several Russian counterparties).

[911] Cohen 9/12/18 302, at 1-4; Cohen 8/7/18 302, at 15.

[912] Cohen 9/12/18 302, at 2, 4.

[913] Cohen 9/12/18 302, at 4.

[914] Cohen 9/12/18 302, at 4, 10.

[915] MDC-H-000618-25 (10/28/15 Letter of Intent, signed by Donald J. Trump, Trump Acquisition, LLC and Andrey Rozov, I.C. Expert Investment Company); Cohen 9/12/18 302, at 3; Written Responses of Donald J. Trump (Nov. 20, 2018), at 15 (Response to Question III, Parts (a) through (g)).

[916] MDC-H-000600 (12/19/15 Email, Sater to Cohen).

[917] Cohen 9/12/18 302, at 5.

U.S. Department of Justice

~~Attorney Work Product // May Contain Material Protected Under Fed. R. Crim. P. 6(e)~~

Peskov, who was Putin's deputy chief of staff and press secretary.[918] On January 20, 2016, Cohen received an email response from Elena Poliakova, Peskov's personal assistant, and phone records confirm that they then spoke for approximately twenty minutes, during which Cohen described the Trump Tower Moscow project and requested assistance in moving the project forward.[919] Cohen recalled briefing candidate Trump about the call soon afterwards.[920] Cohen told Trump he spoke with a woman he identified as "someone from the Kremlin," and Cohen reported that she was very professional and asked detailed questions about the project.[921] Cohen recalled telling Trump he wished the Trump Organization had assistants who were as competent as the woman from the Kremlin.[922]

Cohen thought his phone call renewed interest in the project.[923] The day after Cohen's call with Poliakova, Sater texted Cohen, asking him to "[c]all me when you have a few minutes to chat . . . It's about Putin they called today."[924] Sater told Cohen that the Russian government liked the project and on January 25, 2016, sent an invitation for Cohen to visit Moscow "for a working visit."[925] After the outreach from Sater, Cohen recalled telling Trump that he was waiting to hear back on moving the project forward.[926]

After January 2016, Cohen continued to have conversations with Sater about Trump Tower Moscow and continued to keep candidate Trump updated about those discussions and the status of the project.[927] Cohen recalled that he and Trump wanted Trump Tower Moscow to succeed and that Trump never discouraged him from working on the project because of the campaign.[928] In March or April 2016, Trump asked Cohen if anything was happening in Russia.[929] Cohen also

---

[918] *See* FS00004 (12/30/15 Text Message, Cohen to Sater); TRUMPORG_MC_000233 (1/11/16 Email, Cohen to pr_peskova@prpress.gof.ru); MDC-H-000690 (1/14/16 Email, Cohen to info@prpress.gov.ru); TRUMPORG_MC_000235 (1/16/16 Email, Cohen to pr_peskova@prpress.gov.ru).

[919] 1/20/16 Email, Poliakova to Cohen; Call Records of Michael Cohen. (Showing a 22-minute call on January 20, 2016, between Cohen and the number Poliakova provided in her email); Cohen 9/12/18 302, at 2-3. After the call, Cohen saved Poliakova's contact information in his Trump Organization Outlook contact list. 1/20/16 Cohen Microsoft Outlook Entry (6:22 a.m.).

[920] Cohen 11/20/18 302, at 5.

[921] Cohen 11/20/18 302, at 5-6; Cohen 11/12/18 302, at 4.

[922] Cohen 11/20/18 302, at 5.

[923] Cohen 9/12/18 302, at 5.

[924] FS00011 (1/21/16 Text Messages, Sater & Cohen).

[925] Cohen 9/12/18 302, at 5; 1/25/16 Email, Sater to Cohen (attachment).

[926] Cohen 11/20/18 302, at 5.

[927] Cohen 9/12/18 302, at 6. In later congressional testimony, Cohen stated that he briefed Trump on the project approximately six times after January 2016. *Hearing on Issues Related to Trump Organization Before the House Oversight and Reform Committee*, 116th Cong. (Feb. 27, 2019) (CQ Cong. Transcripts, at 24) (testimony of Michael Cohen).

[928] Cohen 9/12/18 302, at 6.

[929] Cohen 9/18/18 302, at 4.

U.S. Department of Justice

Attorney Work Product // May Contain Material Protected Under Fed. R. Crim. P. 6(e)

recalled briefing Donald Trump Jr. in the spring—a conversation that Cohen said was not "idle chit chat" because Trump Tower Moscow was potentially a $1 billion deal.[930]

Cohen recalled that around May 2016, he again raised with candidate Trump the possibility of a trip to Russia to advance the Trump Tower Moscow project.[931] At that time, Cohen had received several texts from Sater seeking to arrange dates for such a trip.[932] On May 4, 2016, Sater wrote to Cohen, "I had a chat with Moscow. ASSUMING the trip does happen the question is before or after the convention. . . . . Obviously the premeeting trip (you only) can happen anytime you want but the 2 big guys [is] the question. I said I would confirm and revert."[933] Cohen responded, "My trip before Cleveland. Trump once he becomes the nominee after the convention."[934] On May 5, 2016, Sater followed up with a text that Cohen thought he probably read to Trump:

> Peskov would like to invite you as his guest to the St. Petersburg Forum which is Russia's Davos it's June 16-19. He wants to meet there with you and possibly introduce you to either Putin or Medvedev. . . . This is perfect. The entire business class of Russia will be there as well. He said anything you want to discuss including dates and subjects are on the table to discuss.[935]

Cohen recalled discussing the invitation to the St. Petersburg Economic Forum with candidate Trump and saying that Putin or Russian Prime Minister Dmitry Medvedev might be there.[936] Cohen remembered that Trump said that he would be willing to travel to Russia if Cohen could "lock and load" on the deal.[937] In June 2016, Cohen decided not to attend the St. Petersburg Economic Forum because Sater had not obtained a formal invitation for Cohen from Peskov.[938] Cohen said he had a quick conversation with Trump at that time but did not tell him that the project was over because he did not want Trump to complain that the deal was on-again-off-again if it were revived.[939]

During the summer of 2016, Cohen recalled that candidate Trump publicly claimed that he had nothing to do with Russia and then shortly afterwards privately checked with Cohen about the status of the Trump Tower Moscow project, which Cohen found "interesting."[940] At some point

---

[930] Cohen 9/12/18 302, at 10.

[931] Cohen 9/12/18 302, at 7.

[932] Cohen 9/12/18 302, at 7.

[933] FS00015 (5/4/16 Text Message, Sater to Cohen).

[934] FS00015 (5/4/16 Text Message, Cohen to Sater).

[935] FS00016-17 (5/5/16 Text Messages, Sater & Cohen).

[936] Cohen 9/12/18 302, at 7.

[937] Cohen 9/12/18 302, at 7.

[938] Cohen 9/12/18 302, at 7-8.

[939] Cohen 9/12/18 302, at 8.

[940] Cohen 3/19/19 302, at 2.

U.S. Department of Justice

Attorney Work Product // May Contain Material Protected Under Fed. R. Crim. P. 6(e)

that summer, Cohen recalled having a brief conversation with Trump in which Cohen said the Trump Tower Moscow project was going nowhere because the Russian development company had not secured a piece of property for the project.[941] Trump said that was "too bad," and Cohen did not recall talking with Trump about the project after that.[942] Cohen said that at no time during the campaign did Trump tell him not to pursue the project or that the project should be abandoned.[943]

2. Cohen Determines to Adhere to a "Party Line" Distancing Candidate Trump From Russia

As previously discussed, *see* Volume II, Section II.A, *supra*, when questions about possible Russian support for candidate Trump emerged during the 2016 presidential campaign, Trump denied having any personal, financial, or business connection to Russia, which Cohen described as the "party line" or "message" to follow for Trump and his senior advisors.[944]

After the election, the Trump Organization sought to formally close out certain deals in advance of the inauguration.[945] Cohen recalled that Trump Tower Moscow was on the list of deals to be closed out.[946] In approximately January 2017, Cohen began receiving inquiries from the media about Trump Tower Moscow, and he recalled speaking to the President-Elect when those inquiries came in.[947] Cohen was concerned that truthful answers about the Trump Tower Moscow project might not be consistent with the "message" that the President-Elect had no relationship with Russia.[948]

In an effort to "stay on message," Cohen told a New York Times reporter that the Trump Tower Moscow deal was not feasible and had ended in January 2016.[949] Cohen recalled that this was part of a "script" or talking points he had developed with President-Elect Trump and others to

---

[941] Cohen 3/19/19 302, at 2. Cohen could not recall the precise timing of this conversation, but said he thought it occurred in June or July 2016. Cohen recalled that the conversation happened at some point after candidate Trump was publicly stating that he had nothing to do with Russia. Cohen 3/19/19 302, at 2.

[942] Cohen 3/19/19 302, at 2.

[943] Cohen 3/19/19 302, at 2.

[944] Cohen 11/20/18 302, at 1; Cohen 9/18/18 302, at 3, 5; Cohen 9/12/18 302, at 9.

[945] Cohen 9/18/18 302, at 1-2; *see also* Rtskhiladze 4/4/18 302, at 8-9.

[946] Cohen 9/18/18 302, at 1-2.

[947] Cohen 9/18/18 302, at 3.

[948] Cohen 11/20/18 302, at 4.

[949] Cohen 9/18/18 302, at 5. The article was published on February 19, 2017, and reported that Sater and Cohen had been working on plan for a Trump Tower Moscow "as recently as the fall of 2015" but had come to a halt because of the presidential campaign. Consistent with Cohen's intended party line message, the article stated, "Cohen said the Trump Organization had received a letter of intent for a project in Moscow from a Russian real estate developer at that time but determined that the project was not feasible." Megan Twohey & Scott Shane, *A Back-Channel Plan for Ukraine and Russia, Courtesy of Trump Associates*, New York Times (Feb. 19, 2017).

U.S. Department of Justice

~~Attorney Work Product // May Contain Material Protected Under Fed. R. Crim. P. 6(e)~~

dismiss the idea of a substantial connection between Trump and Russia.[950] Cohen said that he discussed the talking points with Trump but that he did not explicitly tell Trump he thought they were untrue because Trump already knew they were untrue.[951] Cohen thought it was important to say the deal was done in January 2016, rather than acknowledge that talks continued in May and June 2016, because it limited the period when candidate Trump could be alleged to have a relationship with Russia to an early point in the campaign, before Trump had become the party's presumptive nominee.[952]

3. Cohen Submits False Statements to Congress Minimizing the Trump Tower Moscow Project in Accordance with the Party Line

In early May 2017, Cohen received requests from Congress to provide testimony and documents in connection with congressional investigations of Russian interference in the 2016 election.[953] At that time, Cohen understood Congress's interest in him to be focused on the allegations in the Steele reporting concerning a meeting Cohen allegedly had with Russian officials in Prague during the campaign.[954] Cohen had never traveled to Prague and was not concerned about those allegations, which he believed were provably false.[955] On May 18, 2017, Cohen met with the President to discuss the request from Congress, and the President instructed Cohen that he should cooperate because there was nothing there.[956]

Cohen eventually entered into a joint defense agreement (JDA) with the President and other individuals who were part of the Russia investigation.[957] In the months leading up to his congressional testimony, Cohen frequently spoke with the President's personal counsel.[958] Cohen

---

[950] Cohen 9/18/18 302, at 5-6.

[951] Cohen 9/18/18 302, at 6.

[952] Cohen 9/12/18 302, at 10.

[953] P-SCO-000000328 (5/9/17 Letter, HPSCI to Cohen); P-SCO-000000331 (5/12/17 Letter, SSCI to Cohen).

[954] Cohen 11/20/18 302, at 2-3.

[955] Cohen 11/20/18 302, at 2-3.

[956] Cohen 11/12/18 302, at 2; Cohen 11/20/19 302, at 3.

[957] Cohen 11/12/18 302, at 2.

[958] Cohen 11/12/18 302, at 2-3; Cohen 11/20/18, at 2-6. Cohen told investigators about his conversations with the President's personal counsel after waiving any privilege of his own and after this Office advised his counsel not to provide any communications that would be covered by any other privilege, including communications protected by a joint defense or common interest privilege. As a result, most of what Cohen told us about his conversations with the President's personal counsel concerned what Cohen had communicated to the President's personal counsel, and not what was said in response. Cohen described certain statements made by the President's personal counsel, however, that are set forth in this section. Cohen and his counsel were better positioned than this Office to evaluate whether any privilege protected those statements because they had knowledge of the scope of their joint defense agreement and access to privileged communications that may have provided context for evaluating the statements they shared. After interviewing Cohen about these matters, we asked the President's personal counsel if he wished to provide information to us about his conversations with Cohen related to Cohen's congressional testimony about

U.S. Department of Justice

~~Attorney Work Product // May Contain Material Protected Under Fed. R. Crim. P. 6(e)~~

said that in those conversations the President's personal counsel would sometimes say that he had just been with the President.[959] Cohen recalled that the President's personal counsel told him the JDA was working well together and assured him that there was nothing there and if they stayed on message the investigations would come to an end soon.[960] At that time, Cohen's legal bills were being paid by the Trump Organization,[961] and Cohen was told not to worry because the investigations would be over by summer or fall of 2017.[962] Cohen said that the President's personal counsel also conveyed that, as part of the JDA, Cohen was protected, which he would not be if he "went rogue."[963] Cohen recalled that the President's personal counsel reminded him that "the President loves you" and told him that if he stayed on message, the President had his back.[964]

In August 2017, Cohen began drafting a statement about Trump Tower Moscow to submit to Congress along with his document production.[965] The final version of the statement contained several false statements about the project.[966] First, although the Trump Organization continued to pursue the project until at least June 2016, the statement said, "The proposal was under consideration at the Trump Organization from September 2015 until the end of January 2016. By the end of January 2016, I determined that the proposal was not feasible for a variety of business reasons and should not be pursued further. Based on my business determinations, the Trump Organization abandoned the proposal."[967] Second, although Cohen and candidate Trump had discussed possible travel to Russia by Trump to pursue the venture, the statement said, "Despite overtures by Mr. Sater, I never considered asking Mr. Trump to travel to Russia in connection with this proposal. I told Mr. Sater that Mr. Trump would not travel to Russia unless there was a definitive agreement in place."[968] Third, although Cohen had regularly briefed Trump on the status

---

Trump Tower Moscow. The President's personal counsel declined and, through his own counsel, indicated that he could not disaggregate information he had obtained from Cohen from information he had obtained from other parties in the JDA. In view of the admonition this Office gave to Cohen's counsel to withhold communications that could be covered by privilege, the President's personal counsel's uncertainty about the provenance of his own knowledge, the burden on a privilege holder to establish the elements to support a claim of privilege, and the substance of the statements themselves, we have included relevant statements Cohen provided in this report. If the statements were to be used in a context beyond this report, further analysis could be warranted.

[959] Cohen 11/20/18 302, at 6.

[960] Cohen 11/20/18 302, at 2, 4.

[961] Cohen 11/20/18 302, at 4.

[962] Cohen 9/18/18 302, at 8; Cohen 11/20/18 302, at 3-4.

[963] Cohen 11/20/18 302, at 4.

[964] Cohen 9/18/18 302, at 11; Cohen 11/20/18 302, at 2.

[965] P-SCO-000003680 and P-SCO-0000003687 (8/16/17 Email and Attachment, Michael Cohen's Counsel to Cohen). Cohen said it was not his idea to write a letter to Congress about Trump Tower Moscow. Cohen 9/18/18 302, at 7.

[966] P-SCO-00009478 (Statement of Michael D. Cohen, Esq. (Aug. 28, 2017)).

[967] P-SCO-00009478 (Statement of Michael D. Cohen, Esq. (Aug. 28, 2017)).

[968] P-SCO-00009478 (Statement of Michael D. Cohen, Esq. (Aug. 28, 2017)).

U.S. Department of Justice

~~Attorney Work Product // May Contain Material Protected Under Fed. R. Crim. P. 6(e)~~

of the project and had numerous conversations about it, the statement said, "Mr. Trump was never in contact with anyone about this proposal other than me on three occasions, including signing a non-binding letter of intent in 2015."[969] Fourth, although Cohen's outreach to Peskov in January 2016 had resulted in a lengthy phone call with a representative from the Kremlin, the statement said that Cohen did "not recall any response to my email [to Peskov], nor any other contacts by me with Mr. Peskov or other Russian government officials about the proposal."[970]

Cohen's statement was circulated in advance to, and edited by, members of the JDA.[971] Before the statement was finalized, early drafts contained a sentence stating, "The building project led me to make limited contacts with Russian government officials."[972] In the final version of the statement, that line was deleted.[973] Cohen thought he was told that it was a decision of the JDA to take out that sentence, and he did not push back on the deletion.[974] Cohen recalled that he told the President's personal counsel that he would not contest a decision of the JDA.[975]

Cohen also recalled that in drafting his statement for Congress, he spoke with the President's personal counsel about a different issue that connected candidate Trump to Russia: Cohen's efforts to set up a meeting between Trump and Putin in New York during the 2015 United Nations General Assembly.[976] In September 2015, Cohen had suggested the meeting to Trump, who told Cohen to reach out to Putin's office about it.[977] Cohen spoke and emailed with a Russian official about a possible meeting, and recalled that Trump asked him multiple times for updates on the proposed meeting with Putin.[978] When Cohen called the Russian official a second time, she told him it would not follow proper protocol for Putin to meet with Trump, and Cohen relayed that

---

[969] P-SCO-00009478 (Statement of Michael D. Cohen, Esq. (Aug. 28, 2017)).

[970] P-SCO-00009478 (Statement of Michael D. Cohen, Esq. (Aug. 28, 2017)).

[971] Cohen 9/12/18 302, at 8-9. Cohen also testified in Congress that the President's counsel reviewed and edited the statement. *Hearing on Issues Related to Trump Organization Before the House Oversight and Reform Committee*, 116th Cong. (Feb. 27, 2019) (CQ Cong. Transcripts, at 24-25) (testimony by Michael Cohen). Because of concerns about the common interest privilege, we did not obtain or review all drafts of Cohen's statement. Based on the drafts that were released through this Office's filter process, it appears that the substance of the four principal false statements described above were contained in an early draft prepared by Cohen and his counsel. P-SCO-0000003680 and P-SCO-0000003687 (8/16/17 Email and Attachment, Cohen's counsel to Cohen).

[972] P-SCO-0000003687 (8/16/17 Draft Statement of Michael Cohen); Cohen 11/20/18 302, at 4.

[973] Cohen 11/20/18 302, at 4. A different line stating that Cohen did "not recall any response to my email [to Peskov in January 2016], nor any other contacts by me with Mr. Peskov or other Russian government officials about the proposal" remained in the draft. *See* P-SCO-0000009478 (Statement of Michael D. Cohen, Esq. (Aug. 28, 2017)).

[974] Cohen 11/20/18 302, at 4.

[975] Cohen 11/20/18 302, at 5.

[976] Cohen 9/18/18 302, at 10-11.

[977] Cohen 9/18/18 302, at 11; Cohen 11/12/18 302, at 4.

[978] Cohen 9/18/18 302, at 11; Cohen 11/12/18 302, at 5.

U.S. Department of Justice

Attorney Work Product // May Contain Material Protected Under Fed. R. Crim. P. 6(e)

message to Trump.[979] Cohen anticipated he might be asked questions about the proposed Trump-Putin meeting when he testified before Congress because he had talked about the potential meeting on Sean Hannity's radio show.[980] Cohen recalled explaining to the President's personal counsel the "whole story" of the attempt to set up a meeting between Trump and Putin and Trump's role in it.[981] Cohen recalled that he and the President's personal counsel talked about keeping Trump out of the narrative, and the President's personal counsel told Cohen the story was not relevant and should not be included in his statement to Congress.[982]

Cohen said that his "agenda" in submitting the statement to Congress with false representations about the Trump Tower Moscow project was to minimize links between the project and the President, give the false impression that the project had ended before the first presidential primaries, and shut down further inquiry into Trump Tower Moscow, with the aim of limiting the ongoing Russia investigations.[983] Cohen said he wanted to protect the President and be loyal to him by not contradicting anything the President had said.[984] Cohen recalled he was concerned that if he told the truth about getting a response from the Kremlin or speaking to candidate Trump about travel to Russia to pursue the project, he would contradict the message that no connection existed between Trump and Russia, and he rationalized his decision to provide false testimony because the deal never happened.[985] He was not concerned that the story would be contradicted by individuals who knew it was false because he was sticking to the party line adhered to by the whole group.[986] Cohen wanted the support of the President and the White House, and he believed that following the party line would help put an end to the Special Counsel and congressional investigations.[987]

Between August 18, 2017, when the statement was in an initial draft stage, and August 28, 2017, when the statement was submitted to Congress, phone records reflect that Cohen spoke with the President's personal counsel almost daily.[988] On August 27, 2017, the day before Cohen

---

[979] Cohen 11/12/18 302, at 5.

[980] Cohen 9/18/18 302, at 11.

[981] Cohen 3/19/19 302, at 2.

[982] Cohen 3/19/19 302, at 2; see Cohen 9/18/18 302, at 11 (recalling that he was told that if he stayed on message and kept the President out of the narrative, the President would have his back).

[983] Cohen 9/12/18 302, at 8; Information at 4-5, United States v. Michael Cohen, 1:18-cr-850 (S.D.N.Y. Nov. 29, 2018), Doc. 2 (Cohen Information).

[984] Cohen 11/20/18 302, at 4.

[985] Cohen 11/20/18 302, at 4; Cohen 11/12/18 302, at 2-3, 4, 6.

[986] Cohen 9/12/18 302, at 9.

[987] Cohen 9/12/18 302, at 8-9.

[988] Cohen 11/12/18 302, at 2-3; Cohen 11/20/18 302, at 5; Call Records of Michael Cohen (Reflecting three contacts on August 18, 2017 (24 seconds; 5 minutes 25 seconds; and 10 minutes 58 seconds); two contacts on August 19 (23 seconds and 24 minutes 26 seconds); three contacts on August 23 (8 seconds; 20 minutes 33 seconds; and 5 minutes 8 seconds); one contact on August 24 (11 minutes 59 seconds); 14 contacts on August 27 (28 seconds; 4 minutes 37 seconds; 1 minute 16 seconds; 1 minutes 35

U.S. Department of Justice

~~Attorney Work Product // May Contain Material Protected Under Fed. R. Crim. P. 6(e)~~

submitted the statement to Congress, Cohen and the President's personal counsel had numerous contacts by phone, including calls lasting three, four, six, eleven, and eighteen minutes.[989] Cohen recalled telling the President's personal counsel, who did not have first-hand knowledge of the project, that there was more detail on Trump Tower Moscow that was not in the statement, including that there were more communications with Russia and more communications with candidate Trump than the statement reflected.[990] Cohen stated that the President's personal counsel responded that it was not necessary to elaborate or include those details because the project did not progress and that Cohen should keep his statement short and "tight" and the matter would soon come to an end.[991] Cohen recalled that the President's personal counsel said "his client" appreciated Cohen, that Cohen should stay on message and not contradict the President, that there was no need to muddy the water, and that it was time to move on.[992] Cohen said he agreed because it was what he was expected to do.[993] After Cohen later pleaded guilty to making false statements to Congress about the Trump Tower Moscow project, this Office sought to speak with the President's personal counsel about these conversations with Cohen, but counsel declined, citing potential privilege concerns.[994]

At the same time that Cohen finalized his written submission to Congress, he served as a source for a Washington Post story published on August 27, 2017, that reported in depth for the first time that the Trump Organization was "pursuing a plan to develop a massive Trump Tower in Moscow" at the same time as candidate Trump was "running for president in late 2015 and early 2016."[995] The article reported that "the project was abandoned at the end of January 2016, just before the presidential primaries began, several people familiar with the proposal said."[996] Cohen recalled that in speaking to the Post, he held to the false story that negotiations for the deal ceased in January 2016.[997]

---

seconds; 6 minutes 16 seconds; 1 minutes 10 seconds; 3 minutes 5 seconds; 18 minutes 55 seconds; 4 minutes 56 seconds; 11 minutes 6 seconds; 8 seconds; 3 seconds; 2 seconds; 2 seconds).

[989] Cohen 11/20/18 302, at 5; Call Records of Michael Cohen. (Reflecting 14 contacts on August 27, 2017 (28 seconds; 4 minutes 37 seconds; 1 minute 16 seconds; 1 minutes 35 seconds; 6 minutes 16 seconds; 1 minutes 10 seconds; 3 minutes 5 seconds; 18 minutes 55 seconds; 4 minutes 56 seconds; 11 minutes 6 seconds; 8 seconds; 3 seconds; 2 seconds; 2 seconds)).

[990] Cohen 11/20/18 302, at 5.

[991] Cohen 11/20/18 302, at 5. Cohen also vaguely recalled telling the President's personal counsel that he spoke with a woman from the Kremlin and that the President's personal counsel responded to the effect of "so what?" because the deal never happened. Cohen 11/20/18 302, at 5.

[992] Cohen 11/20/18 302, at 5.

[993] Cohen 11/20/18 302, at 5.

[994] 2/8/19 email, Counsel for personal counsel to the President to Special Counsel's Office.

[995] Cohen 9/18/18 302, at 7; Carol D. Leonnig et al., *Trump's business sought deal on a Trump Tower in Moscow while he ran for president*, Washington Post (Aug. 27, 2017).

[996] Carol D. Leonnig et al., *Trump's business sought deal on a Trump Tower in Moscow while he ran for president*, Washington Post (Aug. 27, 2017).

[997] Cohen 9/18/18 302, at 7.

U.S. Department of Justice

~~Attorney Work Product // May Contain Material Protected Under Fed. R. Crim. P. 6(e)~~

On August 28, 2017, Cohen submitted his statement about the Trump Tower Moscow project to Congress.[998] Cohen did not recall talking to the President about the specifics of what the statement said or what Cohen would later testify to about Trump Tower Moscow.[999] He recalled speaking to the President more generally about how he planned to stay on message in his testimony.[1000] On September 19, 2017, in anticipation of his impending testimony, Cohen orchestrated the public release of his opening remarks to Congress, which criticized the allegations in the Steele material and claimed that the Trump Tower Moscow project "was terminated in January of 2016; which occurred before the Iowa caucus and months before the very first primary."[1001] Cohen said the release of his opening remarks was intended to shape the narrative and let other people who might be witnesses know what Cohen was saying so they could follow the same message.[1002] Cohen said his decision was meant to mirror Jared Kushner's decision to release a statement in advance of Kushner's congressional testimony, which the President's personal counsel had told Cohen the President liked.[1003] Cohen recalled that on September 20, 2017, after Cohen's opening remarks had been printed by the media, the President's personal counsel told him that the President was pleased with the Trump Tower Moscow statement that had gone out.[1004]

On October 24 and 25, 2017, Cohen testified before Congress and repeated the false statements he had included in his written statement about Trump Tower Moscow.[1005] Phone records show that Cohen spoke with the President's personal counsel immediately after his testimony on both days.[1006]

4. The President Sends Messages of Support to Cohen

In January 2018, the media reported that Cohen had arranged a $130,000 payment during the campaign to prevent a woman from publicly discussing an alleged sexual encounter she had

---

[998] P-SCO-000009477 - 9478 (8/28/17 Letter and Attachment, Cohen to SSCI).

[999] Cohen 11/12/18 302, at 2; Cohen 9/12/18 302, at 9.

[1000] Cohen 9/12/18 302, at 9.

[1001] Cohen 9/18/18 302, at 7; *see, e.g.*, *READ: Michael Cohen's statement to the Senate intelligence committee*, CNN (Sept. 19, 2017).

[1002] Cohen 9/18/18 302, at 7.

[1003] Cohen 9/18/18 302, at 7; Cohen 11/20/18 302, at 6.

[1004] Cohen 11/20/18 302, at 6. Phone records show that the President's personal counsel called Cohen on the morning of September 20, 2017, and they spoke for approximately 11 minutes, and that they had two more contacts that day, one of which lasted approximately 18 minutes. Call Records of Michael Cohen. (Reflecting three contacts on September 20, 2017, with calls lasting for 11 minutes 3 seconds; 2 seconds; and 18 minutes 38 seconds).

[1005] *Cohen* Information, at 4; Executive Session, Permanent Select Committee on Intelligence, U.S. House of Representatives, Interview of Michael Cohen (Oct. 24, 2017), at 10-11, 117-119.

[1006] Call Records of Michael Cohen. (Reflecting two contacts on October 24, 2017 (12 minutes 8 seconds and 8 minutes 27 seconds) and three contacts on October 25, 2017 (1 second; 4 minutes 6 seconds; and 6 minutes 6 seconds)).

U.S. Department of Justice

~~Attorney Work Product // May Contain Material Protected Under Fed. R. Crim. P. 6(e)~~

with the President before he ran for office.[1007] This Office did not investigate Cohen's campaign-period payments to women.[1008] However, those events, as described here, are potentially relevant to the President's and his personal counsel's interactions with Cohen as a witness who later began to cooperate with the government.

On February 13, 2018, Cohen released a statement to news organizations that stated, "In a private transaction in 2016, I used my own personal funds to facilitate a payment of $130,000 to [the woman]. Neither the Trump Organization nor the Trump campaign was a party to the transaction with [the woman], and neither reimbursed me for the payment, either directly or indirectly."[1009] In congressional testimony on February 27, 2019, Cohen testified that he had discussed what to say about the payment with the President and that the President had directed Cohen to say that the President "was not knowledgeable . . . of [Cohen's] actions" in making the payment.[1010] On February 19, 2018, the day after the New York Times wrote a detailed story attributing the payment to Cohen and describing Cohen as the President's "fixer," Cohen received a text message from the President's personal counsel that stated, "Client says thanks for what you do."[1011]

On April 9, 2018, FBI agents working with the U.S. Attorney's Office for the Southern District of New York executed search warrants on Cohen's home, hotel room, and office.[1012] That day, the President spoke to reporters and said that he had "just heard that they broke into the office of one of my personal attorneys—a good man."[1013] The President called the searches "a real disgrace" and said, "It's an attack on our country, in a true sense. It's an attack on what we all

---

[1007] *See, e.g.*, Michael Rothfeld & Joe Palazzolo, *Trump Lawyer Arranged $130,000 Payment for Adult-Film Star's Silence*, Wall Street Journal (Jan. 12, 2018).

[1008] The Office was authorized to investigate Cohen's establishment and use of Essential Consultants LLC, which Cohen created to facilitate the $130,000 payment during the campaign, based on evidence that the entity received funds from Russian-backed entities. Cohen's use of Essential Consultants to facilitate the $130,000 payment to the woman during the campaign was part of the Office's referral of certain Cohen-related matters to the U.S. Attorney's Office for the Southern District of New York.

[1009] *See, e.g.*, Mark Berman, *Longtime Trump attorney says he made $130,000 payment to Stormy Daniels with his money*, Washington Post (Feb. 14, 2018).

[1010] *Hearing on Issues Related to Trump Organization Before the House Oversight and Reform Committee*, 116th Cong. (Feb. 27, 2019) (CQ Cong. Transcripts, at 147-148) (testimony of Michael Cohen). Toll records show that Cohen was connected to a White House phone number for approximately five minutes on January 19, 2018, and for approximately seven minutes on January 30, 2018, and that Cohen called Melania Trump's cell phone several times between January 26, 2018, and January 30, 2018. Call Records of Michael Cohen.

[1011] 2/19/18 Text Message, President's personal counsel to Cohen; *see* Jim Rutenberg et al., *Tools of Trump's Fixer: Payouts, Intimidation and the Tabloids*, New York Times (Feb. 18, 2018).

[1012] Gov't Opp. to Def. Mot. for Temp. Restraining Order, *In the Matter of Search Warrants Executed on April 9, 2018*, 18-mj-3161 (S.D.N.Y. Apr. 13, 2018), Doc. 1 ("On April 9, 2018, agents from the New York field office of the Federal Bureau of Investigation . . . executed search warrants for Michael Cohen's residence, hotel room, office, safety deposit box, and electronic devices.").

[1013] Remarks by President Trump Before Meeting with Senior Military Leadership, White House (Apr. 9, 2018).

U.S. Department of Justice

~~Attorney Work Product // May Contain Material Protected Under Fed. R. Crim. P. 6(e)~~

stand for."[1014] Cohen said that after the searches he was concerned that he was "an open book," that he did not want issues arising from the payments to women to "come out," and that his false statements to Congress were "a big concern."[1015]

A few days after the searches, the President called Cohen.[1016] According to Cohen, the President said he wanted to "check in" and asked if Cohen was okay, and the President encouraged Cohen to "hang in there" and "stay strong."[1017] Cohen also recalled that following the searches he heard from individuals who were in touch with the President and relayed to Cohen the President's support for him.[1018] Cohen recalled that ▮▮▮▮▮▮▮▮, a friend of the President's, reached out to say that he was with "the Boss" in Mar-a-Lago and the President had said "he loves you" and not to worry.[1019] Cohen recalled that ▮▮▮▮▮▮▮▮▮▮ for the Trump Organization, told him, "the boss loves you."[1020] And Cohen said that ▮▮▮▮▮▮▮▮, a friend of the President's, told him, "everyone knows the boss has your back."[1021]

On or about April 17, 2018, Cohen began speaking with an attorney, Robert Costello, who had a close relationship with Rudolph Giuliani, one of the President's personal lawyers.[1022] Costello told Cohen that he had a "back channel of communication" to Giuliani, and that Giuliani had said the "channel" was "crucial" and "must be maintained."[1023] On April 20, 2018, the New York Times published an article about the President's relationship with and treatment of Cohen.[1024] The President responded with a series of tweets predicting that Cohen would not "flip":

> The New York Times and a third rate reporter . . . are going out of their way to destroy Michael Cohen and his relationship with me in the hope that he will 'flip.' They use non-existent 'sources' and a drunk/drugged up loser who hates Michael, a fine person with a wonderful family. Michael is a businessman for his own account/lawyer who I have always liked & respected. Most people will flip if the Government lets them out of trouble, even

---

[1014] Remarks by President Trump Before Meeting with Senior Military Leadership, White House (Apr. 9, 2018).

[1015] Cohen, 10/17/18 302, at 11.

[1016] Cohen 3/19/19 302, at 4.

[1017] Cohen 3/19/19 302, at 4.

[1018] Cohen 9/12/18 302, at 11.

[1019] Cohen 9/12/18 302, at 11.

[1020] Cohen 9/12/18 302, at 11.

[1021] Cohen 9/12/18 302, at 11.

[1022] 4/17/18 Email, Citron to Cohen; 4/19/18 Email, Costello to Cohen; MC-SCO-001 (7/7/18 redacted billing statement from Davidoff, Hutcher & Citron to Cohen).

[1023] 4/21/18 Email, Costello to Cohen.

[1024] See Maggie Haberman et al., *Michael Cohen Has Said He Would Take a Bullet for Trump. Maybe Not Anymore.*, New York Times (Apr. 20, 2018).

U.S. Department of Justice

~~Attorney Work Product // May Contain Material Protected Under Fed. R. Crim. P. 6(e)~~

if it means lying or making up stories. Sorry, I don't see Michael doing that despite the horrible Witch Hunt and the dishonest media![1025]

In an email that day to Cohen, Costello wrote that he had spoken with Giuliani.[1026] Costello told Cohen the conversation was "Very Very Positive[.] You are 'loved'. . . they are in our corner. . . . Sleep well tonight[], you have friends in high places."[1027]

Cohen said that following these messages he believed he had the support of the White House if he continued to toe the party line, and he determined to stay on message and be part of the team.[1028] At the time, Cohen's understood that his legal fees were still being paid by the Trump Organization, which he said was important to him.[1029] Cohen believed he needed the power of the President to take care of him, so he needed to defend the President and stay on message.[1030]

Cohen also recalled speaking with the President's personal counsel about pardons after the searches of his home and office had occurred, at a time when the media had reported that pardon discussions were occurring at the White House.[1031] Cohen told the President's personal counsel he had been a loyal lawyer and servant, and he said that after the searches he was in an uncomfortable position and wanted to know what was in it for him.[1032] According to Cohen, the President's personal counsel responded that Cohen should stay on message, that the investigation was a witch hunt, and that everything would be fine.[1033] Cohen understood based on this conversation and previous conversations about pardons with the President's personal counsel that as long as he stayed on message, he would be taken care of by the President, either through a pardon or through the investigation being shut down.[1034]

[1025] @realDonaldTrump 4/21/18 (9:10 a.m. ET) Tweets.

[1026] 4/21/18 Email, Costello to Cohen.

[1027] 4/21/18 Email, Costello to Cohen. ■■■■■■■■■■

[1028] Cohen 9/12/18 302, at 11.

[1029] Cohen 9/12/18 302, at 10.

[1030] Cohen 9/12/18 302, at 10.

[1031] Cohen 11/20/18 302, at 7. At a White House press briefing on April 23, 2018, in response to a question about whether the White House had "close[d] the door one way or the other on the President pardoning Michael Cohen," Sanders said, "It's hard to close the door on something that hasn't taken place. I don't like to discuss or comment on hypothetical situations that may or may not ever happen. I would refer you to personal attorneys to comment on anything specific regarding that case, but we don't have anything at this point." Sarah Sanders, *White House Daily Briefing*, C-SPAN (Apr. 23, 2018).

[1032] Cohen 11/20/18 302, at 7; Cohen 3/19/19 302, at 3.

[1033] Cohen 3/19/19 302, at 3.

[1034] Cohen 3/19/19 302, at 3-4.

U.S. Department of Justice

~~Attorney Work Product // May Contain Material Protected Under Fed. R. Crim. P. 6(e)~~

On April 24, 2018, the President responded to a reporter's inquiry whether he would consider a pardon for Cohen with, "Stupid question."[1035] On June 8, 2018, the President said he "hadn't even thought about" pardons for Manafort or Cohen, and continued, "It's far too early to be thinking about that. They haven't been convicted of anything. There's nothing to pardon."[1036] And on June 15, 2018, the President expressed sympathy for Cohen, Manafort, and Flynn in a press interview and said, "I feel badly about a lot of them, because I think a lot of it is very unfair."[1037]

5. The President's Conduct After Cohen Began Cooperating with the Government

On July 2, 2018, ABC News reported based on an "exclusive" interview with Cohen that Cohen "strongly signaled his willingness to cooperate with special counsel Robert Mueller and federal prosecutors in the Southern District of New York—even if that puts President Trump in jeopardy."[1038] That week, the media reported that Cohen had added an attorney to his legal team who previously had worked as a legal advisor to President Bill Clinton.[1039]

Beginning on July 20, 2018, the media reported on the existence of a recording Cohen had made of a conversation he had with candidate Trump about a payment made to a second woman who said she had had an affair with Trump.[1040] On July 21, 2018, the President responded: "Inconceivable that the government would break into a lawyer's office (early in the morning)—almost unheard of. Even more inconceivable that a lawyer would tape a client—totally unheard of & perhaps illegal. The good news is that your favorite President did nothing wrong!"[1041] On July 27, 2018, after the media reported that Cohen was willing to inform investigators that Donald Trump Jr. told his father about the June 9, 2016 meeting to get "dirt" on Hillary Clinton,[1042] the President tweeted: "[S]o the Fake News doesn't waste my time with dumb questions, NO, I did NOT know of the meeting with my son, Don jr. Sounds to me like someone is trying to make up

---

[1035] Remarks by President Trump and President Macron of France Before Restricted Bilateral Meeting, The White House (Apr. 24, 2018).

[1036] *President Donald Trump Holds Media Availability Before Departing for the G-7 Summit*, CQ Newsmaker Transcripts (June 8, 2018).

[1037] Remarks by President Trump in Press Gaggle, The White House (June 15, 2018).

[1038] *EXCLUSIVE: Michael Cohen says family and country, not President Trump, is his 'first loyalty'*, ABC (July 2, 2018). Cohen said in the interview, "To be crystal clear, my wife, my daughter and my son, and this country have my first loyalty."

[1039] *See e.g.*, Darren Samuelsohn, *Michael Cohen hires Clinton scandal veteran Lanny Davis*, Politico (July 5, 2018).

[1040] *See, e.g.*, Matt Apuzzo et al., *Michael Cohen Secretly Taped Trump Discussing Payment to Playboy Model*, New York Times (July 20, 2018).

[1041] @realDonaldTrump 7/21/18 (8:10 a.m. ET) Tweet.

[1042] *See, e.g.*, Jim Sciutto, *Cuomo Prime Time Transcript*, CNN (July 26, 2018).

U.S. Department of Justice

~~Attorney Work Product // May Contain Material Protected Under Fed. R. Crim. P. 6(e)~~

stories in order to get himself out of an unrelated jam (Taxi cabs maybe?). He even retained Bill and Crooked Hillary's lawyer. Gee, I wonder if they helped him make the choice!"[1043]

On August 21, 2018, Cohen pleaded guilty in the Southern District of New York to eight felony charges, including two counts of campaign-finance violations based on the payments he had made during the final weeks of the campaign to women who said they had affairs with the President.[1044] During the plea hearing, Cohen stated that he had worked "at the direction of" the candidate in making those payments.[1045] The next day, the President contrasted Cohen's cooperation with Manafort's refusal to cooperate, tweeting, "I feel very badly for Paul Manafort and his wonderful family. 'Justice' took a 12 year old tax case, among other things, applied tremendous pressure on him and, unlike Michael Cohen, he refused to 'break'—make up stories in order to get a 'deal.' Such respect for a brave man!"[1046]

On September 17, 2018, this Office submitted written questions to the President that included questions about the Trump Tower Moscow project and attached Cohen's written statement to Congress and the Letter of Intent signed by the President.[1047] Among other issues, the questions asked the President to describe the timing and substance of discussions he had with Cohen about the project, whether they discussed a potential trip to Russia, and whether the President "at any time direct[ed] or suggest[ed] that discussions about the Trump Moscow project should cease," or whether the President was "informed at any time that the project had been abandoned."[1048]

On November 20, 2018, the President submitted written responses that did not answer those questions about Trump Tower Moscow directly and did not provide any information about the timing of the candidate's discussions with Cohen about the project or whether he participated in any discussions about the project being abandoned or no longer pursued.[1049] Instead, the President's answers stated in relevant part:

> I had few conversations with Mr. Cohen on this subject. As I recall, they were brief, and they were not memorable. I was not enthused about the proposal, and I do not recall any discussion of travel to Russia in connection with it. I do not remember discussing it with

---

[1043] @realDonaldTrump 7/27/18 (7:26 a.m. ET) Tweet; @realDonaldTrump 7/27/18 (7:38 a.m. ET) Tweet; @realDonaldTrump 7/27/18 (7:56 a.m. ET) Tweet. At the time of these tweets, the press had reported that Cohen's financial interests in taxi cab medallions were being scrutinized by investigators. *See, e.g.*, Matt Apuzzo et al., *Michael Cohen Secretly Taped Trump Discussing Payment to Playboy Model*, New York Times (July 20, 2018).

[1044] *Cohen* Information.

[1045] *Cohen* 8/21/18 Transcript, at 23.

[1046] @realDonaldTrump 8/22/18 (9:21 a.m. ET) Tweet.

[1047] 9/17/18 Letter, Special Counsel's Office to President's Personal Counsel (attaching written questions for the President, with attachments).

[1048] 9/17/18 Letter, Special Counsel's Office to President's Personal Counsel (attaching written questions for the President), Question III, Parts (a) through (g).

[1049] Written Responses of Donald J. Trump (Nov. 20, 2018).

anyone else at the Trump Organization, although it is possible. I do not recall being aware at the time of any communications between Mr. Cohen and Felix Sater and any Russian government official regarding the Letter of Intent.[1050]

On November 29, 2018, Cohen pleaded guilty to making false statements to Congress based on his statements about the Trump Tower Moscow project.[1051] In a plea agreement with this Office, Cohen agreed to "provide truthful information regarding any and all matters as to which this Office deems relevant."[1052] Later on November 29, after Cohen's guilty plea had become public, the President spoke to reporters about the Trump Tower Moscow project, saying:

> I decided not to do the project. . . . I decided ultimately not to do it. There would have been nothing wrong if I did do it. If I did do it, there would have been nothing wrong. That was my business. . . . It was an option that I decided not to do. . . . I decided not to do it. The primary reason . . . I was focused on running for President. . . . I was running my business while I was campaigning. There was a good chance that I wouldn't have won, in which case I would've gone back into the business. And why should I lose lots of opportunities?[1053]

The President also said that Cohen was "a weak person. And by being weak, unlike other people that you watch—he is a weak person. And what he's trying to do is get a reduced sentence. So he's lying about a project that everybody knew about."[1054] The President also brought up Cohen's written submission to Congress regarding the Trump Tower Moscow project: "So here's the story: Go back and look at the paper that Michael Cohen wrote before he testified in the House and/or Senate. It talked about his position."[1055] The President added, "Even if [Cohen] was right, it doesn't matter because I was allowed to do whatever I wanted during the campaign."[1056]

In light of the President's public statements following Cohen's guilty plea that he "decided not to do the project," this Office again sought information from the President about whether he participated in any discussions about the project being abandoned or no longer pursued, including when he "decided not to do the project," who he spoke to about that decision, and what motivated

---

[1050] Written Responses of Donald J. Trump (Nov. 20, 2018), at 15 (Response to Question III, Parts (a) through (g)).

[1051] *Cohen* Information; *Cohen* 8/21/18 Transcript.

[1052] Plea Agreement at 4, *United States v. Michael Cohen*, 1 18-cr-850 (S.D.N.Y. Nov. 29, 2018).

[1053] *President Trump Departure Remarks*, C-SPAN (Nov. 29, 2018). In contrast to the President's remarks following Cohen's guilty plea, Cohen's August 28, 2017 statement to Congress stated that Cohen, not the President, "decided to abandon the proposal" in late January 2016; that Cohen "did not ask or brief Mr. Trump . . . before I made the decision to terminate further work on the proposal"; and that the decision to abandon the proposal was "unrelated" to the Campaign. P-SCO-000009477 (Statement of Michael D. Cohen, Esq. (Aug. 28, 2017)).

[1054] *President Trump Departure Remarks*, C-SPAN (Nov. 29, 2018).

[1055] *President Trump Departure Remarks*, C-SPAN (Nov. 29, 2018).

[1056] *President Trump Departure Remarks*, C-SPAN (Nov. 29, 2018).

the decision.[1057] The Office also again asked for the timing of the President's discussions with Cohen about Trump Tower Moscow and asked him to specify "what period of the campaign" he was involved in discussions concerning the project.[1058] In response, the President's personal counsel declined to provide additional information from the President and stated that "the President has fully answered the questions at issue."[1059]

In the weeks following Cohen's plea and agreement to provide assistance to this Office, the President repeatedly implied that Cohen's family members were guilty of crimes. On December 3, 2018, after Cohen had filed his sentencing memorandum, the President tweeted, "'Michael Cohen asks judge for no Prison Time.' You mean he can do all of the TERRIBLE, unrelated to Trump, things having to do with fraud, big loans, Taxis, etc., and not serve a long prison term? He makes up stories to get a GREAT & ALREADY reduced deal for himself, and *get his wife and father-in-law (who has the money?) off Scott Free*. He lied for this outcome and should, in my opinion, serve a full and complete sentence."[1060]

On December 12, 2018, Cohen was sentenced to three years of imprisonment.[1062] The next day, the President sent a series of tweets that said:

> I never directed Michael Cohen to break the law. . . . Those charges were just agreed to by him in order to embarrass the president and get a much reduced prison sentence, which he did—including the fact that *his family was temporarily let off the hook*. As a lawyer, Michael has great liability to me![1063]

On December 16, 2018, the President tweeted, "Remember, Michael Cohen only became a 'Rat' after the FBI did something which was absolutely unthinkable & unheard of until the Witch Hunt was illegally started. They BROKE INTO AN ATTORNEY'S OFFICE! Why didn't they break into the DNC to get the Server, or Crooked's office?"[1064]

In January 2019, after the media reported that Cohen would provide public testimony in a congressional hearing, the President made additional public comments suggesting that Cohen's

---

[1057] 1/23/19 Letter, Special Counsel's Office to President's Personal Counsel.

[1058] 1/23/19 Letter, Special Counsel's Office to President's Personal Counsel.

[1059] 2/6/19 Letter, President's Personal Counsel to Special Counsel's Office.

[1060] @realDonaldTrump 12/3/18 (10:24 a.m. ET and 10:29 a.m. ET) Tweets (emphasis added).

[1061] @realDonaldTrump 12/3/18 (10:48 a.m. ET) Tweet.

[1062] *Cohen* 12/12/18 Transcript.

[1063] @realDonaldTrump 12/13/18 (8:17 a.m. ET, 8:25 a.m. ET, and 8:39 a.m. ET) Tweets (emphasis added).

[1064] @realDonaldTrump 12/16/18 (9:39 a.m. ET) Tweet.

family members had committed crimes. In an interview on Fox on January 12, 2019, the President was asked whether he was worried about Cohen's testimony and responded:

> [I]n order to get his sentence reduced, [Cohen] says "I have an idea, I'll ah, tell—I'll give you some information on the president." Well, there is no information. But *he should give information maybe on his father-in-law because that's the one that people want to look at because where does that money—that's the money in the family. And I guess he didn't want to talk about his father-in-law*, he's trying to get his sentence reduced. So it's ah, pretty sad. You know, it's weak and it's very sad to watch a thing like that.[1065]

On January 18, 2019, the President tweeted, "Kevin Corke, @FoxNews 'Don't forget, Michael Cohen has already been convicted of perjury and fraud, and as recently as this week, the Wall Street Journal has suggested that he may have stolen tens of thousands of dollars. . . .' Lying to reduce his jail time! *Watch father-in-law!*"[1066]

On January 23, 2019, Cohen postponed his congressional testimony, citing threats against his family.[1067] The next day, the President tweeted, "So interesting that bad lawyer Michael Cohen, who sadly will not be testifying before Congress, is using the lawyer of Crooked Hillary Clinton to represent him—Gee, how did that happen?"[1068]

Also in January 2019, Giuliani gave press interviews that appeared to confirm Cohen's account that the Trump Organization pursued the Trump Tower Moscow project well past January 2016. Giuliani stated that "it's our understanding that [discussions about the Trump Moscow project] went on throughout 2016. Weren't a lot of them, but there were conversations. Can't be sure of the exact date. But the president can remember having conversations with him about it. . . . The president also remembers—yeah, probably up—could be up to as far as October, November."[1069] In an interview with the New York Times, Giuliani quoted the President as saying that the discussions regarding the Trump Moscow project were "going on from the day I announced to the day I won."[1070] On January 21, 2019, Giuliani issued a statement that said: "My recent statements about discussions during the 2016 campaign between Michael Cohen and candidate Donald Trump about a potential Trump Moscow 'project' were hypothetical and not based on conversations I had with the president."[1071]

[1065] *Jeanine Pirro Interview with President Trump*, Fox News (Jan. 12, 2019) (emphasis added).

[1066] @realDonaldTrump 1/18/19 (10:02 a.m. ET) Tweet (emphasis added).

[1067] Statement by Lanny Davis, Cohen's personal counsel (Jan. 23, 2019).

[1068] @realDonaldTrump 1/24/19 (7:48 a.m. ET) Tweet.

[1069] Meet the Press Interview with Rudy Giuliani, NBC (Jan. 20, 2019).

[1070] Mark Mazzetti et al., *Moscow Skyscraper Talks Continued Through "the Day I Won,"* Trump *Is Said to Acknowledge*, New York Times (Jan. 20, 2019).

[1071] Maggie Haberman, *Giuliani Says His Moscow Trump Tower Comments Were "Hypothetical"*, New York Times (Jan. 21, 2019). In a letter to this Office, the President's counsel stated that Giuliani's public comments "were not intended to suggest nor did they reflect knowledge of the existence or timing

U.S. Department of Justice

~~Attorney Work Product // May Contain Material Protected Under Fed. R. Crim. P. 6(e)~~

Analysis

In analyzing the President's conduct related to Cohen, the following evidence is relevant to the elements of obstruction of justice.

a.   Obstructive act. We gathered evidence of the President's conduct related to Cohen on two issues: (i) whether the President or others aided or participated in Cohen's false statements to Congress, and (ii) whether the President took actions that would have the natural tendency to prevent Cohen from providing truthful information to the government.

i.   First, with regard to Cohen's false statements to Congress, while there is evidence, described below, that the President knew Cohen provided false testimony to Congress about the Trump Tower Moscow project, the evidence available to us does not establish that the President directed or aided Cohen's false testimony.

Cohen said that his statements to Congress followed a "party line" that developed within the campaign to align with the President's public statements distancing the President from Russia. Cohen also recalled that, in speaking with the President in advance of testifying, he made it clear that he would stay on message—which Cohen believed they both understood would require false testimony. But Cohen said that he and the President did not explicitly discuss whether Cohen's testimony about the Trump Tower Moscow project would be or was false, and the President did not direct him to provide false testimony. Cohen also said he did not tell the President about the specifics of his planned testimony. During the time when his statement to Congress was being drafted and circulated to members of the JDA, Cohen did not speak directly to the President about the statement, but rather communicated with the President's personal counsel—as corroborated by phone records showing extensive communications between Cohen and the President's personal counsel before Cohen submitted his statement and when he testified before Congress.

Cohen recalled that in his discussions with the President's personal counsel on August 27, 2017—the day before Cohen's statement was submitted to Congress—Cohen said that there were more communications with Russia and more communications with candidate Trump than the statement reflected. Cohen recalled expressing some concern at that time. According to Cohen, the President's personal counsel—who did not have first-hand knowledge of the project—responded by saying that there was no need to muddy the water, that it was unnecessary to include those details because the project did not take place, and that Cohen should keep his statement short and tight, not elaborate, stay on message, and not contradict the President. Cohen's recollection of the content of those conversations is consistent with direction about the substance of Cohen's draft statement that appeared to come from members of the JDA. For example, Cohen omitted any reference to his outreach to Russian government officials to set up a meeting between Trump and Putin during the United Nations General Assembly, and Cohen believed it was a decision of

_____

of conversations beyond that contained in the President's [written responses to the Special Counsel's Office]." 2/6/19 Letter, President's Personal Counsel to Special Counsel's Office.

the JDA to delete the sentence, "The building project led me to make limited contacts with Russian government officials."

The President's personal counsel declined to provide us with his account of his conversations with Cohen, and there is no evidence available to us that indicates that the President was aware of the information Cohen provided to the President's personal counsel. The President's conversations with his personal counsel were presumptively protected by attorney-client privilege, and we did not seek to obtain the contents of any such communications. The absence of evidence about the President and his counsel's conversations about the drafting of Cohen's statement precludes us from assessing what, if any, role the President played.

        ii.   **Second, we considered whether the President took actions that would have the natural tendency to prevent Cohen from providing truthful information to criminal investigators or to Congress.**

Before Cohen began to cooperate with the government, the President publicly and privately urged Cohen to stay on message and not "flip." Cohen recalled the President's personal counsel telling him that he would be protected so long as he did not go "rogue." In the days and weeks that followed the April 2018 searches of Cohen's home and office, the President told reporters that Cohen was a "good man" and said he was "a fine person with a wonderful family . . . who I have always liked & respected." Privately, the President told Cohen to "hang in there" and "stay strong." People who were close to both Cohen and the President passed messages to Cohen that "the President loves you," "the boss loves you," and "everyone knows the boss has your back." Through the President's personal counsel, the President also had previously told Cohen "thanks for what you do" after Cohen provided information to the media about payments to women that, according to Cohen, both Cohen and the President knew was false. At that time, the Trump Organization continued to pay Cohen's legal fees, which was important to Cohen. Cohen also recalled discussing the possibility of a pardon with the President's personal counsel, who told him to stay on message and everything would be fine. The President indicated in his public statements that a pardon had not been ruled out, and also stated publicly that "[m]ost people will flip if the Government lets them out of trouble" but that he "d[idn't] see Michael doing that."

After it was reported that Cohen intended to cooperate with the government, however, the President accused Cohen of "mak[ing] up stories in order to get himself out of an unrelated jam (Taxi cabs maybe?)," called Cohen a "rat," and on multiple occasions publicly suggested that Cohen's family members had committed crimes. The evidence concerning this sequence of events could support an inference that the President used inducements in the form of positive messages in an effort to get Cohen not to cooperate, and then turned to attacks and intimidation to deter the provision of information or undermine Cohen's credibility once Cohen began cooperating.

        b.   <u>Nexus to an official proceeding.</u> The President's relevant conduct towards Cohen occurred when the President knew the Special Counsel's Office, Congress, and the U.S. Attorney's Office for the Southern District of New York were investigating Cohen's conduct. The President acknowledged through his public statements and tweets that Cohen potentially could cooperate with the government investigations.

U.S. Department of Justice

~~Attorney Work Product // May Contain Material Protected Under Fed. R. Crim. P. 6(e)~~

   c. Intent. In analyzing the President's intent in his actions towards Cohen as a potential witness, there is evidence that could support the inference that the President intended to discourage Cohen from cooperating with the government because Cohen's information would shed adverse light on the President's campaign-period conduct and statements.

   i. Cohen's false congressional testimony about the Trump Tower Moscow project was designed to minimize connections between the President and Russia and to help limit the congressional and DOJ Russia investigations—a goal that was in the President's interest, as reflected by the President's own statements. During and after the campaign, the President made repeated statements that he had "no business" in Russia and said that there were "no deals that could happen in Russia, because we've stayed away." As Cohen knew, and as he recalled communicating to the President during the campaign, Cohen's pursuit of the Trump Tower Moscow project cast doubt on the accuracy or completeness of these statements.

   In connection with his guilty plea, Cohen admitted that he had multiple conversations with candidate Trump to give him status updates about the Trump Tower Moscow project, that the conversations continued through at least June 2016, and that he discussed with Trump possible travel to Russia to pursue the project. The conversations were not off-hand, according to Cohen, because the project had the potential to be so lucrative. In addition, text messages to and from Cohen and other records further establish that Cohen's efforts to advance the project did not end in January 2016 and that in May and June 2016, Cohen was considering the timing for possible trips to Russia by him and Trump in connection with the project.

   The evidence could support an inference that the President was aware of these facts at the time of Cohen's false statements to Congress. Cohen discussed the project with the President in early 2017 following media inquiries. Cohen recalled that on September 20, 2017, the day after he released to the public his opening remarks to Congress—which said the project "was terminated in January of 2016"—the President's personal counsel told him the President was pleased with what Cohen had said about Trump Tower Moscow. And after Cohen's guilty plea, the President told reporters that he had ultimately decided not to do the project, which supports the inference that he remained aware of his own involvement in the project and the period during the Campaign in which the project was being pursued.

   ii. The President's public remarks following Cohen's guilty plea also suggest that the President may have been concerned about what Cohen told investigators about the Trump Tower Moscow project. At the time the President submitted written answers to questions from this Office about the project and other subjects, the media had reported that Cohen was cooperating with the government but Cohen had not yet pleaded guilty to making false statements to Congress. Accordingly, it was not publicly known what information about the project Cohen had provided to the government. In his written answers, the President did not provide details about the timing and substance of his discussions with Cohen about the project and gave no indication that he had decided to no longer pursue the project. Yet after Cohen pleaded guilty, the President publicly stated that he had personally made the decision to abandon the project. The President then declined to clarify the seeming discrepancy to our Office or answer additional questions. The content and timing of the President's provision of information about his knowledge and actions regarding the Trump Tower Moscow project is evidence that the President may have been concerned about the information that Cohen could provide as a witness.

U.S. Department of Justice

~~Attorney Work Product~~ // ~~May Contain Material Protected Under Fed. R. Crim. P. 6(e)~~

iii.   The President's concern about Cohen cooperating may have been directed at the Southern District of New York investigation into other aspects of the President's dealings with Cohen rather than an investigation of Trump Tower Moscow. There also is some evidence that the President's concern about Cohen cooperating was based on the President's stated belief that Cohen would provide false testimony against the President in an attempt to obtain a lesser sentence for his unrelated criminal conduct. The President tweeted that Manafort, unlike Cohen, refused to "break" and "make up stories in order to get a 'deal.'" And after Cohen pleaded guilty to making false statements to Congress, the President said, "what [Cohen]'s trying to do is get a reduced sentence. So he's lying about a project that everybody knew about." But the President also appeared to defend the underlying conduct, saying, "Even if [Cohen] was right, it doesn't matter because I was allowed to do whatever I wanted during the campaign." As described above, there is evidence that the President knew that Cohen had made false statements about the Trump Tower Moscow project and that Cohen did so to protect the President and minimize the President's connections to Russia during the campaign.

iv.   Finally, the President's statements insinuating that members of Cohen's family committed crimes after Cohen began cooperating with the government could be viewed as an effort to retaliate against Cohen and chill further testimony adverse to the President by Cohen or others. It is possible that the President believes, as reflected in his tweets, that Cohen "ma[d]e[] up stories" in order to get a deal for himself and "get his wife and father-in-law . . . off Scott Free." It also is possible that the President's mention of Cohen's wife and father-in-law were not intended to affect Cohen as a witness but rather were part of a public-relations strategy aimed at discrediting Cohen and deflecting attention away from the President on Cohen-related matters. But the President's suggestion that Cohen's family members committed crimes happened more than once, including just before Cohen was sentenced (at the same time as the President stated that Cohen "should, in my opinion, serve a full and complete sentence") and again just before Cohen was scheduled to testify before Congress. The timing of the statements supports an inference that they were intended at least in part to discourage Cohen from further cooperation.

L.   Overarching Factual Issues

Although this report does not contain a traditional prosecution decision or declination decision, the evidence supports several general conclusions relevant to analysis of the facts concerning the President's course of conduct.

1. Three features of this case render it atypical compared to the heartland obstruction-of-justice prosecutions brought by the Department of Justice.

First, the conduct involved actions by the President. Some of the conduct did not implicate the President's constitutional authority and raises garden-variety obstruction-of-justice issues. Other events we investigated, however, drew upon the President's Article II authority, which raised constitutional issues that we address in Volume II, Section III.B, *infra*. A factual analysis of that conduct would have to take into account both that the President's acts were facially lawful and that his position as head of the Executive Branch provides him with unique and powerful means of influencing official proceedings, subordinate officers, and potential witnesses.

156

Second, many obstruction cases involve the attempted or actual cover-up of an underlying crime. Personal criminal conduct can furnish strong evidence that the individual had an improper obstructive purpose, *see, e.g., United States v. Willoughby*, 860 F.2d 15, 24 (2d Cir. 1988), or that he contemplated an effect on an official proceeding, *see, e.g., United States v. Binday*, 804 F.3d 558, 591 (2d Cir. 2015). But proof of such a crime is not an element of an obstruction offense. *See United States v. Greer*, 872 F.3d 790, 798 (6th Cir. 2017) (stating, in applying the obstruction sentencing guideline, that "obstruction of a criminal investigation is punishable even if the prosecution is ultimately unsuccessful or even if the investigation ultimately reveals no underlying crime"). Obstruction of justice can be motivated by a desire to protect non-criminal personal interests, to protect against investigations where underlying criminal liability falls into a gray area, or to avoid personal embarrassment. The injury to the integrity of the justice system is the same regardless of whether a person committed an underlying wrong.

In this investigation, the evidence does not establish that the President was involved in an underlying crime related to Russian election interference. But the evidence does point to a range of other possible personal motives animating the President's conduct. These include concerns that continued investigation would call into question the legitimacy of his election and potential uncertainty about whether certain events—such as advance notice of WikiLeaks's release of hacked information or the June 9, 2016 meeting between senior campaign officials and Russians—could be seen as criminal activity by the President, his campaign, or his family.

Third, many of the President's acts directed at witnesses, including discouragement of cooperation with the government and suggestions of possible future pardons, occurred in public view. While it may be more difficult to establish that public-facing acts were motivated by a corrupt intent, the President's power to influence actions, persons, and events is enhanced by his unique ability to attract attention through use of mass communications. And no principle of law excludes public acts from the scope of obstruction statutes. If the likely effect of the acts is to intimidate witnesses or alter their testimony, the justice system's integrity is equally threatened.

2. Although the events we investigated involved discrete acts—*e.g.*, the President's statement to Comey about the Flynn investigation, his termination of Comey, and his efforts to remove the Special Counsel—it is important to view the President's pattern of conduct as a whole. That pattern sheds light on the nature of the President's acts and the inferences that can be drawn about his intent.

a. Our investigation found multiple acts by the President that were capable of exerting undue influence over law enforcement investigations, including the Russian-interference and obstruction investigations. The incidents were often carried out through one-on-one meetings in which the President sought to use his official power outside of usual channels. These actions ranged from efforts to remove the Special Counsel and to reverse the effect of the Attorney General's recusal; to the attempted use of official power to limit the scope of the investigation; to direct and indirect contacts with witnesses with the potential to influence their testimony. Viewing the acts collectively can help to illuminate their significance. For example, the President's direction to McGahn to have the Special Counsel removed was followed almost immediately by his direction to Lewandowski to tell the Attorney General to limit the scope of the Russia investigation to prospective election-interference only—a temporal connection that suggests that both acts were taken with a related purpose with respect to the investigation.

157

U.S. Department of Justice

Attorney Work Product // May Contain Material Protected Under Fed. R. Crim. P. 6(e)

The President's efforts to influence the investigation were mostly unsuccessful, but that is largely because the persons who surrounded the President declined to carry out orders or accede to his requests. Comey did not end the investigation of Flynn, which ultimately resulted in Flynn's prosecution and conviction for lying to the FBI. McGahn did not tell the Acting Attorney General that the Special Counsel must be removed, but was instead prepared to resign over the President's order. Lewandowski and Dearborn did not deliver the President's message to Sessions that he should confine the Russia investigation to future election meddling only. And McGahn refused to recede from his recollections about events surrounding the President's direction to have the Special Counsel removed, despite the President's multiple demands that he do so. Consistent with that pattern, the evidence we obtained would not support potential obstruction charges against the President's aides and associates beyond those already filed.

b. In considering the full scope of the conduct we investigated, the President's actions can be divided into two distinct phases reflecting a possible shift in the President's motives. In the first phase, before the President fired Comey, the President had been assured that the FBI had not opened an investigation of him personally. The President deemed it critically important to make public that he was not under investigation, and he included that information in his termination letter to Comey after other efforts to have that information disclosed were unsuccessful.

Soon after he fired Comey, however, the President became aware that investigators were conducting an obstruction-of-justice inquiry into his own conduct. That awareness marked a significant change in the President's conduct and the start of a second phase of action. The President launched public attacks on the investigation and individuals involved in it who could possess evidence adverse to the President, while in private, the President engaged in a series of targeted efforts to control the investigation. For instance, the President attempted to remove the Special Counsel; he sought to have Attorney General Sessions unrecuse himself and limit the investigation; he sought to prevent public disclosure of information about the June 9, 2016 meeting between Russians and campaign officials; and he used public forums to attack potential witnesses who might offer adverse information and to praise witnesses who declined to cooperate with the government. Judgments about the nature of the President's motives during each phase would be informed by the totality of the evidence.

U.S. Department of Justice

~~Attorney Work Product // May Contain Material Protected Under Fed. R. Crim. P. 6(e)~~

III. Legal Defenses To The Application Of Obstruction-Of-Justice Statutes To The President

The President's personal counsel has written to this Office to advance statutory and constitutional defenses to the potential application of the obstruction-of-justice statutes to the President's conduct.[1072] As a statutory matter, the President's counsel has argued that a core obstruction-of-justice statute, 18 U.S.C. § 1512(c)(2), does not cover the President's actions.[1073] As a constitutional matter, the President's counsel argued that the President cannot obstruct justice by exercising his constitutional authority to close Department of Justice investigations or terminate the FBI Director.[1074] Under that view, any statute that restricts the President's exercise of those powers would impermissibly intrude on the President's constitutional role. The President's counsel has conceded that the President may be subject to criminal laws that do not directly involve exercises of his Article II authority, such as laws prohibiting bribing witnesses or suborning perjury.[1075] But counsel has made a categorical argument that "the President's exercise of his constitutional authority here to terminate an FBI Director and to close investigations cannot constitutionally constitute obstruction of justice."[1076]

In analyzing counsel's statutory arguments, we concluded that the President's proposed interpretation of Section 1512(c)(2) is contrary to the litigating position of the Department of Justice and is not supported by principles of statutory construction.

As for the constitutional arguments, we recognized that the Department of Justice and the courts have not definitively resolved these constitutional issues. We therefore analyzed the President's position through the framework of Supreme Court precedent addressing the separation of powers. Under that framework, we concluded, Article II of the Constitution does not categorically and permanently immunize the President from potential liability for the conduct that we investigated. Rather, our analysis led us to conclude that the obstruction-of-justice statutes can

---

[1072] 6/23/17 Letter, President's Personal Counsel to Special Counsel's Office; *see also* 1/29/18 Letter, President's Personal Counsel to Special Counsel's Office; 2/6/18 Letter, President's Personal Counsel to Special Counsel's Office; 8/8/18 Letter, President's Personal Counsel to Special Counsel's Office, at 4.

[1073] 2/6/18 Letter, President's Personal Counsel to Special Counsel's Office, at 2-9. Counsel has also noted that other potentially applicable obstruction statutes, such as 18 U.S.C. § 1505, protect only pending proceedings. 6/23/17 Letter, President's Personal Counsel to Special Counsel's Office, at 7-8. Section 1512(c)(2) is not limited to pending proceedings, but also applies to future proceedings that the person contemplated. *See* Volume II, Section III.A, *supra*.

[1074] 6/23/17 Letter, President's Personal Counsel to Special Counsel's Office, at 1 ("[T]he President cannot obstruct . . . by simply exercising these inherent Constitutional powers.").

[1075] 6/23/17 Letter, President's Personal Counsel to Special Counsel's Office, at 2 n. 1.

[1076] 6/23/17 Letter, President's Personal Counsel to Special Counsel's Office, at 2 n.1 (dashes omitted); *see also* 8/8/18 Letter, President's Personal Counsel to Special Counsel's Office, at 4 ("[T]he obstruction-of-justice statutes cannot be read so expansively as to create potential liability based on facially lawful acts undertaken by the President in furtherance of his core Article II discretionary authority to remove principal officers or carry out the prosecution function.").

U.S. Department of Justice

~~Attorney Work Product // May Contain Material Protected Under Fed. R. Crim. P. 6(e)~~

validly prohibit a President's corrupt efforts to use his official powers to curtail, end, or interfere with an investigation.

A.   Statutory Defenses to the Application of Obstruction-Of-Justice Provisions to the Conduct Under Investigation

The obstruction-of-justice statute most readily applicable to our investigation is 18 U.S.C. § 1512(c)(2). Section 1512(c) provides:

(c) Whoever corruptly—

> (1) alters, destroys, mutilates, or conceals a record, document, or other object, or attempts to do so, with the intent to impair the object's integrity or availability for use in an official proceeding; or

> (2) otherwise obstructs, influences, or impedes any official proceeding, or attempts to do so,

shall be fined under this title or imprisoned not more than 20 years, or both.

The Department of Justice has taken the position that Section 1512(c)(2) states a broad, independent, and unqualified prohibition on obstruction of justice.[1077] While defendants have argued that subsection (c)(2) should be read to cover only acts that would impair the availability or integrity of evidence because that is subsection (c)(1)'s focus, strong arguments weigh against that proposed limitation. The text of Section 1512(c)(2) confirms that its sweep is not tethered to Section 1512(c)(1); courts have so interpreted it; its history does not counsel otherwise; and no principle of statutory construction dictates a contrary view. On its face, therefore, Section 1512(c)(2) applies to all corrupt means of obstructing a proceeding, pending or contemplated— including by improper exercises of official power. In addition, other statutory provisions that are potentially applicable to certain conduct we investigated broadly prohibit obstruction of proceedings that are pending before courts, grand juries, and Congress. *See* 18 U.S.C. §§ 1503, 1505. Congress has also specifically prohibited witness tampering. *See* 18 U.S.C. § 1512(b).

1.   The Text of Section 1512(c)(2) Prohibits a Broad Range of Obstructive Acts

Several textual features of Section 1512(c)(2) support the conclusion that the provision broadly prohibits corrupt means of obstructing justice and is not limited by the more specific prohibitions in Section 1512(c)(1), which focus on evidence impairment.

First, the text of Section 1512(c)(2) is unqualified: it reaches acts that "obstruct[], influence[], or impede[] any official proceeding" when committed "corruptly." Nothing in Section 1512(c)(2)'s text limits the provision to acts that would impair the integrity or availability of evidence for use in an official proceeding. In contrast, Section 1512(c)(1) explicitly includes the requirement that the defendant act "with the intent to impair the object's integrity or availability

---

[1077] *See* U.S. Br., *United States v. Kumar*, Nos. 06–5482–cr(L), 06–5654–cr(CON) (2d Cir. filed Oct. 26, 2007), at pp. 15-28; *United States v. Singleton*, Nos. H-04-CR-514SS, H-06-cr-80 (S.D. Tex. filed June 5, 2006).

for use in an official proceeding," a requirement that Congress also included in two other sections of Section 1512. *See* 18 U.S.C. §§ 1512(a)(2)(B)(ii) (use of physical force with intent to cause a person to destroy an object "with intent to impair the integrity or availability of the object for use in an official proceeding"); 1512(b)(2)(B) (use of intimidation, threats, corrupt persuasion, or misleading conduct with intent to cause a person to destroy an object "with intent to impair the integrity or availability of the object for use in an official proceeding"). But no comparable intent or conduct element focused on evidence impairment appears in Section 1512(c)(2). The intent element in Section 1512(c)(2) comes from the word "corruptly." *See, e.g., United States v. McKibbins*, 656 F.3d 707, 711 (7th Cir. 2011) ("The intent element is important because the word 'corruptly' is what serves to separate criminal and innocent acts of obstruction.") (internal quotation marks omitted). And the conduct element in Section 1512(c)(2) is "obstruct[ing], influenc[ing], or imped[ing]" a proceeding. Congress is presumed to have acted intentionally in the disparate inclusion and exclusion of evidence-impairment language. *See Loughrin v. United States*, 573 U.S. 351, 358 (2014) ("[W]hen 'Congress includes particular language in one section of a statute but omits it in another'—let alone in the very next provision—this Court 'presume[s]' that Congress intended a difference in meaning") (quoting *Russello v. United States*, 464 U.S. 16, 23 (1983)); *accord Digital Realty Trust, Inc. v. Somers*, 138 S. Ct. 767, 777 (2018).

Second, the structure of Section 1512 supports the conclusion that Section 1512(c)(2) defines an independent offense. Section 1512(c)(2) delineates a complete crime with different elements from Section 1512(c)(1)—and each subsection of Section 1512(c) contains its own "attempt" prohibition, underscoring that they are independent prohibitions. The two subsections of Section 1512(c) are connected by the conjunction "or," indicating that each provides an alternative basis for criminal liability. *See Loughrin*, 573 U.S. at 357 ("ordinary use [of 'or'] is almost always disjunctive, that is, the words it connects are to be given separate meanings") (internal quotation marks omitted). In *Loughrin*, for example, the Supreme Court relied on the use of the word "or" to hold that adjacent and overlapping subsections of the bank fraud statute, 18 U.S.C. § 1344, state distinct offenses and that subsection 1344(2) therefore should not be interpreted to contain an additional element specified only in subsection 1344(1). *Id.; see also Shaw v. United States*, 137 S. Ct. 462, 465-469 (2016) (recognizing that the subsections of the bank fraud statute "overlap substantially" but identifying distinct circumstances covered by each).[1078] And here, as in *Loughrin*, Section 1512(c)'s "two clauses have separate numbers, line breaks before, between, and after them, and equivalent indentation—thus placing the clauses visually on an equal footing and indicating that they have separate meanings." 573 U.S. at 359.

Third, the introductory word "otherwise" in Section 1512(c)(2) signals that the provision covers obstructive acts that are different from those listed in Section 1512(c)(1). *See* Black's Law Dictionary 1101 (6th ed. 1990) ("otherwise" means "in a different manner; in another way, or in other ways"); *see also, e.g.*, American Heritage College Dictionary Online ("1. In another way;

[1078] The Office of Legal Counsel recently relied on several of the same interpretive principles in concluding that language that appeared in the first clause of the Wire Act, 18 U.S.C. § 1084, restricting its prohibition against certain betting or wagering activities to "any sporting event or contest," did not apply to the second clause of the same statute, which reaches other betting or wagering activities. *See Reconsidering Whether the Wire Act Applies to Non-Sports Gambling* (Nov. 2, 2018), slip op. 7 (relying on plain language); *id.* at 11 (finding it not "tenable to read into the second clause the qualifier 'on any sporting event or contest' that appears in the first clause"); *id.* at 12 (relying on *Digital Realty*).

U.S. Department of Justice

~~Attorney Work Product // May Contain Material Protected Under Fed. R. Crim. P. 6(e)~~

differently; 2. Under other circumstances"); *see also Gooch v. United States*, 297 U.S. 124, 128 (1936) (characterizing "otherwise" as a "broad term" and holding that a statutory prohibition on kidnapping "for ransom or reward or otherwise" is not limited by the words "ransom" and "reward" to kidnappings for pecuniary benefits); *Collazos v. United States*, 368 F.3d 190, 200 (2d Cir. 2004) (construing "otherwise" in 28 U.S.C. § 2466(1)(C) to reach beyond the "specific examples" listed in prior subsections, thereby covering the "myriad means that human ingenuity might devise to permit a person to avoid the jurisdiction of a court"); *cf. Begay v. United States*, 553 U.S. 137, 144 (2006) (recognizing that "otherwise" is defined to mean "in a different way or manner," and holding that the word "otherwise" introducing the residual clause in the Armed Career Criminal Act, 18 U.S.C. § 924(e)(2)(B)(ii), can, but need not necessarily, "refer to a crime that is similar to the listed examples in some respects but different in others").[1079] The purpose of the word "otherwise" in Section 1512(c)(2) is therefore to clarify that the provision covers obstructive acts *other* than the destruction of physical evidence with the intent to impair its integrity or availability, which is the conduct addressed in Section 1512(c)(1). The word "otherwise" does not signal that Section 1512(c)(2) has less breadth in covering obstructive conduct than the language of the provision implies.

2. Judicial Decisions Support a Broad Reading of Section 1512(c)(2)

Courts have not limited Section 1512(c)(2) to conduct that impairs evidence, but instead have read it to cover obstructive acts in any form.

As one court explained, "[t]his expansive subsection operates as a catch-all to cover 'otherwise' obstructive behavior that might not constitute a more specific offense like document destruction, which is listed in (c)(1)." *United States v. Volpendesto*, 746 F.3d 273, 286 (7th Cir. 2014) (some quotation marks omitted). For example, in *United States v. Ring*, 628 F. Supp. 2d 195 (D.D.C. 2009), the court rejected the argument that "§ 1512(c)(2)'s reference to conduct that 'otherwise obstructs, influences, or impedes any official proceeding' is limited to conduct that is similar to the type of conduct proscribed by subsection (c)(1)—namely, conduct that impairs the integrity or availability of 'record[s], documents[s], or other object[s] for use in an official proceeding." *Id.* at 224. The court explained that "the meaning of § 1512(c)(2) is plain on its face." *Id.* (alternations in original). And courts have upheld convictions under Section 1512(c)(2) that did not involve evidence impairment, but instead resulted from conduct that more broadly thwarted arrests or investigations. *See, e.g., United States v. Martinez*, 862 F.3d 223, 238 (2d Cir. 2017) (police officer tipped off suspects about issuance of arrest warrants before "outstanding warrants could be executed, thereby potentially interfering with an ongoing grand jury proceeding"); *United States v. Ahrensfield*, 698 F.3d 1310, 1324-1326 (10th Cir. 2012) (officer disclosed existence of an undercover investigation to its target); *United States v. Phillips*, 583 F.3d 1261, 1265 (10th Cir. 2009) (defendant disclosed identity of an undercover officer thus preventing him from making controlled purchases from methamphetamine dealers). Those cases illustrate that Section 1512(c)(2) applies to corrupt acts—including by public officials—that frustrate the

---

[1079] In *Sykes v. United States*, 564 U.S. 1, 15 (2011), the Supreme Court substantially abandoned *Begay*'s reading of the residual clause, and in *Johnson v. United States*, 135 S. Ct. 2551 (2015), the Court invalidated the residual clause as unconstitutionally vague. *Begay*'s analysis of the word "otherwise" is thus of limited value.

U.S. Department of Justice

~~Attorney Work Product // May Contain Material Protected Under Fed. R. Crim. P. 6(e)~~

commencement or conduct of a proceeding, and not just to acts that make evidence unavailable or impair its integrity.

Section 1512(c)(2)'s breadth is reinforced by the similarity of its language to the omnibus clause of 18 U.S.C. § 1503, which covers anyone who "corruptly . . . obstructs, or impedes, or endeavors to influence, obstruct, or impede, the due administration of justice." That clause of Section 1503 follows two more specific clauses that protect jurors, judges, and court officers. The omnibus clause has nevertheless been construed to be "far more general in scope than the earlier clauses of the statute." *United States v. Aguilar*, 515 U.S. 593, 599 (1995). "The omnibus clause is essentially a catch-all provision which generally prohibits conduct that interferes with the due administration of justice." *United States v. Brenson*, 104 F.3d 1267, 1275 (11th Cir. 1997). Courts have accordingly given it a "non-restrictive reading." *United States v. Kumar*, 617 F.3d 612, 620 (2d Cir. 2010); *id.* at 620 n.7 (collecting cases from the Third, Fourth, Sixth, Seventh, and Eleventh Circuits). As one court has explained, the omnibus clause "prohibits acts that are similar in result, rather than manner, to the conduct described in the first part of the statute." *United States v. Howard*, 569 F.2d 1331, 1333 (5th Cir. 1978). While the specific clauses "forbid certain means of obstructing justice . . . the omnibus clause aims at obstruction of justice itself, regardless of the means used to reach that result." *Id.* (collecting cases). Given the similarity of Section 1512(c)(2) to Section 1503's omnibus clause, Congress would have expected Section 1512(c)(2) to cover acts that produced a similar result to the evidence-impairment provisions—*i.e.*, the result of obstructing justice rather than covering only acts that were similar in manner. Read this way, Section 1512(c)(2) serves a distinct function in the federal obstruction-of-justice statutes: it captures corrupt conduct, other than document destruction, that has the natural tendency to obstruct contemplated as well as pending proceedings.

Section 1512(c)(2) overlaps with other obstruction statutes, but it does not render them superfluous. Section 1503, for example, which covers pending grand jury and judicial proceedings, and Section 1505, which covers pending administrative and congressional proceedings, reach "*endeavors* to influence, obstruct, or impede" the proceedings—a broader test for inchoate violations than Section 1512(c)(2)'s "attempt" standard, which requires a substantial step towards a completed offense. *See United States v. Sampson*, 898 F.3d 287, 302 (2d Cir. 2018) ("[E]fforts to witness tamper that rise to the level of an 'endeavor' yet fall short of an 'attempt' cannot be prosecuted under § 1512."); *United States v. Leisure*, 844 F.2d 1347, 1366-1367 (8th Cir. 1988) (collecting cases recognizing the difference between the "endeavor" and "attempt" standards). And 18 U.S.C. § 1519, which prohibits destruction of documents or records in contemplation of an investigation or proceeding, does not require the "nexus" showing under *Aguilar*, which Section 1512(c)(2) demands. *See, e.g.*, *United States v. Yielding*, 657 F.3d 688, 712 (8th Cir. 2011) ("The requisite knowledge and intent [under Section 1519] can be present even if the accused lacks knowledge that he is likely to succeed in obstructing the matter."); *United States v. Gray*, 642 F.3d 371, 376-377 (2d Cir. 2011) ("[I]n enacting § 1519, Congress rejected any requirement that the government prove a link between a defendant's conduct and an imminent or pending official proceeding."). The existence of even "substantial" overlap is not "uncommon" in criminal statutes. *Loughrin*, 573 U.S. at 359 n.4; *see Shaw*, 137 S. Ct. at 458-469; *Aguilar*, 515 U.S. at 616 (Scalia, J., dissenting) ("The fact that there is now some overlap between § 1503 and § 1512 is no more intolerable than the fact that there is some overlap between the omnibus clause of § 1503 and the other provisions of § 1503 itself."). But given that Sections 1503, 1505, and

U.S. Department of Justice

~~Attorney Work Product // May Contain Material Protected Under Fed. R. Crim. P. 6(e)~~

1519 each reach conduct that Section 1512(c)(2) does not, the overlap provides no reason to give Section 1512(c)(2) an artificially limited construction. *See Shaw*, 137 S. Ct. at 469.[1080]

3. The Legislative History of Section 1512(c)(2) Does Not Justify Narrowing Its Text

"Given the straightforward statutory command" in Section 1512(c)(2), "there is no reason to resort to legislative history." *United States v. Gonzales*, 520 U.S. 1, 6 (1997). In any event, the legislative history of Section 1512(c)(2) is not a reason to impose extratextual limitations on its reach.

Congress enacted Section 1512(c)(2) as part the Sarbanes-Oxley Act of 2002, Pub. L. No. 107-204, Tit. XI, § 1102, 116 Stat. 807. The relevant section of the statute was entitled "Tampering with a Record *or Otherwise Impeding an Official Proceeding*." 116 Stat. 807 (emphasis added). That title indicates that Congress intended the two clauses to have independent effect. Section 1512(c) was added as a floor amendment in the Senate and explained as closing a certain "loophole" with respect to "document shredding." *See* 148 Cong. Rec. S6545 (July 10, 2002) (Sen. Lott); *id.* at S6549-S6550 (Sen. Hatch). But those explanations do not limit the enacted text. *See Pittston Coal Group v. Sebben*, 488 U.S. 105, 115 (1988) ("[I]t is not the law that a statute can have no effects which are not explicitly mentioned in its legislative history."); *see also Encino Motorcars, LLC v. Navarro*, 138 S. Ct. 1134, 1143 (2018) ("Even if Congress did not foresee all of the applications of the statute, that is no reason not to give the statutory text a fair reading."). The floor statements thus cannot detract from the meaning of the enacted text. *See Barnhart v. Sigmon Coal Co.*, 534 U.S. 438, 457 (2002) ("Floor statements from two Senators cannot amend the clear and unambiguous language of a statute. We see no reason to give greater weight to the views of two Senators than to the collective votes of both Houses, which are memorialized in the unambiguous statutory text."). That principle has particular force where one of the proponents of the amendment to Section 1512 introduced his remarks as only "briefly elaborat[ing] on some of the specific provisions contained in this bill." 148 Cong. Rec. S6550 (Sen. Hatch).

Indeed, the language Congress used in Section 1512(c)(2)—prohibiting "corruptly obstruct[ing], influenc[ing], or imped[ing] any official proceeding" or attempting to do so— parallels a provision that Congress considered years earlier in a bill designed to strengthen protections against witness tampering and obstruction of justice. While the earlier provision is not a direct antecedent of Section 1512(c)(2), Congress's understanding of the broad scope of the

---

[1080] The Supreme Court's decision in *Marinello v. United States*, 138 S. Ct. 1101 (2018), does not support imposing a non-textual limitation on Section 1512(c)(2). *Marinello* interpreted the tax obstruction statute, 26 U.S.C. § 7212(a), to require "a 'nexus' between the defendant's conduct and a particular administrative proceeding." *Id.* at 1109. The Court adopted that construction in light of the similar interpretation given to "other obstruction provisions," *id.* (citing *Aguilar* and *Arthur Andersen*), as well as considerations of context, legislative history, structure of the criminal tax laws, fair warning, and lenity. *Id.* at 1106-1108. The type of "nexus" element the Court adopted in *Marinello* already applies under Section 1512(c)(2), and the remaining considerations the Court cited do not justify reading into Section 1512(c)(2) language that is not there. *See Bates v. United States*, 522 U.S. 23, 29 (1997) (the Court "ordinarily resist[s] reading words or elements into a statute that do not appear on its face.").

U.S. Department of Justice

~~Attorney Work Product // May Contain Material Protected Under Fed. R. Crim. P. 6(e)~~

earlier provision is instructive. Recognizing that "the proper administration of justice may be impeded or thwarted" by a "variety of corrupt methods . . . limited only by the imagination of the criminally inclined," S. Rep. No. 532, 97th Cong., 2d Sess. 17-18 (1982), Congress considered a bill that would have amended Section 1512 by making it a crime, *inter alia*, when a person "corruptly . . . influences, obstructs, or impedes . . . [t]he enforcement and prosecution of federal law," "administration of a law under which an official proceeding is being or may be conducted," or the "exercise of a Federal legislative power of inquiry." *Id.* at 17-19 (quoting S. 2420).

The Senate Committee explained that:

> [T]he purpose of preventing an obstruction of or miscarriage of justice cannot be fully carried out by a simple enumeration of the commonly prosecuted obstruction offenses. There must also be protection against the rare type of conduct that is the product of the inventive criminal mind and which also thwarts justice.

Id. at 18. The report gave examples of conduct "actually prosecuted under the current residual clause [in 18 U.S.C. § 1503], which would probably not be covered in this series [of provisions] without a residual clause." *Id.* One prominent example was "[a] conspiracy to cover up the Watergate burglary and its aftermath by having the Central Intelligence Agency seek to interfere with an ongoing FBI investigation of the burglary." *Id.* (citing *United States v. Haldeman*, 559 F.2d 31 (D.C. Cir. 1976)). The report therefore indicates a congressional awareness not only that residual-clause language resembling Section 1512(c)(2) broadly covers a wide variety of obstructive conduct, but also that such language reaches the improper use of governmental processes to obstruct justice—specifically, the Watergate cover-up orchestrated by White House officials including the President himself. *See Haldeman*, 559 F.3d at 51, 86-87, 120-129, 162.[1081]

4. General Principles of Statutory Construction Do Not Suggest That Section 1512(c)(2) is Inapplicable to the Conduct in this Investigation

The requirement of fair warning in criminal law, the interest in avoiding due process concerns in potentially vague statutes, and the rule of lenity do not justify narrowing the reach of Section 1512(c)(2)'s text.[1082]

a. As with other criminal laws, the Supreme Court has "exercised restraint" in interpreting obstruction-of-justice provisions, both out of respect for Congress's role in defining crimes and in the interest of providing individuals with "fair warning" of what a criminal statute prohibits. *Marinello v. United States*, 138 S. Ct. 1101, 1106 (2018); *Arthur Andersen*, 544 U.S. at 703;

[1081] The Senate ultimately accepted the House version of the bill, which excluded an omnibus clause. *See United States v. Poindexter*, 951 F.2d 369, 382-383 (D.C. Cir. 1991) (tracing history of the proposed omnibus provision in the witness-protection legislation). During the floor debate on the bill, Senator Heinz, one of the initiators and primary backers of the legislation, explained that the omnibus clause was beyond the scope of the witness-protection measure at issue and likely "duplicative" of other obstruction laws, 128 Cong. Rec. 26,810 (1982) (Sen. Heinz), presumably referring to Sections 1503 and 1505.

[1082] In a separate section addressing considerations unique to the presidency, we consider principles of statutory construction relevant in that context. *See* Volume II, Section III.B.1, *infra*.

Aguilar, 515 U.S. at 599-602. In several obstruction cases, the Court has imposed a nexus test that requires that the wrongful conduct targeted by the provision be sufficiently connected to an official proceeding to ensure the requisite culpability. *Marinello*, 138 S. Ct. at 1109; *Arthur Andersen*, 544 U.S. at 707-708; *Aguilar*, 515 U.S. at 600-602. Section 1512(c)(2) has been interpreted to require a similar nexus. *See, e.g., United States v. Young*, 916 F.3d 368, 386 (4th Cir. 2019); *United States v. Petruk*, 781 F.3d 438, 445 (8th Cir. 2015); *United States v. Phillips*, 583 F.3d 1261, 1264 (10th Cir. 2009); *United States v. Reich*, 479 F.3d 179, 186 (2d Cir. 2007). To satisfy the nexus requirement, the government must show as an objective matter that a defendant acted "in a manner that is likely to obstruct justice," such that the statute "excludes defendants who have an evil purpose but use means that would only unnaturally and improbably be successful." *Aguilar*, 515 U.S. at 601-602 (internal quotation marks omitted); *see id.* at 599 ("the endeavor must have the natural and probable effect of interfering with the due administration of justice") (internal quotation marks omitted). The government must also show as a subjective matter that the actor "contemplated a particular, foreseeable proceeding." *Petruk*, 781 F.3d at 445. Those requirements alleviate fair-warning concerns by ensuring that obstructive conduct has a close enough connection to existing or future proceedings to implicate the dangers targeted by the obstruction laws and that the individual actually has the obstructive result in mind.

    b. Courts also seek to construe statutes to avoid due process vagueness concerns. *See, e.g., McDonnell v. United States*, 136 S. Ct. 2355, 2373 (2016); *Skilling v. United States*, 561 U.S. 358, 368, 402-404 (2010). Vagueness doctrine requires that a statute define a crime "with sufficient definiteness that ordinary people can understand what conduct is prohibited" and "in a manner that does not encourage arbitrary and discriminatory enforcement." *Id.* at 402-403 (internal quotation marks omitted). The obstruction statutes' requirement of acting "corruptly" satisfies that test.

    "Acting 'corruptly' within the meaning of § 1512(c)(2) means acting with an improper purpose and to engage in conduct knowingly and dishonestly with the specific intent to subvert, impede or obstruct" the relevant proceeding. *United States v. Gordon*, 710 F.3d 1124, 1151 (10th Cir. 2013) (some quotation marks omitted). The majority opinion in *Aguilar* did not address the defendant's vagueness challenge to the word "corruptly," 515 U.S. at 600 n. 1, but Justice Scalia's separate opinion did reach that issue and would have rejected the challenge, *id.* at 616-617 (Scalia, J., joined by Kennedy and Thomas, JJ., concurring in part and dissenting in part). "Statutory language need not be colloquial," Justice Scalia explained, and "the term 'corruptly' in criminal laws has a longstanding and well-accepted meaning. It denotes an act done with an intent to give some advantage inconsistent with official duty and the rights of others." *Id.* at 616 (internal quotation marks omitted; citing lower court authority and legal dictionaries). Justice Scalia added that "in the context of obstructing jury proceedings, any claim of ignorance of wrongdoing is incredible." *Id.* at 617. Lower courts have also rejected vagueness challenges to the word "corruptly." *See, e.g., United States v. Edwards*, 869 F.3d 490, 501-502 (7th Cir. 2017); *United States v. Brenson*, 104 F.3d 1267, 1280-1281 (11th Cir. 1997); *United States v. Howard*, 569 F.2d 1331, 1336 n.9 (5th Cir. 1978). This well-established intent standard precludes the need to limit the obstruction statutes to only certain kinds of inherently wrongful conduct.[1083]

    [1083] In *United States v. Poindexter*, 951 F.2d 369 (D.C. Cir. 1991), the court of appeals found the term "corruptly" in 18 U.S.C. § 1505 vague as applied to a person who provided false information to Congress. After suggesting that the word "corruptly" was vague on its face, 951 F.2d at 378, the court

U.S. Department of Justice

~~Attorney Work Product // May Contain Material Protected Under Fed. R. Crim. P. 6(e)~~

c. Finally, the rule of lenity does not justify treating Section 1512(c)(2) as a prohibition on evidence impairment, as opposed to an omnibus clause. The rule of lenity is an interpretive principle that resolves ambiguity in criminal laws in favor of the less-severe construction. *Cleveland v. United States*, 531 U.S. 12, 25 (2000). "[A]s [the Court has] repeatedly emphasized," however, the rule of lenity applies only if, "after considering text, structure, history and purpose, there remains a grievous ambiguity or uncertainty in the statute such that the Court must simply guess as to what Congress intended." *Abramski v. United States*, 573 U.S. 169, 188 n.10 (2014) (internal quotation marks omitted). The rule has been cited, for example, in adopting a narrow meaning of "tangible object" in an obstruction statute when the prohibition's title, history, and list of prohibited acts indicated a focus on destruction of records. *See Yates v. United States*, 135 S. Ct. 1074, 1088 (2015) (plurality opinion) (interpreting "tangible object" in the phrase "record, document, or tangible object" in 18 U.S.C. § 1519 to mean an item capable of recording or preserving information). Here, as discussed above, the text, structure, and history of Section 1512(c)(2) leaves no "grievous ambiguity" about the statute's meaning. Section 1512(c)(2) defines a structurally independent general prohibition on obstruction of official proceedings.

5. Other Obstruction Statutes Might Apply to the Conduct in this Investigation

Regardless whether Section 1512(c)(2) covers all corrupt acts that obstruct, influence, or impede pending or contemplated proceedings, other statutes would apply to such conduct in pending proceedings, provided that the remaining statutory elements are satisfied. As discussed above, the omnibus clause in 18 U.S.C. § 1503(a) applies generally to obstruction of pending judicial and grand proceedings.[1084] *See Aguilar*, 515 U.S. at 598 (noting that the clause is "far more general in scope" than preceding provisions). Section 1503(a)'s protections extend to witness tampering and to other obstructive conduct that has a nexus to pending proceedings. *See Sampson*, 898 F.3d at 298-303 & n.6 (collecting cases from eight circuits holding that Section 1503 covers witness-related obstructive conduct, and cabining prior circuit authority). And Section 1505 broadly criminalizes obstructive conduct aimed at pending agency and congressional proceedings.[1085] *See, e.g., United States v. Rainey*, 757 F.3d 234, 241-247 (5th Cir. 2014).

---

concluded that the statute did not clearly apply to corrupt conduct by the person himself and the "core" conduct to which Section 1505 could constitutionally be applied was one person influencing another person to violate a legal duty. *Id.* at 379-386. Congress later enacted a provision overturning that result by providing that "[a]s used in [S]ection 1505, the term 'corruptly' means acting with an improper purpose, personally or by influencing another, including by making a false or misleading statement, or withholding, concealing, altering, or destroying a document or other information." 18 U.S.C. § 1515(b). Other courts have declined to follow *Poindexter* either by limiting it to Section 1505 and the specific conduct at issue in that case, *see Brenson*, 104 F.3d at 1280-1281; reading it as narrowly limited to certain types of conduct, *see United States v. Morrison*, 98 F.3d 619, 629-630 (D.C. Cir. 1996); or by noting that it predated *Arthur Andersen*'s interpretation of the term "corruptly," *see Edwards*, 869 F.3d at 501-502.

[1084] Section 1503(a) provides for criminal punishment of:

> Whoever . . . corruptly or by threats or force, or by any threatening letter or communication, influences, obstructs, or impedes, or endeavors to influence, obstruct, or impede, the due administration of justice.

[1085] Section 1505 provides for criminal punishment of:

167

Finally, 18 U.S.C. § 1512(b)(3) criminalizes tampering with witnesses to prevent the communication of information about a crime to law enforcement. The nexus inquiry articulated in *Aguilar*—that an individual has "knowledge that his actions are likely to affect the judicial proceeding," 515 U.S. at 599—does not apply to Section 1512(b)(3). *See United States v. Byrne*, 435 F.3d 16, 24-25 (1st Cir. 2006). The nexus inquiry turns instead on the actor's intent to prevent communications to a federal law enforcement official. *See Fowler v. United States*, 563 U.S. 668, 673-678 (2011).

* *

In sum, in light of the breadth of Section 1512(c)(2) and the other obstruction statutes, an argument that the conduct at issue in this investigation falls outside the scope of the obstruction laws lacks merit.

B. Constitutional Defenses to Applying Obstruction-Of-Justice Statutes to Presidential Conduct

The President has broad discretion to direct criminal investigations. The Constitution vests the "executive Power" in the President and enjoins him to "take Care that the Laws be faithfully executed." U.S. CONST. ART II, §§ 1, 3. Those powers and duties form the foundation of prosecutorial discretion. *See United States v. Armstrong*, 517 U.S. 456, 464 (1996) (Attorney General and United States Attorneys "have this latitude because they are designated by statute as the President's delegates to help him discharge his constitutional responsibility to 'take Care that the Laws be faithfully executed.'"). The President also has authority to appoint officers of the United States and to remove those whom he has appointed. U.S. CONST. ART II, § 2, cl. 2 (granting authority to the President to appoint all officers with the advice and consent of the Senate, but providing that Congress may vest the appointment of inferior officers in the President alone, the heads of departments, or the courts of law); *see also Free Enterprise Fund v. Public Company Accounting Oversight Board*, 561 U.S. 477, 492-493, 509 (2010) (describing removal authority as flowing from the President's "responsibility to take care that the laws be faithfully executed").

Although the President has broad authority under Article II, that authority coexists with Congress's Article I power to enact laws that protect congressional proceedings, federal investigations, the courts, and grand juries against corrupt efforts to undermine their functions. Usually, those constitutional powers function in harmony, with the President enforcing the criminal laws under Article II to protect against corrupt obstructive acts. But when the President's official actions come into conflict with the prohibitions in the obstruction statutes, any constitutional tension is reconciled through separation-of-powers analysis.

Whoever corruptly . . . influences, obstructs, or impedes or endeavors to influence, obstruct, or impede the due and proper administration of the law under which any pending proceeding is being had before any department or agency of the United States, or the due and proper exercise of the power of inquiry under which any inquiry or investigation is being had by either House, or any committee of either House or any joint committee of the Congress.

U.S. Department of Justice

~~Attorney Work Product // May Contain Material Protected Under Fed. R. Crim. P. 6(e)~~

The President's counsel has argued that "the President's exercise of his constitutional authority . . . to terminate an FBI Director and to close investigations . . . cannot constitutionally constitute obstruction of justice."[1086] As noted above, no Department of Justice position or Supreme Court precedent directly resolved this issue. We did not find counsel's contention, however, to accord with our reading of the Supreme Court authority addressing separation-of-powers issues. Applying the Court's framework for analysis, we concluded that Congress can validly regulate the President's exercise of official duties to prohibit actions motivated by a corrupt intent to obstruct justice. The limited effect on presidential power that results from that restriction would not impermissibly undermine the President's ability to perform his Article II functions.

1. The Requirement of a Clear Statement to Apply Statutes to Presidential Conduct Does Not Limit the Obstruction Statutes

Before addressing Article II issues directly, we consider one threshold statutory-construction principle that is unique to the presidency: "The principle that general statutes must be read as not applying to the President if they do not expressly apply where application would arguably limit the President's constitutional role." OLC, *Application of 28 U.S.C. § 458 to Presidential Appointments of Federal Judges*, 19 Op. O.L.C. 350, 352 (1995). This "clear statement rule," *id.*, has its source in two principles: statutes should be construed to avoid serious constitutional questions, and Congress should not be assumed to have altered the constitutional separation of powers without clear assurance that it intended that result. OLC, *The Constitutional Separation of Powers Between the President and Congress*, 20 Op. O.L.C. 124, 178 (1996).

The Supreme Court has applied that clear-statement rule in several cases. In one leading case, the Court construed the Administrative Procedure Act, 5 U.S.C. § 701 *et seq.*, not to apply to judicial review of presidential action. *Franklin v. Massachusetts*, 505 U.S. 788, 800-801 (1992). The Court explained that it "would require an express statement by Congress before assuming it intended the President's performance of his statutory duties to be reviewed for abuse of discretion." *Id.* at 801. In another case, the Court interpreted the word "utilized" in the Federal Advisory Committee Act (FACA), 5 U.S.C. App., to apply only to the use of advisory committees established directly or indirectly by the government, thereby excluding the American Bar Association's advice to the Department of Justice about federal judicial candidates. *Public Citizen v. United States Department of Justice*, 491 U.S. 440, 455, 462-467 (1989). The Court explained that a broader interpretation of the term "utilized" in FACA would raise serious questions whether the statute "infringed unduly on the President's Article II power to nominate federal judges and violated the doctrine of separation of powers." *Id.* at 466-467. Another case found that an established canon of statutory construction applied with "special force" to provisions that would impinge on the President's foreign-affairs powers if construed broadly. *Sale v. Haitian Centers Council*, 509 U.S. 155, 188 (1993) (applying the presumption against extraterritorial application to construe the Refugee Act of 1980 as not governing in an overseas context where it could affect "foreign and military affairs for which the President has unique responsibility"). *See Application*

[1086] 6/23/17 Letter, President's Personal Counsel to Special Counsel's Office, at 2 n. 1.

U.S. Department of Justice

Attorney Work Product // May Contain Material Protected Under Fed. R. Crim. P. 6(e)

of 28 U.S.C. § 458 to Presidential Appointments of Federal Judges, 19 Op. O.L.C. at 353-354 (discussing *Franklin, Public Citizen,* and *Sale*).

The Department of Justice has relied on this clear-statement principle to interpret certain statutes as not applying to the President at all, similar to the approach taken in *Franklin. See, e.g.,* Memorandum for Richard T. Burress, Office of the President, from Laurence H. Silberman, Deputy Attorney General, *Re: Conflict of Interest Problems Arising out of the President's Nomination of Nelson A. Rockefeller to be Vice President under the Twenty-Fifth Amendment to the Constitution,* at 2, 5 (Aug. 28, 1974) (criminal conflict-of-interest statute, 18 U.S.C. § 208, does not apply to the President). Other OLC opinions interpret statutory text not to apply to certain presidential or executive actions because of constitutional concerns. *See Application of 28 U.S.C. § 458 to Presidential Appointments of Federal Judges,* 19 Op. O.L.C. at 350-357 (consanguinity limitations on court appointments, 28 U.S.C. § 458, found inapplicable to "presidential appointments of judges to the federal judiciary"); *Constraints Imposed by 18 U.S.C. § 1913 on Lobbying Efforts,* 13 Op. O.L.C. 300, 304-306 (1989) (limitation on the use of appropriated funds for certain lobbying programs found inapplicable to certain communications by the President and executive officials).

But OLC has also recognized that this clear-statement rule "does not apply with respect to a statute that raises no separation of powers questions were it to be applied to the President," such as the federal bribery statute, 18 U.S.C. § 201. *Application of 28 U.S.C. § 458 to Presidential Appointments of Federal Judges,* 19 Op. O.L.C. at 357 n.11. OLC explained that "[a]pplication of § 201 raises no separation of powers question, let alone a serious one," because [t]he Constitution confers no power in the President to receive bribes." *Id.* In support of that conclusion, OLC noted constitutional provisions that forbid increases in the President's compensation while in office, "which is what a bribe would function to do," *id.* (citing U.S. CONST. ART. II, § 1, cl. 7), and the express constitutional power of "Congress to impeach [and convict] a President for, *inter alia,* bribery," *id.* (citing U.S. CONST. ART II, § 4).

Under OLC's analysis, Congress can permissibly criminalize certain obstructive conduct by the President, such as suborning perjury, intimidating witnesses, or fabricating evidence, because those prohibitions raise no separation-of-powers questions. *See Application of 28 U.S.C. § 458 to Presidential Appointments of Federal Judges,* 19 Op. O.L.C. at 357 n.11. The Constitution does not authorize the President to engage in such conduct, and those actions would transgress the President's duty to "take Care that the Laws be faithfully executed." U.S. CONST. ART II, §§ 3. In view of those clearly permissible applications of the obstruction statutes to the President, *Franklin's* holding that the President is entirely excluded from a statute absent a clear statement would not apply in this context.

A more limited application of a clear-statement rule to exclude from the obstruction statutes only certain acts by the President—for example, removing prosecutors or ending investigations for corrupt reasons—would be difficult to implement as a matter of statutory interpretation. It is not obvious how a clear-statement rule would apply to an omnibus provision like Section 1512(c)(2) to exclude corruptly motivated obstructive acts only when carried out in the President's conduct of office. No statutory term could easily bear that specialized meaning. For example, the word "corruptly" has a well-established meaning that does not exclude exercises of official power for corrupt ends. Indeed, an established definition states that "corruptly" means action with an

170

U.S. Department of Justice

~~Attorney Work Product // May Contain Material Protected Under Fed. R. Crim. P. 6(e)~~

intent to secure an improper advantage "*inconsistent with official duty* and the rights of others." BALLENTINE'S LAW DICTIONARY 276 (3d ed. 1969) (emphasis added). And it would be contrary to ordinary rules of statutory construction to adopt an unconventional meaning of a statutory term only when applied to the President. *See United States v. Santos*, 553 U.S. 507, 522 (2008) (plurality opinion of Scalia, J.) (rejecting proposal to "giv[e] the same word, in the same statutory provision, different meanings in different factual contexts"); *cf. Public Citizen*, 491 U.S. at 462-467 (giving the term "utilized" in the FACA a uniform meaning to avoid constitutional questions). Nor could such an exclusion draw on a separate and established background interpretive presumption, such as the presumption against extraterritoriality applied in *Sale*. The principle that courts will construe a statute to avoid serious constitutional questions "is not a license for the judiciary to rewrite language enacted by the legislature." *Salinas v. United States*, 522 U.S. 52, 59-60 (1997). "It is one thing to acknowledge and accept . . . well defined (or even newly enunciated), generally applicable, background principles of assumed legislative intent. It is quite another to espouse the broad proposition that criminal statutes do not have to be read as broadly as they are written, but are subject to case-by-case exceptions." *Brogan v. United States*, 522 U.S. 398, 406 (1998).

When a proposed construction "would thus function as an extra-textual limit on [a statute's] compass," thereby preventing the statute "from applying to a host of cases falling within its clear terms," *Loughrin*, 573 U.S. at 357, it is doubtful that the construction would reflect Congress's intent. That is particularly so with respect to obstruction statutes, which "have been given a broad and all-inclusive meaning." *Rainey*, 757 F.3d at 245 (discussing Sections 1503 and 1505) (internal quotation marks omitted). Accordingly, since no established principle of interpretation would exclude the presidential conduct we have investigated from statutes such as Sections 1503, 1505, 1512(b), and 1512(c)(2), we proceed to examine the separation-of-powers issues that could be raised as an Article II defense to the application of those statutes.

2. Separation-of-Powers Principles Support the Conclusion that Congress May Validly Prohibit Corrupt Obstructive Acts Carried Out Through the President's Official Powers

When Congress imposes a limitation on the exercise of Article II powers, the limitation's validity depends on whether the measure "disrupts the balance between the coordinate branches." *Nixon v. Administrator of General Services*, 433 U.S. 425, 443 (1977). "Even when a branch does not arrogate power to itself, . . . the separation-of-powers doctrine requires that a branch not impair another in the performance of its constitutional duties." *Loving v. United States*, 517 U.S. 748, 757 (1996). The "separation of powers does not mean," however, "that the branches 'ought to have no partial agency in, or no controul over the acts of each other.'" *Clinton v. Jones*, 520 U.S. 681, 703 (1997) (quoting James Madison, The Federalist No. 47, pp. 325–326 (J. Cooke ed. 1961) (emphasis omitted)). In this context, a balancing test applies to assess separation-of-powers issues. Applying that test here, we concluded that Congress can validly make obstruction-of-justice statutes applicable to corruptly motivated official acts of the President without impermissibly undermining his Article II functions.

U.S. Department of Justice

~~Attorney Work Product // May Contain Material Protected Under Fed. R. Crim. P. 6(e)~~

a. The Supreme Court's Separation-of-Powers Balancing Test Applies In This Context

A congressionally imposed limitation on presidential action is assessed to determine "the extent to which it prevents the Executive Branch from accomplishing its constitutionally assigned functions," and, if the "potential for disruption is present[,] . . . whether that impact is justified by an overriding need to promote objectives within the constitutional authority of Congress." *Administrator of General Services*, 433 U.S. at 443; *see Nixon v. Fitzgerald*, 457 U.S. 731,753-754 (1982); *United States v. Nixon*, 418 U.S. 683, 706-707 (1974). That balancing test applies to a congressional regulation of presidential power through the obstruction-of-justice laws. [1087]

When an Article II power has not been "explicitly assigned by the text of the Constitution to be within the sole province of the President, but rather was thought to be encompassed within the general grant to the President of the 'executive Power,'" the Court has balanced competing constitutional considerations. *Public Citizen*, 491 U.S. at 484 (Kennedy, J., concurring in the judgment, joined by Rehnquist, C.J., and O'Connor, J.). As Justice Kennedy noted in *Public Citizen*, the Court has applied a balancing test to restrictions on "the President's power to remove Executive officers, a power [that] . . . is not conferred by any explicit provision in the text of the Constitution (as is the appointment power), but rather is inferred to be a necessary part of the grant of the 'executive Power.'" *Id.* (citing *Morrison v. Olson*, 487 U.S. 654, 694 (1988), and *Myers v. United States*, 272 U.S. 52, 115-116 (1926)). Consistent with that statement, *Morrison* sustained a good-cause limitation on the removal of an inferior officer with defined prosecutorial responsibilities after determining that the limitation did not impermissibly undermine the President's ability to perform his Article II functions. 487 U.S. at 691-693, 695-696. The Court has also evaluated other general executive-power claims through a balancing test. For example, the Court evaluated the President's claim of an absolute privilege for presidential communications about his official acts by balancing that interest against the Judicial Branch's need for evidence in a criminal case. *United States v. Nixon, supra* (recognizing a qualified constitutional privilege for presidential communications on official matters). The Court has also upheld a law that provided for archival access to presidential records despite a claim of absolute presidential privilege over the records. *Administrator of General Services*, 433 U.S. at 443-445, 451-455. The analysis in those cases supports applying a balancing test to assess the constitutionality of applying the obstruction-of-justice statutes to presidential exercises of executive power.

Only in a few instances has the Court applied a different framework. When the President's power is "both 'exclusive' and 'conclusive' on the issue," Congress is precluded from regulating its exercise. *Zivotofsky v. Kerry*, 135 S. Ct. 2076, 2084 (2015). In *Zivotofsky*, for example, the Court followed "Justice Jackson's familiar tripartite framework" in *Youngstown Sheet & Tube Co. v. Sawyer*, 343 U.S. 579, 635-638 (1952) (Jackson, J., concurring), and held that the President's

---

[1087] OLC applied such a balancing test in concluding that the President is not subject to criminal prosecution while in office, relying on many of the same precedents discussed in this section. *See A Sitting President's Amenability to Indictment and Criminal Prosecution*, 24 Op. O.L.C. 222, 237-238, 244-245 (2000) (relying on, *inter alia*, *United States v. Nixon*, *Nixon v. Fitzgerald*, and *Clinton v. Jones*, and quoting the legal standard from *Administrator of General Services v. Nixon* that is applied in the text). OLC recognized that "[t]he balancing analysis" it had initially relied on in finding that a sitting President is immune from prosecution had "been adopted as the appropriate mode of analysis by the Court." *Id.* at 244.

U.S. Department of Justice

~~Attorney Work Product // May Contain Material Protected Under Fed. R. Crim. P. 6(e)~~

authority to recognize foreign nations is exclusive. *Id.* at 2083, 2094. *See also Public Citizen* 491 U.S. at 485-486 (Kennedy, J., concurring in the judgment) (citing the power to grant pardons under U.S. CONST., ART. II, § 2, cl. 1, and the Presentment Clauses for legislation, U.S. CONST., ART. I, § 7, Cls. 2, 3, as examples of exclusive presidential powers by virtue of constitutional text).

But even when a power is exclusive, "Congress' powers, and its central role in making laws, give it substantial authority regarding many of the policy determinations that precede and follow" the President's act. *Zivotofsky*, 135 S. Ct. at 2087. For example, although the President's power to grant pardons is exclusive and not subject to congressional regulation, *see United States v. Klein*, 80 U.S. (13 Wall.) 128, 147-148 (1872), Congress has the authority to prohibit the corrupt use of "anything of value" to influence the testimony of another person in a judicial, congressional, or agency proceeding, 18 U.S.C. § 201(b)(3)—which would include the offer or promise of a pardon to induce a person to testify falsely or not to testify at all. The offer of a pardon would precede the act of pardoning and thus be within Congress's power to regulate even if the pardon itself is not. Just as the Speech or Debate Clause, U.S. CONST. ART. I, § 6, cl.1, absolutely protects legislative acts, but not a legislator's "taking or agreeing to take money for a promise to act in a certain way . . . for it is taking the bribe, not performance of the illicit compact, that is a criminal act," *United States v. Brewster*, 408 U.S. 501, 526 (1972) (emphasis omitted), the promise of a pardon to corruptly influence testimony would not be a constitutionally immunized act. The application of obstruction statutes to such promises therefore would raise no serious separation-of-powers issue.

b. The Effect of Obstruction-of-Justice Statutes on the President's Capacity to Perform His Article II Responsibilities is Limited

Under the Supreme Court's balancing test for analyzing separation-of-powers issues, the first task is to assess the degree to which applying obstruction-of-justice statutes to presidential actions affects the President's ability to carry out his Article II responsibilities. *Administrator of General Services*, 433 U.S. at 443. As discussed above, applying obstruction-of-justice statutes to presidential conduct that does not involve the President's conduct of office—such as influencing the testimony of witnesses—is constitutionally unproblematic. The President has no more right than other citizens to impede official proceedings by corruptly influencing witness testimony. The conduct would be equally improper whether effectuated through direct efforts to produce false testimony or suppress the truth, or through the actual, threatened, or promised use of official powers to achieve the same result.

The President's action in curtailing criminal investigations or prosecutions, or discharging law enforcement officials, raises different questions. Each type of action involves the exercise of executive discretion in furtherance of the President's duty to "take Care that the Laws be faithfully executed." U.S. CONST., ART. II, § 3. Congress may not supplant the President's exercise of executive power to supervise prosecutions or to remove officers who occupy law enforcement positions. *See Bowsher v. Synar*, 478 U.S. 714, 726-727 (1986) ("Congress cannot reserve for itself the power of removal of an officer charged with the execution of the laws except by impeachment. . . . [Because t]he structure of the Constitution does not permit Congress to execute the laws, . . . [t]his kind of congressional control over the execution of the laws . . . is constitutionally impermissible."). Yet the obstruction-of-justice statutes do not aggrandize power in Congress or usurp executive authority. Instead, they impose a discrete limitation on conduct

U.S. Department of Justice

Attorney Work Product // May Contain Material Protected Under Fed. R. Crim. P. 6(e)

only when it is taken with the "corrupt" intent to obstruct justice. The obstruction statutes thus would restrict presidential action only by prohibiting the President from acting to obstruct official proceedings for the improper purpose of protecting his own interests. *See* Volume II, Section III.A.3, *supra.*

The direct effect on the President's freedom of action would correspondingly be a limited one. A preclusion of "corrupt" official action is not a major intrusion on Article II powers. For example, the proper supervision of criminal law does not demand freedom for the President to act with the intention of shielding himself from criminal punishment, avoiding financial liability, or preventing personal embarrassment. To the contrary, a statute that prohibits official action undertaken for such personal purposes furthers, rather than hinders, the impartial and evenhanded administration of the law. And the Constitution does not mandate that the President have unfettered authority to direct investigations or prosecutions, with no limits whatsoever, in order to carry out his Article II functions. *See Heckler v. Chaney,* 470 U.S. 821, 833 (1985) ("Congress may limit an agency's exercise of enforcement power if it wishes, either by setting substantive priorities, or by otherwise circumscribing an agency's power to discriminate among issues or cases it will pursue."); *United States v. Nixon,* 418 U.S. at 707 ("[t]o read the Art. II powers of the President as providing an absolute privilege [to withhold confidential communications from a criminal trial] . . . would upset the constitutional balance of 'a workable government' and gravely impair the role of the courts under Art. III").

Nor must the President have unfettered authority to remove all Executive Branch officials involved in the execution of the laws. The Constitution establishes that Congress has legislative authority to structure the Executive Branch by authorizing Congress to create executive departments and officer positions and to specify how inferior officers are appointed. *E.g.,* U.S. CONST., ART. I, § 8, cl. 18 (Necessary and Proper Clause); ART. II, § 2, cl. 1 (Opinions Clause); ART. II, § 2, cl. 2 (Appointments Clause); *see Free Enterprise Fund,* 561 U.S. at 499. While the President's removal power is an important means of ensuring that officers faithfully execute the law, Congress has a recognized authority to place certain limits on removal. *Id.* at 493-495.

The President's removal powers are at their zenith with respect to principal officers—that is, officers who must be appointed by the President and who report to him directly. *See Free Enterprise Fund,* 561 U.S. at 493, 500. The President's "exclusive and illimitable power of removal" of those principal officers furthers "the President's ability to ensure that the laws are faithfully executed." *Id.* at 493, 498 (internal quotation marks omitted); *Myers,* 272 U.S. at 627. Thus, "there are some 'purely executive' officials who must be removable by the President at will if he is able to accomplish his constitutional role." *Morrison,* 487 U.S. at 690; *Myers,* 272 U.S. at 134 (the President's "cabinet officers must do his will," and "[t]he moment that he loses confidence in the intelligence, ability, judgment, or loyalty of any one of them, he must have the power to remove him without delay"); *cf. Humphrey's Executor v. United States,* 295 U.S. 602 (1935) (Congress has the power to create independent agencies headed by principal officers removable only for good cause). In light of those constitutional precedents, it may be that the obstruction statutes could not be constitutionally applied to limit the removal of a cabinet officer such as the Attorney General. *See* 5 U.S.C. § 101; 28 U.S.C. § 503. In that context, at least absent circumstances showing that the President was clearly attempting to thwart accountability for personal conduct while evading ordinary political checks and balances, even the highly limited

174

U.S. Department of Justice

~~Attorney Work Product // May Contain Material Protected Under Fed. R. Crim. P. 6(e)~~

regulation imposed by the obstruction statutes could possibly intrude too deeply on the President's freedom to select and supervise the members of his cabinet.

The removal of inferior officers, in contrast, need not necessarily be at will for the President to fulfill his constitutionally assigned role in managing the Executive Branch. "[I]nferior officers are officers whose work is directed and supervised at some level by other officers appointed by the President with the Senate's consent." *Free Enterprise Fund*, 561 U.S. at 510 (quoting *Edmond v. United States*, 520 U.S. 651, 663 (1997)) (internal quotation marks omitted). The Supreme Court has long recognized Congress's authority to place for-cause limitations on the President's removal of "inferior Officers" whose appointment may be vested in the head of a department. U.S. CONST. ART. II, § 2, cl. 2. *See United States v. Perkins*, 116 U.S. 483, 485 (1886) ("The constitutional authority in Congress to thus vest the appointment [of inferior officers in the heads of departments] implies authority to limit, restrict, and regulate the removal by such laws as Congress may enact in relation to the officers so appointed") (quoting lower court decision); *Morrison*, 487 U.S. at 689 n. 27 (citing *Perkins*); *accord id.* at 723-724 & n.4 (Scalia, J., dissenting) (recognizing that *Perkins* is "established" law); *see also Free Enterprise Fund*, 561 U.S. at 493-495 (citing *Perkins* and *Morrison*). The category of inferior officers includes both the FBI Director and the Special Counsel, each of whom reports to the Attorney General. *See* 28 U.S.C. §§ 509, 515(a), 531; 28 C.F.R. Part 600. Their work is thus "directed and supervised" by a presidentially-appointed, Senate-confirmed officer. *See In re: Grand Jury Investigation*, __ F.3d __, 2019 WL 921692, at *3-*4 (D.C. Cir. Feb. 26, 2019) (holding that the Special Counsel is an "inferior officer" for constitutional purposes).

Where the Constitution permits Congress to impose a good-cause limitation on the removal of an Executive Branch officer, the Constitution should equally permit Congress to bar removal for the corrupt purpose of obstructing justice. Limiting the range of permissible reasons for removal to exclude a "corrupt" purpose imposes a lesser restraint on the President than requiring an affirmative showing of good cause. It follows that for such inferior officers, Congress may constitutionally restrict the President's removal authority if that authority was exercised for the corrupt purpose of obstructing justice. And even if a particular inferior officer's position might be of such importance to the execution of the laws that the President must have at-will removal authority, the obstruction-of-justice statutes could still be constitutionally applied to forbid removal for a corrupt reason.[1088] A narrow and discrete limitation on removal that precluded corrupt action would leave ample room for all other considerations, including disagreement over policy or loss of confidence in the officer's judgment or commitment. A corrupt-purpose prohibition therefore would not undermine the President's ability to perform his Article II functions. Accordingly, because the separation-of-powers question is "whether the removal restrictions are of such a nature that they impede the President's ability to perform his constitutional duty," *Morrison*, 487 U.S. at 691, a restriction on removing an inferior officer for a

---

[1088] Although the FBI director is an inferior officer, he is appointed by the President and removable by him at will, *see* 28 U.S.C. § 532 note, and it is not clear that Congress could constitutionally provide the FBI director with good-cause tenure protection. *See* OLC, *Constitutionality of Legislation Extending the Term of the FBI Director*, 2011 WL 2566125, at *3 (O.L.C. June 20, 2011) ("tenure protection for an officer with the FBI Director's broad investigative, administrative, and policymaking responsibilities would raise a serious constitutional question whether Congress had 'impede[d]' the President's ability to perform his constitutional duty' to take care that the laws be faithfully executed") (quoting *Morrison*, 487 U.S. at 691).

U.S. Department of Justice

Attorney Work Product // May Contain Material Protected Under Fed. R. Crim. P. 6(e)

corrupt reason—a reason grounded in achieving personal rather than official ends—does not seriously hinder the President's performance of his duties. The President retains broad latitude to supervise investigations and remove officials, circumscribed in this context only by the requirement that he not act for corrupt personal purposes.[1089]

c. Congress Has Power to Protect Congressional, Grand Jury, and Judicial Proceedings Against Corrupt Acts from Any Source

Where a law imposes a burden on the President's performance of Article II functions, separation-of-powers analysis considers whether the statutory measure "is justified by an overriding need to promote objectives within the constitutional authority of Congress." *Administrator of General Services*, 433 U.S. at 443. Here, Congress enacted the obstruction-of-justice statutes to protect, among other things, the integrity of its own proceedings, grand jury investigations, and federal criminal trials. Those objectives are within Congress's authority and serve strong governmental interests.

i. Congress has Article I authority to define generally applicable criminal law and apply it to all persons—including the President. Congress clearly has authority to protect its own legislative functions against corrupt efforts designed to impede legitimate fact-gathering and lawmaking efforts. *See Watkins v. United States*, 354 U.S. 178, 187, 206-207 (1957); *Chapman v. United States*, 5 App. D.C. 122, 130 (1895). Congress also has authority to establish a system of federal courts, which includes the power to protect the judiciary against obstructive acts. *See* U.S. CONST. ART. I, § 8, cls. 9, 18 ("The Congress shall have Power ... To constitute Tribunals inferior to the supreme Court" and "To make all Laws which shall be necessary and proper for carrying into Execution the foregoing powers"). The long lineage of the obstruction-of-justice statutes, which can be traced to at least 1831, attests to the necessity for that protection. *See An Act Declaratory of the Law Concerning Contempts of Court*, 4 Stat. 487-488 § 2 (1831) (making it a crime if "any person or persons shall corruptly ... endeavor to influence, intimidate, or impede any juror, witness, or officer, in any court of the United States, in the discharge of his duty, or shall, corruptly ... obstruct, or impede, or endeavor to obstruct or impede, the due administration of justice therein").

ii. The Article III courts have an equally strong interest in being protected against obstructive acts, whatever their source. As the Supreme Court explained in *United States v. Nixon*, a "primary constitutional duty of the Judicial Branch" is "to do justice in criminal prosecutions." 418 U.S. at 707; *accord Cheney v. United States District Court for the District of Columbia*, 542 U.S. 367, 384 (2004). In *Nixon*, the Court rejected the President's claim of absolute executive privilege because "the allowance of the privilege to withhold evidence that is demonstrably

---

[1089] The obstruction statutes do not disqualify the President from acting in a case simply because he has a personal interest in it or because his own conduct may be at issue. As the Department of Justice has made clear, a claim of a conflict of interest, standing alone, cannot deprive the President of the ability to fulfill his constitutional function. *See, e.g.*, OLC, *Application of 28 U.S.C. § 458 to Presidential Appointments of Federal Judges*, 19 O.L.C. Op. at 356 (citing Memorandum for Richard T. Burress, Office of the President, from Laurence H. Silberman, Deputy Attorney General, *Re: Conflict of Interest Problems Arising out of the President's Nomination of Nelson A. Rockefeller to be Vice President under the Twenty-Fifth Amendment to the Constitution*, at 2, 5 (Aug. 28, 1974)).

U.S. Department of Justice

~~Attorney Work Product // May Contain Material Protected Under Fed. R. Crim. P. 6(e)~~

relevant in a criminal trial would cut deeply into the guarantee of due process of law and gravely impair the basic function of the courts." 407 U.S. at 712. As *Nixon* illustrates, the need to safeguard judicial integrity is a compelling constitutional interest. *See id.* at 709 (noting that the denial of full disclosure of the facts surrounding relevant presidential communications threatens "[t]he very integrity of the judicial system and public confidence in the system").

iii. Finally, the grand jury cannot achieve its constitutional purpose absent protection from corrupt acts. Serious federal criminal charges generally reach the Article III courts based on an indictment issued by a grand jury. *Cobbledick v. United States*, 309 U.S. 323, 327 (1940) ("The Constitution itself makes the grand jury a part of the judicial process."). And the grand jury's function is enshrined in the Fifth Amendment. U.S. CONST. AMEND. V. ("[n]o person shall be held to answer" for a serious crime "unless on a presentment or indictment of a Grand Jury"). "[T]he whole theory of [the grand jury's] function is that it belongs to no branch of the institutional government, serving as a kind of buffer or referee between the Government and the people," *United States v. Williams*, 504 U.S. 36, 47 (1992), "pledged to indict no one because of prejudice and to free no one because of special favor." *Costello v. United States*, 350 U.S. 359, 362 (1956). If the grand jury were not protected against corrupt interference from all persons, its function as an independent charging body would be thwarted. And an impartial grand jury investigation to determine whether probable cause exists to indict is vital to the criminal justice process.

*   *

The final step in the constitutional balancing process is to assess whether the separation-of-powers doctrine permits Congress to take action within its constitutional authority notwithstanding the potential impact on Article II functions. *See Administrator of General Services*, 433 U.S. at 443; *see also Morrison*, 487 U.S. at 691-693, 695-696; *United States v. Nixon*, 418 U.S. at 711-712. In the case of the obstruction-of-justice statutes, our assessment of the weighing of interests leads us to conclude that Congress has the authority to impose the limited restrictions contained in those statutes on the President's official conduct to protect the integrity of important functions of other branches of government.

A general ban on corrupt action does not unduly intrude on the President's responsibility to "take Care that the Laws be faithfully executed." U.S. CONST. ART II, §§ 3.[1090] To the contrary, the concept of "faithful execution" connotes the use of power in the interest of the public, not in the office holder's personal interests. *See* 1 Samuel Johnson, *A Dictionary of the English Language* 763 (1755) ("faithfully" def. 3: "[w]ith strict adherence to duty and allegiance"). And immunizing the President from the generally applicable criminal prohibition against corrupt obstruction of official proceedings would seriously impair Congress's power to enact laws "to promote objectives within [its] constitutional authority," *Administrator of General Services*, 433 U.S. at 425—*i.e.*, protecting the integrity of its own proceedings and the proceedings of Article III courts and grand juries.

[1090] As noted above, the President's selection and removal of principal executive officers may have a unique constitutional status.

U.S. Department of Justice

Attorney Work Product // May Contain Material Protected Under Fed. R. Crim. P. 6(e)

Accordingly, based on the analysis above, we were not persuaded by the argument that the President has blanket constitutional immunity to engage in acts that would corruptly obstruct justice through the exercise of otherwise-valid Article II powers. [1091]

3. Ascertaining Whether the President Violated the Obstruction Statutes Would Not Chill his Performance of his Article II Duties

Applying the obstruction statutes to the President's official conduct would involve determining as a factual matter whether he engaged in an obstructive act, whether the act had a nexus to official proceedings, and whether he was motivated by corrupt intent. But applying those standards to the President's official conduct should not hinder his ability to perform his Article II duties. *Cf. Nixon v. Fitzgerald*, 457 U.S. at 752-753 & n.32 (taking into account chilling effect on the President in adopting a constitutional rule of presidential immunity from private civil damages action based on official duties). Several safeguards would prevent a chilling effect: the existence of settled legal standards, the presumption of regularity in prosecutorial actions, and the existence of evidentiary limitations on probing the President's motives. And historical experience confirms that no impermissible chill should exist.

a. As an initial matter, the term "corruptly" sets a demanding standard. It requires a concrete showing that a person acted with an intent to obtain an "improper advantage for [him]self or someone else, inconsistent with official duty and the rights of others." BALLENTINE'S LAW DICTIONARY 276 (3d ed. 1969); *see United States v. Pasha*, 797 F.3d 1122, 1132 (D.C. Cir. 2015); *Aguilar*, 515 U.S. at 616 (Scalia, J., concurring in part and dissenting in part). That standard parallels the President's constitutional obligation to ensure the faithful execution of the laws. And virtually everything that the President does in the routine conduct of office will have a clear governmental purpose and will not be contrary to his official duty. Accordingly, the President has no reason to be chilled in those actions because, in virtually all instances, there will be no credible basis for suspecting a corrupt personal motive.

That point is illustrated by examples of conduct that would and would not satisfy the stringent corrupt-motive standard. Direct or indirect action by the President to end a criminal investigation into his own or his family members' conduct to protect against personal embarrassment or legal liability would constitute a core example of corruptly motivated conduct. So too would action to halt an enforcement proceeding that directly and adversely affected the President's financial interests for the purpose of protecting those interests. In those examples,

---

[1091] A possible remedy through impeachment for abuses of power would not substitute for potential criminal liability after a President leaves office. Impeachment would remove a President from office, but would not address the underlying culpability of the conduct or serve the usual purposes of the criminal law. Indeed, the Impeachment Judgment Clause recognizes that criminal law plays an independent role in addressing an official's conduct, distinct from the political remedy of impeachment. *See* U.S. CONST. ART. I, § 3, cl. 7. Impeachment is also a drastic and rarely invoked remedy, and Congress is not restricted to relying only on impeachment, rather than making criminal law applicable to a former President, as OLC has recognized. *A Sitting President's Amenability to Indictment and Criminal Prosecution*, 24 Op. O.L.C. at 255 ("Recognizing an immunity from prosecution for a sitting President would not preclude such prosecution once the President's term is over or he is otherwise removed from office by resignation or impeachment.").

official power is being used for the purpose of protecting the President's personal interests. In contrast, the President's actions to serve political or policy interests would not qualify as corrupt. The President's role as head of the government necessarily requires him to take into account political factors in making policy decisions that affect law-enforcement actions and proceedings. For instance, the President's decision to curtail a law-enforcement investigation to avoid international friction would not implicate the obstruction-of-justice statutes. The criminal law does not seek to regulate the consideration of such political or policy factors in the conduct of government. And when legitimate interests animate the President's conduct, those interests will almost invariably be readily identifiable based on objective factors. Because the President's conduct in those instances will obviously fall outside the zone of obstruction law, no chilling concern should arise.

b. There is also no reason to believe that investigations, let alone prosecutions, would occur except in highly unusual circumstances when a credible factual basis exists to believe that obstruction occurred. Prosecutorial action enjoys a presumption of regularity: absent "clear evidence to the contrary, courts presume that [prosecutors] have properly discharged their official duties." *Armstrong,* 517 U.S. at 464 (*quoting United States v. Chemical Foundation, Inc.,* 272 U.S. 1, 14–15 (1926)). The presumption of prosecutorial regularity would provide even greater protection to the President than exists in routine cases given the prominence and sensitivity of any matter involving the President and the likelihood that such matters will be subject to thorough and careful review at the most senior levels of the Department of Justice. Under OLC's opinion that a sitting President is entitled to immunity from indictment, only a successor Administration would be able to prosecute a former President. But that consideration does not suggest that a President would have any basis for fearing abusive investigations or prosecutions after leaving office. There are "obvious political checks" against initiating a baseless investigation or prosecution of a former President. *See Administrator of General Services,* 433 U.S. at 448 (considering political checks in separation-of-powers analysis). And the Attorney General holds "the power to conduct the criminal litigation of the United States Government," *United States v. Nixon,* 418 U.S. at 694 (citing 28 U.S.C. § 516), which provides a strong institutional safeguard against politicized investigations or prosecutions. [1092]

[1092] Similar institutional safeguards protect Department of Justice officers and line prosecutors against unfounded investigations into prosecutorial acts. Prosecutors are generally barred from participating in matters implicating their personal interests, *see* 28 C.F.R. § 45.2, and are instructed not to be influenced by their "own professional or personal circumstances," Justice Manual § 9-27.260, so prosecutors would not frequently be in a position to take action that could be perceived as corrupt and personally motivated. And if such cases arise, criminal investigation would be conducted by responsible officials at the Department of Justice, who can be presumed to refrain from pursuing an investigation absent a credible factual basis. Those facts distinguish the criminal context from the common-law rule of prosecutorial immunity, which protects against the threat of suit by "a defendant [who] often will transform his resentment at being prosecuted into the ascription of improper and malicious actions." *Imbler v. Pachtman,* 424 U.S. 409, 425 (1976). As the Supreme Court has noted, the existence of civil immunity does not justify criminal immunity. *See O'Shea v. Littleton,* 414 U.S. 488, 503 (1974) ("Whatever may be the case with respect to civil liability generally, . . . we have never held that the performance of the duties of judicial, legislative, or executive officers, requires or contemplates the immunization of otherwise criminal deprivation of constitutional rights.") (citations omitted).

U.S. Department of Justice

~~Attorney Work Product // May Contain Material Protected Under Fed. R. Crim. P. 6(e)~~

These considerations distinguish the Supreme Court's holding in *Nixon v. Fitzgerald* that, in part because inquiries into the President's motives would be "highly intrusive," the President is absolutely immune from private civil damages actions based on his official conduct. 457 U.S. at 756-757. As *Fitzgerald* recognized, "there is a lesser public interest in actions for civil damages than, for example, in criminal prosecutions." *Fitzgerald*, 457 U.S. at 754 n.37; *see Cheney*, 542 U.S. at 384. And private actions are not subject to the institutional protections of an action under the supervision of the Attorney General and subject to a presumption of regularity. *Armstrong*, 517 U.S. at 464.

c. In the rare cases in which a substantial and credible basis justifies conducting an investigation of the President, the process of examining his motivations to determine whether he acted for a corrupt purpose need not have a chilling effect. Ascertaining the President's motivations would turn on any explanation he provided to justify his actions, the advice he received, the circumstances surrounding the actions, and the regularity or irregularity of the process he employed to make decisions. But grand juries and courts would not have automatic access to confidential presidential communications on those matters; rather, they could be presented in official proceedings only on a showing of sufficient need. *Nixon*, 418 U.S. at 712; *In re Sealed Case*, 121 F.3d 729, 754, 756-757 (D.C. Cir. 1997); *see also Administrator of General Services*, 433 U.S. at 448-449 (former President can invoke presidential communications privilege, although successor's failure to support the claim "detracts from [its] weight").

In any event, probing the President's intent in a criminal matter is unquestionably constitutional in at least one context: the offense of bribery turns on the corrupt intent to receive a thing of value in return for being influenced in official action. 18 U.S.C. § 201(b)(2). There can be no serious argument against the President's potential criminal liability for bribery offenses, notwithstanding the need to ascertain his purpose and intent. *See* U.S. CONST. ART. I, § 3; ART. II, § 4; *see also Application of 28 U.S.C. § 458 to Presidential Appointments of Federal Judges*, 19 Op. O.L.C. at 357 n.11 ("Application of § 201 [to the President] raises no separation of powers issue, let alone a serious one.").

d. Finally, history provides no reason to believe that any asserted chilling effect justifies exempting the President from the obstruction laws. As a historical matter, Presidents have very seldom been the subjects of grand jury investigations. And it is rarer still for circumstances to raise even the possibility of a corrupt personal motive for arguably obstructive action through the President's use of official power. Accordingly, the President's conduct of office should not be chilled based on hypothetical concerns about the possible application of a corrupt-motive standard in this context.

In sum, contrary to the position taken by the President's counsel, we concluded that, in light of the Supreme Court precedent governing separation-of-powers issues, we had a valid basis for investigating the conduct at issue in this report. In our view, the application of the obstruction statutes would not impermissibly burden the President's performance of his Article II function to supervise prosecutorial conduct or to remove inferior law-enforcement officers. And the protection of the criminal justice system from corrupt acts by any person—including the President accords with the fundamental principle of our government that "[n]o [person] in this

U.S. Department of Justice

~~Attorney Work Product // May Contain Material Protected Under Fed. R. Crim. P. 6(e)~~

country is so high that he is above the law." *United States v. Lee*, 106 U.S. 196, 220 (1882); *see also Clinton v. Jones*, 520 U.S. at 697; *United States v. Nixon, supra.*

IV. CONCLUSION

Because we determined not to make a traditional prosecutorial judgment, we did not draw ultimate conclusions about the President's conduct. The evidence we obtained about the President's actions and intent presents difficult issues that would need to be resolved if we were making a traditional prosecutorial judgment. At the same time, if we had confidence after a thorough investigation of the facts that the President clearly did not commit obstruction of justice, we would so state. Based on the facts and the applicable legal standards, we are unable to reach that judgment. Accordingly, while this report does not conclude that the President committed a crime, it also does not exonerate him.

Appendix A

Office of the Deputy Attorney General
Washington, D.C. 20530

ORDER NO. 3915-2017

APPOINTMENT OF SPECIAL COUNSEL
TO INVESTIGATE RUSSIAN INTERFERENCE WITH THE
2016 PRESIDENTIAL ELECTION AND RELATED MATTERS

By virtue of the authority vested in me as Acting Attorney General, including 28 U.S.C. §§ 509, 510, and 515, in order to discharge my responsibility to provide supervision and management of the Department of Justice, and to ensure a full and thorough investigation of the Russian government's efforts to interfere in the 2016 presidential election, I hereby order as follows:

(a)   Robert S. Mueller III is appointed to serve as Special Counsel for the United States Department of Justice.

(b)   The Special Counsel is authorized to conduct the investigation confirmed by then-FBI Director James B. Comey in testimony before the House Permanent Select Committee on Intelligence on March 20, 2017, including:

      (i)   any links and/or coordination between the Russian government and individuals associated with the campaign of President Donald Trump; and

      (ii)   any matters that arose or may arise directly from the investigation; and

      (iii)   any other matters within the scope of 28 C.F.R. § 600.4(a).

(c)   If the Special Counsel believes it is necessary and appropriate, the Special Counsel is authorized to prosecute federal crimes arising from the investigation of these matters.

(d)   Sections 600.4 through 600.10 of Title 28 of the Code of Federal Regulations are applicable to the Special Counsel.

_____5/17/17_____
Date

Rod J. Rosenstein
Acting Attorney General

U.S. Department of Justice

Attorney Work Product // May Contain Material Protected Under Fed. R. Crim. P. 6(e)

Appendix B

APPENDIX B: GLOSSARY

The following glossary contains names and brief descriptions of individuals and entities referenced in the two volumes of this report. It is not intended to be comprehensive and is intended only to assist a reader in the reading the rest of the report.

Referenced Persons

Agalarov, Aras	Russian real-estate developer (owner of the Crocus Group); met Donald Trump in connection with the Miss Universe pageant and helped arrange the June 9, 2016 meeting at Trump Tower between Natalia Veselnitskaya and Trump Campaign officials.
Agalarov, Emin	Performer, executive vice president of Crocus Group, and son of Aras Agalarov; helped arrange the June 9, 2016 meeting at Trump Tower between Natalia Veselnitskaya and Trump Campaign officials.
Akhmetov, Rinat	Former member in the Ukrainian parliament who hired Paul Manafort to conduct work for Ukrainian political party, the Party of Regions.
Akhmetshin, Rinat	U.S. lobbyist and associate of Natalia Veselnitskaya who attended the June 9, 2016 meeting at Trump Tower between Veselnitskaya and Trump Campaign officials.
Aslanov, Dzheykhun (Jay)	Head of U.S. department of the Internet Research Agency, which engaged in an "active measures" social media campaign to interfere in the 2016 U.S. presidential election.
Assange, Julian	Founder of WikiLeaks, which in 2016 posted on the internet documents stolen from entities and individuals affiliated with the Democratic Party.
Aven, Petr	Chairman of the board of Alfa-Bank who attempted outreach to the Presidential Transition Team in connection with anticipated post-election sanctions.
Bannon, Stephen (Steve)	White House chief strategist and senior counselor to President Trump (Jan. 2017 – Aug. 2017); chief executive of the Trump Campaign.
Baranov, Andrey	Director of investor relations at Russian state-owned oil company, Rosneft, and associate of Carter Page.
Berkowitz, Avi	Assistant to Jared Kushner.
Boente, Dana	Acting Attorney General (Jan. 2017 – Feb. 2017); Acting Deputy Attorney General (Feb. 2017 – Apr. 2017).
Bogacheva, Anna	Internet Research Agency employee who worked on "active measures" social media campaign to interfere in in the 2016 U.S. presidential election; traveled to the United States under false pretenses in 2014.
Bossert, Thomas (Tom)	Former homeland security advisor to the President who also served as a senior official on the Presidential Transition Team.

Boyarkin, Viktor	Employee of Russian oligarch Oleg Deripaska.
Boyd, Charles	Chairman of the board of directors at the Center for the National Interest, a U.S.-based think tank with operations in and connections to Russia.
Boyko, Yuriy	Member of the Ukrainian political party Opposition Bloc and member of the Ukrainian parliament.
Brand, Rachel	Associate Attorney General (May 2017 – Feb. 2018).
Browder, William (Bill)	Founder of Hermitage Capital Management who lobbied in favor of the Magnitsky Act, which imposed financial and travel sanctions on Russian officials.
Bulatov, Alexander	Russian intelligence official who associated with Carter Page in 2008.
Burchik, Mikhail	Executive director of the Internet Research Agency, which engaged in an "active measures" social media campaign to interfere in the 2016 U.S. presidential election.
Burck, William	Personal attorney to Don McGahn, White House Counsel.
Burnham, James	Attorney in the White House Counsel's Office who attended January 2017 meetings between Sally Yates and Donald McGahn.
Burt, Richard	Former U.S. ambassador who had done work Alfa-Bank and was a board member of the Center for the National Interest.
Bystrov, Mikhail	General director of the Internet Research Agency, which engaged in an "active measures" social media campaign to interfere in the 2016 U.S. presidential election.
Calamari, Matt	Chief operating officer for the Trump Organization.
Caputo, Michael	Trump Campaign advisor.
Chaika, Yuri	Prosecutor general of the Russian Federation who also maintained a relationship with Aras Agalarov.
Christie, Chris	Former Governor of New Jersey.
Clapper, James	Director of National Intelligence (Aug. 2010 – Jan. 2017).
Clovis, Samuel Jr.	Chief policy advisor and national co-chair of the Trump Campaign.
Coats, Dan	Director of National Intelligence.
Cobb, Ty	Special Counsel to the President (July 2017 – May 2018).
Cohen, Michael	Former vice president to the Trump Organization and special counsel to Donald Trump who spearheaded an effort to build a Trump-branded property in Moscow. He admitted to lying to Congress about the project.
Comey, James Jr.	Director of the Federal Bureau of Investigation (Sept. 4, 2013 – May 9, 2017).

U.S. Department of Justice

~~Attorney Work Product // May Contain Material Protected Under Fed. R. Crim. P. 6(e)~~

Conway, Kellyanne	Counselor to President Trump and manager of the Trump Campaign.
Corallo, Mark	Spokesman for President Trump's personal legal team (June 2017 – July 2017).
Corsi, Jerome	Author and political commentator who formerly worked for WorldNetDaily and InfoWars. ███████
Costello, Robert	Attorney who represented he had a close relationship with Rudolph Giuliani, the President's personal counsel.
Credico, Randolph (Randy)	Radio talk show host who interviewed Julian Assange in 2016. ████
Davis, Richard (Rick) Jr.	Partner with Pegasus Sustainable Century Merchant Bank, business partner of Paul Manafort, and co-founder of the Davis Manafort lobbying firm.
Dearborn, Rick	Former White House deputy chief of staff for policy who previously served as chief of staff to Senator Jeff Sessions.
Dempsey, Michael	Office of Director of National Intelligence official who recalled discussions with Dan Coats after Coats's meeting with President Trump on March 22, 2017.
Denman, Diana	Delegate to 2016 Republican National Convention who proposed a platform plank amendment that included armed support for Ukraine.
Deripaska, Oleg	Russian businessman with ties to Vladimir Putin who hired Paul Manafort for consulting work between 2005 and 2009.
Dhillon, Uttam	Attorney in the White House Counsel's Office (Jan. 2017 – June 2018).
Dmitriev, Kirill	Head of the Russian Direct Investment Fund (RDIF); met with Erik Prince in the Seychelles in January 2017 and, separately, drafted a U.S.-Russia reconciliation plan with Rick Gerson.
Donaldson, Annie	Chief of staff to White House Counsel Donald McGahn (Jan. 2017 – Dec. 2018).
Dvorkovich, Arkady	Deputy prime minister of the Russian Federation and chairman of the board of directors of the New Economic School in Moscow. He met with Carter Page twice in 2016.
Dvoskin, Evgeney	Executive of Genbank in Crimea and associate of Felix Sater.
Eisenberg, John	Attorney in the White House Counsel's Office and legal counsel for the National Security Council.
Erchova, Lana (a/k/a Lana Alexander)	Ex-wife of Dmitry Klokov who emailed Ivanka Trump to introduce Klokov to the Trump Campaign in the fall of 2015.

Fabrizio, Anthony (Tony)	Partner at the research and consulting firm Fabrizio, Lee & Associates. He was a pollster for the Trump Campaign and worked with Paul Manafort on Ukraine-related polling after the election.
Fishbein, Jason	Attorney who performed worked for Julian Assange and also sent WikiLeaks a password for an unlaunched website PutinTrump.org on September 20, 2016.
Flynn, Michael G. (a/k/a Michael Flynn Jr.)	Son of Michael T. Flynn, National Security Advisor (Jan. 20, 2017 – Feb. 13, 2017).
Flynn, Michael T.	National Security Advisor (Jan. 20, 2017 – Feb. 13, 2017), Director of the Defense Intelligence Agency (July 2012 – Aug. 7, 2014), and Trump Campaign advisor. He pleaded guilty to lying to the FBI about communications with Ambassador Sergey Kislyak in December 2016.
Foresman, Robert (Bob)	Investment banker who sought meetings with the Trump Campaign in spring 2016 to discuss Russian foreign policy, and after the election met with Michael Flynn.
Futerfas, Alan	Outside counsel for the Trump Organization and subsequently personal counsel for Donald Trump Jr.
Garten, Alan	General counsel of the Trump Organization.
Gates, Richard (Rick) III	Deputy campaign manager for Trump Campaign, Trump Inaugural Committee deputy chairman, and longtime employee of Paul Manafort. He pleaded guilty to conspiring to defraud the United States and violate U.S. laws, as well as making false statements to the FBI.
Gerson, Richard (Rick)	New York hedge fund manager and associate of Jared Kushner. During the transition period, he worked with Kirill Dmitriev on a proposal for reconciliation between the United States and Russia.
Gistaro, Edward	Deputy Director of National Intelligence for Intelligence Integration.
Glassner, Michael	Political director of the Trump Campaign who helped introduce George Papadopoulos to others in the Trump Campaign.
Goldstone, Robert	Publicist for Emin Agalarov who contacted Donald Trump Jr. to arrange the June 9, 2016 meeting at Trump Tower between Natalia Veselnitskaya and Trump Campaign officials.
Gordon, Jeffrey (J.D.)	National security advisor to the Trump Campaign involved in changes to the Republican party platform and who communicated with Russian Ambassador Sergey Kislyak at the Republican National Convention.
Gorkov, Sergey	Chairman of Vnesheconombank (VEB), a Russian state-owned bank, who met with Jared Kushner during the transition period.
Graff, Rhona	Senior vice-president and executive assistant to Donald J. Trump at the Trump Organization.

U.S. Department of Justice

~~Attorney-Work-Product // May-Contain-Material-Protected-Under-Fed. R. Crim. P. 6(e)~~

███████████   ████████████████████████████████████

Hawker, Jonathan   Public relations consultant at FTI Consulting; worked with Davis Manafort International LLC on public relations campaign in Ukraine.

Heilbrunn, Jacob   Editor of the National Interest, the periodical that officially hosted candidate Trump's April 2016 foreign policy speech.

Hicks, Hope   White House communications director (Aug. 2017 – Mar. 2018) and press secretary for the Trump Campaign.

Holt, Lester   NBC News anchor who interviewed President Trump on May 11, 2017.

Hunt, Jody   Chief of staff to Attorney General Jeff Sessions (Feb. 2017 – Oct. 2017).

Ivanov, Igor   President of the Russian International Affairs Council and former Russian foreign minister. Ivan Timofeev told George Papadopoulos that Ivanov advised on arranging a "Moscow visit" for the Trump Campaign.

Ivanov, Sergei   Special representative of Vladimir Putin, former Russian deputy prime minister, and former FSB deputy director. In January 2016, Michael Cohen emailed the Kremlin requesting to speak to Ivanov.

Kasowitz, Marc   President Trump's personal counsel (May 2017 – July 2017).

Katsyv, Denis   Son of Peter Katsyv; owner of Russian company Prevezon Holdings Ltd. and associate of Natalia Veselnitskaya.

Katsyv, Peter   Russian businessman and father of Denis Katsyv.

███████████   ████████████████████████████████████

Kaveladze, Irakli (Ike)   Vice president at Crocus Group and Aras Agalarov's deputy in the United States. He participated in the June 9, 2016 meeting at Trump Tower between Natalia Veselnitskaya and Trump Campaign officials.

Kaverzina, Irina   Employee of the Internet Research Agency, which engaged in an "active measures" social media campaign to interfere in the 2016 U.S. presidential election.

Kelly, John   White House chief of staff (July 2017 – Jan. 2019).

Khalilzad, Zalmay   U.S. special representative to Afghanistan and former U.S. ambassador. He met with Senator Jeff Sessions during foreign policy dinners put together through the Center for the National Interest.

Kilimnik, Konstantin   Russian-Ukrainian political consultant and long-time employee of Paul Manafort assessed by the FBI to have ties to Russian intelligence.

Kislyak, Sergey   Former Russian ambassador to the United States and current Russian senator from Mordovia.

Klimentov, Denis   Employee of the New Economic School who informed high-ranking Russian government officials of Carter Page's July 2016 visit to Moscow.

U.S. Department of Justice

~~Attorney-Work-Product // May Contain Material Protected Under Fed. R. Crim. P. 6(e)~~

Klimentov, Dmitri	Brother of Denis Klimentov who contacted Kremlin press secretary Dmitri Peskov about Carter Page's July 2016 visit to Moscow.
Klokov, Dmitry	Executive for PJSC Federal Grid Company of Unified Energy System and former aide to Russia's minister of energy. He communicated with Michael Cohen about a possible meeting between Vladimir Putin and candidate Trump.
Kobyakov, Anton	Advisor to Vladimir Putin and member of the Roscongress Foundation who invited candidate Trump to the St. Petersburg International Economic Forum.
Krickovic, Andrej	Professor at the Higher School of Economics who recommended that Carter Page give a July 2016 commencement address in Moscow.
Krylova, Aleksandra	Internet Research Agency employee who worked on "active measures" social media campaign to interfere in the 2016 U.S. presidential election; traveled to the United States under false pretenses in 2014.
Kushner, Jared	President Trump's son-in-law and senior advisor to the President.
Kuznetsov, Sergey	Russian government official at the Russian Embassy to the United States who transmitted Vladimir Putin's congratulations to President-Elect Trump for his electoral victory on November 9, 2016.
Landrum, Pete	Advisor to Senator Jeff Sessions who attended the September 2016 meeting between Sessions and Russian Ambassador Sergey Kislyak.
Lavrov, Sergey	Russian minister of foreign affairs and former permanent representative of Russia to the United Nations.
Ledeen, Barbara	Senate staffer and associate of Michael Flynn who sought to obtain Hillary Clinton emails during the 2016 U.S. presidential campaign period.
Ledeen, Michael	Member of the Presidential Transition Team who advised on foreign policy and national security matters.
Ledgett, Richard	Deputy director of the National Security Agency (Jan. 2014 – Apr. 2017); present when President Trump called Michael Rogers on March 26, 2017.
Lewandowski, Corey	Campaign manager for the Trump Campaign (Jan. 2015 – June 2016).
Luff, Sandra	Legislative director for Senator Jeff Sessions; attended a September 2016 meeting between Sessions and Russian Ambassador Sergey Kislyak.
Lyovochkin, Serhiy	Member of Ukrainian parliament and member of Ukrainian political party, Opposition Bloc Party.
Magnitsky, Sergei	Russian tax specialist who alleged Russian government corruption and died in Russian police custody in 2009. His death prompted passage of

U.S. Department of Justice

Attorney-Work-Product // May-Contain-Material-Protected-Under Fed. R. Crim. P. 6(e)

	the Magnitsky Act, which imposed financial and travel sanctions on Russian officials.
Malloch, Theodore (Ted)	Chief executive officer of Global Fiduciary Governance and the Roosevelt Group. He was a London-based associate of Jerome Corsi.
Manafort, Paul Jr.	Trump campaign member (March 2016 – Aug. 2016) and chairman and chief strategist (May 2016 – Aug. 2016).
Mashburn, John	Trump administration official and former policy director to the Trump Campaign.
McCabe, Andrew	Acting director of the FBI (May 2017 – Aug. 2017); deputy director of the FBI (Feb. 2016 – Jan. 2018).
McCord, Mary	Acting Assistant Attorney General (Oct. 2016 – May 2017).
McFarland, Kathleen (K.T.)	Deputy White House National Security Advisor (Jan. 2017 – May 2017).
McGahn, Donald (Don)	White House Counsel (Jan. 2017 – Oct. 2018).
Medvedev, Dmitry	Prime Minister of Russia.
Melnik, Yuriy	Spokesperson for the Russian Embassy in Washington, D.C., who connected with George Papadopoulos on social media.
Mifsud, Joseph	Maltese national and former London-based professor who, immediately after returning from Moscow in April 2016, told George Papadopoulos that the Russians had "dirt" in the form of thousands of Clinton emails.

Miller, Stephen	Senior advisor to the President.
Millian, Sergei	Founder of the Russian American Chamber of Commerce who met with George Papadopoulos during the campaign.
Mnuchin, Steven	Secretary of the Treasury.
Müller-Maguhn, Andrew	Member of hacker association Chaos Computer Club and associate of Julian Assange, founder of WikiLeaks.
Nader, George	Advisor to the United Arab Emirates's Crown Prince who arranged a meeting between Kirill Dmitriev and Erik Prince during the transition period.
Netyksho, Viktor	Russian military officer in command of a unit involved in Russian hack-and-release operations to interfere in the 2016 U.S. presidential election.

U.S. Department of Justice

~~Attorney Work Product // May Contain Material Protected Under Fed. R. Crim. P. 6(e)~~

Oganov, Georgiy   Advisor to Oleg Deripaska and a board member of investment company Basic Element. He met with Paul Manafort in Spain in early 2017.

Oknyansky, Henry (a/k/a Henry Greenberg)   Florida-based Russian individual who claimed to have derogatory information pertaining to Hillary Clinton. He met with Roger Stone in May 2016.

Page, Carter   Foreign policy advisor to the Trump Campaign who advocated pro-Russian views and made July 2016 and December 2016 visits to Moscow.

Papadopoulos, George   Foreign policy advisor to the Trump Campaign who received information from Joseph Mifsud that Russians had "dirt" in the form of thousands of Clinton emails. He pleaded guilty to lying to the FBI about his contact with Mifsud.

Parscale, Bradley   Digital media director for the 2016 Trump Campaign.

Patten, William (Sam) Jr.   Lobbyist and business partner of Konstantin Kilimnik.

Peskov, Dmitry   Deputy chief of staff of and press secretary for the Russian presidential administration.

Phares, Walid   Foreign policy advisor to the Trump Campaign and co-secretary general of the Transatlantic Parliamentary Group on Counterterrorism (TAG).

Pinedo, Richard   U.S. person who pleaded guilty to a single-count information of identity fraud.

Podesta, John Jr.   Clinton campaign chairman whose email account was hacked by the GRU. WikiLeaks released his stolen emails during the 2016 campaign.

Podobnyy, Victor   Russian intelligence officer who interacted with Carter Page while operating inside the United States; later charged in 2015 with conspiring to act as an unregistered agent of Russia.

Poliakova, Elena   Personal assistant to Dmitry Peskov who responded to Michael Cohen's outreach about the Trump Tower Moscow project in January 2016.

Polonskaya, Olga   Russian national introduced to George Papadopoulos by Joseph Mifsud as an individual with connections to Vladimir Putin.

Pompeo, Michael   U.S. Secretary of State; director of the Central Intelligence Agency (Jan. 2017 – Apr. 2018).

Porter, Robert   White House staff secretary (Jan. 2017 – Feb. 2018).

Priebus, Reince   White House chief of staff (Jan. 2017 – July 2017); chair of the Republican National Committee (Jan. 2011 – Jan. 2017).

Prigozhin, Yevgeniy   Head of Russian companies Concord Catering and Concord Management and Consulting; supported and financed the Internet Research Agency, which engaged in an "active measures" social media campaign to interfere in the 2016 U.S. presidential election.

U.S. Department of Justice

~~Attorney Work Product // May Contain Material Protected Under Fed. R. Crim. P. 6(e)~~

Prikhodko, Sergei	First deputy head of the Russian Government Office and former Russian deputy prime minister. In January 2016, he invited candidate Trump to the St. Petersburg International Economic Forum.
Prince, Erik	Businessman and Trump Campaign supporter who met with Presidential Transition Team officials after the election and traveled to the Seychelles to meet with Kirill Dmitriev in January 2017.
Raffel, Josh	White House communications advisor (Apr. 2017 – Feb. 2018).
Rasin, Alexei	Ukrainian associate of Henry Oknyansky who claimed to possess derogatory information regarding Hillary Clinton.
Rogers, Michael	Director of the National Security Agency (Apr. 2014 – May 2018).
Rosenstein, Rod	Deputy Attorney General (Apr. 2017 – present); Acting Attorney General for the Russian election interference investigation (May 2017 – Nov. 2018).
Rozov, Andrei	Chairman of I.C. Expert Investment Company, a Russian real-estate development corporation that signed a letter of intent for the Trump Tower Moscow project in 2015.
Rtskhiladze, Giorgi	Executive of the Silk Road Transatlantic Alliance, LLC who communicated with Cohen about a Trump Tower Moscow proposal.
Ruddy, Christopher	Chief executive of Newsmax Media and associate of President Trump.
Rybicki, James	FBI chief of staff (May 2015 – Feb. 2018).
Samochornov, Anatoli	Translator who worked with Natalia Veselnitskaya and attended a June 9, 2016 meeting at Trump Tower between Veselnitskaya and Trump Campaign officials.
Sanders, Sarah Huckabee	White House press secretary (July 2017 – present).
Sater, Felix	Real-estate advisor who worked with Michael Cohen to pursue a Trump Tower Moscow project.
Saunders, Paul J.	Executive with the Center for the National Interest who worked on outlines and logistics of candidate Trump's April 2016 foreign policy speech.
Sechin, Igor	Executive chairman of Rosneft, a Russian-stated owned oil company.
Sessions, Jefferson III (Jeff)	Attorney General (Feb. 2017 – Nov. 2018); U.S. Senator (Jan. 1997 – Feb. 2017); head of the Trump Campaign's foreign policy advisory team.
Shoygu, Sergey	Russian Minister of Defense.
Simes, Dimitri	President and chief executive officer of the Center for the National Interest.

Smith, Peter	Investment banker active in Republican politics who sought to obtain Hillary Clinton emails during the 2016 U.S. presidential campaign period.
Spicer, Sean	White House press secretary and communications director (Jan. 2017 – July 2017).
Stone, Roger	Advisor to the Trump Campaign ███████████████
Tillerson, Rex	U.S. Secretary of State (Feb. 2017 – Mar. 2018).
Timofeev, Ivan	Director of programs at the Russian International Affairs Council and program director of the Valdai Discussion Club who communicated in 2016 with George Papadopoulos, attempting to arrange a meeting between the Russian government and the Trump Campaign.
Trump, Donald Jr.	President Trump's son; trustee and executive vice president of the Trump Organization; helped arrange and attended the June 9, 2016 meeting at Trump Tower between Natalia Veselnitskaya and Trump Campaign officials.
Trump, Eric	President Trump's son; trustee and executive vice president of the Trump Organization.
Trump, Ivanka	President Trump's daughter; advisor to the President and former executive vice president of the Trump Organization.
Ushakov, Yuri Viktorovich	Aide to Vladimir Putin and former Russian ambassador to the United States; identified to the Presidential Transition Team as the proposed channel to the Russian government.
Vaino, Anton	Chief of staff to Russian president Vladimir Putin.
Van der Zwaan, Alexander	Former attorney at Skadden, Arps, Slate, Meagher & Flom, LLP; worked with Paul Manafort and Rick Gates.
Vargas, Catherine	Executive assistant to Jared Kushner.
Vasilchenko, Gleb	Internet Research Agency employee who engaged in an "active measures" social media campaign to interfere in the 2016 U.S. presidential election.
Veselnitskaya, Natalia	Russian attorney who advocated for the repeal of the Magnitsky Act and was the principal speaker at the June 9, 2016 meeting at Trump Tower with Trump Campaign officials.
Weber, Shlomo	Rector of the New Economic School (NES) in Moscow who invited Carter Page to speak at NES commencement in July 2016.
Yanukovych, Viktor	Former president of Ukraine who had worked with Paul Manafort.

Yates, Sally	Acting Attorney General (Jan. 20, 2017 – Jan. 30, 2017); Deputy Attorney General (Jan. 10, 2015 – Jan. 30, 2017).
Yatsenko, Sergey	Deputy chief financial officer of Gazprom, a Russian state-owned energy company, and associate of Carter Page.
Zakharova, Maria	Director of the Russian Ministry of Foreign Affair's Information and Press Department who received notification of Carter Page's speech in July 2016 from Denis Klimentov.
Zayed al Nahyan, Mohammed bin	Crown Prince of Abu Dhabi and deputy supreme commander of the United Arab Emirates (UAE) armed forces.

Entities and Organizations

Alfa-Bank	Russia's largest commercial bank, which is headed by Petr Aven.
Center for the National Interest (CNI)	U.S.-based think tank with expertise in and connections to Russia. CNI's publication, the National Interest, hosted candidate Trump's foreign policy speech in April 2016.
Concord	Umbrella term for Concord Management and Consulting, LLC and Concord Catering, which are Russian companies controlled by Yevgeniy Prigozhin.
Crocus Group or Crocus International	A Russian real-estate and property development company that, in 2013, hosted the Miss Universe Pageant, and from 2013 through 2014, worked with the Trump Organization on a Trump Moscow project.
DCLeaks	Fictitious online persona operated by the GRU that released stolen documents during the 2016 U.S. presidential campaign period.
Democratic Congressional Campaign Committee	Political committee working to elect Democrats to the House of Representatives; hacked by the GRU in April 2016.
Democratic National Committee	Formal governing body for the Democratic Party; hacked by the GRU in April 2016.
Duma	Lower House of the national legislature of the Russian Federation.
Gazprom	Russian oil and gas company majority-owned by the Russian government.
Global Energy Capital, LLC	Investment and management firm founded by Carter Page.
Global Partners in Diplomacy	Event hosted in partnership with the U.S. Department of State and the Republican National Convention. In 2016, Jeff Sessions and J.D. Gordon delivered speeches at the event and interacted with Russian Ambassador Sergey Kislyak.

Guccifer 2.0	Fictitious online persona operated by the GRU that released stolen documents during the 2016 U.S. presidential campaign period.
I.C. Expert Investment Company	Russian real-estate and development corporation that signed a letter of intent with a Trump Organization subsidiary to develop a Trump Moscow property.
Internet Research Agency (IRA)	Russian entity based in Saint Petersburg and funded by Concord that engaged in an "active measures" social media campaign to interfere in the 2016 U.S. presidential election.
KLS Research LLC	Business established by an associate of and at the direction of Peter Smith to further Smith's search for Hillary Clinton emails.
Kremlin	Official residence of the president of the Russian Federation; it is used colloquially to refer to the office of the president or the Russian government.
LetterOne	Company that includes Petr Aven and Richard Burt as board members. During a board meeting in December 2016, Aven asked for Burt's help to make contact with the Presidential Transition Team.
Link Campus University	University in Rome, Italy, where George Papadopoulos was introduced to Joseph Mifsud.
London Centre of International Law Practice (LCILP)	International law advisory organization in London that employed Joseph Mifsud and George Papadopoulos.
Main Intelligence Directorate of the General Staff (GRU)	Russian Federation's military intelligence agency.
New Economic School in Moscow (NES)	Moscow-based school that invited Carter Page to speak at its July 2016 commencement ceremony.
Opposition Bloc	Ukrainian political party that incorporated members of the defunct Party of Regions.
Party of Regions	Ukrainian political party of former President Yanukovych. It was generally understood to align with Russian policies.
Pericles Emerging Market Partners LLP	Company registered in the Cayman Islands by Paul Manafort and his business partner Rick Davis. Oleg Deripaska invested in the fund.
Prevezon Holdings Ltd.	Russian company that was a defendant in a U.S. civil action alleging the laundering of proceeds from fraud exposed by Sergei Magnitsky.
Roscongress Foundation	Russian entity that organized the St. Petersburg International Economic Forum.
Rosneft	Russian state-owned oil and energy company.
Russian Direct Investment Fund	Sovereign wealth fund established by the Russian Government in 2011 and headed by Kirill Dmitriev.

U.S. Department of Justice

~~Attorney Work Product // May Contain Material Protected Under Fed. R. Crim. P. 6(e)~~

Russian International Affairs Council	Russia-based nonprofit established by Russian government decree. It is associated with the Ministry of Foreign Affairs, and its members include Ivan Timofeev, Dmitry Peskov, and Petr Aven.
Silk Road Group	Privately held investment company that entered into a licensing agreement to build a Trump-branded hotel in Georgia.
St. Petersburg International Economic Forum	Annual event held in Russia and attended by prominent Russian politicians and businessmen.
Tatneft	Russian energy company.
Transatlantic Parliamentary Group on Counterterrorism	European group that sponsored a summit between European Parliament lawmakers and U.S. persons. George Papadopoulos, Sam Clovis, and Walid Phares attended the TAG summit in July 2016.
Unit 26165 (GRU)	GRU military cyber unit dedicated to targeting military, political, governmental, and non-governmental organizations outside of Russia. It engaged in computer intrusions of U.S. persons and organizations, as well as the subsequent release of the stolen data, in order to interfere in the 2016 U.S. presidential election.
Unit 74455 (GRU)	GRU military unit with multiple departments that engaged in cyber operations. It engaged in computer intrusions of U.S. persons and organizations, as well as the subsequent release of the stolen data, in order to interfere in the 2016 U.S. presidential election.
Valdai Discussion Club	Group that holds a conference attended by Russian government officials, including President Putin.
WikiLeaks	Organization founded by Julian Assange that posts information online, including data stolen from private, corporate, and U.S. Government entities. Released data stolen by the GRU during the 2016 U.S. presidential election.

Index of Acronyms

CNI	Center for the National Interest
DCCC	Democratic Congressional Campaign Committee
DNC	Democratic National Committee
FBI	Federal Bureau of Investigation
FSB	Russian Federal Security Service
GEC	Global Energy Capital, LLC
GRU	Russian Federation's Main Intelligence Directorate of the General Staff
HPSCI	U.S. House of Representatives Permanent Select Committee on Intelligence
HRC	Hillary Rodham Clinton
IRA	Internet Research Agency
LCILP	London Centre of International Law Practice
NATO	North Atlantic Treaty Organization
NES	New Economic School
NSA	National Security Agency
ODNI	Office of the Director of National Intelligence
PTT	Presidential Transition Team
RDIF	Russian Direct Investment Fund
RIAC	Russian International Affairs Council
SBOE	State boards of elections
SCO	Special Counsel's Office
SJC	U.S. Senate Judiciary Committee
SSCI	U.S. Senate Select Committee on Intelligence
TAG	Transatlantic Parliamentary Group on Counterterrorism
VEB	Vnesheconombank

Appendix C

APPENDIX C

INTRODUCTORY NOTE

The President provided written responses through his personal counsel to questions submitted to him by the Special Counsel's Office. We first explain the process that led to the submission of written questions and then attach the President's responses.

Beginning in December 2017, this Office sought for more than a year to interview the President on topics relevant to both Russian-election interference and obstruction-of-justice. We advised counsel that the President was a "subject" of the investigation under the definition of the Justice Manual—"a person whose conduct is within the scope of the grand jury's investigation." Justice Manual § 9-11.151 (2018). We also advised counsel that "[a]n interview with the President is vital to our investigation" and that this Office had "carefully considered the constitutional and other arguments raised by . . . counsel, and they d[id] not provide us with reason to forgo seeking an interview."[1] We additionally stated that "it is in the interest of the Presidency and the public for an interview to take place" and offered "numerous accommodations to aid the President's preparation and avoid surprise."[2] After extensive discussions with the Department of Justice about the Special Counsel's objective of securing the President's testimony, these accommodations included the submissions of written questions to the President on certain Russia-related topics.[3]

We received the President's written responses in late November 2018.[4] In December 2018, we informed counsel of the insufficiency of those responses in several respects.[5] We noted, among other things, that the President stated on more than 30 occasions that he "does not 'recall' or 'remember' or have an 'independent recollection'" of information called for by the questions.[6] Other answers were "incomplete or imprecise."[7] The written responses, we informed counsel, "demonstrate the inadequacy of the written format, as we have had no opportunity to ask follow-up questions that would ensure complete answers and potentially refresh your client's recollection or clarify the extent or nature of his lack of recollection."[8] We again requested an in-person interview, limited to certain topics, advising the President's counsel that "[t]his is the President's

---

[1] 5/16/18 Letter, Special Counsel to the President's Personal Counsel, at 1.

[2] 5/16/18 Letter, Special Counsels's Office to the President's Personal Counsel, at 1; see 7/30/18 Letter, Special Counsel's Office to the President's Personal Counsel, at 1 (describing accommodations).

[3] 9/17/18 Letter, Special Counsel's Office to the President's Personal Counsel, at 1 (submitting written questions).

[4] 11/20/18 Letter, President's Personal Counsel to the Special Counsel's Office (transmitting written responses of Donald J. Trump).

[5] 12/3/18 Letter, Special Counsel's Office to the President's Personal Counsel, at 3.

[6] 12/3/18 Letter, Special Counsel's Office to the President's Personal Counsel, at 3.

[7] 12/3/18 Letter, Special Counsel's Office to the President's Personal Counsel, at 3; see (noting, "for example," that the President "did not answer whether he had at any time directed or suggested that discussions about the Trump Moscow Project should cease . . . but he has since made public comments about that topic").

[8] 12/3/18 Letter, Special Counsel's Office to the President's Personal Counsel, at 3.

opportunity to voluntarily provide us with information for us to evaluate in the context of all of the evidence we have gathered."[9] The President declined.[10]

Recognizing that the President would not be interviewed voluntarily, we considered whether to issue a subpoena for his testimony. We viewed the written answers to be inadequate. But at that point, our investigation had made significant progress and had produced substantial evidence for our report. We thus weighed the costs of potentially lengthy constitutional litigation, with resulting delay in finishing our investigation, against the anticipated benefits for our investigation and report. As explained in Volume II, Section II.B., we determined that the substantial quantity of information we had obtained from other sources allowed us to draw relevant factual conclusions on intent and credibility, which are often inferred from circumstantial evidence and assessed without direct testimony from the subject of the investigation.

*   *   *

---

[9] 12/3/18 Letter, Special Counsel to the President's Personal Counsel.

[10] 12/12/18 Letter, President's Personal Counsel to the Special Counsel's Office, at 2.

[11]

[12]

U.S. Department of Justice

~~Attorney Work Product // May Contain Material Protected Under Fed. R. Crim. P. 6(e)~~

WRITTEN QUESTIONS TO BE ANSWERED UNDER OATH BY PRESIDENT DONALD J. TRUMP

I.   **June 9, 2016 Meeting at Trump Tower**

   a.   When did you first learn that Donald Trump, Jr., Paul Manafort, or Jared Kushner was considering participating in a meeting in June 2016 concerning potentially negative information about Hillary Clinton? Describe who you learned the information from and the substance of the discussion.

   b.   Attached to this document as Exhibit A is a series of emails from June 2016 between, among others, Donald Trump, Jr. and Rob Goldstone. In addition to the emails reflected in Exhibit A, Donald Trump, Jr. had other communications with Rob Goldstone and Emin Agalarov between June 3, 2016, and June 9, 2016.
      i.   Did Mr. Trump, Jr. or anyone else tell you about or show you any of these communications? If yes, describe who discussed the communications with you, when, and the substance of the discussion(s).
      ii.   When did you first see or learn about all or any part of the emails reflected in Exhibit A?
      iii.   When did you first learn that the proposed meeting involved or was described as being part of Russia and its government's support for your candidacy?
      iv.   Did you suggest to or direct anyone not to discuss or release publicly all or any portion of the emails reflected in Exhibit A? If yes, describe who you communicated with, when, the substance of the communication(s), and why you took that action.

   c.   On June 9, 2016, Donald Trump, Jr., Paul Manafort, and Jared Kushner attended a meeting at Trump Tower with several individuals, including a Russian lawyer, Natalia Veselnitskaya (the "June 9 meeting").
      i.   Other than as set forth in your answers to I.a and I.b, what, if anything, were you told about the possibility of this meeting taking place, or the scheduling of such a meeting? Describe who you discussed this with, when, and what you were informed about the meeting.
      ii.   When did you learn that some of the individuals attending the June 9 meeting were Russian or had any affiliation with any part of the Russian government? Describe who you learned this information from and the substance of the discussion(s).
      iii.   What were you told about what was discussed at the June 9 meeting? Describe each conversation in which you were told about what was discussed at the meeting, who the conversation was with, when it occurred, and the substance of the statements they made about the meeting.

U.S. Department of Justice

Attorney Work Product // May Contain Material Protected Under Fed. R. Crim. P. 6(e)

   iv. Were you told that the June 9 meeting was about, in whole or in part, adoption and/or the Magnitsky Act? If yes, describe who you had that discussion with, when, and the substance of the discussion.

  d. For the period June 6, 2016 through June 9, 2016, for what portion of each day were you in Trump Tower?

   i. Did you speak or meet with Donald Trump, Jr., Paul Manafort, or Jared Kushner on June 9, 2016? If yes, did any portion of any of those conversations or meetings include any reference to any aspect of the June 9 meeting? If yes, describe who you spoke with and the substance of the conversation.

  e. Did you communicate directly or indirectly with any member or representative of the Agalarov family after June 3, 2016? If yes, describe who you spoke with, when, and the substance of the communication.

  f. Did you learn of any communications between Donald Trump, Jr., Paul Manafort, or Jared Kushner and any member or representative of the Agalarov family, Natalia Veselnitskaya, Rob Goldstone, or any Russian official or contact that took place after June 9, 2016 and concerned the June 9 meeting or efforts by Russia to assist the campaign? If yes, describe who you learned this information from, when, and the substance of what you learned.

  g. On June 7, 2016, you gave a speech in which you said, in part, "I am going to give a major speech on probably Monday of next week and we're going to be discussing all of the things that have taken place with the Clintons."

   i. Why did you make that statement?
   ii. What information did you plan to share with respect to the Clintons?
   iii. What did you believe the source(s) of that information would be?
   iv. Did you expect any of the information to have come from the June 9 meeting?
   v. Did anyone help draft the speech that you were referring to? If so, who?
   vi. Why did you ultimately not give the speech you referenced on June 7, 2016?

  h. Did any person or entity inform you during the campaign that Vladimir Putin or the Russian government supported your candidacy or opposed the candidacy of Hillary Clinton? If yes, describe the source(s) of the information, when you were informed, and the content of such discussion(s).

  i. Did any person or entity inform you during the campaign that any foreign government or foreign leader, other than Russia or Vladimir Putin, had provided, wished to provide, or offered to provide tangible support to your campaign, including by way of offering to provide negative information on Hillary Clinton? If

U.S. Department of Justice

Attorney Work Product // May Contain Material Protected Under Fed. R. Crim. P. 6(e)

yes, describe the source(s) of the information, when you were informed, and the content of such discussion(s).

II.   Russian Hacking / Russian Efforts Using Social Media / WikiLeaks

a. On June 14, 2016, it was publicly reported that computer hackers had penetrated the computer network of the Democratic National Committee (DNC) and that Russian intelligence was behind the unauthorized access, or hack. Prior to June 14, 2016, were you provided any information about any potential or actual hacking of the computer systems or email accounts of the DNC, the Democratic Congressional Campaign Committee (DCCC), the Clinton Campaign, Hillary Clinton, or individuals associated with the Clinton campaign? If yes, describe who provided this information, when, and the substance of the information.

b. On July 22, 2016, WikiLeaks released nearly 20,000 emails sent or received by Democratic party officials.
     i.   Prior to the July 22, 2016 release, were you aware from any source that WikiLeaks, Guccifer 2.0, DCLeaks, or Russians had or potentially had possession of or planned to release emails or information that could help your campaign or hurt the Clinton campaign? If yes, describe who you discussed this issue with, when, and the substance of the discussion(s).
     ii. After the release of emails by WikiLeaks on July 22, 2016, were you told that WikiLeaks possessed or might possess additional information that could be released during the campaign? If yes, describe who provided this information, when, and what you were told.

c. Are you aware of any communications during the campaign, directly or indirectly, between Roger Stone, Donald Trump, Jr., Paul Manafort, or Rick Gates and (a) WikiLeaks, (b) Julian Assange, (c) other representatives of WikiLeaks, (d) Guccifer 2.0, (e) representatives of Guccifer 2.0, or (f) representatives of DCLeaks? If yes, describe who provided you with this information, when you learned of the communications, and what you know about those communications.

d. On July 27, 2016, you stated at a press conference: "Russia, if you're listening, I hope you're able to find the 30,000 emails that are missing. I think you will probably be rewarded mightily by our press."
     i.   Why did you make that request of Russia, as opposed to any other country, entity, or individual?
     ii. In advance of making that statement, what discussions, if any, did you have with anyone else about the substance of the statement?
     iii. Were you told at any time before or after you made that statement that Russia was attempting to infiltrate or hack computer systems or email accounts of Hillary Clinton or her campaign? If yes, describe who provided this information, when, and what you were told.

U.S. Department of Justice

Attorney Work Product // May Contain Material Protected Under Fed. R. Crim. P. 6(e)

e. On October 7, 2016, emails hacked from the account of John Podesta were released by WikiLeaks.

  i. Where were you on October 7, 2016?

  ii. Were you told at any time in advance of, or on the day of, the October 7 release that WikiLeaks possessed or might possess emails related to John Podesta? If yes, describe who told you this, when, and what you were told.

  iii. Are you aware of anyone associated with you or your campaign, including Roger Stone, reaching out to WikiLeaks, either directly or through an intermediary, on or about October 7, 2016? If yes, identify the person and describe the substance of the conversations or contacts.

f. Were you told of anyone associated with you or your campaign, including Roger Stone, having any discussions, directly or indirectly, with WikiLeaks, Guccifer 2.0, or DCLeaks regarding the content or timing of release of hacked emails? If yes, describe who had such contacts, how you became aware of the contacts, when you became aware of the contacts, and the substance of the contacts.

g. From June 1, 2016 through the end of the campaign, how frequently did you communicate with Roger Stone? Describe the nature of your communication(s) with Mr. Stone.

  i. During that time period, what efforts did Mr. Stone tell you he was making to assist your campaign, and what requests, if any, did you make of Mr. Stone?

  ii. Did Mr. Stone ever discuss WikiLeaks with you or, as far as you were aware, with anyone else associated with the campaign? If yes, describe what you were told, from whom, and when.

  iii. Did Mr. Stone at any time inform you about contacts he had with WikiLeaks or any intermediary of WikiLeaks, or about forthcoming releases of information? If yes, describe what Stone told you and when.

h. Did you have any discussions prior to January 20, 2017, regarding a potential pardon or other action to benefit Julian Assange? If yes, describe who you had the discussion(s) with, when, and the content of the discussion(s).

i. Were you aware of any efforts by foreign individuals or companies, including those in Russia, to assist your campaign through the use of social media postings or the organization of rallies? If yes, identify who you discussed such assistance with, when, and the content of the discussion(s).

U.S. Department of Justice

~~Attorney Work Product // May Contain Material Protected Under Fed. R. Crim. P. 6(e)~~

III. The Trump Organization Moscow Project

a. In October 2015, a "Letter of Intent," a copy of which is attached as Exhibit B, was signed for a proposed Trump Organization project in Moscow (the "Trump Moscow project").

    i. When were you first informed of discussions about the Trump Moscow project? By whom? What were you told about the project?

    ii. Did you sign the letter of intent?

b. In a statement provided to Congress, attached as Exhibit C, Michael Cohen stated: "To the best of my knowledge, Mr. Trump was never in contact with anyone about this proposal other than me on three occasions, including signing a non-binding letter of intent in 2015." Describe all discussions you had with Mr. Cohen, or anyone else associated with the Trump Organization, about the Trump Moscow project, including who you spoke with, when, and the substance of the discussion(s).

c. Did you learn of any communications between Michael Cohen or Felix Sater and any Russian government officials, including officials in the office of Dmitry Peskov, regarding the Trump Moscow project? If so, identify who provided this information to you, when, and the substance of what you learned.

d. Did you have any discussions between June 2015 and June 2016 regarding a potential trip to Russia by you and/or Michael Cohen for reasons related to the Trump Moscow project? If yes, describe who you spoke with, when, and the substance of the discussion(s).

e. Did you at any time direct or suggest that discussions about the Trump Moscow project should cease, or were you informed at any time that the project had been abandoned? If yes, describe who you spoke with, when, the substance of the discussion(s), and why that decision was made.

f. Did you have any discussions regarding what information would be provided publicly or in response to investigative inquiries about potential or actual investments or business deals the Trump Organization had in Russia, including the Trump Moscow project? If yes, describe who you spoke with, when, and the substance of the discussion(s).

g. Aside from the Trump Moscow project, did you or the Trump Organization have any other prospective or actual business interests, investments, or arrangements with Russia or any Russian interest or Russian individual during the campaign? If yes, describe the business interests, investments, or arrangements.

U.S. Department of Justice

Attorney Work Product // May Contain Material Protected Under Fed. R. Crim. P. 6(e)

IV. Contacts with Russia and Russia-Related Issues During the Campaign

a. Prior to mid-August 2016, did you become aware that Paul Manafort had ties to the Ukrainian government? If yes, describe who you learned this information from, when, and the substance of what you were told. Did Mr. Manafort's connections to the Ukrainian or Russian governments play any role in your decision to have him join your campaign? If yes, describe that role.

b. Were you aware that Paul Manafort offered briefings on the progress of your campaign to Oleg Deripaska? If yes, describe who you learned this information from, when, the substance of what you were told, what you understood the purpose was of sharing such information with Mr. Deripaska, and how you responded to learning this information.

c. Were you aware of whether Paul Manafort or anyone else associated with your campaign sent or directed others to send internal Trump campaign information to any person located in Ukraine or Russia or associated with the Ukrainian or Russian governments? If yes, identify who provided you with this information, when, the substance of the discussion(s), what you understood the purpose was of sharing the internal campaign information, and how you responded to learning this information.

d. Did Paul Manafort communicate to you, directly or indirectly, any positions Ukraine or Russia would want the U.S. to support? If yes, describe when he communicated those positions to you and the substance of those communications.

e. During the campaign, were you told about efforts by Russian officials to meet with you or senior members of your campaign? If yes, describe who you had conversations with on this topic, when, and what you were told.

f. What role, if any, did you have in changing the Republican Party platform regarding arming Ukraine during the Republican National Convention? Prior to the convention, what information did you have about this platform provision? After the platform provision was changed, who told you about the change, when did they tell you, what were you told about why it was changed, and who was involved?

g. On July 27, 2016, in response to a question about whether you would recognize Crimea as Russian territory and lift sanctions on Russia, you said: "We'll be looking at that. Yeah, we'll be looking." Did you intend to communicate by that statement or at any other time during the campaign a willingness to lift sanctions and/or recognize Russia's annexation of Crimea if you were elected?

U.S. Department of Justice

Attorney Work Product // May Contain Material Protected Under Fed. R. Crim. P. 6(e)

    i. What consideration did you give to lifting sanctions and/or recognizing Russia's annexation of Crimea if you were elected? Describe who you spoke with about this topic, when, the substance of the discussion(s).

V.   Contacts with Russia and Russia-Related Issues During the Transition

a. Were you asked to attend the World Chess Championship gala on November 10, 2016? If yes, who asked you to attend, when were you asked, and what were you told about about why your presence was requested?

    i. Did you attend any part of the event? If yes, describe any interactions you had with any Russians or representatives of the Russian government at the event.

b. Following the Obama Administration's imposition of sanctions on Russia in December 2016 ("Russia sanctions"), did you discuss with Lieutenant General (LTG) Michael Flynn, K.T. McFarland, Steve Bannon, Reince Priebus, Jared Kushner, Erik Prince, or anyone else associated with the transition what should be communicated to the Russian government regarding the sanctions? If yes, describe who you spoke with about this issue, when, and the substance of the discussion(s).

c. On December 29 and December 31, 2016, LTG Flynn had conversations with Russian Ambassador Sergey Kislyak about the Russia sanctions and Russia's response to the Russia sanctions.

    i. Did you direct or suggest that LTG Flynn have discussions with anyone from the Russian government about the Russia sanctions?

    ii. Were you told in advance of LTG Flynn's December 29, 2016 conversation that he was going to be speaking with Ambassador Kislyak? If yes, describe who told you this information, when, and what you were told. If no, when and from whom did you learn of LTG Flynn's December 29, 2016 conversation with Ambassador Kislyak?

    iii. When did you learn of LTG Flynn and Ambassador Kislyak's call on December 31, 2016? Who told you and what were you told?

    iv. When did you learn that sanctions were discussed in the December 29 and December 31, 2016 calls between LTG Flynn and Ambassador Kislyak? Who told you and what were you told?

d. At any time between December 31, 2016, and January 20, 2017, did anyone tell you or suggest to you that Russia's decision not to impose reciprocal sanctions was attributable in any way to LTG Flynn's communications with Ambassador Kislyak? If yes, identify who provided you with this information, when, and the substance of what you were told.

e. On January 12, 2017, the Washington Post published a column that stated that LTG Flynn phoned Ambassador Kislyak several times on December 29, 2016. After learning of the column, did you direct or suggest to anyone that LTG Flynn should deny that he discussed sanctions with Ambassador Kislyak? If yes, who did you make this suggestion or direction to, when, what did you say, and why did you take this step?
   i. After learning of the column, did you have any conversations with LTG Flynn about his conversations with Ambassador Kislyak in December 2016? If yes, describe when those discussions occurred and the content of the discussions.

f. Were you told about a meeting between Jared Kushner and Sergei Gorkov that took place in December 2016?
   i. If yes, describe who you spoke with, when, the substance of the discussion(s), and what you understood was the purpose of the meeting.

g. Were you told about a meeting or meetings between Erik Prince and Kirill Dmitriev or any other representative from the Russian government that took place in January 2017?
   If yes, describe who you spoke with, when, the substance of the discussion(s), and what you understood was the purpose of the meeting(s).

h. Prior to January 20, 2017, did you talk to Steve Bannon, Jared Kushner, or any other individual associated with the transition regarding establishing an unofficial line of communication with Russia? If yes, describe who you spoke with, when, the substance of the discussion(s), and what you understood was the purpose of such an unofficial line of communication.

RESPONSES OF PRESIDENT DONALD J. TRUMP

I.   June 9, 2016 Meeting at Trump Tower

a.   When did you first learn that Donald Trump, Jr., Paul Manafort, or Jared Kushner was considering participating in a meeting in June 2016 concerning potentially negative information about Hillary Clinton? Describe who you learned the information from and the substance of the discussion.

b.   Attached to this document as Exhibit A is a series of emails from June 2016 between, among others, Donald Trump, Jr. and Rob Goldstone. In addition to the emails reflected in Exhibit A, Donald Trump, Jr. had other communications with Rob Goldstone and Emin Agalarov between June 3, 2016, and June 9, 2016.

     i.   Did Mr. Trump, Jr. or anyone else tell you about or show you any of these communications? If yes, describe who discussed the communications with you, when, and the substance of the discussion(s).

     ii.   When did you first see or learn about all or any part of the emails reflected in Exhibit A?

     iii.   When did you first learn that the proposed meeting involved or was described as being part of Russia and its government's support for your candidacy?

     iv.   Did you suggest to or direct anyone not to discuss or release publicly all or any portion of the emails reflected in Exhibit A? If yes, describe who you communicated with, when, the substance of the communication(s), and why you took that action.

c.   On June 9, 2016, Donald Trump, Jr., Paul Manafort, and Jared Kushner attended a meeting at Trump Tower with several individuals, including a Russian lawyer, Natalia Veselnitskaya (the "June 9 meeting").

     i.   Other than as set forth in your answers to I.a and I.b, what, if anything, were you told about the possibility of this meeting taking place, or the scheduling of such a meeting? Describe who you discussed this with, when, and what you were informed about the meeting.

     ii.   When did you learn that some of the individuals attending the June 9 meeting were Russian or had any affiliation with any part of the Russian government? Describe who you learned this information from and the substance of the discussion(s).

U.S. Department of Justice

Attorney Work Product // May Contain Material Protected Under Fed. R. Crim. P. 6(e)

        iii.   What were you told about what was discussed at the June 9 meeting? Describe each conversation in which you were told about what was discussed at the meeting, who the conversation was with, when it occurred, and the substance of the statements they made about the meeting.

        iv.   Were you told that the June 9 meeting was about, in whole or in part, adoption and/or the Magnitsky Act? If yes, describe who you had that discussion with, when, and the substance of the discussion.

d.   For the period June 6, 2016 through June 9, 2016, for what portion of each day were you in Trump Tower?

        i.   Did you speak or meet with Donald Trump, Jr., Paul Manafort, or Jared Kushner on June 9, 2016? If yes, did any portion of any of those conversations or meetings include any reference to any aspect of the June 9 meeting? If yes, describe who you spoke with and the substance of the conversation.

e.   Did you communicate directly or indirectly with any member or representative of the Agalarov family after June 3, 2016? If yes, describe who you spoke with, when, and the substance of the communication.

f.   Did you learn of any communications between Donald Trump, Jr., Paul Manafort, or Jared Kushner and any member or representative of the Agalarov family, Natalia Veselnitskaya, Rob Goldstone, or any Russian official or contact that took place after June 9, 2016 and concerned the June 9 meeting or efforts by Russia to assist the campaign? If yes, describe who you learned this information from, when, and the substance of what you learned.

g.   On June 7, 2016, you gave a speech in which you said, in part, "I am going to give a major speech on probably Monday of next week and we're going to be discussing all of the things that have taken place with the Clintons."

        i.   Why did you make that statement?

        ii.   What information did you plan to share with respect to the Clintons?

        iii.   What did you believe the source(s) of that information would be?

        iv.   Did you expect any of the information to have come from the June 9 meeting?

        v.   Did anyone help draft the speech that you were referring to? If so, who?

        vi.   Why did you ultimately not give the speech you referenced on June 7, 2016?

h.   Did any person or entity inform you during the campaign that Vladimir Putin or the Russian

U.S. Department of Justice

Attorney Work Product // May Contain Material Protected Under Fed. R. Crim. P. 6(e)

government supported your candidacy or opposed the candidacy of Hillary Clinton? If yes, describe the source(s) of the information, when you were informed, and the content of such discussion(s).

i. Did any person or entity inform you during the campaign that any foreign government or foreign leader, other than Russia or Vladimir Putin, had provided, wished to provide, or offered to provide tangible support to your campaign, including by way of offering to provide negative information on Hillary Clinton? If yes, describe the source(s) of the information, when you were informed, and the content of such discussion(s).

Response to Question 1, Parts (a) through (c)

I have no recollection of learning at the time that Donald Trump, Jr., Paul Manafort, or Jared Kushner was considering participating in a meeting in June 2016 concerning potentially negative information about Hillary Clinton. Nor do I recall learning during the campaign that the June 9, 2016 meeting had taken place, that the referenced emails existed, or that Donald J. Trump, Jr., had other communications with Emin Agalarov or Robert Goldstone between June 3, 2016 and June 9, 2016.

Response to Question 1, Part (d)

I have no independent recollection of what portion of these four days in June of 2016 I spent in Trump Tower. This was one of many busy months during a fast-paced campaign, as the primary season was ending and we were preparing for the general election campaign.

I am now aware that my Campaign's calendar indicates that I was in New York City from June 6 – 9, 2016. Calendars kept in my Trump Tower office reflect that I had various calls and meetings scheduled for each of these days. While those calls and meetings may or may not actually have taken place, they do indicate that I was in Trump Tower during a portion of each of these working days, and I have no reason to doubt that I was. When I was in New York City, I stayed at my Trump Tower apartment.

My Trump Organization desk calendar also reflects that I was outside Trump Tower during portions of these days. The June 7, 2016 calendar indicates I was scheduled to leave Trump Tower in the early evening for Westchester where I gave remarks after winning the California, New Jersey, New Mexico, Montana, and South Dakota Republican primaries held that day. The June 8, 2016 calendar indicates a scheduled departure in late afternoon to attend a ceremony at my son's school. The June 9, 2016 calendar indicates I was scheduled to attend midday meetings and a fundraising luncheon at the Four Seasons Hotel. At this point, I do not remember on what dates these events occurred, but I do not currently have a reason to doubt that they took place as scheduled on my calendar.

Widely available media reports, including television footage, also shed light on my activities during these days. For example, I am aware that my June 7, 2016 victory remarks at the Trump

National Golf Club in Briarcliff Manor, New York, were recorded and published by the media. remember winning those primaries and generally recall delivering remarks that evening.

At this point in time, I do not remember whether I spoke or met with Donald Trump, Jr., Paul Manafort, or Jared Kushner on June 9, 2016. My desk calendar indicates I was scheduled to meet with Paul Manafort on the morning of June 9, but I do not recall if that meeting took place. It was more than two years ago, at a time when I had many calls and interactions daily.

Response to Question I, Part (e)

I have no independent recollection of any communications I had with the Agalarov family or anyone I understood to be a representative of the Agalarov family after June 3, 2016 and before the end of the campaign. While preparing to respond to these questions, I have become aware of written communications with the Agalarovs during the campaign that were sent, received, and largely authored by my staff and which I understand have already been produced to you.

In general, the documents include congratulatory letters on my campaign victories, emails about a painting Emin and Aras Agalarov arranged to have delivered to Trump Tower as a birthday present, and emails regarding delivery of a book written by Aras Agalarov. The documents reflect that the deliveries were screened by the Secret Service.

Response to Question I, Part (f)

I do not recall being aware during the campaign of communications between Donald Trump, Jr., Paul Manafort, or Jared Kushner and any member or representative of the Agalarov family, Robert Goldstone, Natalia Veselnitskaya (whose name I was not familiar with), or anyone I understood to be a Russian official.

Response to Question I, Part (g)

In remarks I delivered the night I won the California, New Jersey, New Mexico, Montana, and South Dakota Republican primaries, I said, "I am going to give a major speech on probably Monday of next week and we're going to be discussing all of the things that have taken place with the Clintons." In general, I expected to give a speech referencing the publicly available, negative information about the Clintons, including, for example, Mrs. Clinton's failed policies, the Clintons' use of the State Department to further their interests and the interests of the Clinton Foundation, Mrs. Clinton's improper use of a private server for State Department business, the destruction of 33,000 emails on that server, and Mrs. Clinton's temperamental unsuitability for the office of President.

In the course of preparing to respond to your questions, I have become aware that the Campaign documents already produced to you reflect the drafting, evolution, and sources of information for the speech I expected to give "probably" on the Monday following my June 7, 2016 comments. These documents generally show that the text of the speech was initially drafted by Campaign staff with input from various outside advisors and was based on publicly available material, including, in particular, information from the book *Clinton Cash* by Peter Schweizer.

The Pulse Nightclub terrorist attack took place in the early morning hours of Sunday, June 12, 2016. In light of that tragedy, I gave a speech directed more specifically to national security and terrorism than to the Clintons. That speech was delivered at the Saint Anselm College Institute of Politics in Manchester, New Hampshire, and, as reported, opened with the following:

> This was going to be a speech on Hillary Clinton and how bad a President, especially in these times of Radical Islamic Terrorism, she would be. Even her former Secret Service Agent, who has seen her under pressure and in times of stress, has stated that she lacks the temperament and integrity to be president. There will be plenty of opportunity to discuss these important issues at a later time, and I will deliver that speech soon. But today there is only one thing to discuss: the growing threat of terrorism inside of our borders.

I continued to speak about Mrs. Clinton's failings throughout the campaign, using the information prepared for inclusion in the speech to which I referred on June 7, 2016.

Response to Question I, Part (h)

I have no recollection of being told during the campaign that Vladimir Putin or the Russian government "supported" my candidacy or "opposed" the candidacy of Hillary Clinton. However, I was aware of some reports indicating that President Putin had made complimentary statements about me.

Response to Question I, Part (i)

I have no recollection of being told during the campaign that any foreign government or foreign leader had provided, wished to provide, or offered to provide tangible support to my campaign.

II. Russian Hacking / Russian Efforts Using Social Media / WikiLeaks

a. On June 14, 2016, it was publicly reported that computer hackers had penetrated the computer network of the Democratic National Committee (DNC) and that Russian intelligence was behind the unauthorized access, or hack. Prior to June 14, 2016, were you provided any information about any potential or actual hacking of the computer systems or email accounts of the DNC, the Democratic Congressional Campaign Committee (DCCC), the Clinton Campaign, Hillary Clinton, or individuals associated with the Clinton campaign? If yes, describe who provided this information, when, and the substance of the information.

U.S. Department of Justice

Attorney Work Product // May Contain Material Protected Under Fed. R. Crim. P. 6(e)

b.   On July 22, 2016, WikiLeaks released nearly 20,000 emails sent or received by Democratic party officials.

    i.   Prior to the July 22, 2016 release, were you aware from any source that WikiLeaks, Guccifer 2.0, DCLeaks, or Russians had or potentially had possession of or planned to release emails or information that could help your campaign or hurt the Clinton campaign? If yes, describe who you discussed this issue with, when, and the substance of the discussion(s).

    ii.   After the release of emails by WikiLeaks on July 22, 2016, were you told that WikiLeaks possessed or might possess additional information that could be released during the campaign? If yes, describe who provided this information, when, and what you were told.

c.   Are you aware of any communications during the campaign, directly or indirectly, between Roger Stone, Donald Trump, Jr., Paul Manafort, or Rick Gates and (a) WikiLeaks, (b) Julian Assange, (c) other representatives of WikiLeaks, (d) Guccifer 2.0, (e) representatives of Guccifer 2.0, or (f) representatives of DCLeaks? If yes, describe who provided you with this information, when you learned of the communications, and what you know about those communications.

d.   On July 27, 2016, you stated at a press conference: "Russia, if you're listening, I hope you're able to find the 30,000 emails that are missing. I think you will probably be rewarded mightily by our press."

    i.   Why did you make that request of Russia, as opposed to any other country, entity, or individual?

    ii.   In advance of making that statement, what discussions, if any, did you have with anyone else about the substance of the statement?

    iii.   Were you told at any time before or after you made that statement that Russia was attempting to infiltrate or hack computer systems or email accounts of Hillary Clinton or her campaign? If yes, describe who provided this information, when, and what you were told.

e.   On October 7, 2016, emails hacked from the account of John Podesta were released by WikiLeaks.

    i.   Where were you on October 7, 2016?

    ii.   Were you told at any time in advance of, or on the day of, the October 7 release that WikiLeaks possessed or might possess emails related to John Podesta? If yes, describe who told you this, when, and what you were told.

U.S. Department of Justice

~~Attorney Work Product // May Contain Material Protected Under Fed. R. Crim. P. 6(e)~~

iii.   Are you aware of anyone associated with you or your campaign, including Roger Stone, reaching out to WikiLeaks, either directly or through an intermediary, on or about October 7, 2016? If yes, identify the person and describe the substance of the conversations or contacts.

f.   Were you told of anyone associated with you or your campaign, including Roger Stone, having any discussions, directly or indirectly, with WikiLeaks, Guccifer 2.0, or DCLeaks regarding the content or timing of release of hacked emails? If yes, describe who had such contacts, how you became aware of the contacts, when you became aware of the contacts, and the substance of the contacts.

g.   From June 1, 2016 through the end of the campaign, how frequently did you communicate with Roger Stone? Describe the nature of your communication(s) with Mr. Stone.

i.   During that time period, what efforts did Mr. Stone tell you he was making to assist your campaign, and what requests, if any, did you make of Mr. Stone?

ii.   Did Mr. Stone ever discuss WikiLeaks with you or, as far as you were aware, with anyone else associated with the campaign? If yes, describe what you were told, from whom, and when.

iii.   Did Mr. Stone at anytime inform you about contacts he had with WikiLeaks or any intermediary of WikiLeaks, or about forthcoming releases of information? If yes, describe what Stone told you and when.

h.   Did you have any discussions prior to January 20, 2017, regarding a potential pardon or other action to benefit Julian Assange? If yes, describe who you had the discussion(s) with, when, and the content of the discussion(s).

i.   Were you aware of any efforts by foreign individuals or companies, including those in Russia, to assist your campaign through the use of social media postings or the organization of rallies? If yes, identify who you discussed such assistance with, when, and the content of the discussion(s).

Response to Question II, Part (a)

I do not remember the date on which it was publicly reported that the DNC had been hacked, but my best recollection is that I learned of the hacking at or shortly after the time it became the subject of media reporting. I do not recall being provided any information during the campaign about the hacking of any of the named entities or individuals before it became the subject of media reporting.

U.S. Department of Justice

~~Attorney Work Product // May Contain Material Protected Under Fed. R. Crim. P. 6(e)~~

Response to Question II, Part (b)

I recall that in the months leading up to the election there was considerable media reporting about the possible hacking and release of campaign-related information and there was a lot of talk about this matter. At the time, I was generally aware of these media reports and may have discussed these issues with my campaign staff or others, but at this point in time – more than two years later – I have no recollection of any particular conversation, when it occurred, or who the participants were.

Response to Question II, Part (c)

I do not recall being aware during the campaign of any communications between the individuals named in Question II (c) and anyone I understood to be a representative of WikiLeaks or any of the other individuals or entities referred to in the question.

Response to Question II, Part (d)

I made the statement quoted in Question II (d) in jest and sarcastically, as was apparent to any objective observer. The context of the statement is evident in the full reading or viewing of the July 27, 2016 press conference, and I refer you to the publicly available transcript and video of that press conference. I do not recall having any discussion about the substance of the statement in advance of the press conference. I do not recall being told during the campaign of any efforts by Russia to infiltrate or hack the computer systems or email accounts of Hillary Clinton or her campaign prior to them becoming the subject of media reporting and I have no recollection of any particular conversation in that regard.

Response to Question II, Part (e)

I was in Trump Tower in New York City on October 7, 2016. I have no recollection of being told that WikiLeaks possessed or might possess emails related to John Podesta before the release of Mr. Podesta's emails was reported by the media. Likewise, I have no recollection of being told that Roger Stone, anyone acting as an intermediary for Roger Stone, or anyone associated with my campaign had communicated with WikiLeaks on October 7, 2016.

Response to Question II, Part (f)

I do not recall being told during the campaign that Roger Stone or anyone associated with my campaign had discussions with any of the entities named in the question regarding the content or timing of release of hacked emails.

Response to Question II, Part (g)

I spoke by telephone with Roger Stone from time to time during the campaign. I have no recollection of the specifics of any conversations I had with Mr. Stone between June 1, 2016 and

U.S. Department of Justice

Attorney Work Product // May Contain Material Protected Under Fed. R. Crim. P. 6(e)

November 8, 2016. I do not recall discussing WikiLeaks with him, nor do I recall being aware of Mr. Stone having discussed WikiLeaks with individuals associated with my campaign, although I was aware that WikiLeaks was the subject of media reporting and campaign-related discussion at the time.

Response to Question II, Part (h)

I do not recall having had any discussion during the campaign regarding a pardon or action to benefit Julian Assange.

Response to Question II, Part (i)

I do not recall being aware during the campaign of specific efforts by foreign individuals or companies to assist my campaign through the use of social media postings or the organization of rallies.

III.   The Trump Organization Moscow Project

a.   In October 2015, a "Letter of Intent," a copy of which is attached as Exhibit B, was signed for a proposed Trump Organization project in Moscow (the "Trump Moscow project").

    i.   When were you first informed of discussions about the Trump Moscow project? By whom? What were you told about the project?

    ii.   Did you sign the letter of intent?

b.   In a statement provided to Congress, attached as Exhibit C, Michael Cohen stated: "To the best of my knowledge, Mr. Trump was never in contact with anyone about this proposal other than me on three occasions, including signing a non-binding letter of intent in 2015." Describe all discussions you had with Mr. Cohen, or anyone else associated with the Trump Organization, about the Trump Moscow project, including who you spoke with, when, and the substance of the discussion(s).

c.   Did you learn of any communications between Michael Cohen or Felix Sater and any Russian government officials, including officials in the office of Dmitry Peskov, regarding the Trump Moscow project? If so, identify who provided this information to you, when, and the substance of what you learned.

d.   Did you have any discussions between June 2015 and June 2016 regarding a potential trip to Russia by you and/or Michael Cohen for reasons related to the Trump Moscow project? If yes, describe who you spoke with, when, and the substance of the discussion(s).

e.   Did you at any time direct or suggest that discussions about the Trump Moscow project

U.S. Department of Justice

~~Attorney Work Product // May Contain Material Protected Under Fed. R. Crim. P. 6(e)~~

should cease, or were you informed at any time that the project had been abandoned? If yes, describe who you spoke with, when, the substance of the discussion(s), and why that decision was made.

f.   Did you have any discussions regarding what information would be provided publicly or in response to investigative inquiries about potential or actual investments or business deals the Trump Organization had in Russia, including the Trump Moscow project? If yes, describe who you spoke with, when, and the substance of the discussion(s).

g.   Aside from the Trump Moscow project, did you or the Trump Organization have any other prospective or actual business interests, investments, or arrangements with Russia or any Russian interest or Russian individual during the campaign? If yes, describe the business interests, investments, or arrangements.

Response to Question III, Parts (a) through (g)

Sometime in 2015, Michael Cohen suggested to me the possibility of a Trump Organization project in Moscow. As I recall, Mr. Cohen described this as a proposed project of a general type we have done in the past in a variety of locations. I signed the non-binding Letter of Intent attached to your questions as Exhibit B which required no equity or expenditure on our end and was consistent with our ongoing efforts to expand into significant markets around the world.

I had few conversations with Mr. Cohen on this subject. As I recall, they were brief, and they were not memorable. I was not enthused about the proposal, and I do not recall any discussion of travel to Russia in connection with it. I do not remember discussing it with anyone else at the Trump Organization, although it is possible. I do not recall being aware at the time of any communications between Mr. Cohen or Felix Sater and any Russian government official regarding the Letter of Intent. In the course of preparing to respond to your questions, I have become aware that Mr. Cohen sent an email regarding the Letter of Intent to "Mr. Peskov" at a general, public email account, which should show there was no meaningful relationship with people in power in Russia. I understand those documents already have been provided to you.

I vaguely remember press inquiries and media reporting during the campaign about whether the Trump Organization had business dealings in Russia. I may have spoken with campaign staff or Trump Organization employees regarding responses to requests for information, but I have no current recollection of any particular conversation, with whom I may have spoken, when, or the substance of any conversation. As I recall, neither I nor the Trump Organization had any projects or proposed projects in Russia during the campaign other than the Letter of Intent.

IV.   Contacts with Russia and Russia-Related Issues During the Campaign

a.   Prior to mid-August 2016, did you become aware that Paul Manafort had ties to the Ukrainian government? If yes, describe who you learned this information from, when, and the substance of what you were told. Did Mr. Manafort's connections to the Ukrainian or

U.S. Department of Justice

Attorney Work Product // May Contain Material Protected Under Fed. R. Crim. P. 6(e)

Russian governments play any role in your decision to have him join your campaign? If yes, describe that role.

b. Were you aware that Paul Manafort offered briefings on the progress of your campaign to Oleg Deripaska? If yes, describe who you learned this information from, when, the substance of what you were told, what you understood the purpose was of sharing such information with Mr. Deripaska, and how you responded to learning this information.

c. Were you aware of whether Paul Manafort or anyone else associated with your campaign sent or directed others to send internal Trump campaign information to any person located in Ukraine or Russia or associated with the Ukrainian or Russian governments? If yes, identify who provided you with this information, when, the substance of the discussion(s), what you understood the purpose was of sharing the internal campaign information, and how you responded to learning this information.

d. Did Paul Manafort communicate to you, directly or indirectly, any positions Ukraine or Russia would want the U.S. to support? If yes, describe when he communicated those positions to you and the substance of those communications.

e. During the campaign, were you told about efforts by Russian officials to meet with you or senior members of your campaign? If yes, describe who you had conversations with on this topic, when, and what you were told.

f. What role, if any, did you have in changing the Republican Party platform regarding arming Ukraine during the Republican National Convention? Prior to the convention, what information did you have about this platform provision? After the platform provision was changed, who told you about the change, when did they tell you, what were you told about why it was changed, and who was involved?

g. On July 27, 2016, in response to a question about whether you would recognize Crimea as Russian territory and lift sanctions on Russia, you said: "We'll be looking at that. Yeah, we'll be looking." Did you intend to communicate by that statement or at any other time during the campaign a willingness to lift sanctions and/or recognize Russia's annexation of Crimea if you were elected?

    i. What consideration did you give to lifting sanctions and/or recognizing Russia's annexation of Crimea if you were elected? Describe who you spoke with about this topic, when, the substance of the discussion(s).

Response to Question IV, Parts (a) through (d)

Mr. Manafort was hired primarily because of his delegate work for prior presidential candidates, including Gerald Ford, Ronald Reagan, George H.W. Bush, and Bob Dole. I knew that Mr. Manafort had done international consulting work and, at some time before Mr. Manafort left the

U.S. Department of Justice

~~Attorney Work Product // May Contain Material Protected Under Fed. R. Crim. P. 6(e)~~

campaign, I learned that he was somehow involved with individuals concerning Ukraine, but I do not remember the specifics of what I knew at the time.

I had no knowledge of Mr. Manafort offering briefings on the progress of my campaign to an individual named Oleg Deripaska, nor do I remember being aware of Mr. Manafort or anyone else associated with my campaign sending or directing others to send internal Trump Campaign information to anyone I knew to be in Ukraine or Russia at the time or to anyone I understood to be a Ukrainian or Russian government employee or official. I do not remember Mr. Manafort communicating to me any particular positions Ukraine or Russia would want the United States to support.

Response to Question IV, Part (e)

I do not recall being told during the campaign of efforts by Russian officials to meet with me or with senior members of my campaign. In the process of preparing to respond to these questions, I became aware that on March 17, 2016, my assistant at the Trump Organization, Rhona Graff, received an email from a Sergei Prikhodko, who identified himself as Deputy Prime Minister of the Russian Federation, Foundation Roscongress, inviting me to participate in the St. Petersburg International Economic Forum to be held in June 2016. The documents show that Ms. Graff prepared for my signature a brief response declining the invitation. I understand these documents already have been produced to you.

Response to Question IV, Part (f)

I have no recollection of the details of what, when, or from what source I first learned about the change to the platform amendment regarding arming Ukraine, but I generally recall learning of the issue as part of media reporting. I do not recall being involved in changing the language to the amendment.

Response to Question IV, Part (g)

My statement did not communicate any position.

V.   Contacts with Russia and Russia-Related Issues During the Transition

a.   Were you asked to attend the World Chess Championship gala on November 10, 2016? If yes, who asked you to attend, when were you asked, and what were you told about about [*sic*] why your presence was requested?

  i.   Did you attend any part of the event? If yes, describe any interactions you had with any Russians or representatives of the Russian government at the event.

U.S. Department of Justice

~~Attorney Work Product // May Contain Material Protected Under Fed. R. Crim. P. 6(e)~~

Response to Question V, Part (a)

I do not remember having been asked to attend the World Chess Championship gala, and I did not attend the event. During the course of preparing to respond to these questions, I have become aware of documents indicating that in March of 2016, the president of the World Chess Federation invited the Trump Organization to host, at Trump Tower, the 2016 World Chess Championship Match to be held in New York in November 2016. I have also become aware that in November 2016, there were press inquiries to my staff regarding whether I had plans to attend the tournament, which was not being held at Trump Tower. I understand these documents have already been provided to you.

Execut d on **NOVEMBER 20**, 2018

DONALD J. TRUMP
President of the United States

U.S. Department of Justice

Appendix D

U.S. Department of Justice

Attorney Work Product // May Contain Material Protected Under Fed. R. Crim. P. 6(e)

APPENDIX D

SPECIAL COUNSEL'S OFFICE TRANSFERRED, REFERRED, AND COMPLETED CASES

This appendix identifies matters transferred or referred by the Special Counsel's Office, as well as cases prosecuted by the Office that are now completed.

A. Transfers

The Special Counsel's Office has concluded its investigation into links and coordination between the Russian government and individuals associated with the Trump Campaign. Certain matters assigned to the Office by the Acting Attorney General have not fully concluded as of the date of this report. After consultation with the Office of the Deputy Attorney General, the Office has transferred responsibility for those matters to other components of the Department of Justice and the FBI. Those transfers include:

1. United States v. Bijan Rafiekian and Kamil Ekim Alptekin

    U.S. Attorney's Office for the Eastern District of Virginia
    (Awaiting trial)

The Acting Attorney General authorized the Special Counsel to investigate, among other things, possible criminal conduct by Michael Flynn in acting as an unregistered agent for the Government of Turkey. *See* August 2, 2017 Memorandum from Rod J. Rosenstein to Robert S. Mueller, III. The Acting Attorney General later confirmed the Special Counsel's authority to investigate Rafiekian and Alptekin because they "may have been jointly involved" with Flynn in FARA-related crimes. *See* October 20, 2017 Memorandum from Associate Deputy Attorney General Scott Schools to Deputy Attorney General Rod J. Rosenstein.

On December 1, 2017, Flynn pleaded guilty to an Information charging him with making false statements to the FBI about his contacts with the Russian ambassador to the United States. As part of that plea, Flynn agreed to a Statement of the Offense in which he acknowledged that the Foreign Agents Registration Act (FARA) documents he filed on March 7, 2017 "contained materially false statements and omissions." Flynn's plea occurred before the Special Counsel had made a final decision on whether to charge Rafiekian or Alptekin. On March 27, 2018, after consultation with the Office of the Deputy Attorney General, the Special Counsel's Office referred the investigation of Rafiekian and Alptekin to the National Security Division (NSD) for any action it deemed appropriate. The Special Counsel's Office determined the referral was appropriate because the investigation of Flynn had been completed, and that investigation had provided the rationale for the Office's investigation of Rafiekian and Alptekin. At NSD's request, the Eastern District of Virginia continued the investigation of Rafiekian and Alptekin.

2. United States v. Michael Flynn

    U.S. Attorney's Office for the District of Columbia
    (Awaiting sentencing)

U.S. Department of Justice

~~Attorney Work Product // May Contain Material Protected Under Fed. R. Crim. P. 6(e)~~

3. United States v. Richard Gates

   U.S. Attorney's Office for the District of Columbia
   (Awaiting sentencing)

4. United States v. Internet Research Agency, et al. (Russian Social Media Campaign)

   U.S. Attorney's Office for the District of Columbia
   National Security Division
   (Post-indictment, pre-arrest & pre-trial[1])

5. United States v. Konstantin Kilimnik

   U.S. Attorney's Office for the District of Columbia
   (Post-indictment, pre-arrest)

6. United States v. Paul Manafort

   U.S. Attorney's Office for the District of Columbia
   U.S. Attorney's Office for the Eastern District of Virginia
   (Post-conviction)

7. United States v. Viktor Netyksho, et al. (Russian Hacking Operations)

   U.S. Attorney's Office for the Western District of Pennsylvania
   National Security Division
   (Post-indictment, pre-arrest)

8. United States v. William Samuel Patten

   U.S. Attorney's Office for the District of Columbia
   (Awaiting sentencing)

The Acting Attorney General authorized the Special Counsel to investigate aspects of Patten's conduct that related to another matter that was under investigation by the Office. The investigation uncovered evidence of a crime; the U.S. Attorney's Office for the District of Columbia handled the prosecution of Patten.

9. ██████████████████████████████████████
   ████████████████████████████

(Investigation ongoing)

The Acting Attorney General authorized the Special Counsel to investigate, among other things, crime or crimes arising out of payments Paul Manafort received from the Ukrainian government before and during the tenure of President Viktor Yanukovych. *See* August 2, 2017 Memorandum from Rod J. Rosenstein to Robert S. Mueller, III. The Acting Attorney General

---

[1] One defendant, Concord Management & Consulting LLC, appeared through counsel and is in pre-trial litigation.

later confirmed ██
██
██

On October 27, 2017, Paul Manafort and Richard Gates were charged in the District of Columbia with various crimes (including FARA) in connection with work they performed for Russia-backed political entities in Ukraine. On February 22, 2018, Manafort and Gates were charged in the Eastern District of Virginia with various other crimes in connection with the payments they received for work performed for Russia-backed political entities in Ukraine. During the course of its ███████████████, the Special Counsel's Office developed substantial evidence with respect to individuals and entities that wer ██████████████████████████
██████████████.[2] On February 23, 2018, Gates pleaded guilty in the District of Columbia to a multi-object conspiracy and to making false statements; the remaining charges against Gates were dismissed.[3] Thereafter, in consultation with the Office of the Deputy Attorney General, the Special Counsel's Office closed the ████████████████████ and referred them █████ for further investigation as it deemed appropriate. The Office based its decision to close those matters on its mandate, the indictments of Manafort, Gates's plea, and its determination as to how best to allocate its resources, among other reasons; ███
████████████████████████ At ██████████████████████████████████ continued the investigation of those closed matters.

10. United States v. Roger Stone

U.S. Attorney's Office for the District of Columbia
(Awaiting trial)

11. ██
██████████████████████████████████████

(Investigation ongoing)

B. Referrals

During the course of the investigation, the Office periodically identified evidence of potential criminal activity that was outside the scope of the Special Counsel's jurisdiction established by the Acting Attorney General. After consultation with the Office of the Deputy Attorney General, the Office referred that evidence to appropriate law enforcement authorities, principally other components of the Department of Justice and the FBI. Those referrals, listed

---

[2] ██
██

[3] Manafort was ultimately convicted at trial in the Eastern District of Virginia and pleaded guilty in the District of Columbia. *See* Vol. I, Section IV.A.8. The trial and plea happened after the transfer decision described here.

alphabetically by subject, are summarized below.

1.

2. Michael Cohen

During the course of the investigation, the Special Counsel's Office uncovered evidence of potential wire fraud and FECA violations pertaining to Michael Cohen. That evidence was referred to the U.S. Attorney's Office for the Southern District of New York and the FBI's New York Field Office.

3.

4.

5. Gregory Craig▮▮▮▮▮▮▮▮ Skadden, Arps, Slate, Meagher & Flom LLP

During the course of the FARA investigation of Paul Manafort and Rick Gates, the Special Counsel's Office uncovered evidence of potential FARA violations pertaining ▮▮▮▮▮▮ Gregory Craig, Skadden, Arps, Slate, Meagher & Flom LLP (Skadden), and their work on behalf of the government of Ukraine.

After consultation with the NSD, the evidence regarding Craig ▮▮▮▮▮▮▮▮ was referred to NSD, and NSD elected to partner with the U.S. Attorney's Office for the Southern District of New York and the FBI's New York Field Office. NSD later elected to partner on the Craig matter with the U.S. Attorney's Office for the District of Columbia. NSD retained and handled issues relating to Skadden itself.

6.

U.S. Department of Justice

~~Attorney Work Product // May Contain Material Protected Under Fed. R. Crim. P. 6(e)~~

U.S. Department of Justice

Attorney Work Product // May Contain Material Protected Under Fed. R. Crim. P. 6(e)

C. Completed Prosecutions

In three cases prosecuted by the Special Counsel's Office, the defendants have completed or are about to complete their terms of imprisonment. Because no further proceedings are likely in any case, responsibility for them has not been transferred to any other office or component.

1. United States v. George Papadopoulos

   Post-conviction, Completed term of imprisonment (December 7, 2018)

2. United States v. Alex van der Zwaan

   Post-conviction, Completed term of imprisonment (June 4, 2018)

3. United States v. Richard Pinedo

   Post-conviction, Currently in Residential Reentry Center (release date May 13, 2019)

59913481R00139

Made in the USA
Columbia, SC
09 June 2019